W9-CPF-064

GOD'S BULLIES

ALSO BY PERRY DEANE YOUNG

Two of the Missing
The David Kopay Story (with David Kopay)

GOD'S BULLIES

Native Reflections on Preachers and Politics

PERRY DEANE YOUNG

HOLT, RINEHART AND WINSTON New York

Published by Holt, Rinehart and Winston,
383 Madison Avenue, New York, New York 10017.

Published simultaneously in Canada by Holt, Rinehart and
Winston of Canada, Limited.

LIBRARY OF CONGRESS CATALOGING IN PUBLICATION DATA

Young, Perry Deane.
  God's bullies.

  Includes index.
  1. Christianity and politics. 2. United States—
Religion—1960–   . 3. Conservatism—United States.
4. Moral Majority, Inc. 5. Falwell, Jerry. I. Title.
BR115.P7Y68   261.7'0973   82-6087   AACR2
ISBN: 0-03-059706-4

First Edition
Designer: Christopher Simon
Printed in the United States of America

10 9 8 7 6 5 4 3 2 1

ISBN 0-03-059706-4

To the memory of my father,
Robert Finley Young, 1889–1958.
And for my mother,
Rheba Maphry Tipton Young Stanton,
Whose best advice to me was:
"Now don't *you* be a 'Preacher Sam.' "

CONTENTS

CONTENTS

PART FIVE

FOREWORD

It was more accurate for me to avoid all titles of the people discussed in this book. Some of them called themselves "reverend" when clearly they were not. Others had been given "doctorates" when they hadn't earned one, much less three, college degrees. Will Rogers said it best when he was offered an honorary degree: "What are you trying to do, make a joke out of college degrees? They are in bad enough repute as it is. . . . I got too much respect for people that work and earn 'em to see 'em handed around to every notorious character."

I have not meant to embarrass anybody or to hold any person or group up to ridicule by the information disclosed in this book. After all, I begin with myself and my own family. While there is much about us that is boorish and ridiculous, we are not without some strains of decency and integrity, too. My intention has been to try to understand my family and in turn to understand the leaders of the new right and religious right who claim to speak for people like them. I can no more change the fact that I was born among them than I can change the color of my eyes or skin. Furthermore, I wouldn't if I could.

If I found a situation that was humorous, however, I have not hesitated to describe it as I saw it. I learned my lesson in this regard at a torchlight ceremony one night among the beautiful people on the Hindu island of Bali. Dressed in proper sarong and cummerbund, I stood among the crowds in an open temple, with anthropology texts coursing through my brain. As the gamelan orchestra of primitive xylophones reached a crescendo behind me, an old man picked up a spear and danced in a trance directly in front of me. The young friends and family of my guide suddenly started laughing uproariously at this most religious moment. If Margaret Mead had mentioned laughter, I had missed it. "Why are they laughing?" I asked my young guide. "Because what the man is doing is funny." And so it was; I soon found myself laughing along with my native hosts.

When I first began this book, a reporter told me I'd be surprised to find that the conservatives were easier to deal with than the liberals. To a man, they were courteous, respectful, and cooperative with me, and I am grateful to them for it. I have been careful to distinguish my own deeply felt opinions and conclusions about what they are doing from how they see themselves. My maxim has been what Edward Heath said when asked if he was being vindictive in his campaign against Harold Wilson. "One need not be vindictive," he said, "one need only be fair to the man."

As for homosexuality, I would wish that I never had to hear or write that word again. I believe a person's private life should be just that; it's nobody's business how or with whom you have sex, especially the government's. But the parent new-right groups and their religious offspring have made this a major political issue. I could not avoid the subject in this book because I was forced to face it every way I turned. In many important ways, what these people are saying about homosexuals reveals just how far they are willing to go in changing the rest of society to fit their molds. Their use of this issue also reveals aspects of their own characters that many of them would obviously prefer to leave hidden.

A homosexual has a right to any political beliefs he wants, but I found it an interesting and important part of the story that so many homosexuals kept turning up as leaders of the new right. I do not refer to mere foot soldiers; I am speaking of some of the key architects and masterminds of the movement. As a homosexual myself, my first impulse would be to protect anybody who might suffer as a result of the disclosure of his or her private sex life. However, in writing a book, I feel, my first obligation is to the reader. I would have been guilty of withholding information I considered key and vital to understanding these people's motivations and actions if I had not shared with the reader what I was privileged to know about their sexual orientation.

That some of the people responsible for the vicious anti-homosexual campaigns being waged in this country now—either directly or by supporting others involved—are themselves homosexual was a fact I happened to know. I could not, in good conscience, withhold such information from the reader. It is just as relevant as it would be if a crusading anti-Semite were found to be a Jew; or if a leading anti-abortionist had secretly had an abortion herself. It is not their homosexuality I am disclosing but their repression of feelings I regard as natural. It is, finally, not their homosexuality that is worth noting, but their hypocrisy. Theirs is a kind of sultan's morality, which publicly seeks to punish others for the same "vices" they are secretly indulging in. More fascinating to me is the fact that they are joining forces with those who would destroy them and their—our—kind.

While the subjects of this book are not Caesars and I am not Suetonius, they certainly are men of extraordinary power in our country today and I am a writer recording the facts of their lives. Like Suetonius, the Roman biographer of the twelve Caesars, I simply felt that whether my subjects were married or single, whether they preferred sex with men or women or enjoyed both, were all facts that must be included in any record of their lives.

As to the frequent historical references in this book, I should explain that I am neither a professional historian nor a true scholar. However, I have been interested in history from a very early age, and have collected letters, diaries, newspapers, and documents dating back to 1704. I share the sentiments William F. Buckley, Jr. expressed in the foreword to his 1951 book, *God and Man at Yale*: "I cannot claim to have approached this project with the diligence and patience of a professional scholar. As far as pure scholarship is concerned, it is best said of me that I have the profoundest respect for it, and no pretension to it."

At the back of the book, I have also included some samples of the direct mail being sent out by these new-right groups, because it has to be seen to be believed.

I have included the texts of four speeches—by Barry M. Goldwater and Thomas J. McIntyre in the U.S. Senate, by A. Bartlett Giamatti, president of Yale University, and by Jerry Falwell, pastor of Thomas Road Baptist Church in Lynchburg, Virginia. It seemed to me that the authors of these speeches approached the same subject as this book but with perspectives uniquely their own. I especially recommend Falwell's sermon, delivered in 1965, at the height of the civil rights movement, because it documents the man's inherent racism and anti-Semitism; it also provides an excellent argument as to why preachers should stick to their vocations and stay out of politics.

Last, I have ended the appendixes and the book itself with some of the writings of Thomas Jefferson on the subject of religion and government in America. The leaders of the new right are constantly speaking of taking us back to the simple truths of our founding fathers. I could not agree with them more.

—Perry Deane Young
Washington, D.C.
April 1982

PART ONE

1

COPING WITH A REDNECK RENAISSANCE

Like Barry Goldwater, I sometimes feel my life is on a gigantic wheel that has turned full circle—or else the world around me has changed enough to make me feel as though I'm back where I started. Goldwater says everybody used to say he was behind the times and now they tell him he was ahead of his time. Previously regarded as a reactionary, he suddenly began to hear people describing him, in retrospect, as a prophet.

Goldwater has witnessed the happy realization of his dreams of a conservative government. My own cycle has not been so pleasant; for me, it has been the recurrence of a nightmare of hate-filled voices come back to haunt not just me but an entire country.

When I was a teenager, there was nothing you could be in this country that was worse than what I was: white, Anglo-Saxon, Protestant, Southern, "redneck," to use a word I rather like now. (Its origins, after all, are quite noble, referring to farmers like my father whose necks were colored through honest labor.)

In those days, however, the mere sound of our voices evoked universally despised images of night riders in bedsheets. I didn't like being branded a racist bigot just because of the way I talked. In the sense that it is all-inclusive, the stereotype of the redneck was unfair to some, but I knew it was nonetheless true for many. Racism was a way of life. It was wrong then and it's wrong now. Ignorance of history and science was wrong then and it's wrong now. A culture built on hate and intolerance is no culture at all.

Imagine my consternation in suddenly finding that what I had struggled so hard to overcome had overcome me. The accent that was so unfashionable and disdained during my formative years was now in the news, on stage, in the White House. By the late 1970s, I could turn on the radio in New York City and hear Conway Twitty and Loretta Lynn singing "You're the Reason Our Kids Are Ugly."

But there is a dark side to this redneck renaissance that reflects no new recognition of a neglected "silent" majority. Using God and morality as a smoke screen, a powerful group of political activists is trying to reinstate the same old bigotry, intolerance, and racism that prevailed when I was a child. What a bitter irony of history that in 1980 Ronald Reagan would choose a group of ministers in Texas before whom to assert his anti-intellectualism similar to those John F. Kennedy had chosen to hear his thoughts on religious tolerance and enlightenment just twenty years earlier.

While I am pleased to see my culture suddenly appreciated, my kinsmen regarded as whole human beings for a change, I am saddened by the way it is taking place. Racism is no different if it is spoken bluntly by my Uncle Lo (for Lorenzo Dow) in his Klan robes than if it is couched in polite phrases by the rich young rulers of the new right. There were—and there remain—sound, solid reasons for despising, if not rednecks themselves, then certainly their ignorance and intolerance. In creating a movement that feeds on these people's hate and fear, the leaders of the new right are only carrying on a tradition of demagoguery that we have long known in the South. But it is a shameful tradition that is unworthy of the ideals expressed in our founding documents.

If my language is strong in response to all this, it's because my feelings are as well. When I speak of rednecks and all those the "moral majority" claims to represent, I'm not talking about exotic figures in a foreign land. I mean the people I know best, my family and myself.

I was born into as narrow and superstitious a community as that presided over by Jerry Falwell. In my travels since leaving home, I have been more struck by the similarities than by the differences in people in other countries or in other sections of this country. I find a special comfort in the common origins of our seemingly different rituals—a feast of lights driving off the dark of winter, a dance of joy welcoming the warmth of springtime. We all still knock on wood in unwitting tribute to the faith of our Druid ancestors.

To me, the rituals of the absolute believers—Muslim, Jew, Christian, Mormon, Hindu—and the taboos they impose are only slight variations on the same primitive themes. This is never more dramatically felt than when you arrive as a cultural outsider between the lines in Northern Ireland or in the Middle East. The people on both sides look alike and their scriptures sound as though they came from the very same source, even if they're pronounced in different accents. None of it seems worth fighting over. You realize, then, that people see God through mirrors—and the reflection is often that fearsome, intolerant beast inside all of us. I've never been nearly so worried about the existence or nonexistence of God as I have been about what so many people will try to do in His name. A psychiatrist friend of mine puts it this way: "If you take away the God part, why did Abraham want to kill his son?"

As much as I might fear what many of the religious have done and continue to do, I think it is at our own peril that we regard them as so exotic and separate from ourselves we fail to see what it is in them that is also in us. Young Catholics, Jews, and Mormons in recent times have been able to look back on a history of intolerance and hatred toward their people without ever having to consider what it might have been in them that caused such feelings. If the opposition to them was all bad, they seem to think, then they must be all right.

I'm now grateful that I was never allowed the luxury of looking beyond myself for blame. From the moment I first talked among outlanders, my intellect was suspect purely because of my Southern accent. I had no intention of staying among the "hills-bound, world-lost" people (as Thomas Wolfe described our mutual cousins) I had been born to. I could see that much of what they said and did and felt was not me. But neither did I want to pose as somebody I wasn't or couldn't be. Being blindly patronizing can be just as false as being blindly prejudiced.

I had to figure out what was good and bad in my history; I had to understand what I should rightly be ashamed of and what I should hold onto and recall with pride. You can never overcome anything by pretending it's not there. That's why Martin Luther King, Jr. always said integration would be healthier in the South when it came because

Southerners had been more open about their true feelings. My goal was to become myself. I think the experience was a healthy one. I emerged from it with an attitude similar to that attributed by André Maurois to Benjamin Disraeli's writer father, Isaac D'Israeli: "He, for his part, felt no shame in being a Jew. On the contrary, he spoke with pride of the history of his race. But he held it utterly ridiculous to maintain, in an age of reason, practices and beliefs which had been adapted to the needs of a tribe of Arab nomads several thousands of years earlier."

Liberals hear the words of Moral Majority, Inc., and see a monster. I see only a stern old stick man who lived his life without humor or music in solemn service to the Lord Jesus and who was known to me until very recently as my grandfather. He had caused my real grandfather to be sentenced to the chain gang for a very natural act of love that produced my mother. My journey of self-discovery began many years ago with an attempt to understand what sort of man this tyrannical Baptist preacher was who had such a profound influence on my mother's life and in turn on mine. The hatred I felt for the old bastard and everything he stood for was enough to have altered my own life at one time. I had to understand him and "where he was coming from," as we phrased it in the 1960s, or I would never figure out where I had come from and wanted to go.

I was caught between the mind-crippling force of fundamentalism on the one hand and the promise of freedom and life through learning and education on the other. If that conflict has often been painfully frustrating and confusing, it has never been dull.

By facing up to and overcoming the very real hatred I felt for my preacher "granddaddy" and his kind, I was able finally to understand and love those people, my people. It was necessary to hate the man in order to love him, necessary to become a non-Christian in order to understand and appreciate the enduring truth and beauty of the teachings of Christ himself.

When I first began to hear the words of Jimmy Carter and Anita Bryant and Jerry Falwell and others like them, I thought I was hearing ghosts. Like Ibsen's Mrs. Alving, I knew the real people had to be dead, and yet I could hear their very same words and sentences spoken in the same accents.

I was born on a hilltop farm a few miles north of Asheville, North Carolina. The farm came to mean only hard times and bad feelings for me, but it was picturesque to outsiders who envied our "simple" lifestyle and wished they had our view of the mountains. A Jewish boy from a fancy part of town came out once and watched our cows being milked. "They must be awfully poor to have to get their milk that way," he said. While the grown-ups laughed, I thought how nice it would be to trade the smelly barn and cows for his neat cartons and nice warm kitchen.

The people in my world thought mainly of clawing their way out, and never mind which of their brothers and sisters—or parents—got stepped on in the process. I'm the youngest of thirteen, a fact that never fails to bring a warm smile from those who automatically envision "one big happy family." Would that the sequence of adjectives were always appropriate. There is no photograph of my several brothers and sisters together; we've never been in the same room or even in the same building at one time, except briefly in church for the funeral of the patriarch, and that would surely have turned violent if it had lasted any longer. With the old man laid out dead in the front hall, two of my brothers squared off and slugged it out in the backyard over the impropriety of one's having dug the grave, the only means he, the poorest one, had of contributing toward the funeral expenses. Except for one sister whose Iowa-born husband was appalled by the inane bickering, the others talked a lot and did nothing. I entered the University of North Carolina at Chapel Hill later that year with a savings of $175, a self-help scholarship, a job, and a room to call home in the house of compassionate strangers who became "like family," treating me with greater respect and kindness than I had ever known at home.

That's why I can't agree with Tolstoy's famous dictum on unhappy families being different—or interesting—in their own ways. In my attempts to record and codify my past, I'm constantly reminded of the banality of so much of it. I had to go around the world, it seemed, to appreciate that there are only so many kinds of good and evil, and all of it was back there at our house around suppertime every evening. The silly squabbles and grudges (some so old that nobody knew their origins) came down to ridiculously insignificant insults that involved trifling amounts of money or property not worth fighting over. My father specified in his will that every penny his sons had ever given him was to be paid back. The farm had to be sold to do this, but it was done.

By comparison only, we were the landed gentry. Nearly everybody

7

in the community except the Youngs worked at the cotton mill, the casket plant, the bleacheries, or the lumber mills. My father and his brothers all had farms; three of them also had general stores that still stocked high-topped shoes and kerosene lamps into the 1950s. The community was called Woodfin after an early landowner, a cousin of the "New South" editor, Henry Woodfin Grady. It is now incorporated as a town, but there were distinct boundaries to it even then. The French Broad River eased by on the west, and on the east was an upper-middle-class development where the nearest houses faced away from Woodfin to improve their value.

The place had a rough reputation that was surely more ferocious than any individual could have been. Our boys who had survived the war came back revved up to keep on fighting. One of them smashed his plane in the front yard doing a stunt for his wife; three or four others died in car crashes, going full speed through dead-man's curves that were treacherous even to the sober and slow. The boys from out in Woodfin would take no gaff from anybody, especially the uptown crowd. Not being tough myself, I liked this image, although I still had a country boy's shame for my origins.

One forest ranger and two sometime deputy sheriffs lived among us, but we existed almost totally outside the law. Rather, we had a law unto ourselves. Calling in the law was unthinkable unless outsiders were involved.

There was a very definite sense of what was meet and proper, although nobody stopped to think about what that was or wasn't. We were all white and—nominally—all Protestant Christians, meaning Methodists, Baptists, and Holy Rollers. The Presbyterians and all others were in town. It was hardly a level society, even though everybody worked either on farms or in the factories. There was the aristocracy of strength and looks that exists everywhere. Here, the high school athletes were at the top because in the wintertime the entire community followed our championship girls' and boys' basketball teams wherever they went. This was only a passing honor, however. The athletes soon learned that nothing happens after the game, and their hero's slot is quickly filled by another.

The principal of the school was a figure of such authority he functioned almost as a mayor of the community. To be punished by him for an infraction at school meant you'd be punished twice as much at home for the public embarrassment. Our teachers were the only people in our world who had been to college. They were our ultimate authorities on just about everything, and most of them handled their superior roles with grace. At school we had prayers and Bible readings and, every month or so, a "sword drill." With the class divided up as if for a spelling bee, we stood facing each other and "fenced" with verses from the Bible. One student would yell, "John Three Sixteen," and the opponent had to fire back with "forgodsolovedtheworld. . . ." I can't remember why it was necessary to say it so fast.

To outsiders, the churches might have seemed the center of such a community. Certainly the preachers would have put themselves up front, out center, and on top of any list. But that was not the reality of it. In more than a few cases the preachers had used their religion and their families to avoid military service, and that left a taint of cowardice on their names from then on. The preachers also seemed to be the kind who always knew how to get out of work—and yet they drove around in fancy cars as if they'd earned them. There was no honor in this among physical laborers. Mainly, the preachers were a humorless lot, generally of lower intelligence and intellect than the ones they were trying to lead. As self-described examples of all that is good and righteous, they were carefully examined by their neighbors and found wanting. The preachers in our society were more often the butt of jokes than the objects of affection and admiration. I remember an old fellow saying, "The church is the last place where a fool can stand up and talk for a half hour without having anybody tell him to shut up and sit down."

A stranger pulled up and asked crazy Bob one time where was the Church of God. Bob scratched his head and said he didn't rightly know. "Up yunder's the Methodist Church and that's Preacher Dawkins's, and down the other way's the Baptists, and that's Preacher Sprinkles's.

"But if God's got a church around here, I don't know about it."

" 'What makes you think you're called to be a preacher?' "
"The country boy just grinned kind of foolish. 'Well, I got the biggest prick in the neighborhood,' says he, 'and a terrible craving for fried chicken.' " (From *Pissing in the Snow & Other Ozark Folktales* by Vance Randolph.)

9

I remember one preacher and his wife in particular. They lived in a low little cottage behind a thick hedge so high that it almost obscured any view of the tiny yard and house. They also had put up an expensive ten-foot-high fence around their garden.

Every Halloween we'd get even in a ritual more sacred to us than Easter is to Catholics. We would gather up sacks full of leftover eggplant and bell peppers—hard enough to pick up and throw, but squishy enough to make a good mess. Meanwhile, the preacher and his wife would have made their preparations too. Sometimes these would be an elaborate arrangement of wires in the hedge; other times they would spend hours placing white lollipop sticks in neat rows in the yard. They would tell us the hedge or yard was "wired" and we'd be electrocuted if we tried to cross over for trick or treat.

Throughout the evening, with hordes of happy younger kids veering around the danger, the preacher and his wife would take turns sitting in a straight chair on a spotlit front porch, a shotgun resting on their laps. It was a portrait of the original homesteaders defending their little speck of ground. It would be one, two, and sometimes three A.M. before they finally got tired enough to call off their guard; sometimes they would just have stepped inside for a few minutes. That was when we'd fire a wicked barrage of rotten eggs and whatever produce we had scavenged from our fields. We felt good afterwards; maybe the preacher did too, as he spent the next day undoing the wires and sticks and scrubbing off the smelly opinions of others, confirming his own goodness by these evil attacks. The law was never called, nobody was ever punished or even scolded; our parents quietly agreed that hypocrisy was getting what it deserved.

The real measure of worth in our community, and, I believe, in much of America, was the opposite of pretension and meanness. A good person could go far, but a good, honest, and strong person would go further still. There is a primitive respect for being fair and just and honest about who you are and what you want that transcends all religions in this country. To step over that line is a far worse transgression than anything on that other list of what the religious call "sins." A "sense of decency" is more important to us than a chest full of badges for going to church every Sunday.

In Woodfin, there were the "good Christians," who truly lived their religion, secure enough not to have to prance around with their piety on their sleeves. There was a special kind of reverence for these people who went about the drudgery of their daily lives uncomplaining and yet somehow at peace. The most hated people, the ones who got the choicest batch of rotten eggs at Halloween, were the legalistic ones who saw the world in severe terms of right and wrong, good and evil. To take a drink or smoke tobacco were sins they spoke about as if they were murder. Sex was something filthy and vile even when your parents did it in the bedroom with the lights off and the doors closed. It was not a subject for mixed company, and was only to be giggled about in separate groups of girls and boys.

In the face of these sour-faced nay-sayers stood a happy number of individuals who were the real heroes in our community, who believed that smoking a cigarette was not the same thing as murder, and neither was drinking a beer; they knew from their experience that some people actually liked the taste. And they didn't get struck by lightning or suffer the agonies of hell. In fact, they seemed to be having a happier time of it than the religious were. When you examined the straight and narrow lives of the preachers, you had to wonder if it was all worth it. If heaven was as joyless and somber a place as this road to it, maybe it wasn't worth the sacrifices necessary to get there after all. A stereotype among us was the preacher's kid who grew up bad, having suffered enough already from being good.

My mother—reared as a preacher's child—was usually not very interested in religion, but even if she didn't go to church, she always felt she should, and I was sent off to Sunday school whether my parents went or not. My mother was haunted by the hard-shell Baptist faith of her childhood, and this had a profound effect on me.

I remember one time old man Dorsey put up a revival tent up the road from our pasture. My mother was in bed with another sick headache or case of nerves or something the doctors couldn't diagnose. I could hear her moaning to God in her agony, "The noise, the noise." It was coming from the loudspeakers on top of Dorsey's tent, echoing up the valley and from out of my mother's own past. "Come on out and hear the word of God. Singing and praying all night. Preaching like you never heard before. I'll fly away, oh, Jesus, I'll fly away. . . ." I couldn't have been more than seven or eight, but I rushed out of the house and down the hill with the imagined strength of little David the giant killer. Two plans were battling inside my head. I was going to rush in and smash the machine just to stop the noise, or I was going to move slowly up the sawdust aisle to the front, seize the microphone,

11

and tell them the truth about Jesus. It is a recurring fantasy of mine, to this day. What I actually did was go to a quiet place where I knew nobody could find me, and stare off at the hazy mountains, dreaming of what lay beyond them.

I was twelve years old when I couldn't handle the conflicts anymore and sought an answer in the most obvious place that culture offered. Billy Graham, whose mountaintop estate is just outside Asheville, was bringing his crusade to our city auditorium. I had heard the first thrilling episodes on the radio: so many people attending, so many conversions to Christ. And when our next-door neighbor said she wanted to go, I knew it was destiny leading me there, too.

Graham was already some sort of religious wonder boy. His candidate, Eisenhower, had won the presidency and his crusades had the blessings of the Hearst newspapers and Henry Luce's *Time* magazine. The Asheville newspapers welcomed him home as if he were a native-born pope; they wrote about his crusade as if they were being paid well to publicize it.

I knew that Graham's following included a disproportionate number of women. Marshall Frady in his superb biography, *Billy Graham: A Parable of American Righteousness*, sets the figure at 60 percent. What I did not know until recently was that a heavy percentage of his converts were also very young adolescents. The 1951 Seattle crusade produced 6,354 "decisions for Christ." Of that number, only 3,349 followed up a referral to a local church. Of that number, one-third, or 1,155, were under fourteen.

In Asheville, that afternoon in 1953, I was one of that number. Nettie McElrath and I sat speechless through the whole show—huge choirs singing, Billy resplendent in pastels with his powerful build and delivery, milking sexuality out of every word about *Jeeeeeeesus*. When it came time for the countdown, I raised my hand. I didn't know then, of course, that all of this was very carefully orchestrated. Billy asked the choir to keep singing the invitational hymn: "Just as I am without one plea . . . O Lamb of God, I come, ahhhhhh come." As the man himself intoned the familiar code words that triggered whatever hidden guilt and shame might propel you out of your seat and down to the front, the choir kept singing, "I come, I come." And Billy pleaded softly: "Nobody looking, nobody leaving, everybody giving their heart to the Lord Jesus. If there is trouble in your life, if you're so weary you feel you can't carry on, then come on down and give your heart to Jesus and know what a full life can be, I want you to raise your hand and come on down. . . ." At that signal, the paid staff members began moving from the back of the auditorium as if they were going down to be saved. I was caught up in the moment; my head was swimming with delicious throbs of guilt. Masturbation loomed large among those guilts. Playing around with a neighbor boy loomed even larger. My fantasies of naked men (of Graham himself) pushed me out of the seat and down the aisle. I confessed, I repented, I asked forgiveness. I wanted to change. I wanted to be good. I wanted not to be confused anymore. There was a prayer for all of us huddled in front of the stage at eye level with Billy's feet. And then we walked back to our seats, feeling a bit wet and strange but trying to reassure ourselves that it was all going to be different now.

But nothing happened; nothing changed. I followed up with my down-front counselor, a busy young man registered at the old YMCA. He was annoyed at seeing me and he had no time for talk. I should just go to church and pray and get lost.

Even at that age, a part of me knew it was all a lie, but another part of me was still scared—suppose those people are right.

In 1970, as a reporter for the *New York Post* covering Graham's New York crusade, I had a private interview with him in a suite he often uses at the Salisbury Hotel, which is wrapped around and on top of a Baptist church in mid-Manhattan. I wanted to confront him with my own experience; I had been through it and I knew it was a sham. I also wanted to tell him I felt he was one person who might have helped keep the calm and saved us from the bloodshed and violence that wracked the South during the 1960s. Graham seemed to spend a lot of time in the Bahamas in those years. And at that time, Graham was appearing with Richard Nixon every chance he got, cheering on the war effort, all in the name of the Prince of Peace. But I couldn't get through to Graham. He had a forceful, if indirect, answer to every accusation I made. He has practiced that intense holy look too long not to be effective. I left feeling empty and lost, as though I'd been duped once again by the same guy who "saved" me back in Asheville. Saved me from what?

But in Frady's biography, I was pleased to find that someone had gotten to Graham: his most beloved partner, Charles (Chuck) Templeton, with whom he had started out on the road, sharing hotel rooms and ice cream pastel suits and flowered ties. Two virile, handsome men, they had wowed the crowds from London to Los Angeles. Then Templeton went to Princeton University's graduate school, while Graham—who'd been satisfied with a degree from a Bible school diploma mill—stayed on the road. Graham's wife, Ruth, had "tart" words for this former evangelist who now works as a radio personality in Toronto, living the life of a bon vivant, bachelor boulevardier, as Frady describes him.

Graham himself, however, continues to defend Templeton. "I love Chuck to this very day. He's one of the few men I've ever loved in my life. He and I had been so close. But then all of a sudden our paths were parting. He began to be a little cool to me then. I think . . . Chuck was always sorry for me."

Templeton, said Frady, began to look back on his evangelizing as some kind of "frenetic mummery, really a matter of all those people, woeful for something to answer the dull vacancy in their lives and in their hearts, drum-majored and razzle-dazzled into a romance with Jesus.

"While he was at Princeton, he and Billy began to hold periodic exhaustive binges of discussion, prayer, debate, in a small wan twin-bedded room at the Taft Hotel in New York. . . ."

In a memorable session, Templeton confronted Graham with the truth of the Great Commandment: "What is it, Billy? It's to love the Lord thy God, not only with all thy heart and all thy soul, but all thy *mind*. All thy mind! And not to think, Billy, is a sin against the Great Commandment. Deliberately, I mean to *decide* not to think—that's a sin against God's will, against His word, that's disobedience, that's rebellion, that's unfaithfulness." Then he hit Graham with a wallop that hurt: "You really want to know what you've done, Billy? You've committed intellectual suicide—that's what."

The resulting confusion caused Billy terrible headaches, and riding across the Great Salt Lake Desert with his assistant, Grady Wilson, Graham broke down and cried until they stopped the car and walked into the desert. It was so hot they took off their shirts and knelt there for two hours praying aloud that God would end this confusion in Billy's head. Soon it was over. Billy said, "All right, let's go! Let's go!" Graham was never troubled by doubts about God or himself after that. He could see in Richard Nixon a great President and a good and decent man. He could see anything he wanted to, because he had chosen not to see at all.

For me, the latest resurgence of the impulse to mix religion and government, to put preachers into politics, did not begin with Jerry Falwell and the elections of 1980. Billy Graham had been doing it for years, of course. But long before I first heard of Jerry Falwell, I listened as Anita Bryant and Jimmy Carter held forth on the importance of "God's law." Carter, I know, would describe himself as a progressive and a liberal. However, stripped of the crowd-pleasing rhetoric, his fundamentalist faith was the same old absolutist view of right and wrong, good and evil that had been an omnipresent shadow of terror and doom over my childhood and that of countless others. When Carter was elected, a Southern writer friend of mine quipped: "Let all those other people get a taste of what it is to live under these fundamentalists. . . ."

It was not Falwell, but Carter and Bryant who first tried to popularize the theme that the American family is threatened by decadence at every turn. I know a family can be a beautiful and positive institution, but my experience teaches me that a family can also impose the worst kind of imprisonment wherein are practiced the most unspeakable cruelties known to man.

Nothing a homosexual does or thinks is as unnatural as forcing a person to live as a heterosexual contrary to his or her wants and needs. Nothing a promiscuous heterosexual does is as immoral as forcing a healthy, normal man or woman into a condition of celibacy out of church-imposed strictures against birth control and abortion. How many acts of violence, all in the family, have been—and continue to be—committed by these intensely oppressed people who simply did not fit in the role of husband, wife, or parent?

Those who are attempting to impose God's law on the rest of us who prefer living under the Constitution of the United States refuse to understand that there were sound, enduring reasons why our founding fathers deliberately chose not to mention God in that sacred document. To tamper with that great tradition of separation of church and state is to risk on a purely practical level the kind of sectarian warfare that characterized European history prior to the founding of this country. What these people are proposing is a radical change not just in our tradition of law, but in the very form of government itself. Although their approach is from a different direction, it would be just as radical a change as communism because it would require the same kind of totalitarian, police-state control.

What it comes down to is not—as the religious right proclaims—a battle between God and Satan, good and evil, but the ancient conflict between tyranny and freedom, between ignorance and enlightenment. I know that there is much good that has been done and is being done in the name of God. However, I also know that there is an untold amount of evil being perpetrated by mere humans presuming to speak for God.

The timing of this latest attempt to put God—as a minority of people see him—in charge of the government is odd in that we are confronted almost daily with news from halfway around the world, where such religious states already exist. We are appalled by the inhumanities committed daily in God's name in Iran, but we don't stop to think that the very same things could easily happen here if these radical forces have their way.

The same people who, in the 1960s, said "Love it or Leave it," are now issuing worse denunciations of our country than we ever heard from the left. Jerry Falwell says that "godless, spineless leaders have brought our nation floundering to the brink of death...." James Robison, a Texas evangelist and major force in the new right, says: "America is corrupt. She's drunk, duped, sinful, perverted, and Godless, and her doom is as certain as God unless she turns in repentance and comes to the altar of God in complete confession...."

These preachers may hold their audiences with such talk, but it just isn't true. Their own polls show that this remains the most religious—in terms of private belief and actual church attendance—country in the Western world. They are obviously talking about something other than our religious state. If you do not believe that a Christian dictatorship is what they have in mind, then hear the words of James Robison again: "Let me tell you something else about the character of God. If necessary, God would raise up a tyrant, a man who might not have the best ethics, to protect the freedom interests of the ethical and the godly."

We have the awesome example of God's law in Iran, but we have an even more extreme example of the same tyranny, which grew directly out of the fundamentalist culture right here in America. I am referring to the mass murder-suicides of 912 innocent Americans at Jonestown in Guyana. It should be remembered that by the time a preacher named Jim Jones took those people's lives, he had already taken their money—millions of dollars accumulated out of pathetically small welfare and social security checks. It was God's will, he said, that they give everything to him (Jones, not God), and that included their lives.

In a pointed column about hearing Jones's exhortations through tapes found in the ruins of Jonestown, Darrell Laurent wrote in Jerry Falwell's hometown newspaper, the *Lynchburg* (Virginia) *News*: "Whether Jones began as a well-intentioned messiah or a sort of cosmic con man is unimportant. What matters is that when he turned from his original path and began wandering in ideological circles, 912 people fell off a cliff with him. . . . Those who feel the world is better off without the Jonestown victims might remember that children as well as rats followed the Pied Piper of Hamelin. . . ."

Although Jones was clearly crazed toward the end of his life, he had earlier been praised widely for his good work, even by Rosalynn Carter. Much of what he has to say to his people in those tapes makes no sense at all; a chilling amount of it, however, is the stock fundamentalist or absolutist mentality at work. Conservatives are forever saying that communism is the logical end of liberalism. Well, fascism is the logical end of what many of them are trying to do. If you speak of absolute control—of children's minds, adults' behavior—it doesn't matter whether you start from the right or left, you end up with the same totalitarian state.

As if the 1980 elections validated their cause, the leaders of the new right were quick to take credit for "creating" Ronald Reagan. The opposite is closer to the truth. The absolutist attitudes expressed by these people have been a part of our history from the beginning; what is new is the respectability and visibility given them by nods of approval from the President and various members of Congress who ought to know better.

These "social" issues from the new right were not that important to Reagan; in fact, his own life and lifestyle are obviously inconsistent with many of them. Reagan's main interests were the economy and national defense. If it would bring in another category of voters, he seems to have reasoned, why not tell them he supported the teaching of "creationism" and mandatory prayers in the public schools? He supported them not out of any real conviction, but because he didn't think they were very important, one way or the other.

"It isn't that he's a bad guy really," an actress friend of Ronald Reagan's was quoted as saying in an *Esquire* article in August 1980. "I really don't even think he realizes how dangerous the things he does really are."

But if Reagan has unwittingly promoted this new bigotry and intolerance, what will it matter if we gain the mightiest military force and the healthiest economy—only to have lost our very spirit and our soul?

2

PREACHER PRESIDENT

Limping back home in defeat once again, Jimmy Carter must surely have wondered, as Billy Graham did once when he got the flu: "Lord, what have I ever done to deserve this?" Here he was the first born-again Baptist President in history; he told us he prayed twenty-five times a day at least; every night, he and his wife read a chapter of the Bible before going to bed. They went to church every Sunday, taught Sunday School, even preached on some occasions; they forbade the drinking of hard liquor in their White House.

And yet it was supposedly their own people, in a tidal wave of fundamentalism, that drove them out. The winner, meanwhile, was a lukewarm Presbyterian, a Hollywood actor with two wives still living and two sets of children who don't seem to like each other. He is known to dance on Sunday sometimes and to take a drink when he feels like it and not to worry if others want to drink. As a governor, he signed the most liberal abortion law in the country and later, in his newspaper column, he said there was no need for a law barring homosexuals from teaching in public schools. If Ronald and Nancy Reagan have ever read the Bible at bedtime, they have had the grace not to mention it.

From the once-again-remote village of Plains, Georgia, Carter and his wife now speak bitterly of the religious-right forces that take credit for driving them out of the White House. Dotson Rader, a free-lance writer and the son of an evangelist himself, was the first to interview them after the crushing defeat.

Writing in the July 19, 1981, issue of *Parade* magazine, Rader said:

Because Carter was probably the first self-confessed born-again Christian to sit in the Oval Office, I wondered about the attacks on him—a fellow religionist—by the Moral Majority and their allies on the religious right.

"We went through a phase in 1980, which I hope was a peak," Carter said. . . . "I believe the dominance of the rightist element in the religious community will wane. We've seen this before when very effective religious spokesmen, quite often using the electronic media, were highly racist in their profession, as you know. It's a sordid side of human nature, but it's effective. . . ."

As he spoke, Rosalynn Carter walked in the room. He continued his thought. ". . . for a while. If you read the history of the South in particular, you'll see how effective it was. If anyone professed to be a moderate on the race issue, he was shot down, quite often by religious forces. So it's not at all a new factor on the American scene."

"But it was a factor in your defeat," I said.

"It had a high level of influence in the 1980 presidential election, yes."

"Jerry Falwell's fought Jimmy as long and as hard as he could," Mrs. Carter said.

"Yes, that's right. In 1976, Jerry Falwell was a bitter antagonist of mine."

"I thought Reverend Falwell only emerged recently," I said.

"No, he was just not as powerful . . ." said Rosalynn.

"Or as well known . . ." said Jimmy.

" . . . in 1976 as he was in 1980," added Rosalynn. "He had the West Coast then—Washington, Oregon, probably California too. He said bad things about us everywhere then. I had a friend in Oregon whom I'd call and he'd tell me the bad things Jerry Falwell had said about us that week."

"But doesn't this attack, coming from an alleged Christian leader, have an effect on your faith as a Christian?" I asked. Rosalynn glanced at her husband. "It had an effect on our children." "I've never equated my faith with that of the Jerry Falwells or the Gerald L. K. Smiths," Carter explained.

But if religion was a force that removed them from power, it had been just as important in getting them that power in the first place. If it hadn't been for Carter's religious pose, Jerry Falwell would have had no common ground for attacking him. And, more important, the media would have had no legitimate reason for reporting what an unknown evangelist had to say about a candidate for President. These reports about Falwell and Carter caught the eye of the political professionals in Washington, and that was the specific origin of Falwell's Moral Majority, Inc.

At first, Carter explained in that interview with Dotson Rader, "there was a compensating political advantage" to his religion, "in being different. Being Southern. Being Baptist. That aroused a curiosity about me . . . and I undoubtedly got a lot of publicity when I desperately needed it—when nobody knew who I was—that paid off later."

At the time, however, Carter and his aides avoided what one of them called "the religious nut factor" as if the candidate had a bad disease. Religion was a double-edged sword that could just as easily be turned against them. But they were not unaware of the polls that showed that there were millions of Americans out there who shared Carter's faith.

Whatever the reasoning behind the move, Carter went public about his religious beliefs on March 18, 1976, during the North Carolina primary at a speech in Winston-Salem. He said: "I spent more time on my knees the four years I was governor in the seclusion of a little private room off the governor's office than I did in all the rest of my life put together because I felt so heavily on my shoulders the decisions I made might very well affect many, many people. I recognized for the first time that I had lacked something very precious—a complete commitment to Christ, a presence of the Holy Spirit in my life in a more profound and personal way. And since then I've had an inner peace and inner conviction and assurance that transformed my life for the better."

At a press conference the next day, he talked further about his religion. "In 1967, I realized my own relationship with God was a very superficial one. . . . I began to realize that my Christian life, which I had always professed to be preeminent, had really been a secondary interest in my life, and I formed a very close, personal, intimate relationship with God through Christ that has given me a great deal of peace, equanimity. . . . It was not a profound stroke, a voice of God from heaven. It was not anything of that kind. It wasn't anything mysterious. It was the same kind of experience that many have who become Christians in a deeply personal way and it has given me a deep feeling of equanimity and peace."

Now if Carter had honestly wanted to dispense with his private beliefs as an issue in the campaign, he could have done precisely what John F. Kennedy did in 1960. Many Americans had legitimate fears about a Catholic serving as President. In one speech, delivered before the Greater Houston Ministerial Association, September 12, 1960, Kennedy addressed those fears and talked about his faith and how it would and would not affect his presidency. Kennedy then went on with his campaign, seeing no reason to explain further about his religion.

Carter, however, saw it as something that made him interesting to reporters. When asked how many times he prayed each day, he could easily have said that was a matter between him and his God. In fact, that's exactly how Gerald Ford did handle questions about his and his wife's religion. What he said was, "We don't wear our religion on our sleeves."

Did how many times he prayed each day or how much he prayed while governor have anything whatsoever to do with how effective a leader he could be? Carter and his wife obviously felt that it did. History was to prove how wrong they were. In fact, the Carters had to talk about religion because there was nothing else extraordinary about the man. There was nothing unusual or outstanding in his career as navy officer, governor, husband, father, peanut farmer. But he had once taken a walk in a piney woods his family owned over in Webster County, Georgia. And *there* was a tale to tell.

After losing his first campaign for governor, in 1966, Jimmy Carter suffered what his psychiatrist friend, Peter Bourne, described as "an acute reactive depression." The sermon one Sunday at Plains Baptist asked the question: "If you were arrested for being a Christian, would there be enough evidence to convict you?" Carter said he had to answer no.

Then, one day in the late fall of the same year, Carter and his sister, a self-styled psychologist-evangelist, Ruth Stapleton, took a walk in the woods. That's about all the two agree upon in their separate accounts. She says he knelt and cried at one point; he says he didn't cry. She asked if he would give up everything for the Lord; he said yes. Even politics? she asked. He couldn't answer that one. But, from later accounts, this was the turning point, this was when he was "born again." Like so much the Carters did, it wasn't the thing itself that seemed strange, it was the way they handled it. They talked about it as if they knew the rest of us thought it was weird, as if they themselves thought it was something he perhaps ought to be ashamed of.

The strangest part of the whole Carter religious picture ensued from this walk in the woods. He resolved to get more involved in his church. He spent a year doing "mission" work in Pennsylvania and Massachusetts. People in those states may well wonder where or who were the natives who needed converting to the Southern Baptist faith. Carter came with a list.

In their book *Jimmy Carter*, Bruce Mazlish and Edwin Diamond give Carter's own account of one of his sojourns into the mining country around Lock Haven, Pennsylvania. (The ellipses are theirs.) "I'm not sure about the year . . . May 1967. (It was) what we call a pioneer mission. Before I went, there had been identified 100 families of non-believers . . . I was assigned the responsibility along with another person, Milo Pennington, from Texas, to go into these homes and explain our own faith and seek their conversion. Milo Pennington was not well educated. He happens to be a peanut farmer—there aren't very many of them in Texas—and he did the work and talking. It seemed to me he was the most inept person I had ever known in expressing himself. He fumbled and didn't know what to say and I thought, 'Oh, I could do much better. . . .' But he had done it before and he was a deeply committed person."

According to Carter, Pennington managed to convert fifteen or twenty families to the way of the Southern Baptists. "The whole week was almost a miracle to me. I felt the sense of the presence of God's influence in my life. I called my wife on the phone one night and she said, 'Jimmy, you don't sound like the same person. You sound almost like you're intoxicated.' . . . And I said, 'Well, in a way I am.' "

When Carter got around to writing his national campaign biography, *Why Not the Best?*, what had previously been a turning point in his life was reduced to this meager sentence: "My church life became far more meaningful to me, and every year I went with other laymen on pioneer mission trips to other states or to special areas of Georgia."

It never left my mind that the finger so near the button for four years had so recently been pushing doorbells for Christ in Pennsylvania. There was no way he could describe this as a sane and sensible act. It sounded strange—hell, it was strange. If Carter's purpose had been to serve humankind in the manner of Christ, then there was no reason for him to go all the way to Lock Haven, Pennsylvania, to do it. One of the most bitter and bloody battlefields of the civil rights movement was in Americus, Georgia, where Plains people go to shop. Here was a whole seedbed of anger, hate, and frustration right in his own backyard while Carter was off seeking sinners up North.

I lived in Georgia when Carter was governor. I knew firsthand that he had been a caretaker at best. He was certainly never a farsighted liberal, as he tried to depict himself to the national press corps in 1976. Otherwise, somebody might have guessed who he was or what he did when he appeared on the television show "What's My Line?" while he was governor.

When I read that Carter's church still refused to admit blacks as late as 1976, I could not understand why so many Northern liberals believed what he was saying about his record on racial questions. He was an avowed "conservative," the code word in those days for a segregationist. There were many courageous white Southerners who took a stand against segregation years before, and they had faced the very real dangers that went with speaking out. Jimmy Carter was not among them.

A distinguished black legislator in Georgia, Julian Bond, wrote about Carter's real record in *The Nation*, April 17, 1976. Bond said that as a candidate for governor, "Carter courted the Wallace vote, and said nice things about Lester Maddox. . . . Carter let Georgia's white voters know he could win 'without a single black vote.' He won the primary with less than 10 percent of that vote." At the June 1972 Democratic Governors' Conference in Omaha, Nebraska, Bond said, Carter introduced resolutions urging that Vietnam not be an issue in the 1972 campaign, praising J. Edgar Hoover for his service to the nation, and urging the racist governors of Mississippi and Alabama to come back into the Democratic Party.

"Southern Baptists are fond of saying that 'prayer changes things,' " wrote Bond. "Jimmy Carter's religiosity has certainly had that effect on him, in fact has changed him from Left to Right to Center so many times that converts to the Carter cause ought to take a cue from an earlier apostle—Thomas, who doubted."

Carter's religiosity, however, was to prove his most valuable weapon in the campaign for black votes nationwide. His wife was commissioned to go among the black churches and spread the word.

One would like to feel some kind of sympathy for Rosalynn Carter. She was, at first, carried along as the unwilling helpmate of her husband's ambition. The pictures of her in the early Georgia gubernatorial campaigns show a plain, ordinary housewife—which she was—frightened and harassed in the role she was having to play. But gradually she warmed to it so that her husband's ambition became hers, until now the two quite literally finish each other's sentences and talk as one.

Lillian Carter would always vow not to speak of her daughter-in-law, but a few of her choice sentences about Rosalynn did make it into print, and they offer an incisive portrait of a cold, cold woman. "She's very ambitious. And Rosalynn will be a force to be reckoned with in the White House, you'll see. She has more influence on Jimmy than anyone else. Even if I, his mother, want Jimmy to do something, I ask Rosalynn first. She can do anything in the world with Jimmy. He listens to her. He thinks she has a great mind. I admire her, of course, but I have never seen her let her hair down. I've never heard her tell a joke."

Howard Norton, a writer for Christian publications, tells about going with Rosalynn to a black church in Baltimore in his book, *Rosalynn, a Portrait*. She had already addressed two other black congregations that morning when she took the pulpit at Gillies Memorial Community Church. "It is pleasant to be here this morning and to join you in praising the Lord, and to have the opportunity to say a few words about my husband, Jimmy Carter, who is running for President."

Then she routinely invoked the name of Martin Luther King, Sr., father of the civil rights leader. She said she sat with King after his wife had been killed by a crazed gunman during a morning worship service. "And Dr. King told me that day that he thought my husband would be a great president and that he was with him all the way. . . . Another thing I want you to know about my husband is that he's a Christian man. He has told me many times that he spent more time on his knees as governor of Georgia, than in all the rest of his life put together."

The congregation, said Norton, responded with "Yes, yes! Praise the Lord. Thank you, God!"

Norton's Christian perspective takes some odd turns in his book. He praises Richard Nixon, for example, for not protesting that the 1960 election was stolen from him, because that would have been divisive. He describes the Kennedy "Camelot" as "a political era well-named because it ended, in real life, as in the fictional story that created the name, with infidelity, immorality and human misery. . . ."

But the Carters, Norton felt, had been sent by God. "Many Christians believed that the Lord's timing of the Carter takeover was not without purpose, and offers a great potential for good. With the American family on the decline, what could be better for the nation than to have the close-knit, God-fearing Carters in the White House, a living example of what a family could and should be?"

The whole emphasis on the family as a political issue did not begin with Moral Majority, Inc.; it started with Jimmy Carter in 1976. Said Norton: "Reporters who covered the Carter campaign, and I was one of them, believe that it was Rosalynn's idea to make morality, or the lack of it, an issue in 1976."

Having secured the Democratic nomination for President, Carter opened his campaign with a speech on the family that Jerry Falwell could easily have written. "The breakdown of the American family has reached extremely dangerous proportions. There can be no more urgent priority for the next administration than to see that every decision our administration makes is designed to honor and support and strengthen the American family." After he was President, on February 10, 1977, he told employees of the Department of Housing and Urban Development: "I think it is very important that all of us in government not forget that no matter how dedicated we might be, and how eager to perform well, that we need a stable family life to make us better servants of the people. . . . So those of you who are living in sin, I hope you'll get married. Those of you who have left your spouse, get reacquainted. I think it's very important that we have stable family lives. And I am serious about that." Just how serious was emphasized that week when one of his assistants publicly announced that he was marrying the woman he lived with.

In an editorial titled, "Getting God's Kingdom into Politics," in the September 19, 1980, *Christianity Today*, it was recalled that 1976 was the "year of the evangelical. That was the year evangelicals exulted in born-again Jimmy Carter's election to the presidency, the year they put up their feet and said, 'Well, it's about time the world took notice of us.' They basked in all the exposure they were getting."

And so the Carters came to Washington, making cracks about "Georgetown parties" before they'd ever been to one, saying a hefty portion of our population was living in sin, and promising never to serve hard liquor in the White House. Rosalynn explained the latter by saying she was actually saving the taxpayers money, adding: "They [magazine articles] make me sound like a real prude. I'm not a prude. . . . Jimmy promised his father that he wouldn't smoke and he never has. And in a strict home like mine, alcohol wasn't allowed in the house. But that doesn't make me a prude. I don't care what other people do, or say, or think, we are going to do what we feel is right. And I hope they won't call me a prude for doing it."

Well, she was a prude and he was a weak, indecisive, and inept President. They were also bad neighbors who took little or no interest in the city they lived in for four years. The truth was they didn't know how. Every time I saw one of them get up in public, I always felt a peculiar shame for them, as if it were a relative of mine who had gotten on stage at an opera and didn't know how to sing, or had arrived at a formal dress dinner in overalls. We Americans are self-contradictory about class. We tell ourselves we don't believe in it, but we do. We want to be led by leaders, by people who are stronger and smarter than we are. I remember a column Pete Hamill wrote once about a candidate for mayor of New York. He would never win, said Hamill, because he had no class. He didn't mean class in the sense of who your father was or even how much money you had, he meant class in the sense of knowing what's appropriate. The Carters could do a simple thing like turning on the Christmas tree lights—or not turning them on, as the case was—and make you feel embarrassed for them. They never seemed to fit in because they didn't fit. They were ill suited for the position, and they knew it as well as we did.

So great was our relief—even though an actor was replacing a peanut farmer—that you could almost feel a collective sigh in Washington when the Carters left town. Gone was that strange disconnected grin. "When Reagan smiles, you feel like he means it," explained a White House guard to me. "He actually laughs sometimes."

Whenever I think of the Carters' attempts to catch up on their lack of education and sophistication, I am reminded of Art Buchwald's "Six-Minute Louvre." Buchwald had a friend who said that the only things Americans wanted to see in the famed museum were the Mona Lisa, the Winged Victory, and the Venus de Milo, just so they could say they'd been there. He timed it: you could leave a taxi waiting and make it in a sprint, six minutes flat. Oh, yes, we were in Paris and we went to the Louvre and we saw . . .

During Carter's navy days, he and Rosalynn enrolled in one of those at-home study courses on the "great books of the world" and then they liked that so much that they did another on the "great painters of the world." In the White House, Rosalynn organized Spanish lessons from nine to noon three days a week for herself and certain staff members. Dinners with the Carters ended early on Tuesday nights because that was when Jimmy, Rosalynn, and Amy had their speed-reading lessons. When I read that the Carters also played classical music "as background," like Muzak in elevators or dentists' offices, I wondered if they didn't also get tapes of Beethoven's symphonies, for example, and speed them up as they pored over the world's great books and pictures.

There would be something admirable in all this self-improvement if it had remained confined to an ordinary house and family in Plains, Georgia, but it was somehow not worthy of the house once lived in by Thomas Jefferson. We pride ourselves on the fact that America is the place where anybody can become President, but every time it happens, we become sickened by the reflection of ourselves.

"How could we have known?" was the collective question asked by three of the best political reporters in Washington at a seminar I attended after Carter's defeat. They said he talked all right as a candidate in 1976; his position papers and statements read okay; the Democratic platform was a first-rate progressive program. But none of that revealed the man himself. None of that foretold that he would be inept as President.

I think the key to the man was his religion, and I think that explained him from the beginning. However, respect for another person's religion is almost as sacred a tradition in America as religion itself. The reporters were too polite to question or probe too deeply into Carter's beliefs because it just isn't done. It is a part of the television code that one does not criticize anything religious on the air.

Meanwhile, Carter himself was showing no corresponding restraint. He talked about God every chance he got. He taught Sunday School in Washington, and always led the prayers at church when he was home in Plains. Also, as President, he delivered three actual sermons—at two national prayer breakfasts and before the Southern Baptist Brotherhood Commission in Atlanta, of which he had been a member for six years.

Garry Wills was one of the few journalists to explore the delicate question as to the substance of Carter's faith. Wills wrote in the June 1976 issue of *The Atlantic*: "There is concern over Carter's religion that is not mere bigotry. It may seem unjust to punish real religion when we reward empty religiosity; but the thing makes sense. When Birch Bayh goes to his native hamlet and says he never feels closer to God than when he is there, we do not care because we know he does not mean it. When Nixon used Billy Graham to bless the billy clubs of the sixties, the insincerity gave us at least the relief of mockery. Kennedy's Catholicism was made up of gestures. But when a man *means* what he says in this awesome area, he drifts outside the ties and shared weaknesses that keep us in touch with each other."

In a television interview, Bill Moyers asked Carter if he ever had any doubts about himself, about God or life. "I can't think of any," answered Carter. "I obviously don't know all the answers to philosophical questions and theological questions—the kind of questions that are contrived, but the things that I haven't been able to answer in a theory or supposition—I just accept them, and go on. Things that I can't influence and change. . . . But doubt about my faith—no. Doubt about my purpose in life—I don't have any doubts about that."

Carter's sincerity thus became a real issue in the campaign. Facing Gerald Ford, who singlehandedly restored a sense of decency—and sanity—to the White House, Carter tried to make it a crusade of honesty against corruption. "I will never lie to you," he said with Nixonian earnestness. Who ever expected him to lie?

Carter's sincerity was a screen behind which he could hide the most important issue in any campaign—what kind of man he was. He said he was sincere.

But if you move beyond the carefully prepared campaign statements

29

and speeches to the interviews in which Carter was often caught off guard about his religion, you find exposed a mind that is just as narrow and limited as Jerry Falwell's.

PLAYBOY: We'd like to ask you a blunt question: Isn't it just these views about what's "sinful" and what's "immoral" that contribute to the feeling that you might get a call from God, or get inspired and push the wrong button? More realistically, wouldn't we expect a puritanical tone to be set in the White House if you're elected?

CARTER: Harry Truman was a Baptist. Some people get very abusive about the Baptist faith. If people want to know about it, they can read the New Testament. The main thing is that we don't think we're better than anyone else. We are taught not to judge other people. But as to some of the behavior you've mentioned, I can't change the teachings of Christ. I can't change the teachings of Christ! I believe in them, and a lot of people in this country do as well.

"Read the Bible, read the New Testament." How many times have I had that thrown back at me whenever I asked a sensible question about a fundamentalist's beliefs.

Carter told the "couples' class" at First Baptist in Washington on February 20, 1977, that "God's law doesn't change, no matter if one is in Plains, Georgia, Washington, the Soviet Union, China, or Pakistan. Congress meets and goes home. God's law doesn't change." Rosalynn said, "I think, after all our battles, Jimmy's election to the presidency proves to us and to the world that you don't have to compromise with God's law to get ahead, even in this sinful world." They never did explain what they meant by God's law or how they intended to enforce it.

The Carters expected us to believe these blatant contradictions: While presenting himself as a man of tolerance when among liberals, Carter was telling his own people that he was a firm believer in the absolutes; with a remarkably simplistic interpretation of the Bible, he also tried to suggest that he was some kind of scholar who understood the danger in too literal an interpretation of the scriptures.

"He is a man who reads the Bible every day," wrote Garry Wills, "and has taught it all his adult life. I asked him if he ever entertained, in Sunday school classes or private study, the 'form criticism' of the New Testament. 'What is that?' he asked. A bit dumbfounded, I said, 'The kind of textual analysis Rudolf Bultmann did.' He knew that name, but could not remember if he had read anything by Bultmann.

For a bright and educated modern man, dealing with the thing he says matters most to him, he shows an extraordinarily reined-in curiosity. It suggests a kind of willed narrowness of mastery."

I, for one, never believed in Jimmy Carter's piety or his sincerity. He could lie to us because he had lied to himself. As Thomas Paine wrote in *Age of Reason*, if a man begins with so important a false-hood—about God—then he is capable of any kind of corruption after that. It would almost have been comforting to know that Carter knew and accepted that it was a lie he was carrying on about religion. If he was as secure in his faith as he said he was, why did he have to talk about it so much? Did we really need to know how often he prayed or read the Bible? I had known Jimmy Carter's kind of pious phony all my life; I had despised them from the moment I figured out what they were up to. In the name of Jesus and God, they had perpetrated all kinds of little cruelties on others and had meanwhile fooled themselves into thinking they could do no wrong because they were always carrying out God's will.

"The bugger was drinking a double martini" was how one fellow explained it to me the night of Carter's defeat. What do you mean? I asked. When he was told that he was not only going to lose the election, but lose badly, Carter was aboard Air Force One and, according to *Time*, "had just finished a double martini." He was a "kitchen drinker" all along; a hypocrite, in other words.

We can't say that Carter's brother, Billy, didn't warn us. It must be difficult for those outside the Bible barrens to understand how a beer in the hand could ever symbolize so much in a culture. But among fundamentalists, a man who would "take a drink" was not just an outlaw risking the scorn of his pious neighbors; he was in danger of eternal damnation to the fires of hell.

Some of the beer drinkers were ordinary folks who couldn't cope, addicts to whatever would get them away from their drab lives. But others were genuine heroes because they recognized how silly all that talk about sin was. They flaunted their beer cans, in other words. They had known the pious ones before and after salvation, and they knew they hadn't changed; they'd just found a rationale for the same old selfishness. That the religious were so concerned about other people's drinking habits and sex lives said much more about them and their own minds than it did about those they regarded as sinners.

What I remember about those few who would be themselves no

matter what the cost, who'd take a drink if they felt like it, was that they were the real victors. The religious ones had denied themselves a few pleasures in favor of a bitter outlook on life. It was also obvious that they had occupied their minds with superficial prohibitions while ignoring the more important teachings of love and compassion, not to mention joy, in the Bible.

That is why Jimmy Carter might get himself elected President, but in Plains, he would never be the man his brother Billy was. Billy might take a drink, but he wasn't stingy or selfish; he didn't take himself so seriously that he couldn't take a joke. There was no evidence that the preacher President even had a sense of humor, especially about himself.

In that interview with Dotson Rader, Carter offers a revealing story about his own self-image: " 'My mother, even back when I was a young person, was always interested in people different from her—an inquisitive person. In fact, she *favors* people who are different in preference to those who are not!' Carter laughed somewhat ruefully. 'And I'm one of the people, to be truthful about it, who is not very different. I'm more . . . well, orthodox in my attitudes and habits than are my sisters and brothers.' "

If John Kennedy or nearly any political figure of our time had claimed a rabbit swam out to attack him while he was out in a boat fishing, as Carter did, we would have laughed, but not the same way or for the same reasons we did when we heard about Carter's rabbit. We weren't laughing with Carter; we were laughing at him. He was the kind of person who would be frightened by a rabbit attack. With Kennedy, we would have laughed at the rabbit.

Later, of course, poor Billy would turn sour in the heat of the limelight. But in the beginning he offered a happy balance to Carter's somber piety. In *Redneck Power: The Wit and Wisdom of Billy Carter*, Jeremy Rifkin and Ted Howard wrote: "He has become a friend and neighbor to millions of people he will probably never even shake hands with. That's because, when you get right down to it, Billy makes a lot of sense, and in these times, that's something."

When Billy said, "I'm not the Carter that doesn't tell a lie," we knew he was the one who told the truth. "You know all that stuff about my sister being a faith healer," he said. "I went down to see her and she couldn't do me a bit of good [for a hangover]."

His most famous paragraph about his family was concise and devastating: "I got a mama who joined the Peace Corps when she was sixty-eight. I got one sister who's a Holy Roller preacher. Another wears a helmet and rides a motorcycle. And my brother thinks he's going to be President. So that makes me the only sane one in the family. . . . We're not a dynasty or anything. Just average folks in Plains."

Billy's beer can became a symbol of defiance, a banner of common sense flying in the face of that "bunch of damned hypocrites down there at that Baptist Church." He said, "I catch hell for my beer drinking from some folks, but I bet 80 percent of them go out of town and do their drinking there. They're what we call kitchen drinkers."

What is so striking about Billy's words, on reflection, is that he was obviously trying to tell us something. His brother was one of those down at the Baptist Church; his brother went out of town to drink; his brother was average, no matter what he said. This was never more clearly articulated by Billy than at a press conference he staged the day he would lose the election for mayor of Plains.

"What happens if you lose?" he was asked.

"If I lose, I celebrate."

"And if you win?"

"I celebrate. I promise you one thing I won't do, I won't get out and walk in the woods if I lose." If he wasn't saying his brother was a hypocrite, what did he mean by all those remarks?

Whatever his conscious reasoning, I think Billy was out to expose his brother as the phony he knew he was—even if he had to go to Libya to do it. I'll never believe that Billy himself didn't know that what he was doing with those Libyan agents was embarrassing to the President and possibly dangerous to the country. It wasn't a question of Carter's being able to control his brother's behavior. It was a serious matter of influence and leadership. Here was a man presuming to lead a whole country when he couldn't even keep his own brother out of what could have been a serious international incident. Likewise, he hadn't been able to convince a tiny church congregation that segregation was wrong, 111 years after the Civil War ended, and 22 years after the *Brown* v. *Board of Education* Supreme Court decision on integration.

Jimmy Carter had run for President and won for the simple reason that he wanted it more than anybody else did. He explained his ruthless ambition as God's will. But, as Edwin Diamond and Bruce Mazlish conclude in their book, "Someone convinced he stands on the side of God and the People can be a potent force in the Presidency, but only if his goodness is harnessed to experience and ability," neither of which Carter possessed.

In trying to please everybody, Carter pleased nobody. In trying to take all sides, stand for everything, he stood for nothing. His own fundamentalist brethren were among the first to turn on him. Liberals felt betrayed because Carter had convinced them he was one of them when he wasn't; conservative fundamentalists felt betrayed because they had accepted him at his word when he spoke of morality and the family and the absolutes of God's law.

"I've had about all the born-again diplomacy I can stand," said the pastor of Forest Hills Baptist Church in Decatur, Georgia, where two hundred Georgia preachers gathered during the 1980 campaign to mobilize forces against Carter. This preacher said he had been "thrilled at the thought of a born-again in the White House." But his disillusionment began with Carter's inaugural speech when he "mentioned the Lord's name less often than any other President."

These Georgians had the professional counsel of right-wing activist Paul Weyrich, the lead-off speaker at this meeting in Decatur. And the Reagan campaign had provided them with copies of a tract called "Ronald Reagan: A Man of Faith." According to this, Reagan supported aid to private Christian schools, prayers in public schools, and was against abortion and homosexuality. Reagan is quoted in the tract as saying, "The time has come to turn to God and reassert our trust in Him for the healing of America."

Meanwhile, one of the new Christian activist groups, called Christian Voice Moral Government Fund, opened its 1980 campaign with a newspaper advertisement asserting: "In 1976 millions of Christians provided Jimmy Carter with his edge of victory. This time things will be different. Jimmy Carter has betrayed the Christian community on prayer in the schools, the ERA, abortion, 'gay' rights, and on Christian schools.

"Governor Reagan will win the majority of the newly awakened Christian vote in 1980 (we will help see to that), and in so doing, win the election. We believe that he is the only candidate who can do so."

Reagan did win that vote and also the election. Groups like Christian Voice have been around throughout American history; their recent rise to prominence is largely the result of candidates blindly promising to carry through on single-issue legislation with no regard for history or fear of what this could lead to in the future. But if Reagan courted and won "the newly awakened Christian vote," he was not the first. That honor—in our time, at least—goes to Jimmy Carter, a defeated candidate back home in Plains again.

After four years of the Carter presidency, *Time* magazine concluded: "In a peculiar way Jimmy Carter is consumed by himself. His world still resembles the small stretch of Plains, Georgia. His goodness becomes an end in itself, defined in the Main Street encounters where his audiences are people with names and problems that are manageable. This does little, however, to define the tastes of the presidency, where decisions must have heroic dimensions, where leaders must balance their immense egos against a deeper understanding that they are but specks of dust in the ultimate sweep of history, where the future must be just as real as the present."

Many people were surprised that the Carters could so easily return to their ordinary lives in Plains. The truth is they never really left the place.

3

VICTORY IN MIAMI:
First Beachhead of the New Right

They sit you down and ask you, "Do you know what these homos do?" And then they tell you—in lip-smacking detail.

—A Miami reporter quoted by Lindsy van Gelder
Ms., September 1977

Like jungle cats sniffing the wind and taking off in the direction of fresh blood, the right-wing political professionals flocked to Miami for the Anita Bryant crusade in early 1977. After the Miami-Dade Council voted to include homosexuals in the city-county civil rights laws, Bryant had felt called by God to lead what she called "a battle of the agnostics, the atheists, and the ungodly on one side, and God's people on the other." Only four years later, when Bryant herself confessed her sins, did we learn to what extent she and that seemingly local movement had been nurtured and manipulated by others with larger prey than Miami's voters in mind.

Ronald Reagan, then a mere ex-governor with dreams of the presidency, flew in for Anita's birthday tribute with some oranges from California. This was a many-layered joke that would have been mean in a lesser comic's hands. Bryant had said the drought that did mild damage to California's citrus crop was God's judgment for the state's tolerance of homosexuals; then came the devastating freeze that did severe damage to the orange crop in Florida.

Jesse Helms made available his Senate staff for research and also the resources of his multimillion-dollar fund for right-wing campaigns, the Congressional Club, for Bryant's crusade. Helms wrote in his widely syndicated column: "I am proud of Anita Bryant. In my several conversations with her in recent weeks, I have pledged my full support to her. . . . She is fighting for decency and morality in America—and that makes her, in my book, an all-American lady."

She may have earned herself a dubious position in the psychosexual history of America, but Anita Bryant's role in the rise of the religious right is prominent and secure. She provided the national publicity they couldn't have gotten otherwise. Hers was the first successful coalition of right-wing Baptist fundamentalists with conservative Jews and Catholics. The first victory in Miami provided the beachhead without which other major developments might not have happened.

Twenty-eight of the thirty-four Miami rabbis who took a stand on the homosexual rights issue sided with Bryant. Bob Slidell, handsome young president of the Miami Beach B'nai B'rith, posed proudly as an officer of Bryant's Save Our Children, Inc., for a full-page advertisement in the newspapers. At the organizational meeting of this group in Bryant's Miami Beach mansion, the Catholic archbishop, Coleman F. Carroll, gave his blessing and swore to defy the law if anybody tried to enforce it in Catholic schools. Carroll also ordered a letter attacking the law to be read in all Catholic churches. A Catholic monsignor, Peter Reilly, led the prayers at the last major rally of the anti-homosexual forces.

Jerry Falwell and many of the other television evangelists flew in to give their support to Bryant, although the media paid scant attention to them in those days. Political activists from Christian Cause/Christian Voice Inc. in California came in with professional advice. John Briggs, the state legislator who sponsored a referendum to bar homosexual teachers or "anyone who advocates the homosexual lifestyle" from California's public schools, was also there. Bryant's organization (later renamed Protect the Children, Inc., and then Anita Bryant Ministries, Inc.) gave financial and other aid to the later California crusade, where the anti-homosexual measure was defeated. H. Edward Rowe of the Christian Leadership Foundation in Washington came down to be director of Anita Bryant Ministries, Inc., and then went back to become executive director of Religious Roundtable, Inc. Mike Thompson, who produced Bryant's television commercials, went on to do similar work for the American Conservative Union and for Christian Voice in Washington. Thompson did the devastating spots shown at the end of the 1980 presidential campaign, which depicted Jimmy Carter as soft on homosexuals: "They elected a mayor in San Francisco, now they're trying to elect a President."

In homosexuality, the politicians had found an issue that cut across religious, racial, and ethnic lines. Everybody might not out-and-out hate homosexuals as people, but few politicians would be willing to risk "endorsing" homosexuality. It was both smoke screen and scapegoat all in one neat package, and furthermore, it was an issue that guaranteed headlines in the newspapers and time on the radio and television talk shows.

To Anita Bryant and her husband, a former disc jockey named Bob Green, the most important arrival in Miami was B. Larry Coy, a Christian psychological counselor who came to them directly from Jerry Falwell's ministries in Lynchburg, Virginia. According to Bryant's confession later, Coy took over her ministries and her private life as well. Both ended in a shambles and, again according to Bryant, she lost "millions of dollars" in the process.

By the time I read of Bryant's spectacular turnaround on the subject of homosexuality and women's rights in an article published in the January 1981 *Ladies' Home Journal*, I was not surprised by anything she said or did. From the beginning of her crusade, I had been drawn to her antics as one is drawn to a particularly dangerous or foolish act being played out in public. Distance leaves you helpless to stop it, and yet you cannot turn your eyes away from it. The more jokes about her and the more ridiculous phrases I heard attributed to Bryant, the more intrigued I became with the woman.

I went to my neighborhood library and made Xerox copies of every article listed about her in American magazines from 1950 through 1977. Friends at the *Miami Herald*, *The New York Times*, *The Washington Post*, and the *Washington Star* also helped me copy their entire files on Bryant. Another friend in one of the gay organizations provided me with the clippings from six hundred newspapers nationwide for 1977 on the subject of Bryant and homosexuality. Then, by a telling coincidence, another friend passed along an incredible assortment of material from Bryant's own files—including pictures of naked boys and various marked pages from pornographic magazines. Bryant had sent this material to my friend, a reporter who had interviewed her.

And therein lay an explanation of Anita Bryant's motives. This reporter was clearly not in sympathy with what Bryant was doing. And yet Bryant literally reached out to her, touching her arms frequently during the long interview, begging for approval or any kind of response, even laughter. With elaborate inscriptions of love and caring, she presented the reporter with copies of all eight of her books, which were passed along for me to read. The article my friend wrote about Bryant had obviously held her up to ridicule through her own words, but she continued to write to my reporter friend and send articles, brochures, letters (from Helms's staff, for example), and clippings.

Ken Kelly, whose interview with Bryant in *Playboy* exposed her to further ridicule through her naïve musings about sex, came away with even stronger feelings for and about Bryant. He had despised her husband and what both of them were doing and saying, but at close range he could only feel pity for the woman herself. For weeks after Kelly did the interview, he would get phone calls from Bryant. There was no reason for them—she just wanted to talk with somebody.

It finally dawned on me and others that the woman was lonely. She was starved for affection and had serious sexual problems of her own. Hers was the shrill voice of sexual repression. She was a far worse victim of oppression than most of us homosexuals are. We all have suspicions of such motivations every time we hear somebody raging on about other people's sex lives, but rarely has anyone defined and explained them as bluntly as Bryant has.

On March 25, 1940, in her grandparents' house in Barnsdall, Oklahoma (population then: 1,831; in 1970: 641), Anita Jane Bryant was born dead. She told about this in the May 1978 *Playboy* interview, and in her book, *Mine Eyes Have Seen the Glory*, published in 1970. She was "black and swollen with poison" and the doctor pronounced her hopeless. Her grandfather wasn't yet born again, so he called the doctor some very bad words and threatened to kill him if he didn't put life into that baby girl. Although she was later—publicly, at least—a teetotaler, she admits that she would have stayed dead if the doctor hadn't forced a shot of whiskey down her baby throat, causing her to regurgitate the poison.

Her parents were Warren Gene and Lenora Bryant. Her father was an oil-field roustabout, and when they were getting along, the family lived in a two-room trailer with no toilet. When they moved into a house, Anita nearly scalded herself in the shower because she had never seen one and didn't know how it worked.

Anita made her singing debut at the age of two with a performance of "Jesus Loves Me" in her grandfather's church. Not long after her younger sister, Sandra Jean, was born, her parents were divorced. Eighteen months later they remarried. They divorced again when Anita was thirteen. She asks in one of her books: "Did the breakup happen because of the excessive strains placed on our family by my own deep-felt hunger to perform?" Although she describes her childhood—and her marriage—in pretty phrases in her books, in interviews she says it was a bitter time. While her mother worked, she and her sister were passed around to various relatives, where there was sometimes nothing more to eat than milk gravy and crackers.

When she was three, Anita appeared in an operetta at the high school. "I liked the costume and loved the applause," she said later. "My parents were divorced and I had this need to be accepted, to be loved." She started singing songs she heard on the radio; her favorites were Little Jimmy Dickens's "Take an Old Cold Tater and Wait" and "Sleepin' at the Foot of the Bed," both about grinning in the face of bitter poverty.

Her grandfather became a born-again Christian after being blinded in an oil-refinery accident, and Anita, too, became a devout fundamentalist at the very early age of eight. She told *Newsweek* that was when she knew she was going to be a star because "I met the creator of stars, Jesus Christ Our Lord."

She had a regular spot on "Gizmo Goodkin's Talent Show" in Oklahoma City; she was Red Feather Girl for the United Community Appeal; a majorette in the American Legion band; and a frequent performer on the "Sooner Shindig" and Scotty Harrell shows. "What stands out most of all in my memory are my feelings of intense ambition, and a relentless drive to succeed at doing well the thing I loved," she wrote of this period.

In 1957, Anita knew she would win the local contest for the Arthur Godfrey's "Talent Scouts," and she did. She worried about going to the sinful city of New York, but she put the matter in God's hands, and as He was to do throughout her career, God told her to go ahead and do what she wanted to do. At eighteen, she went from being Miss Tulsa to Miss Oklahoma. She came in third ("second runner-up") in the Miss America contest, but this, again, was a blessing. If she had won she wouldn't have been able to pursue her recording career. At nineteen, she recorded "Till There Was You," the first of three gold records.

On a promotional tour in Miami, she met Bob Green, a handsome young blond who squired her around in his monogrammed Thunderbird. She thought he was too good-looking to be nice. But she noticed that Green neither smoked nor drank, and she later admitted to sexual stirrings in response to him. They were to be married June 25, 1960, in Tulsa, but there was a last-minute hitch. Bob had fulfilled all requirements for heavenly grace according to a certain Lutheran church in the Bronx, but not according to Anita. The night before their wedding, Anita got him down on his knees beside her and a woman friend, and in a matter of minutes Green was born again in time for the next day's ceremony. It was a bad honeymoon and a bad marriage from the start, she says now. But they kept up the happy front for almost twenty years. Although her interviews are full of vague references to her marital discord, her books depict her life with Green as perfect bliss. She explains that she wrote that way because she wanted it to be true.

Bryant was so successful that she and her manager-husband were able to buy a $300,000 estate on the bay side of Miami Beach. It was built in low Spanish style and featured a heart-shaped sunken bathtub indoors and a regular swimming pool outdoors, along with banyan trees and waterfalls and a private dock with a Bertram Cruiser. The couple adopted a first child and then had three of their own. Like her own birth, Anita attributed her twins' survival of a complicated delivery to a miracle from God.

Although she would not appear in nightclubs because of her religious scruples, Bryant's association with Billy Graham (starting in 1963) brought her into contact with politicians. She sang in the White House sixteen times, by her count. She also began doing television commercials and landed a $100,000-a-year contract from the Florida State Citrus Commission. Other sponsors included Coca-Cola, Kraft Foods, Holiday Inns, and Tupperware.

Since Kate Smith was old and ailing, Bryant's husband saw the bicentennial year as her big chance. "The Battle Hymn of the Republic" became her "God Bless America," and she sang it and sang it.

Back in 1973, after singing the song as Lyndon Johnson's casket was lowered into the Texas soil, she went straight to California and checked herself into a Christian psychiatric center. She had reached this point with virtually no real education in books or the world about her; she led a sheltered life, going from one performance to another and living in a big house with four servants to look after the children. She knew she needed help when she became hysterical after viewing her grandfather's body and had to be quieted on a pew beside his casket at the funeral. Her hatred for her father and men in general, she said, was "poisoning my marriage and my relationship with people around me." The main problem, she told *Playboy*, was that "because of my father, I basically had a hate for men. I mean, there were times when I literally *hated* my husband—and I couldn't help it."

So here she was on a talk show in 1977, the wholesome gal in the commercials for Coca-Cola and orange juice and Tupperware. Gore Vidal, who was slated to appear on the same show, might well have said to her what he said to Mary Hartman: "You *are* America." Instead, Bryant dodged Vidal and he went on immediately after her and compared her with Adolf Hitler. It had all begun at a revival meeting at the Northside Baptist Church, where Anita's pastor told her about a law being considered by the city-county council that would include homosexuals in the civil rights code. The preacher said he'd burn the place down before he let homosexuals teach in the church's school. Bryant was amazed, stunned, and heartsick. The idea of homosexuals being allowed to teach and serve as role models and maybe even molest her children aroused her fighting spirit. She finally had a cause that would take her mind outside her own problems by focusing on somebody else's.

It was one of the more curious media phenomena in recent history: a serious local controversy over the legal rights of homosexuals somehow developed into a nationwide debate jokingly characterized as "the Anita Bryant thing," or—as a nice lady in the records office of Northwestern University phrased it even more delicately when I inquired about Bryant's student days there—"the orange juice thing." (Bryant referred to herself as a regular college student; in fact, she merely audited three noncredit courses and never finished those.)

When she began her crusade to repeal the Miami ordinance banning discrimination against homosexuals in housing and employment, Anita Bryant was admittedly, unashamedly ignorant of the many changes in attitudes about sexual behavior that had taken place in America in her lifetime.

Anyone familiar with the thirty-year-old Kinsey reports knows that the major change was that people were finally beginning to talk about what they had secretly been doing and thinking all along. In her book about the crusade, Bryant actually says, "I was not smart enough or informed enough" to deal with the subject of homosexuality. In another place she says, "I was only a woman."

But that didn't stop her. More importantly, her ignorance did not keep her from becoming the central focus of media attention during this time when homosexuality was discussed throughout the country as it never had been before. Her clipping service told Bryant that only the President had more stories than she did during one week of 1977.

Anita Bryant provided a national forum on the subject, which homosexuals had never been able to achieve on their own. The news business is a form of entertainment, and Anita Bryant has been a professional entertainer since she was a child. She knows how to get the media's attention and hold it. The reporters knew she was far more interesting to viewers and readers than a boring bunch of authoritative sources whose only claim to the limelight is that they happen to know what they are talking about.

However, there is such serious disagreement among professional psychiatrists and psychologists regarding homosexuality that it was shocking to see an uneducated singer step forth with a specific set of answers and explanations—and even more shocking to see how many people were so anxious to believe the worst about homosexuals that they accepted whatever she said without ever questioning the truth of it.

On a visit to Miami in March 1977, I made the following notes after visiting the *Miami Herald* newsroom and after talking with various supporters of Bryant. "A sad, sick feeling overcomes me as I think about what is going on here. I know that what those people are saying is not true of me or any other homosexual. I know that the prejudices about us are just as unfounded as those I grew up with about blacks being rapists and inferior beasts. Anita quotes the Bible as saying we should be put to death, and the reporters—my friends—copy the words with no more feeling than if she were talking about rats or guinea pigs. A Jew must have felt the same way in Munich in the early 1920s, overhearing a war-shocked bum named Hitler raving on a street corner and seeing a crowd gathering around, taking him seriously, believing his words."

The press kit that Bryant's group gave to visiting reporters contained a paper entitled "Why Certain Sexual Deviations Are Punishable by Death." It purported to be a "Christian viewpoint" on sex. "As barnyard animals become restless, confused, and panicky just before a hurricane, tornado, or earthquake, so too these vile beastly creatures evidently sense the coming judgment. Their frantic efforts to obtain acceptance and public approval and their worldwide shameless marches . . . are evidence of this as it was in ancient Sodom and Gomorrah." This paper also condemned "racial mixing of human seed" and numerous explicit sexual acts such as "Cunnilingus. Oral sex where the tongue is used to stimulate the female clitoris producing an orgasm and the discharge eaten. Also a form of vampirism or eating of blood. Such degeneracy produces a taste and craving for the effects as does liquor and narcotics. The depravity of the individual became so perverted and degenerate in the scriptural record that finally through judgment God allowed them to eat their own children."

A survivor of one of the death camps in Germany said, "Freedom means not having to lie about who you are." I know that comparison of homosexuals to Jews makes liberals nervous, but I also know that it is accurate. I'm not referring so much to the "moral degenerates" who died along with the Jews in Germany, but more to the way the Jews had to live when they, too, were regarded as outlaws and degenerates. They said of them as they said of us just ten or fifteen years ago: "You can tell by their eyes." It is this constant terror of being "found out" that has caused too many good and decent people to kill themselves. Everybody knows of the small number of alleged Communists who were blacklisted during the 1950s witch hunts; forgotten are more than ten thousand government employees accused of being homosexual and fired without any recourse to public opinion or justice of any sort.

Although I firmly believe that the widespread public debate was wholesome and the eventual results will be healthy, it was frustrating to see oneself falsely depicted in story after story, broadcast after broadcast. It began with the names chosen for Bryant's organization. Every time the newspapers printed the words, "Save Our Children" or "Protect Our Children," the impression was left that there was a threat to children in the homosexual rights laws.

Bryant herself had started this by saying, "Homosexuals can't reproduce, so they have to recruit." The word "recruit" thus became a

44

euphemism for sexual abuse and child molestation. The illogic in the statement was rarely challenged by reporters. It implied that one's being homosexual also meant that one was impotent and sterile with the opposite sex. The head of the Miami gay rights group at the time was the father of four children; the head of the National Gay Task Force had fathered two children.

Not surprisingly, the people who were most disturbed by the widespread acceptance of this myth about child molestation were the professional physicians and social workers whose lives are devoted to helping the victims of this very serious national problem. It would be a great convenience if all child abuse and molestation could be blamed on sinister men in overcoats lurking outside the school grounds. But the truth is that most of these cases involve people who are parents, and most of them are heterosexual. It does not help the victims of child abuse for anyone to pretend that the abuse is coming from outside the family; it only disrupts the efforts of those who are seriously concerned about a national tragedy.

To be accused of such a crime is no laughing matter. But in that year, I watched in mounting dismay as the debate over homosexual rights became a national joke about Anita Bryant. While her lines inspired an endless fund of material for the stand-up comics, they also aroused widespread fears and ugly prejudices that are not based on truth and have done too much damage in the past. The Ku Klux Klan came back to life in at least three places with Bryant's anti-homosexual cause as their rallying cry. Their newspapers called for the death penalty for homosexuals. The legislatures in a dozen states reacted to Bryant's crusade by either stopping action on pending homosexual rights bills or by enacting laws (in Oklahoma, Arkansas, Florida, and Pennsylvania) that further restricted the rights of homosexuals.

While I could appreciate Bryant's creating a forum on the subject, I found it disturbing that it was largely a forum of one. Only one of the national magazines that published lengthy interviews with Bryant bothered to follow that up with articles putting her claims within the context of scientific and medical knowledge. To me, this was just as irresponsible as publishing unchallenged the claims made by Southern racists—and they had plenty of "authorities" to back them up, including the Bible—that blacks were an inferior race inclined toward rape.

I suspected that a number of reporters and editors were so anxious to attack homosexuality (which they couldn't do directly) that they ignored certain obvious facts in order to give Anita Bryant her say. A careful reading of the files I assembled proved this to be correct.

In her first press conference, Bryant waved a leaflet published by the gay coalition in Miami and said, "The homosexuals' recruitment has begun." She implied that the leaflet was obscene and said it was being passed out at schools (a statement she later had to retract). None of the news stories pointed out that the leaflet was not obscene, but was a simple informational sheet, and that there was no reason why it couldn't be given to schoolchildren.

I began to see a pattern in Bryant's assertions, which I recognized from my own fundamentalist background. She would "tell a lie when the truth would do." Even with a substantial amount of source material to support her viewpoint, she always had to go beyond that. She couldn't resist the exaggeration that led to another distortion and finally to an outright lie.

The first advertisement of Save Our Children, Inc. stated that "The Los Angeles Police Department recently reported that 25,000 boys seventeen years old or younger in that city alone have been recruited into a homosexual ring to provide sex for adult male customers." I called up the LAPD and talked with Lieutenant Dan Cooke in the public information office. "That is incorrect," he said. "There is no homosexual ring; there isn't even a ring." I talked with a man in Bryant's office and he said, "Oh, somebody sent us that out of a newspaper in Minnesota." Another ad featured a letter from the head of Big Brothers of Minneapolis endorsing the Miami crusade and saying his city's anti-discrimination laws had prohibited Big Brothers from telling a parent that a prospective Big Brother was homosexual. (The *Wall Street Journal* quickly followed this up with an editorial column saying what a shame that discrimination laws were forcing people to do such things.) But the story was not true. The president of the Minneapolis City Council, Louis G. Demars, wrote to the *Miami Herald*: "Big Brothers now has the right and duty to disclose the sexual and affectional preference of all prospective big brothers to the little brothers and their families. The ordinance in Minneapolis is a good one. It has served as our recognition that all citizens regardless of their sexual or affectional preference are entitled to equal rights and protection under the law." His letter took up one paragraph of newsprint; the ad had spread the first letter across a full page.

On a more personal level, Bryant began to talk of the dangers she faced in speaking out. It became part of the ritual. Before she would sing her battle hymn, she would announce that there had been bomb threats but she was not afraid. Finally, reporters from the *Miami Herald* tracked down four of these "threats" and confronted Bryant with the lack of evidence. There had been no threats and nobody had told her there had been. "Are you sure?" she asked in answer.

The climax of the Anita Bryant crusade came when "in a stroke of Nixonian genius," as *New Times* called it, Bryant herself decided she was the victim of discrimination by gays. She read a solemn statement to the press about how she was being blacklisted, just as liberal entertainers had been in the 1950s. She said that homosexuals had pressured the Singer Company into canceling a contract she had to do a pilot for a television talk show, the dream of her life. Nearly every gay spokesman in America decried the canceling of that contract. Nearly every newspaper carried editorials critical of gays for causing Bryant to lose the contract.

In fact, there had been no pressure on the Singer Company and there couldn't have been because nobody knew about such a contract until it was canceled. Likewise, the pathetic attempts by some gays in some places to organize a boycott of Florida orange juice never had the support of the more responsible organizations and leaders. The spokesman for the Florida citrus industry supported Bryant's right to speak out throughout the crusade. Interestingly enough, he said, sales actually increased by 25 percent during that time.

In most parts of Miami, the final vote showed overwhelming support for Anita Bryant's successful drive to overturn the homosexual rights ordinance. One exception was in Precinct 37, North Dade Condominium, a retirement community mostly made up of Jews. The *Miami Herald* had assigned reporters to interview voters on their way out of the polls to ask how they had voted and why.

" 'What you have here is old people, many from the old country, and they know what discrimination is,' said Bea Goldberg, a resident of the community and chief poll clerk for nine years. 'Many of them are from Hitler's camps.' " The old people voted 597 against repeal, 299 for—that is, two out of three voted for homosexual rights. I wondered how the young president of Miami Beach B'nai B'rith felt, reading the wisdom of his elders:

"He was seventy-eight years old, a short, meek retired merchant with bushy eyebrows who had emigrated to New York from Russia as a child. 'We knew persecution,' he said, and he voted to uphold the gay rights ordinance. . . .

" 'I think the gays have a right to do whatever they damn well please,' said Esther Robinson, seventy-four.

" 'I didn't like her—Bryant,' said Minnie Koplowitz, seventy-five. 'Anybody who talks to God has a guilty conscience. God is in your heart.' "

Perhaps the funniest response to Bryant was a letter from Joseph J. Jaffa of Baltimore, Maryland, in the May 2, 1977, *Newsweek*: "I'm certain that if God really did have his hand on her, as Bryant states, it would be over her mouth."

Whatever Bryant's stated motives at the time, she naïvely and unwittingly laid bare her psychosexual problems as few other public figures have in our time. Although she and I were born a year and a day and several hundred miles apart, our families shared similar attitudes, especially about sex. We got our education out behind the barn. There was no such thing as a healthy attitude about sex; how could there be when you couldn't even talk about it?

Something even deeper was at work on Anita, however. Here she was, living in the lap of luxury, and yet she was consistently inventing "suffering" in order to fit the life of guilt and shame prescribed by her religion. Hadn't Jesus had his tormentors and people who made fun of him? Bryant loved the idea of bomb threats and the fact that people were making fun of her; it was confirmation that she was indeed on the straight and narrow, being a good girl, enjoying poor health.

Her fear of homosexuals was her fear of men in general. She never once spoke of homosexuals as anything but males unless she was specifically asked about lesbians. She writes in every one of her books about her mistrust of men and their "ulterior motives." In interview after interview, she spoke of her hatred for her father and her problems with her husband. Once, she said, they were separated "in body and soul" for several years; another time, she says it was only "God's law" against divorce that kept them together.

For people who abhorred homosexuality, Bryant and her husband evinced a peculiarly public obsession with the "nitty-gritty" (her words) details of it. My favorite quotation appeared in the *Washington Star*: "The reason homosexuals are called fruits is because God says in the Bible that men are trees, and new life is the fruit of the womb. You are forbidden to eat new life—the sperm."

Lindsy van Gelder offered the following explanation of the Miami crusade in the September, 1977, *Ms.* It was not "an issue of religion; only 30 percent of Miamians go to church on Easter, and while the Book of Leviticus, endlessly cited by Bryant as the last word on morality, also includes scriptures against eating snails and shaving beards, no one was taking to the streets to close down the city's French restaurants and barbershops. It should not even have been an issue of child molesting, since in eleven out of twelve cases such crimes are committed by heterosexual men against young girls. The campaign was about one thing: irrational sexual fear.

"The majority, as we all know by now, frequently holds up the dark mirror of its own projected guilts and fantasies and then blames minorities for the traits assigned to them. In much the same way that blacks are perceived as rapists and women as temptresses, homosexuals are seen as people whose lives revolve around sex, and are therefore subhuman. Gays easily become a convenient scapegoat for everyone from premature ejaculators and involuntary celibates to those who fear their own sexual desires."

Before my friend Lindsy wrote those words, we talked at length about what we had seen and felt in Miami. We agreed that the person with a problem was Anita Bryant herself. But neither of us could have predicted that Bryant would ever admit that.

"I often wonder what she is hiding," wrote S. Myman in the letters column of the *Miami News*. And in that extraordinary interview published in *Ladies' Home Journal*, Anita Bryant told all.

She said she and her husband were married for the wrong reasons. "Physical attraction was Bob's overriding virtue. He looked like Robert Redford and he was the first man I ever slept with. I was lonely and needy, very naïve and unhappy, which clouded my ability to look at what you should look at in a man. I had such doubts about getting married and I was depressed all through the honeymoon. Our problems never ended after that. It was obvious to anyone around us by the way we cut up each other verbally and embarrassed each other in public. . . . Someone can say he loves you, but when his treatment of you is diabolical, when you are used and abused, how can you believe that? Underneath Bob had a hate, a contempt for me. Who can withstand constant rejection—no respect, no trust, no affection, no love life, no recognition as a worthwhile human being? Something's got to give."

Bryant began taking sleeping pills and drinking wine in greater quantities to ease her mind. She had severe headaches, chest pains, difficulty swallowing food. On a tour of the Holy Land in the summer of 1978, she had to be hospitalized with a mysterious paralysis from the neck down that lasted for twenty-four hours.

What finally brought about her break with her husband and their "ministries" was Bryant's realization that there was a "satanically self-righteous conspiracy" to use her. It involved a "devil's triangle" among her husband, herself, and their fundamentalist marriage counselor, B. Larry Coy, who by this time was also in charge of Anita Bryant Ministries. Bryant says she tried to fire Coy, but by then the votes were stacked against her.

The showdown came at a board meeting of the ministries. The night before, Bryant had called Coy to tell him that she either had to get a divorce or she was going to die of a heart attack; she promised not to go public about it. At the board meeting, she said, "It was amazing the lies they accused me of, like a bunch of self-righteous Pharisees. They had already judged me. Bob made copies of letters written to me privately and they were read to the board. There was a threat that if I did not submit to my husband they would have me 'excommunicated.' Larry Coy even repeated my phone call saying, 'Anita told me last night she was going to get a divorce—openly. Now, Anita, do you have scriptural grounds for divorce?' "

Bryant scoffed at their efforts to get her to repent and renounce her evil ways, and finally stormed out of the meeting with the parting shot: "Good luck with the 'Bob Green ministries.' "

And what does Bryant think of fundamentalists and homosexuals now that she's been forced to admit in public that she's a victim herself? "Fundamentalists have their head in the sand. The church is sick right now and I have to say I'm even part of that sickness. . . . The answers don't seem quite so simple now. I guess I can better understand the gays' and the feminists' anger and frustration. As for the gays, the church needs to be more loving, unconditionally, and willing to see these people as human beings, to minister to them and try to understand. . . . I could see that a lot of people got involved in the crusade who had a personal vendetta about gays. They harbored hatreds.

They were as wrong as the gay extremists and they're going to hate Anita Bryant for saying that."

It was a scary time for a while, and in many ways the very real threat to our lives and freedom is still there, but the most heartening thing is that in spite of multimillion-dollar efforts, Bryant's crusade did not catch fire throughout the country. There is strong evidence that the extensive free and open debate on the subject changed public opinion toward more understanding of homosexuality than any of us ever expected to see in our lifetimes. I offer Anita Bryant's own change of heart as the most wonderful example of that.

However, as public opinion turns increasingly against the forces of the religious right and their true minority status is confirmed time and again, they have frantically renewed their attacks on homosexuals. In the direct-mail business, that means only one thing: somebody out there is responding more to this issue (with cold cash) than any other. The public may well begin to ask, as that letter writer did of Anita Bryant in Miami: What are they hiding?

In light of the continuing crusades against homosexuals, I think it is important to recall certain scientific and medical knowledge on the subject. The pioneer study was that of Alfred Kinsey, *Sexual Behavior in the Human Male*, published in 1948. Remarkably, the statistics from that study have endured the many assaults and revisions that succeeded it. But more important, the humanity expressed almost in a wilderness by Kinsey at that time has also gained ground in the succeeding years.

Kinsey concluded: "There are those who will contend that the immorality of homosexual behavior calls for its suppression no matter what the facts are concerning the incidence and frequency of such activity in the population. Some have demanded that homosexuality be completely eliminated from society by a concentrated attack upon it at every point, and the 'treatment' or isolation of all individuals with any homosexual tendencies. Whether such a program is morally desirable is a matter on which a scientist is not qualified to pass judgment; but whether such a program is physically feasible is a matter for scientific determination.

"The evidence that we now have on the incidence and frequency of homosexual activity indicates that at least a third of the male population would have to be isolated from the rest of the community, if all those with any homosexual capacities were to be so treated. It means that at least 13 percent of the male population (rating four to six on the heterosexual-homosexual scale), would have to be institutionalized and isolated, if all persons who were predominantly homosexual were to be handled in that way. Since about 34 percent of the total population of the United States are adult males, this means that there are about six and a third million males in this country who would need such isolation.

"If all persons with any trace of homosexual history, or those who were predominantly homosexual, were eliminated from the population today, there is no reason for believing that the incidence of the homosexual in the next generation would be materially reduced. The homosexual has been a significant part of human sexual activity ever since the dawn of history, primarily because it is an expression of capacities that are basic in the human animal."

PLAYBOY: As far back as 1948, Dr. Alfred Kinsey showed that, from his research, two out of every five American males had committed a homosexual act. You've heard of his research, we assume.

BRYANT: Not that much, no. But, of course, we know where *he* was coming from, personally.

PLAYBOY: What does that mean?

BRYANT: Well, I mean, he had no spiritual beliefs, no religious beliefs.

Bryant also says in her book that the American Psychiatric Association's removal of homosexuality from its list of mental illnesses did not reflect a majority of the membership. In fact, the members voted 5,854 in favor of the move, 3,810 voted against, and 367 abstained.

One of the most important comments on the subject came from within the Catholic church and was published almost simultaneously with Bryant's crusade in 1977. This was *Human Sexuality: New Directions in American Catholic Thought, a Study Commissioned by the Catholic Theological Society of America*, from the Paulist Press.

This study spoke directly to the fears voiced in Miami. Even discussing the subject of homosexuality, it said, subjected the study to "the prejudice and passionate hostility it invariably generates, attitudes born of ignorance and fear. Particularly for people not altogether secure in their own sexual identity, homosexuality is a highly emotional subject, not easily permitting of concrete objective discussion. What gross unfairness can be committed, for example, by those who see all homosexuals as child molesters or constituents of some subversive underground. . . . For too long homosexuals have been the victims not only of misunderstanding but also of silence and neglect on the part of theologians and those charged with pastoral care within the Church. . . .

"There is no doubt but that the Old Testament condemns homosexual practice with the utmost severity. The reason for the condemnation, however, and the severity of the punishment cannot be appreciated apart from the historical background that gave rise to them. Simply citing verses from the Bible outside of their historical context and then blithely applying them to homosexuals today does grave injustice both to Scripture and to people who have already suffered a great deal from the travesty of Biblical interpretation. . . .

"Above all, there are matters of justice to be recognized. The alienation, loneliness, and discrimination suffered by homosexuals can be attributed in no little part to the attitudes of the Church. . . ."

Just one victim of these attitudes was Ovidio (Herbie) Ramos. I happened to be in Miami the morning Ramos's body was found— empty bottles of sleeping pills and whiskey beside him, a fired revolver in his hand. I sat in mourning with his best friend and heard the story.

It began on Monday night, March 14, 1977, when both sides of the controversy were scheduled to appear on the Spanish-language radio talk show "Studio Uno." Bryant's Latin delegation would not appear unless the homosexuals repented their "sins" and agreed to seek treatment. When they refused, the anti-homosexual group sent a tape recording to represent their side.

Because both sides were not in the studio, the moderator would not allow the six men and women from Latins for Human Rights to answer the attacks on them being called in by listeners. These six were the only ones in an organization of twenty who were willing to risk public disclosure by going on the radio. Two of these would not use their real names on the program.

Herbie Ramos, twenty-eight, had always been effeminate; he had always been homosexual. Recently he had had violent conflicts with his family over his homosexuality. His father was constantly berating him for not being like his older brother, who was married and had children.

Ramos must have known before about the hostile feelings that exist toward homosexuals, but he sat there not believing the insults people were calling in. One woman—an immigrant herself—said homosexuals should all be deported. Another said homosexuals should be put in concentration camps or put to death. Men calling in made fun of homosexuals as sissies who swished like ducks. Herbie told his best friend, "I didn't know they hated us so much."

The next night, Herbie took a large quantity of Valium and drank a lot of whiskey. But the mixture failed to kill him. It was not the first time he had failed at suicide.

On Wednesday night, March 16, Herbie Ramos put a pistol to his head and this time succeeded in ending the conflicts in his life. The next morning, Jesse Monteagudo sat trying to describe him to me. "He was very effeminate, I guess. And, you know, campy. Some people didn't like him maybe. But, but . . ." Tears came to his eyes and he choked on the words.

"But he had a right to live," I said.

PART TWO

4

CREATING A "MORAL MAJORITY"

It was the truths that made the people grotesque ... the moment one of the people took one of the truths to himself, called it his truth, and tried to live his life by it, he became a grotesque and the truth he embraced became a falsehood.

—from *Winesburg, Ohio* by Sherwood Anderson

H. L. Mencken warned us about sending the firemen home too early. We assumed the flames of backwoods fundamentalism were put out during that famous exchange between William Jennings Bryan and Clarence Darrow in Dayton, Tennessee, in July 1925. The brilliant Darrow's arguments were so eloquent and convincing, we thought he must have won the case. It sure seemed that way in the book, the play, the movie.

In fact, Darrow lost. The young biology teacher, John Scopes, was convicted of teaching the theory of evolution and was ordered to pay court costs and a fine. The law restricting teachers in Tennessee remained in force. Darrow, nonetheless, felt he had won a larger victory by gaining an international audience for this showdown between enlightenment and ignorance, climaxed by that wonderful moment when old Bryan could take it no longer and shouted, red-faced, exasperated:

"The purpose is to cast ridicule on everybody who believes in the Bible, and I am perfectly willing that the world shall know that these gentlemen have no other purpose than ridiculing every Christian who believes in the Bible."

Convinced he'd won the day, Darrow shot back: "We have the purpose of preventing bigots and ignoramuses from controlling the education of the United States and you know it, and that is all."

But I am here quoting from the memorial biography published by Bryan's friends shortly after his death—in Tennessee, five days after the Scopes trial ended. They weren't ashamed of his words, and neither was Bryan. He thought he had won, in fact and in effect, and so did his fundamentalist brothers and sisters throughout the country. The very same arguments that served to convince some of us how wrong "those people" were only reassured them as to how right they must be.

Bryan had come very close to being President of the United States. But he lived long enough for people to be thankful for the boring but safe likes of Harding and Coolidge, said Mencken. Dullness moved into the White House, "but there is at least nothing to compare to the intolerable buffoonery that went on in Tennessee. The President of the United States doesn't believe that the earth is square, and that witches should be put to death, and that Jonah swallowed the whale. The Golden Text is not painted weekly on the White House wall, and there is no need to keep ambassadors waiting while Pastor Simpson, of Smithville, prays for rain in the Blue Room. We have escaped something—by a narrow margin, but still safely."

It was a temporary escape. Fifty years later, there was no need for Pastor Simpson to pray in the Blue Room; there was a lay preacher praying in the President's office. And every way you look, the ghost of William Jennings Bryan now stalks the land in a hundred different new embodiments. Standing where Bryan stood in the old Dayton courthouse, Jerry Falwell mounted a major nationwide television appeal in late 1981 for funds to defend new anti-evolution laws in twenty-two states. At a meeting of fundamentalist ministers in Dallas during the 1980 campaign, the actor who would replace the preacher President assured his audience that he was with them, that he, too, favored the teaching of "creationism" in public schools.

For at least two generations we had regarded that Mencken story out of a Tennessee hill town as a dated piece of fiction, a classic bit of local color, an isolated period piece. The absurdity of arguing about evolution versus the creation story in Genesis seemed as remote from our highly developed technological times as the Salem witch trials. But Mencken himself saw that fundamentalism was far from dead after Clarence Darrow's arguments exposed it to enlightenment.

"It is too early, it seems to me, to send the firemen home," wrote Mencken. "The fire is still burning on many a far-flung hill, and it may begin to roar again at any moment. . . . Heave an egg out of a Pullman window and you will hit a Fundamentalist almost anywhere in the United States today. They swarm in the country towns, inflamed by their pastors. . . . They are thick in the mean streets behind the gasworks. They are everywhere that learning is too heavy a burden for mortal minds, even the vague pathetic learning on tap in little red schoolhouses. They march with the Klan, with the Christian Endeavor Society . . . with all the rococo bands that poor and unhappy folk organize to bring some light of purpose into their lives. . . ."

We are told that out of this same tradition that Mencken described, a new and powerful force known variously as "the new Christian right" or "the religious right" or "the moral majority" has emerged. We are led to believe that these groups, or this movement, sprang naturally from the fundamentalist soil. But such is not the case.

A fundamentalist is generally defined as one who believes in adult baptism (that one should have a choice in the matter and be old enough to know what he is doing), in a literal interpretation of the Bible, and in being "reborn" or "born again" through a personal experience in accepting Jesus Christ as one's personal Savior. This definition does not begin to cover all those in the religious right. There are Orthodox Jewish rabbis on nearly every one of these groups' boards of advisers. In most cases, the groups themselves were set up by Catholics. The idea for Moral Majority, Inc., and the name itself came from two political operatives in Washington—one a Jew, the other a Catholic.

The most effective leaders of the new right are nearly all Catholics. The following are only a few of them: Phyllis Schlafly of Eagle Forum, Terry Dolan of National Conservative Political Action Committee, Robert Boege of the National Conservative Foundation, Robert Bauman, former national chairman of both Young Americans for Freedom and American Conservative Union, and Richard A. Viguerie, whose direct-mail expertise made winners of them all.

This odd ecumenicism of convenience was best described by Gerald Schomp, a recruiter for the John Birch Society, in his book, *Birchism*

Was My Business: ". . . on Sundays I went to a Catholic church to worship and to a Baptist church to be seen by all my close Birch friends. The sermons at this particular church were right-wing harangues and it was just like attending a chapter meeting." Schomp, of course, does not go into why he was so comfortable in the Catholic faith or discuss the possibility that his brand of politics might have grown out of such a rigidly defined belief.

The part of this so-called fundamentalist movement that is most upsetting to me and many others who descend from that culture is that these people are betraying their own best traditions. While I don't espouse the imposition of anybody's faith on our pluralistic society, I do think that this country grew out of that Protestant mentality which emphasized independence of thought, personal freedom, and the right to communicate with one's God directly without interference from the state or intervention by any earthly intermediaries of the church. Gore Vidal has a character in his novel *Burr* watching the immigrants getting off the boats in New York and saying that it won't be long before the Catholics have taken over the country. And, he muses, it is a contradiction for a person to be an American and a Catholic. I think that is an extreme view, true only when such a person begins to see the larger society in terms of his own religion, and begins to feel (as many thousands of Catholics now do on the subject of abortion) that the rest of society must be changed in order to conform with his own narrow faith.

Such rigidity of belief is precisely what defines the new right and its religious progeny for the moment, but it also explains that the movement carries with it the seeds of its own destruction. What may seem to outsiders as minor differences of language and interpretation of the same scriptures, are matters of deeply felt dogma to the firm believers—matters, to some, of life and death. And if one doesn't think such differences are the stuff people kill and die for, then he need only read the day's reports out of Northern Ireland and the Middle East.

However, the coalition that is the subject of this book did not take those differences into account. In fact, what defines this movement is its adherents' absolutist view of the world and the way life ought to be in the United States. For that reason, one cannot separate the new-right political groups from the religious groups that were set up by them. They made a very public show of solidarity with each other in the beginning.

It is impossible to say precisely when the new right had its beginnings, since it dates from a primitive attitude that was part of America's heritage all along. When I first began work on this book, I thought I would be hopelessly lost in a maze of attitudes, issues, people, and organizations. However, I soon realized that the subject was not nearly so complicated as it first appeared to be. Certain patterns quickly became apparent and I recognized that the new right consisted of a remarkably small number of leaders, issues, and attitudes.

In the interviews for the portraits of the new right leadership in the following chapters, there was always a point where the subject would stop me and assume the air of a kindly professor explaining life itself to a fresh young student. "You know, there are three kinds of government," he would say—never four or five or two, always three. Numbers two and three sometimes varied, but number one was always the same. (I later discovered these people had borrowed their list from the conservative author Russell Kirk, and he attributed it to Edmund Burke.) There are, according to the new right, those who believe that all authority comes from (1.) God (these are conservatives or the right); (2.) the government (liberals or Communists); (3.) the individual (anarchists or libertarians).

I couldn't believe I was hearing this the first time, but by the fourth time I had stopped taking notes and listened intently to be sure the person was actually reciting the same list, defending the divine right of kings by saying all power comes from God. They ignored or were ignorant of the fact that our founding fathers had rejected such a doctrine and that this country would not exist if its founders had held to this absolutist faith in divine rights. "It is not God and country, it is God," proclaimed Bailey Smith, president of the Southern Baptist Convention, at that historic Religious Roundtable meeting in Dallas which Ronald Reagan also addressed in the 1980 campaign.

In order to hold such precise views of who and what God—and, in turn, God's law—is, one must naturally claim to be in a privileged position, to be some sort of conduit or spokesman for God. Presuming to speak for God—or to know what He wants—is only a step away from presuming to be God. It is the rationale of vigilantes and dictators throughout history.

There were two strains of thought that ran through every interview I had with these leaders. The first was that there is no room for compromise; we must "get back to" the basic truths of good and evil. Every single person I interviewed used this sentence, almost word for word, at some point: "Peaceful coexistence won't work for us." (I wondered what they planned to do next, if they couldn't live at peace with the rest of us.)

The second was the spokesmen's view that only radical change will save us. The latter was also the thinking that Whittaker Chambers noted with reference to the American Communists in his book, *Witness*: "The tie that binds them across the frontiers of nations, across barriers of language and differences of class and education, in defiance of religion, morality, truth, law, honor, the weaknesses of the body and the irresolutions of the mind, even unto death, is a simple conviction: it is necessary to change the world."

Sitting across from several of the intense young men who are leaders of the new right, I came to the conclusion that with their uncompromising world-view, they could just as easily be Communists. They were, in effect, talking about the same sort of control of people's lives, the same totalitarian state, although they would never use such words to describe the world they want.

In his introduction to Richard A. Viguerie's *The New Right: We're Ready to Lead*, Jerry Falwell declares: ". . . it is no wonder that we find America depraved, decadent, and demoralized today. . . . The godless minority of treacherous individuals who have been permitted to formulate national policy must now realize they do not represent the majority. They must be made to see that moral Americans are a powerful group who will no longer permit them to destroy our country with their godless, liberal philosophies."

I think this celebration of our decline and fall is much too premature. We are still one of the most religious countries in the world. In his *Democracy in America*, written about a visit he made in 1831–33, Alexis de Tocqueville said: "America is still the place where the Christian religion has kept the greatest real power over men's souls. . . . The religious atmosphere of the country was the first thing that struck me on arrival in the United States. The longer I stayed in the country, the more conscious I became of the important political consequences resulting from this novel situation."

At the same time that the religious politicians rage on about our moral degeneracy and spiritual decline, they contradict such talk by their own polls and statements that most Americans are, in fact, religious and moral. They also selectively quote from parts of a poll conducted by Research and Forecasts, Inc. of New York City for Connecticut Mutual Life Insurance Co. on "American Values in the '80s."

As quoted in Religious Roundtable's newsletter, the survey showed that "74 percent of all Americans consider themselves religious. A total of 73 percent frequently feel that God loves them, and approximately half of all Americans frequently engage in prayer and attend religious services. The study identified 26 percent of the population, nearly forty-five million people, as a 'cohesive and powerful group' of intensely religious Americans."

This newsletter and every other religious-right publication that quoted from that survey blithely ignored the fine points that explained it and the dire warnings contained in its conclusions. Ten moral issues were used to gauge opinion in the survey: adultery, use of hard drugs, homosexuality, having sex before the age of sixteen, lesbianism, pornographic movies, abortion, smoking marijuana, living with someone of the opposite sex without being married, sex between two single people. The findings were hardly as simplistic as the religious press rendered them:

"The report observes that while a mere 3 percent of the public find none of the ten activities included in the survey to be 'morally wrong,' it is not at all clear that there is indeed a 'moral majority' in the nation. In fact, the report reveals that Americans who are strictest in their moral judgments, i.e., who believe that all ten of the activities are morally wrong, are in the minority. This 'moral minority' is about a quarter of the population (24 percent). Clearly, the vast majority of Americans prefer to evaluate each moral issue individually."

In conclusion, the report said: "The opportunity lies in the opening for a visionary leader to mobilize large numbers of people for national programs of self-sacrifice and devotion to shared goals. The danger lies in the opening for a divisive leader to mobilize large numbers in the service of a partisan campaign to blame the nation's troubles on one group or another labeled 'immoral.' "

The most significant finding of this survey—and, to liberals, the most frightening—was that the one-fourth who considered themselves deeply religious were much more likely to vote: 77 percent, compared with 49 percent. Considering that only 51 percent of the Americans old enough to vote in the 1980 presidential elections actually voted, this means that the country could conceivably be taken over and controlled by a "moral minority."

Falwell and his new-right colleagues are fully aware—from their own polls, if from nowhere else—that America is not the immoral mess they say it is. But they also know that their continuing popularity and their financial empires depend on this hyped-up sense of crisis. They are playing on a fanatic fear that God's people are under attack by atheistic Communists from within and from abroad. They may not all go so far as the John Birch Society's Robert Welch in saying that we are already 80–90 percent under Communist domination in this country and that Dwight D. Eisenhower was a Communist dupe, but that difference is only a matter of degree.

As McCarthy did before them, these people of the new right lose sight of the fact that their own tactics would destroy the very same freedoms they claim to be defending. Commenting on the "antics of McCarthy," in an editorial published March 19, 1950, *The New York Times* said: "There is a security inherent in democracy itself which may be lost if we lose faith in free institutions. There is a security in the existence of intelligent men and women willing to make their own moral and intellectual decisions and abide by the consequences. . . . [It] would be far better for a few secrets to leak out than for this nation to imitate the Communist or Fascist pattern and suppress, in the private citizen or the office holder, the right of private conscience."

What the right wing in this country is afraid of is not any real Communist threat. As Dalton Trumbo wrote in *The Time of the Toad*, about the McCarthy period: "The hard-headed, rock-ribbed gentlemen of the far American Right had known what they wanted all along, and their methods, though cruder and more brutal than their opponents', were expertly chosen for the job at hand. The anti-Communist campaign they had inaugurated on that cold January dawn in 1920 had been aimed at the entire left wing of American political life, and only incidentally at Communists. . . . The whole campaign had been a fraud, and it still is. The American Communist Party, unarmed, fluid in its membership to the point of instability, outmanned 80,000 to 131,000,000 at its peak, posed about as grave a threat of revolution as the Ancient Arabic Order of the Nobles of the Mystic Shrine, which outmanned it ten to one and had much more fun."

The religious right has come up with a 1980s equivalent for "Communist" in labeling everything liberal as "humanistic." The ignorant misuse of the word would be laughable if it weren't for the awesome possibilities posed by the very stupidity of those who use it.

What the rightists fear is freedom itself. This is suggested in an anthem of a precursor of Moral Majority, Moral Re-Armament, whose Up With People singers proclaimed: "Freedom Isn't Free." It is explicitly stated by leaders of various new-right and religious groups in candid moments when their true feelings come through the polite phrases they use on the talk shows and in interviews with the national media.

Rich Anquin, president of the Minnesota branch of Moral Majority, has said: "Freedom of speech has never been right. We've never had freedom of speech in this country and we never should have." A national officer of Moral Majority named Charles Stanley says: "We do not want a democracy in this land because if we have a democracy a majority rules." Jerry Falwell, in his *Listen, America!*, paraphrases the early essays of Robert Welch in his simplistic explanations that ours was never meant to be a democracy but a republic.

The reactionary sentiments expressed in such statements reflect a nostalgia for a time of white supremacy in matters of race and male chauvinism in the areas of sexuality and sex roles. The attitudes that most threaten the security of these new-right spokesmen are those that have brought about societal changes reflecting greater compassion and humanity regarding racial minorities, women, and homosexuals.

In the one brief decade of the 1960s, we finally resolved our Civil War on the side of humanity. The successful battles for the rights and dignity of black Americans led to other changes. What some people derisively call the "me decade," the 1970s, was, I think, a healthy time of introspection, focusing attention inward on the same questions we had asked of society in the 1960s. What resulted was greater freedom of personal expression on a private level and greater tolerance of other people's problems and peculiarities on a social level. In a moment of history, we moved from the unnatural barbarity of medieval attitudes and laws regarding sexuality and sex roles into a new kind of humanity that once seemed impossible. I think the mislabeled "moral majority" is a moral minority, as that Connecticut Life survey defines it. As anxious as we may be about the future, I don't believe the real majority of Americans want to return to the 1950s, much less to the 1590s. The "moral majority" will have its few seconds of fame and power and then fade from the scene as surely as the "Know-Nothings" did a hundred and thirty years ago.

It is a wild assortment of single issues that is brought together in this religious coalition created by the new right. One of the spokesmen I interviewed said everything the government did could be classified as a moral issue—including national defense and the budget. Such thinking was the subject of a letter written by Thomas Jefferson, the founding father most often quoted—although with extreme selectivity—by conservatives themselves.

I am aware that arguments may be found which may twist a thread of politics into the cord of religious duties. So may they for every other branch of human art or science. Thus, for example, it is a religious duty to obey the laws of our country; the teacher of religion, therefore, must instruct us in those laws, that we may know how to obey them. It is a religious duty to assist our sick neighbors; the preacher must, therefore, teach us medicine, that we may do it understandingly. It is a religious duty to preserve our own health; our religious teacher, then, must tell us what dishes are wholesome and give us recipes in cookery, that we may learn how to prepare them.

And so, ingenuity, by generalizing more and more, may amalgamate all the branches of science into any one of them; and the physician who is paid to visit the sick may give a sermon instead of medicine and the merchant to whom money is sent for a hat may send a handkerchief instead. But notwithstanding this possible confusion of all sciences into one, common sense draws lines between them sufficiently distinct for the general purposes of life; and no one is at a loss to understand that a recipe in medicine or cookery, or a demonstration in geometry, is not a lesson in religion.

In general, the major "social" issues of the new right are all about control—of children's minds, adults' behavior, and everybody's private sex lives, except for the sponsors' own, of course. Ronald Reagan called his encounter with conservatism a "rendezvous with destiny"; I would call my year among these people a rendezvous with hypocrisy. Under the guise of "getting the federal government off our backs," they have invited even more interference and intervention than we have ever known with liberals in charge. In fact, liberals now seem to have taken over the old conservative role of defending individual freedoms and the right to privacy.

The most extreme measure proposed by the new right is an omnibus bill called the Family Protection Act. Connaught (Connie) Marshner, the Roman Catholic mother of two children who was formerly with Young Americans for Freedom and then the Heritage Foundation, and who is now with the Committee for the Survival of a Free Congress, was the major author of this proposal. She has explained: "The bill came about because a group of Christian leaders and people with political experience and Christian values got together and worked for about a year in an ad hoc task force hammering out what were the biggest problems and seeking solutions for them through federal legislation."

The original conservative signers of the bill, which was first introduced in 1978, included a congressman who was so involved in a tawdry netherworld of homosexual intrigue that the FBI exposed him as a prime target for blackmailers; another signer was among the six conservative lawmakers involved in extramarital sexual play with the blonde lobbyist Paula Parkinson—he was the only one who filmed his exploit on videotape. The man who introduced the Family Protection Act in the Senate in 1978 and again in 1980 was President Reagan's best friend, Paul Laxalt, former governor of Nevada and owner of a gambling casino, who was involved in a bitter divorce some years ago with a wife who presumably considered him something less than the perfect family protector.

But the Family Protection Act is not only impractical in its attempt to cure all of society's ills through the government bureaucracy; it is also irresponsible. That is not just my opinion, but also that of many leading conservatives. If this is a conservative measure, wrote the erudite columnist James J. Kilpatrick, then "I have wasted my adult life in understanding and promoting the conservative cause. The bill is a hodgepodge of good intentions and bad law. . . . The sponsors of this misbegotten bill would involve 'recognized religious groups' in decisions relating to courses that touched upon religious beliefs. They would require 'parental review' of textbooks prior to adoption. They would intrude upon the right and power of the states to fix certification requirements for teachers. They would snatch funds from any state that prohibited 'voluntary prayer' on the premises of any public building.

"What in the world, we may gently inquire, has become of the conservative's traditional dedication to states' rights? What of the wall that conservatives insist should be maintained between church and state? . . . The bill is hopeless. It attempts to cover everything under moon or sun, from legal services to abortions to sex education to trust funds to private schools to food stamps for college students. In one way or another, the bill violates just about every precept of a conservative political philosophy. Legislatively speaking, it is so much junk. It ought to be quietly scrapped."

This view from another conservative shows just how extreme the social forces of the new right are in relation to the overall conservative political spectrum. It should be noted that Kilpatrick's column was written in response to the bill's introduction in the 1980 Congress; the new-right leaders had spent a full year drafting the measure for introduction in 1978, and when no action was taken on it then, they spent another two years revising it. And Kilpatrick still called it junk.

The most volatile issues rallied to by the new right came about through two Supreme Court decisions in 1973: the first one cleared the way for legal abortions throughout the country; the second mandated busing as the means by which local school districts were to carry out a strict quota system of school integration.

As for abortion, I know from my own background and from my coverage of anti-abortion and pro-life rallies in the past year that this is almost strictly an issue of the Roman Catholic faith, and possibly of only a small but strident percentage of its members. When George McGovern was running for reelection to the Senate in 1980, he spent an afternoon with the new Catholic bishop in South Dakota; they agreed on nearly every issue until they came to abortion. When McGovern said he felt it was a woman's right, the Catholic bishop said he was sorry, but he could not support him.

When I moved among the thousands of marchers who came to Washington for the "pro-life" rally in early 1981, I found that all but an insignificant number of them were Roman Catholics. So severe were their attitudes and so inflexible their spoken opinions, I felt for all the world as though I were back in the South, covering the Ku Klux Klan again. On stage there were some token fundamentalists—Jerry Falwell and James Robison usually show up, and this time there

was even a Jewish man (with no arms and crippled legs) who had converted to Christianity at the age of twelve and now made a living as a
folk singer at religious rallies. But among the marchers themselves I
was able to find only one or two Protestants. When I interviewed the
Catholics, I would ask first about abortion and then move on to other
issues that are identified with them. What about birth-control pills and
devices? What about divorce? Unless it was an experienced activist
who'd been interviewed before and knew where my line of questioning
was leading, they responded to a man and woman: yes, these too
should be against the law because "they're against my religion."

That is why I think responsible Catholic leaders are making a
dreadful mistake in not trying to calm these protests instead of inciting
their followers to more and more violent confrontations and conflicts.
Even a vast majority of those who define themselves as conservative in
this country are in favor of legalized abortion. The Catholics speak of
abortion as murder, but meanwhile support murder through capital
punishment, and by their refusal to support gun control and international arms limitation. They speak of the rights of the unborn, but never of the rights of the more than ten million women who have had
abortions in this country. I have heard Catholic sociologists cite the
church's own polls revealing that more than 80 percent of American
Catholics ignore the edicts regarding birth control.

I don't believe the Supreme Court will ever reverse its decision on
abortion, although a conservative Congress may well try to force the
issue. Most of the people in this country support the court in this particular case, and I think the Catholic church itself will suffer most in
any prolonged and bitter struggle over abortion. The church may well
find itself in the same position in America as in its native Italy, where
the voters recently reaffirmed their support of legalized abortion by an
overwhelming majority. In my childhood, one of the many horror stories that was spread about Catholics was that the baby would be saved
first if it came to a choice between its life and the mother's. That, you
see, was murder to us—because the baby, even at that stage, was not
yet born, not yet a person. I had wondered if I would ever find a contemporary illustration for this point, and suddenly it presented itself at
a Moral Majority training session. A Baptist preacher and local Moral
Majority official stood up and said, "I just got a call from my mother
this morning and she tells me my little sister, age fifteen, is pregnant
and she's going to have an abortion." A Catholic priest's little sister

would have had no such option. The fundamentalists have simply latched on to another issue that puts them in the limelight. They appear at these Catholic anti-abortion rallies, but the absence of their followers in the audiences confirms my point that most Protestants do not share the Catholics' passion for this particular issue.

An even more divisive issue than abortion is that of school busing. One can only grieve at the widespread abandonment of the public schools in America. If, as Jefferson believed, the hope of our democracy lies in universal education, then the fear of its downfall must surely accompany the abandonment of such education. If the new right has its way, the government will soon be subsidizing private schools and the only children left in the public schools will be those of poor blacks.

I once spent an afternoon talking with Federal Judge J. R. McMillan, in Charlotte, North Carolina, who made the ruling that the Supreme Court later upheld on busing.

There was, the judge told me sadly, "simply no other way to do it." Even after the Supreme Court had flatly ruled that Southerners could no longer continue with separate and unequal education for blacks and whites, segregation continued to be practiced. McMillan had spent months going over various plans for integrating school systems. In every case, the plans were merely another device for slowing the process down. The only fair way, McMillan decided, was to impose a strict quota system based on the percentages of blacks and whites in the district. In our mobile society, there was an obvious answer as to how to achieve racial balance: busing.

Although I finished high school five years after the Supreme Court's desegregation ruling, real integration was another ten years off in the district where I went to school. Still, we had a busing problem. As now, our parents protested that it would destroy our community to bus all the children across the river to school. They were right, to a certain extent, but many other factors had already started to tear at the cohesiveness of the community by then. As everybody began to own cars, we had greater mobility in our immediate area; and television gave us access to the rest of the world.

The county school superintendent explained the problems he faced in terms of cold hard cash: there was only so much money for new schools. In order to have new schools of any quality at all, we would have to settle for regional schools; and we would have to get to them on buses. We accepted that, of course, because we were still being transported to all-white schools. Now I hear people (in Boston and Los Angeles instead of the South, where integration has been achieved) saying that race has nothing to do with it; it's the busing they're opposed to. Nonsense. No racist ever called himself that.

The most specific illustration of this point is that the so-called "Christian academies" set up throughout the South and elsewhere in America in order to avoid integrated public schools also employ buses as a means of getting students to school. In many, perhaps most, cases the students travel farther than they would to the public schools. When politicians speak of supporting such schools, they are talking about subsidizing racism and encouraging the further abandonment of the public schools.

Many of the issues of the new right involve public schools, although these people are in the forefront of the private-school movement. They want to be able to censor books used in the schools, and to mandate prayers and Bible readings as part of the curriculum, in which they would also include the teaching of "creationism."

As for prayers in the schools, a liberal congressman from Oregon, Les AuCoin, has this answer for those who write to him in support of Jesse Helms's bill to try to prohibit federal courts from hearing any case involving school prayer. "I and the majority of U.S. religious organizations and church groups . . . oppose this bill. The focus of our opposition is not school prayer. What we oppose is a bill that would make it impossible for the federal courts and the U.S. Supreme Court ever to hear any case involving school activities that may infringe on our constitutional protection against 'an establishment of religion' by federal or state government or its agencies. The real danger of the Helms bill is this: if Congress can throw up obstacles to subvert constitutional rights in matters of religion, then it can do the same thing when constitutional protections involving freedom of speech or assembly are at stake."

AuCoin goes on to explain that the 1962 Supreme Court ruling on prayers simply struck down mandatory prayers in schools. Nothing in that ruling prohibits voluntary prayer by individual students. And, asks the congressman, wasn't that what Jesus had in mind in his words quoted in Matthew 6:5–6: "And when thou prayest, thou shalt not be as the hypocrites are: for they love to pray standing in the synagogues and in the corners of the streets, that they may be seen of men. Verily I say unto you, They have their reward. But thou, when thou prayest, enter into thy closet and when thou has shut thy door, pray to thy Father which is in secret; and thy Father which seeth in secret shall reward you openly."

As for Bible reading in schools, an editorial in *Christian Century* dated October 24, 1962, spoke to the questions raised by this issue even before the Supreme Court had ruled against it:

> If the court should decide that the reading of the Bible as a devotional exercise and the repetition of the Lord's Prayer are practices consistent with the intent of the First Amendment, tormenting and divisive questions will rise: what version of the Bible will be used—the Douay, the King James, the Revised Standard? Who will decide what ten verses should be read? The teacher? Can a public school teacher, an employee of the state, select a passage of scripture for a public school class without violating the Constitution? Shall the children select the reading? Imaginative young people have been known to select passages of Scripture which appeal to their prurient rather than to their spiritual interests. Would not Jews demand readings from the Old Testament; Christian Scientists readings from *Science and Health*; Mormons from the *Book of Mormon*? Which Lord's Prayer? When the Roman Catholic children complete their Pater Noster will they remain reverently quiet while the Protestant children add "... the kingdom and the power and the glory forever ..."? Meanwhile, what about the Jews, the Unitarians, the atheists, the Moslems, the Hindus—have they no choice but to listen daily to Christian prayer or to suffer the embarrassment of withdrawing from the presence of their schoolmates? Why should random passages of Scripture be read to children without comment? Is the Bible a talisman, a cabalistic charm? There will be no end to such questions and no end to the controversies they will raise. It seems entirely unlikely that a Supreme Court which has repeatedly restored the wall between church and state, which has been consistently faithful to the First Amendment, will now open a Pandora's box by legalizing the use of sectarian scriptures and prayers in public schools.

The logic suggested in that *Christian Century* editorial was followed by the court, and mandatory prayers and Bible readings were subsequently banned from public schools as violations of the First Amendment. Many of the fundamentalists see this as a contradiction. They think only in terms of the rights of the religious or the freedom of religious expression; they don't seem to understand that in the context of the times of our founding fathers, freedom of religion also meant freedom *from* religion.

The Supreme Court, as of this writing, has yet to rule on another emotional issue involving religion and education—the teaching of evolution in public schools. Although they make every effort to be diplomatic on the subject, the religious-right leaders are not speaking of teaching the story of the Creation in Genesis alongside Darwin's theory; they want it taught instead of evolution. A headline in Religious Roundtable's newsletter that read "Get Evolution Out of Our Schools" let that fact slip.

In Lynchburg, Virginia, a biology teacher at Jerry Falwell's Liberty College met his counterpart from the more liberal Lynchburg College one day. The fundamentalist said it really was a shame that the other teacher's students didn't at least get a chance to hear about "creationism," the newly coined word used to describe the Genesis story. "You know, you're absolutely right," said the other biology teacher. "And then I'd like the same chance to come and tell your students about evolution." Suddenly the fundamentalist grew quiet, his face reddened with anger, and he walked off.

This rigid attitude has emerged in all of the debates and court cases involving the issue of evolution and creationism in the past two years. The proponents of the Genesis story first talk of the free exchange of ideas and how they just want their children to have a choice, to have both evolution and the Creation story taught them, but gradually it becomes obvious that they are really talking about imposing their belief about how the world was created on a school course designed to explain scientifically how life has evolved on the planet. There is no argument among scientists as to whether evolution took place, but only *how*.

In a court opinion fully worthy of the best of our country's enlightened traditions, a federal judge in Arkansas in 1981 overturned that state's "anti-evolution" law and said its proponents were staging "a religious crusade coupled with a desire to conceal this fact." Judge William Overton said the Arkansas law violated all three tests laid down by the Supreme Court for deciding whether a law violates the First

73

Amendment: it had a religious purpose basically; it had no secular educational purpose; and it would involve the state in religious judgments.

Furthermore, Overton said, the law's definition of creation science "simply makes a bald assertion. It explains nothing and refers to no scientific fact or theory." He said the creationists did not take data and "weigh it against the opposing scientific data.... Instead, they take the literal wording of the Book of Genesis and attempt to find scientific support for it."

Stephen Jay Gould, a widely published author who is also a paleontologist and professor of geology at Harvard University, wrote in the January 12, 1982, *New York Times*: "The issue is not religion versus science, for no such opposition exists, but a particular, narrow sectarianism opposed to knowledge and learning in general...."

Gould, who testified against the anti-evolution law at the trial, noted that twelve of the seventeen individual plaintiffs were ministers. He asked an important question for our times: "We professional evolutionists are obviously concerned and angry about the creationist resurgence, but why should anyone else view it with more than mild amusement?

"First, although the etymology of the argument pits creation against evolution, the attack is directed against all science; if the earth is but ten thousand years old, then most of physics falls with the invalidation of radioactive decay as a method of dating, and nearly all of astronomy goes in rebutting the claim that light from distant galaxies takes millions of years to reach us. Creationism can only flourish in an ambiance of unquestioning authoritarianism. Second, the growth of creationism reflects no increased force of argument but the successes of a larger political program (identified with the Moral Majority and other rightist groups) that include defeat of the Equal Rights Amendment and a total ban on abortion. Jesters often prepare the way for heavy roles.

"This political setting also guarantees that creationism will not quietly recede after this recent, rousing defeat.... Eternal vigilance, to quote the old cliche, is indeed the price of liberty."

Jerry Falwell himself, in a sermon he distributed in 1965, pointed up the absurdity of taking the Bible literally. Falwell actually pleaded for a kind of humanistic reasoning in interpreting the scriptures. "If we are going to lift out of the Old Testament things that are convenient for proving our contentions, we are also forced to accept other things. For instance, we would be forced to stone to death everybody who does any work on the Sabbath, or who commits adultery, or who fails to tithe. You can see how absurd such applications are under the Grace of God. . . . One atheist said that he could prove anything by the Bible. This is true, if you are not fair to the full and complete revelation."

Falwell was subsequently able to curb this trend toward logic. He now dismisses that sermon as "false prophecy." In his 1980 book, he states without equivocation: "The Bible is absolutely infallible, without error in all matters pertaining to faith and practice, as well as in areas such as geography, science, history, etc." The "etc." is presumably meant to cover such biblical science as the "fact" that the earth is square and the sun goes around that square. But how do Falwell and other literalists explain the fact that in Genesis 1, God created man in his own image, while in Genesis 2, God made man from a handful of dust?

Much of Leviticus, you will find, is full of blood and gore. Here it is explained exactly how the preachers are to slice off the heads of little doves before the altar and to chop up live baby lambs and bullocks and goats. You're supposed to put the head over here, put the liver and kidneys someplace else, let the blood drain off into a bucket for some other reason, and then take the entrails outside and bury them somewhere. It is the word of God, God's law, but I did not find these laws being obeyed at Jerry Falwell's church the Sunday I attended. The church didn't even have an altar for such sacrificial bloodletting.

Fundamentalists don't slaughter lambs and goats on their altars, and yet they do seize on the story of the Creation as the inspired word of God, the absolute truth. But as these people rage on about creationism, I cannot imagine for one second that any of them would ever urge our Defense Department to shelve its modern warheads and go back to the spear, the slingshot, and the chariot—as it would be required to do if we were restricted to the science and technology set forth in the Bible.

As *The Washington Post* noted in an editorial hailing the Arkansas ruling: "There are encouraging signs that an opposition is at last beginning to organize to meet a threat it failed for too long to take seriously. The Arkansas ruling provides powerful support for these efforts. But it will be no substitute for them. In terms of determination, dedication, and all the other elements that create political clout, the creationists are still ahead."

The real struggle, noted this same editorial writer, "is being waged at the local level by parents, teachers, school board members and other citizens. They, in turn, powerfully influence textbook publishers, who determine what students will read. It is at this level that creationists have scored their greatest successes and that scientists and others interested in sound education have been most remiss."

In communities throughout the country, an incredibly small number of activist parents have marched into school libraries and set themselves up as censorship committees. With little or no visible opposition to their efforts, the school boards and teachers have had no choice in many places but to give in to their efforts. It is a struggle that would be laughable if it did not strike at the very heart of our free society. On many of the forbidden-book lists of these book banners, you will find that all but a few of the titles are those of black activists from the 1960s. The censors would swear that their intention is not racist, but that certainly is the effect of what they're doing. And once they get into the banning business, they just don't seem to know where to stop. For example, the word went out about certain definitions in *The American Heritage Dictionary*—and so, in a scattered bunch of communities, children are now denied access to one of the better dictionaries published in this country.

One book puzzled me every time I saw it on these lists: John Steinbeck's *The Grapes of Wrath*. It had been a while since I had read the book, so I pulled it down from my shelf and reread it. I had to laugh. The old preacher, of course, was what had them so upset. He'd been one of the best of the hellfire-and-brimstone exhorters, but he had finally admitted the error of his ways and given up preaching for good. The Joads still wanted him to pray over them in their various crises, although he explained that at his best he was a phony and a fraud and didn't know any more about God than they did. My niece, who teaches school in Asheville, North Carolina, tells me there was one happy result of the local crusade to ban Steinbeck from the school library shelves. The kids all rushed to read him while they could.

As for the new right's use of the issue of homosexuality, I have discussed that at some length in other parts of this book. However, three specific points need to be made about the subject as an issue:

1. The new right mistakenly claims that including homosexuals in civil rights laws would impose quotas in hiring—as with blacks and women. But the homosexual rights statutes all specifically prohibit such quotas for a very practical reason: it would require some sort of census of the number of homosexuals, and nobody wants that, even if it could be done.

2. The fears of what homosexuals might do to children are based on lies and distortions that fly in the face of all available medical and sociological knowledge. They also speak of a homosexual lifestyle as if it were something that could be controlled or changed through legislation. But that could never come about without some sort of police state; and they should also know that the lifestyle of Jerry Falwell and his kind is far more reprehensible to many people than anything done by homosexuals.

3. While they often say they "love the sinner but hate the sin" (incorrectly attributing a saying of Mahatma Gandhi to Jesus), they simply could not accomplish the elimination of homosexuality without isolating or eliminating homosexuals themselves. Many of them have been candid about their opinion that the death penalty should be reinstated to get rid of homosexuals. Dean Wycoff of Moral Majority in Santa Clara County, California, has said: "I agree with capital punishment and I believe that homosexuality . . . could be coupled with murder and other sins. It would be the government that sits upon this land who will be executing the homosexuals." James Robison has said of homosexuals: "You say, 'Don't you care about those people [who] have the problem?' Yes, I do. But the cure to cancer is not to ignore it—remove it."

Homosexuality is one thing only to the new right: an effective political issue. There are enough homosexuals holding leadership and staff positions in these groups for all of them to know that the threats they speak of are not real. What the issue means was spelled out by Robert Billings, first executive director of Moral Majority, at an organizational meeting of the group's Pennsylvania chapter, Pennsylvanians for Biblical Morality, in Emmanuel Baptist Church in Shermantown. Another minister who was there was privately appalled by what Billings was suggesting in the name of Jesus. Although he was in no position to speak out on the subject, he said, he did take notes on what Billings said and—when he heard I was writing this book—repeated the words for me to use. Billings said: "I know what you and I feel about these queers, these fairies. We wish we could get in our cars and run them down while they march. . . . We need an emotionally charged issue to stir up people and get them mad enough to get up from watching TV and do something. I believe that the homosexual issue is the issue we should use." Dan Hummel, the minister who is head of the Pennsylvania group, followed up Billings's remarks by saying: "Some say we should hate the sin and love the sinner. Well, men, we know what we hate and who we hate."

But these kinds of issues, which brought the divergent groups of the new right together into what seemed such a workable coalition in 1980, are also what render the movement ineffective, according to William Brock, former chairman of the Republican National Committee. "You can't build a party around those emotional social issues," Brock has said, "and I'm not sure government can solve them. The new-right groups are competitive not only in that they draw away money from us, but they draw away attention in Congress from the broad issues of tax reduction, job creation, health care, housing—the 'American dream' issues. We can only become a majority party by bringing together people around those issues."

The new-right leaders I spoke with would not be the least bit upset by such criticism as Brock's. While nominally Republicans, every one of them places "philosophy" or "ideology" above party politics. They have infuriated regular party officials time and again by crossing over and supporting Democratic candidates who agreed with their views. One of their prime targets in 1982 is Lowell Weicker, the liberal Republican senator from Connecticut.

Historically, these people should not be considered in the mainstream of two-party politics. They descend—in spirit and, in many cases, in fact—from the more radical fringe groups throughout history and from the periodic efforts to found a third political party by drawing on the ever-present forces of racism, nativism, or—in recent years—anti-communism, a respectable cover-phrase for all kinds of ulterior motives.

Their shared view of absolute right and wrong is what has provided the new right with a kind of ecumenical umbrella under which a Catholic archbishop, a Jewish rabbi, and a fundamentalist preacher can sit comfortably with members of the John Birch Society, the followers of Korean evangelist-entrepreneur Sun Myung Moon, and the Ku Klux Klan or the (white) Citizens' Council. The right-wing political professionals are, of course, very sensitive about being lumped together with all these different groups. But the connections are there.

The prevalence of John Birch Society members surprised me at first, but you will find references to the Birch Society in just about every biography of a new-right leader. John Rousselot, a new-right congressman from California, was formerly public relations director for the Birchers; Larry McDonald of Georgia, a stalwart fixture of the new right and a member of several groups' advisory boards, is also a proud member of the Birch Society's national council. The late Texas oil tycoon H. L. Hunt contributed to the Birch Society and to various other right-wing political groups; his son, Bunker, now serves on the society's national council. Bunker Hunt also contributed a million dollars to Moral Majority last year.

That a key leader of the new right started his career by working in the senatorial campaign of another prominent member of the Birch Society does not necessarily mean that he completely supported the Birchers' views, but he obviously didn't loathe them either. That a Birch Society editor was called in to advise Jerry Falwell does not mean that the two agreed on everything, but it does mean that they didn't exactly despise each other's philosophy. Likewise, that a delegation of Moonies attended the annual Conservative Political Action Conference in 1981 did not mean that the others attending endorsed Moon's brand of political religion. But I didn't see anybody trying to throw the Moonies out of the banquet hall as right-winger Larry McDonald did do to a reporter from the socialist paper *Progressive*, who showed up at one of his events.

As for the Klan, I don't think there will ever come a day when the new right will welcome these fellows in costume, but otherwise the ideology is so similar that I know from my own background that many members of the Klan are also members of Moral Majority—and vice versa.

Just two of the prominent Southern racists from the old segregationist days who are among the elder statesmen and heroes of the new right are Strom Thurmond of South Carolina, who led the Dixiecrat secession from the Democratic Party in 1948, and Jesse Helms of North Carolina, who started his political career in 1950 as an aide to Willis Smith in his bitterly racist but successful campaign for the U.S. Senate. That campaign included a disgraceful attack on the distinguished former president of the University of North Carolina, Frank Porter Graham, who later became moderator of the United Nations.

Willis Smith's newspaper ads screamed that "The South Is Under Attack." His campaign brochures said, "White People Wake Up," and asked such questions as these: "Do you want Negroes riding beside you, your wife, and your daughters in buses, cabs, and trains? Negroes going to white schools and white children going to Negro schools? Negroes to occupy the same hospital rooms with you and your wife and daughter?" After working in Smith's office in Washington, Helms returned to North Carolina and worked on newspapers for a while and then made a name for himself as a television editorialist by red-baiting the University of North Carolina at Chapel Hill, tearing away at the reputation the school had gained as an oasis of reason and tolerance in the South. He also voiced consistent and virulent opposition to the attempts by black people to secure their legal rights and equal opportunities.

Interestingly, Strom Thurmond also attempted to have the tax-exempt status of the National Council of Churches removed because of its involvement in "politics," meaning the civil rights movement. One of the early causes of the John Birch Society was also to bar church groups from political and social action—again, because of liberals involved in the civil rights cause.

In a book called *The Radical Right*, published in 1966, Benjamin R. Epstein and Arnold Forster observed: "Perhaps the most consistent target of the Radical Right's negative propaganda has been the churches—particularly when they espouse social applications of Christian teaching." At that time, Jerry Falwell was preaching a similar opinion to his congregation in Lynchburg, Virginia. But the times change, and the preachers and politicians change with them.

Only in rare candid moments will you hear any member of the new right publicly admit that these earlier arguments on the separation of church and state were really a cover for racism. They would have us believe that there is no connection between the new right and the old racism. But I contend that there is. In fact, one of the original masterminds of the new right is M. Stanton Evans, whose own life and career bridge the time separating these similar movements.

Evans is the son of Medford B. Evans, and as such is a second-generation right-wing activist. The elder Evans started out as a field worker for the original John Birch Society, then moved over to edit H. L. Hunt's *Facts Forum News*. In 1962, Medford Evans assisted former army major general Edwin Walker in his testimony before the Senate Special Preparedness Subcommittee. Walker had been relieved of his command in Germany because of his aggressive propaganda activities among his troops, using material supplied by the Birch Society. After that, Evans began work in Jackson, Mississippi, with the Citizens' Councils of America. (For public relations reasons the group had removed "White" from its name.) In 1966, he became editor of the Citizens' Councils' monthly journal.

The younger Evans, meanwhile, was working his way up the ladder of what he was one of the first to call "the new right." Like many other new-right leaders, Evans was among the ninety-three conservative college students who met in September 1960 at William F. Buckley, Jr.'s family estate in Sharon, Connecticut, to form a movement on the right to counter the "new left" on college campuses. The "Sharon Statement," the founding document of Young Americans for Freedom, was written by the son of the Citizens' Councils' editor, Medford B. Evans. In it, the young conservatives declared that "the forces of international Communism are, at present, the greatest single threat" to our liberties in America, and "the United States should stress victory over, rather than co-existence with, this menace. . . ." In a book he wrote later, *Revolt on the Campus*, Evans said the student conservative "believes the nature of the adversary is such that we cannot co-exist with it, but we must defeat it, if we are to survive."

The original members of Young Americans for Freedom were the real radicals in colleges in the early 1960s. To be any sort of leftist, however radical, was somewhat fashionable; it meant you'd get invited to the best parties and meet the most glamorous celebrities who came to visit the school. To be a reactionary in a time of forward motion was to swim against the current—and the YAF members felt stronger and all the more committed because of the very differences that set them apart.

The youthful radical-right movement would march on to victory in only twenty years. "The Republican platform [of 1980] reads like a YAF tract from around 1963," boasted its national chairman, James Lacy, a young Los Angeles attorney. "We feel we've basically got control of the party now and we're not going to let it go."

In March 1981, I went to the group's celebration of the presidential victory and the new senatorial majority. This was the annual Conservative Political Action Conference staged by YAF and the American Conservative Union. The ACU had been founded, Lacy explained, "when we decided we needed a senior organization."

The group boasted of a twenty-year high in membership, with 80,000. In Virginia alone, the group's national headquarters, there are 3,000 YAF members. The largest single campus chapter in Virginia and the country is at Jerry Falwell's Liberty College, where 400 students belong to YAF.

At an opening press conference for this event, Lacy discovered that he had scheduled it in a spacious first-floor room the hotel had rented to somebody else. With Lacy in the lead, we went up on the elevator and wound around a dark corridor until we came to a tiny meeting room that looked like an ordinary hotel bedroom without the furniture. Lacy quipped as he entered, "Reminds me of the pre-power days."

The high point of "CPAC '81" was the banquet speech by Ronald Reagan, who had addressed the conference every year for eight years, since its founding. The printed program listed the current national advisory board of Young Americans for Freedom, including the President and six members of his cabinet, along with 19 senators and 102 representatives. The days of being the odd conservative on campus were long gone; the "yaffers" had arrived in force.

5

A COMPANY CALLED
RICHARD A. VIGUERIE

Richard A. Viguerie was a name none of the founders of Young Americans for Freedom had ever heard, so, of course, he was not invited to their original meeting. This is a telling fact recorded by Viguerie in *The New Right: We're Ready to Lead*, his history of himself, his direct-mail empire, and a political movement that caught on and made money. If the business of government is business, as conservatives are forever saying, then the business of the new right is a company called the Richard A. Viguerie Company, or RAVCO, and more recently just The Viguerie Company.

The implication of Viguerie's absence at the Sharon meeting is that the real messiah of the new right had still not emerged from Texas. The YAF founders would learn soon enough who was the most important person to their movement.

Lost in a maze of names and organizations when I first began this book, I kept coming back to one: Richard A. Viguerie. He was born September 23, 1933, in Golden Acres, near Houston, Texas. His parents were from Louisiana, of French descent, and Roman Catholic. They had one other child, a daughter, Annette. The mother worked in a paper mill during World War II, and the father started out as a construction worker at Shell Oil and worked his way up to an executive position.

Young Richard attended public schools except for part of one year at a Catholic school. He was a strict believer in Catholicism, but he was always comfortable among the more devout Baptist fundamentalists, with whom he also attended college. His dream was to earn an engineering degree, go to South America, and make a fortune so he could come back, run for Congress, and serve there for the rest of his life. But his problems with college algebra convinced him he was no builder of bridges. He carried his dream of a career in politics with him to law school, after earning a B.S. in political science at the University of Houston. Here again, it seemed he could make a "C" but never better. As he tells it, "I woke up to the fact that I was not going to be a second Clarence Darrow."

Viguerie's poor aptitude for algebra and the law didn't keep him out of politics, at least as a campaigner. He worked for Eisenhower in 1952 and then became president of the Young Republicans Club in Houston.

In 1960, Viguerie worked for John Tower in his campaign against Lyndon Johnson—who won reelection to the Senate the same year he won the vice-presidency. Although he wasn't invited to the founding, Viguerie did inadvertently end up with YAF. In 1961, he answered an ad in the *National Review* calling for a field man to work for an unidentified national conservative organization. He didn't know about YAF and so assumed it was the older Americans for Constitutional Action.

But when he got to New York City he found that he was to be executive secretary of the younger group, and that it faced an indebtedness of $20,000, with almost no money in the bank. Viguerie has described himself as a shy person who didn't take to the kind of face-to-face, door-to-door pitches that were necessary to fund raising in those days.

He reasoned that if he couldn't do it comfortably in person, maybe he would do better writing letters. Out of that simple inspiration, as Viguerie himself tells his story, came the enormously successful direct-mail operations that helped change the character of American politics and in the process managed to overburden the postal service with billions of extra pieces of mail written by a computer and read by only a small fraction of the millions of people who receive them.

When YAF moved to Washington, D.C., in 1962, Viguerie and his wife, the former Elaine O'Leary of Houston, moved with it. (They now have three children.) This job lasted until December 1964, when—according to Alan Crawford, a former "yaffer" himself, writing in *Thunder on the Right*—Viguerie left YAF and carried the mailing list with him.

According to Viguerie, his famous lists did not begin with the one he took from YAF, but with Barry Goldwater's. In those pre-Watergate days, the only requirements about reporting campaign contributions were that all those who had given over fifty dollars should be listed in a report to the House clerk. The names had to be copied by hand, and Viguerie said he and "several women" did the work.

Although Viguerie describes himself in his book as a son of Barry Goldwater, the senator does not return the favor. Goldwater is a party man with no taste for most of the issues that bother the new-right leaders. It is hard now to determine which came first, Viguerie's attitude about the Republican National Committee or its officials' attitude about him. In any event, he has never managed to win the very lucrative fund-raising and promotional accounts of the party's campaigns for President. Losing those obviously rankled. And Viguerie now explains that "I was always a conservative first."

He also once said: "I don't believe in my lifetime you will ever be able to successfully market the word 'Republican.' You could as easily sell the Edsel or Typhoid Mary. The Republican Party is like a disabled tank on the bridge, impeding the troops from crossing to the other side. You've got to take that tank and throw it in the river."

Wayne A. Stewart III, a former executive at Viguerie's company who became a fund raiser for the Republican National Committee, says Viguerie "set a course at that time to destroy the Republican Party. . . . I'd never question his integrity, not from any of the dealings I've had with him. But instead of helping to make things work, he wants to tear it down, destroy what's there and start from scratch."

One ludicrous moment in Viguerie's career came in 1976, when he offered himself as a vice-presidential candidate for the American Independent Party. He withdrew when the convention nominated Lester Maddox for President, not because of the candidate's avowed racism, but because he considered him a hopeless candidate. That same year, Viguerie had tried to get George Wallace interested in heading up a strong third-party movement, but the ailing Wallace was not interested. In his book, Viguerie mentions a friendly visit to Wallace in Alabama—with two other new-right leaders, Paul Weyrich and Jeffrey St. John—and speaks of his disappointment that they couldn't work together on a new party; again, he doesn't mention Wallace's racism. In fact, he says they agreed on nearly every issue they discussed.

Viguerie himself would ascribe his phenomenal success to his dedication to a cause or to his "philosophy." He has, in a very short number of years, amassed a fortune and a true business empire of his very own. He had started out in three rooms over a drugstore on Capitol Hill. In 1982, he has 275 employees and he plans to move his operations into his own nine-million-dollar building in suburban Virginia.

To get there, he tells of many years with no vacations, and seven-day weeks with many ten- and fourteen-hour days. I don't think politics alone can explain such fanatical drive. I think Viguerie is a self-defined failure who has achieved wealth and power the only way he could. He couldn't succeed at politics the way he dreamed of as a child—by becoming an engineer and retiring to Congress, or by becoming a lawyer. He wasn't good enough or smart enough for either of those routes, he says. But with hard work and cunning, he could become a real power behind the throne, the key man in everybody else's campaign, the one who can bring in the money.

He had never risked such a public show of failure before that debacle in 1976 at the American Independent Party convention, and it's difficult to imagine that he would ever take such a risk again. And yet he has described himself as "like the Kennedys in one regard. I'm very competitive and I hate to lose. I can be playing a fourteen-year-old kid on the pinball machine in the basement and I want to beat him." He is the fiercest kind of competitor, one who won't risk actual defeat in an ordinary contest, one who is competing with himself.

There seems to be a darker side to Viguerie, an important gap in who he says he is and the man others describe. Some interviewers have hinted at this, but nobody has reached this mysterious part of the man, possibly because he hasn't discovered it himself. The only hints have come when he has committed such a seemingly uncharacteristic act as his attempt to run for Vice-President. One unexplained incident was when Viguerie took his children out of one of the best schools in suburban Washington and put them in a Christian academy in Virginia. Another odd fact is that although they're strict Roman Catholics, the Vigueries also believe in the spiritualism of Edgar Cayce and in reincarnation.

Robert Timberg of the *Baltimore Sun* wrote that "to understand Mr. Viguerie, one must look beyond the trim, balding man in the pleasant suburban office and see the world as he sees it, as a dangerous place where things go bump in the night." Says Viguerie: "We feel the Soviets are knocking at the door. We're at war with the Soviets right now. The only people who don't recognize that are the liberals in the Western world."

His heroes to this day are "the two Macs" of the 1950s. "I was very angry over the firing of [Douglas] MacArthur, who wanted to win the Korean War and beat the Communists. And I felt the same way about Joe [McCarthy]—he was a fighter fighting Communism." He has said that McCarthy was right "even when he was inaccurate."

In 1973, George Wallace's brother asked Viguerie if he would take charge of raising the funds to pay off Wallace's 1972 presidential campaign debt. Viguerie raised eight million dollars in three years; more important to his business, he emerged with the name and address of every person in America who had responded to the appeal for funds for Wallace. Added to the Goldwater list and others, this became the core of Viguerie's famous conservative lists. In 1980, Viguerie sent out more than seventy million letters through one hundred different lists and raised more than twenty million dollars for conservative candidates.

A sales packet for potential customers shows just how extensive the mailing lists of the Richard A. Viguerie Company are. This packet, which I obtained at the company's exhibit at the Conservative Political Action Conference in Washington in 1981, indicates how much these customers must pay just to rent the lists alone. Additional costs involve the writing of the letter and sample tryouts to see what wording is most effective; then there are other costs for postage and handling, for paper, and for the use of the machines.

Most of the categories are predictable—donors to conservative candidates, the subscription list of *Conservative Digest* (owned and published by Viguerie), Americans Against Gun Control—but many of them are not: those who buy family history books, for example.

A list of 204,000 "affluent farmers" rented for $32.50 per thousand names; 1,300,000 names and addresses of boat owners went for $28 per thousand; 170,000 names and addresses of "donors to needy children" rented for $30 a thousand. One recommended list was of "Donors of $15 (average) to one or more charitable appeals concerned with missionary work, health and welfare, veterans' assistance, and social morals." There were 219,000 of those renting for $35 per thousand.

Viguerie achieved his power not just through making his magic lists available to individual conservative candidates; he also had a major assist in 1974 from the reformed election laws enacted by a Democratic Congress to correct the kind of abuses Republicans made famous in the 1972 Nixon campaign. A small number of individual investors had contributed the monumental amounts that made Nixon's amazingly expensive (considering the odds were always in his favor) campaign possible. The new laws prohibited individual contributions of more than one thousand dollars directly to a campaign. Direct mail thus became the only feasible way to go after the larger numbers of smaller contributions. Viguerie insists there's nothing new in what he's doing, he just does more of it and more effectively. In his book, he names the liberal George McGovern as an early collector of mailing lists and advocate of direct-mail campaigning. He also says McGovern talked to him about working for his 1968 senatorial campaign. Viguerie declined, but says another direct-mail company raised twenty million dollars for McGovern in 1972.

The political action committees that had such an important impact on the 1980 campaigns were almost all set up to take advantage of the new reform laws, although unions and other special interest groups had had such committees for many years. These PACs became one of the major sources of revenue for the Richard A. Viguerie Company.

In his book, Viguerie names four people as the main architects and commanding generals of the new right: himself, of course, and three other men, all of whom are founders and current presidents of political action committees. They are Howard Phillips of The Conservative Caucus, Paul Weyrich of the Committee for the Survival of a Free Congress, and John Terry Dolan of the National Conservative Political Action Committee (NCPAC, pronounced "nikpak"). The only other conservative group in their league of spending and influence is the Congressional Club set up by Jesse Helms of North Carolina. All of these groups, including Helms's, started out as and have remained clients of the Richard A. Viguerie Company.

Being a writer and a collector of letters—historic and recent ones from special friends—I find "direct mail" more disturbing than others who have been closer to the development of computers might. In effect, computers are now talking to each other through this dehumanized form of communication. Millions of Americans are receiving letters signed by people who have not only not written the letters, but in most cases have never even read the words over their signatures. This was explained to me by Robert Boege, president of the National Conservative Foundation, a subsidiary of NCPAC: "Those people who sign those things don't read them; they [he, of course, meant "we"] don't have time." Many of the letters come equipped with post-cards to send to Washington, or self-addressed envelopes to return to the senders. In every case, the returned letters are processed by computers printing out personalized thank-you letters from the President or a congressman or a candidate, which none of them ever saw or signed.

Viguerie has outlined a set formula for the effective letter:

1.   It must be personal, written from a recognizable figure to anybody and everybody, but with the receiver's name at the top and written in a casual, conversational (and often ungrammatical) style.

2.   It must involve the reader—by telling him his contribution will carry with it a seat on an advisory committee, or the letter itself will ostensibly contain some "confidential report" meant only for this person's eyes.

3.   It must appear creditable and authoritative. I have been on twenty of these lists for the past year. Every letter I received was on longer-than-letter-sized paper, folded twice, and the message was typed single-spaced, starting at the top of the first page and continuing for four pages (two sheets, back and front) to the very bottom of the last. The message is full of facts and figures and quotations along with every sort of dire warning as to what will happen if the receiver's urgently needed contribution is not sent by return mail.

4.   Last, but most important, Viguerie says, "the successful direct-mail fund-raising letter must evoke a strong emotional response."

After reading some of this stuff, you have the impression the letters are asking for more than a contribution; they seem to be asking for blood. NCPAC's Terry Dolan told Alan Crawford that the point of direct mail is to "make them angry" and "stir up hostilities." He said the "shriller you are" the more effective you are; "that's the nature of the beast."

In an interview with Nick Kotz published in *The Atlantic*, Viguerie said, "The interesting thing about direct mail is that when it's professionally done, it has a devastating impact. It's like using a water moccasin for a watchdog—it's very quiet." He also said, "We didn't invent playing to fears. The liberals try to scare [their] people as we do ours. People vote *against* long before they vote *for*. People aren't interested in sending money for good government; that is something they expect. They will give money quicker to defeat someone who is opposed to their beliefs."

Thus, you find a U.S. Senator, Jesse Helms, explaining in a mailing of March 1976 why he helped to organize NCPAC. "Why? Because right now your tax dollars are being doled out to people who are perfectly able to work, but *refuse* to. Because your tax dollars are being used to pay for grade school courses that teach our children that *cannabalism* [sic], *wife swapping*, and the *murder* of infants and the elderly are acceptable behavior. . . ." (It took a while, but I finally tracked this one to its source—a National Science Foundation series of sociological studies for advanced high school students, which in no way advocated the practices described.) Toward the end of page four, Helms gets to the point of it all: "But I'll be honest with you. I don't know if NCPAC is going to be able to keep on going. Because, sad to say, it takes money to keep going. So if we don't receive financial support from you and other concerned Americans we will have to stop everything. . . ."

In Virginia, a fund-raising letter went out over the signature of a young bachelor legislator, John S. Buckley, warning that the U.S. Department of Education "could force your child or grandchild to sit in a classroom and hear that homosexuality is natural and decent." The department, said the letter, is "fueled by ultra-liberal, special interest money, militant homosexuals, and 'sex counsellors.'" Buckley—former national chairman of YAF and a cousin of columnist William F. Buckley, Jr.—later explained that "these folks [his direct-mail advisers] wanted to send out the letter this way. . . . They assured me the facts were documented, and I said, 'Okay by me.' This was not something I initiated." In other words, ideas and facts that were not his were sent out in a letter that he did not write—but that bore his signature. And the young legislator saw nothing unusual in any of that.

The number of political action committees operating in elections has grown from 608 in 1975 to 2,785 in the 1979–1980 election cycle; the amount of money they have spent on elections has grown from $12.5 million for 1974 to more than $131 million for the 1980 elections. Nine of the top ten biggest spenders were conservative organizations. NCPAC spent $7.5 million for 1980 and the Congressional Club spent $7.2 million.

I began to wonder about these figures after a young man with Jesse Helms's Congressional Club proudly told me (at the CPAC meeting) that "we had to spend over four million to make six million." But, I asked him, how did they account for that expenditure? Were the people contributing funds being told that most of that money was not going to conservative candidates, but to fund-raising operations? "Oh, yes," said the fellow from the Congressional Club, "one of our brochures shows that in one of those pie-graphs." He picked up the brochure he had just described and looked at it and then at me, aghast—there was no way in this accounting that the contributor could have known that two-thirds of the money was going for direct-mail and other expenses.

Alan Crawford writes in his book, *Thunder on the Right*: "Huge amounts of money have been raised by the New Right PACs, but relatively meager amounts have actually been received by the candidates for whom the money is raised. By and large, the worst offenders have been PACs using RAVCO as their fund raiser." In 1976, the Committee for the Survival of a Free Congress "raised" $1.7 million, but only $265,000 of that amount went to candidates; in 1978, the same group raised $1.2 million and gave just $127,000 to candidates. The National Conservative Political Action Committee raised $2.5 million in 1976, with $386,800 going to candidates; in 1978, NCPAC raised $1.5 million, with $212,000 going to candidates. Republican fund raiser Wyatt Stewart says Viguerie's charges of at least 50 percent are way too high. Stewart charged only 25 percent.

Still, Viguerie's supporters are as absolute in their loyalty to him as they are to their cause. He may cost more, says Paul Weyrich, but he gets the job done. Weyrich describes Viguerie's role as that of a "catalyst. He is somebody who taught the conservative movement to dress for success. He made us think in terms of winning."

Their first big winning season was in 1978. The major new-right cause that year was to block Senate approval of the Panama Canal treaty. Conservative Caucus mailed three million letters against the treaty and conducted anti-treaty rallies in fifty states; NCPAC sent out half a million letters; the American Conservative Union raised one million dollars through a half-hour television documentary, and also mailed out two million letters. According to Viguerie, new-right groups mailed out between seven and nine million letters concerning this one issue in less than a year.

Viguerie quotes a startling set of figures in his book, which explains where much of the money is coming from, if not why so much of it is going to the conservatives. In 1976, the political action committee of the Chicago & Northwestern Transportation Company gave 92.9 percent of its political contributions to liberal candidates, but in 1978 only 17 percent went to liberals; the National Forest Products Association gave 100 percent to liberals in 1976, but only 17 percent two years later; Weyerhauser Corporation gave 61.9 percent to liberals in 1976, 17 percent in 1978; Georgia Pacific gave 44.8 percent to liberals in 1976, but only 16 percent in 1978.

Viguerie concludes: "Conservatives will dominate the 1980s, I predict, because most of our leaders are now coming into their own, while most of the liberal leaders are dead, retired, or just too tired to compete in the demanding decade before us." That may be true, but it might also be that these corporations are simply following a prevailing wind and they would just as easily shift back to support of liberals if those candidates show signs of being able to win elections next time.

The innocent contributor to new-right causes apparently has no assurance as to how his funds will be used. Even if one-half or two-thirds of the amount he thinks he's contributing directly to a cause or candidate is diverted to the fund raiser, no law has been broken; there's no such thing as "false advertising" in political campaigns.

However, there is one area where Viguerie's fund-raising techniques have come under scrutiny and failed the test. His mailings for charitable groups were found, in a New York investigation, to be "instruments calculated to deceive the contributing public into believing that the greater portion of the dollar contributed would be expended for the specified and represented program services." The New York State Office of Charities Registrations audited Viguerie's work with certain groups in that state between 1971 and 1973. Working with Citizens for Decency, Viguerie retained 93 percent, 84 percent, and 69 percent of the funds he raised for three years. With another group, Americans for Effective Law Enforcement, in 1974, Viguerie retained 90 percent of what he raised; in 1975, he raised $5.4 million for the National Rifle Association and kept $3 million—possibly a contributing factor in his break with that group and his organization of a rival group, Gun Owners of America.

In 1977, Viguerie's work with two groups affiliated with Sun Myung Moon caused him additional troubles in New York. The Korean Culture and Freedom Foundation was prohibited from further solicitations because in 1975, of $1.5 million raised, more than $900,000 went to Viguerie. That same year, the Children's Relief Fund—whose president is Moon's right-hand man and preaching interpreter—sent out a letter through Viguerie that said: "As I write you this letter, thousands of little boys and girls are suffering from the terminal forms of malnutrition. . . . What better gift could you give than a gift to fight suffering and death?" A New York attorney general's report of this Viguerie operation said: "The disproportionate and wholly inadequate expenditures for program services ($95,674), was the direct result of the unconscionably high fees of $920,302 (60 percent of expenses) disbursed to the professional fund raiser, Viguerie. . . ." In Ohio, a similar investigation of the same group found that its financial report was "inaccurate, false, and misleading" and that the fund-raising drive itself had caused "substantial annoyance, inconvenience, and pecuniary injury to residents."

There was another Viguerie client whose stated purpose was to collect money for distributing Bibles in Asia. No Bibles ever got there through Viguerie's efforts; he charged 12 percent more than the total amount collected. "It's easy to demagogue on that," scoffs Viguerie, "but we were out there prospecting." Such attacks, he added, had only forced him to stop helping charities—at least two of them had left him for other fund raisers anyhow.

Viguerie still thinks of himself as some kind of missionary. He speaks of sacrificing time with his family and vacations in order to "organize the movement" after Gerald Ford named the liberal Nelson Rockefeller—"it might as well have been Teddy Kennedy," said Viguerie—as his Vice-President. He says from the moment he wakes up he thinks about what can he do to change the country. "I wouldn't just want to be manufacturing widgets. I like the fact that I can combine a successful business with politics and I can help orphans and people who have leprosy in India and whatever." There's no evidence he's ever done either of these things, or of how much he would charge if he did.

But Lyn Meyerhoff of Baltimore, a fund raiser for national GOP candidates, says: "He's not a force, he's a service—he's a service you buy." And Robert Boege of NCPAC's National Conservative Foundation told me what he thought of all the direct-mail experts: "Those people have no politics, no philosophy—save Mammon's."

Although Viguerie and his new-right generals lost a battle over the Panama Canal treaty in 1978, they felt they were headed toward victory in the war by drawing so much attention to their cause. They also made substantial headway in two successful campaigns that unseated the prominent liberal senators, Dick Clark of Iowa and Thomas J. McIntyre of New Hampshire. A coalition of "Stop ERA, pro-gun, prolife, right to work" had won for the conservatives, says Viguerie. And the religious were emerging as a whole new source of political power. The Sunday before the elections in Iowa, new-right forces manned the church doors to give out anti-abortion leaflets after mass to the Catholics, and to distribute other leaflets promoting different causes to Protestants.

Richard A. Viguerie, the "godfather" and King Midas of the new right, was also present for the birth of the religious offspring of his movement. His name does not appear on any of their boards, but they are all clients of his direct-mail business. It can also be assumed that Viguerie was involved in the original discussions that led to these groups, since all three of the major ones were created out of Viguerie-related organizations. Religious Roundtable was set up by Edward McAteer and Howard Phillips of The Conservative Caucus, and Phillips and CSFC's Paul Weyrich were the ones who thought up Moral Majority; Gary Jarmin of the American Conservative Union helped set up Christian Voice.

The following chapters profile each of these men and show how their lives led to the religious right. NCPAC's Terry Dolan is also included. In recent months, Dolan has diplomatically tried to put some distance between himself and the religious groups, but he told me he was close to them and involved in nearly everything they're doing. Also, it was the new right's self-proclaimed founder, Richard A. Viguerie, who said in his book that Dolan was one of the four rulers of the new "social conservatives" in America.

Out there were millions of people just waiting to be called—"an army that meets every Sunday," as one new-right leader phrased it. All that was needed was a man to lead them and an organization with a catchy name they could rally around. The new right was ready with the man, with a name for the group, and with all manner of experience in raising money and keeping in the news.

MUTUAL FUNDS

The following chart is designed to show the interrelationships among the leaders and groups of the new right who are discussed in this book. The U.S. congressmen are designated by a single asterisk (*); the U.S. senators by a dagger (†).

THE CONSERVATIVE CAUCUS

Charles Black, Joseph Coors, Dan Crane*, Bob Dornan*, Jerry Falwell, George Hansen*, Jesse Helms†, Gordon Humphrey†, Eddie McAteer, Larry McDonald*, Howard Phillips, Steve Symms†, Richard A. Viguerie, Paul Weyrich.

THE ROUNDTABLE
(formerly Religious Roundtable)

Phil Crane*, Jerry Falwell, Jesse Helms†, Gordon Humphrey†, Eddie McAteer, Larry McDonald*, Howard Phillips, Richard A. Viguerie.

COMMITTEE FOR THE SURVIVAL OF A FREE CONGRESS

Joseph Coors, Bob Dornan*, Jerry Falwell, George Hansen*, Orrin Hatch†, Jesse Helms†, Gordon Humphrey†, Roger Jepsen†, Paul Laxalt†, Larry McDonald*, Howard Phillips, Steve Symms†, Richard A. Viguerie, Paul Weyrich.

MORAL MAJORITY, INC.

Terry Dolan, Jerry Falwell, Jesse Helms†, Eddie McAteer, Howard Phillips, Richard A. Viguerie, Paul Weyrich.

THE VIGUERIE COMPANY

CHRISTIAN VOICE

John M. Ashbrook*, Dan Crane*, Phil Crane*, Colonel V. Doner, George Hansen*, Orrin Hatch†, Larry McDonald*, Mike Thompson, Guy Vander Jagt*, Richard A. Viguerie.

NATIONAL CONSERVATIVE POLITICAL ACTION COMMITTEE

John M. Ashbrook*, Bob Bauman*, Charles Black, Joseph Coors, Dan Crane*, Phil Crane*, Terry Dolan, Bob Dornan*, Jerry Falwell, George Hansen*, Orrin Hatch†, Jesse Helms†, Gordon Humphrey†, Roger Jepsen†, Paul Laxalt†, Larry McDonald*, Steve Symms†, Guy Vander Jagt*, Richard A. Viguerie.

AMERICAN CONSERVATIVE UNION

John M. Ashbrook*, Bob Bauman*, Charles Black, Joseph Coors, Dan Crane*, Phil Crane*, Terry Dolan, Colonel V. Doner, M. Stanton Evans, Jesse Helms†, Gary Jarmin, Paul Laxalt†, Larry McDonald*, Howard Phillips, Steve Symms†, Mike Thompson, Richard A. Viguerie.

YOUNG AMERICANS FOR FREEDOM

John M. Ashbrook*, Bob Bauman*, Charles Black, Dan Crane*, Phil Crane*, Terry Dolan, Bob Dornan*, M. Stanton Evans, George Hansen*, Orrin Hatch†, Jesse Helms†, Gordon Humphrey†, Roger Jepsen†, Paul Laxalt†, Larry McDonald*, Howard Phillips, Steve Symms†, Richard A. Viguerie.

The membership of the advisory committee of the National Defeat Legal Services Committee shows just how close the relationship is between the new-right and religious-right leaders. The members are: Neal Blair, president of Free the Eagle; Paul A. Brown, director of the Life Amendment Political Action Committee; John T. (Terry) Dolan, chairman of the National Conservative Political Action Committee; William D'Onofrio, president of the National Association for Neighborhood Schools; Peter Gamma, executive director of the National Pro-Life Political Action Committee; Ron Godwin, executive vice-president of Moral Majority, Inc.; Robert C. Heckman, executive director of Young Americans for Freedom; Tim LaHaye, founder of Family Life Seminars; Gary North, director of the Institute for Christian Economics; Harry Schultz, president of the International Harry Schultz Letter; Don Todd, executive director of American Conservative Union; Richard A. Viguerie, publisher of *Conservative Digest*; Paul M. Weyrich, director of the Committee for the Survival of a Free Congress. Howard Phillips of The Conservative Caucus served as chairman of this committee; Lawrence J. Straw, Jr. was treasurer.

6

SKELETONS ON THE LINE
AT CHRISTIAN VOICE

NO MORE CONCEPTS. I stared at the slogan blankly. It was ap-
pealing in a strange sort of way, a refreshing release from my
past, the many years when questioning and answering yielded
only more confusion and despair. "No more concepts." I re-
peated it slowly in my mind over and over, savoring those pre-
cious words.

—Christopher Edwards, writing about his six months as
a follower of Sun Myung Moon in *Crazy for God.*

"Choo-choo-choo,   choo-choo-choo,   choo-choo-choo.   Yay,
yay—Pow!"

—Greeting chant among Moonies,
quoted throughout *Crazy for God.*

Among liberals on Capitol Hill, Gary Jarmin is the most despised
and feared activist of the religious right. Like the Irish hit men hired
by the Mafia, he goes about his work—quiet, but deadly—virtually ignored by the media. There is a rare mention of him in *Time* or *Newsweek*; his name does not appear in the *Reader's Guide to Periodical
Literature.*

As legislative director of Christian Voice and author of the "Report
Cards" on the "Christian/Moral" votes of congressmen, he is several
times as effective as Jerry Falwell. The amazing amount of space de-

voted to Falwell in the press is not nearly so hard to understand as the near-total lack of attention paid to Gary Jarmin.

It isn't just that he's a powerful political operative; he's also an interesting character. Tall and ruggedly handsome, he looks like a real cowboy alongside the usual biscuit-faced lobbyists one sees in Washington. About halfway through our three-hour interview, Jarmin stopped and explained why he was telling me about his unconventional—and criminal—background. "I've never hidden any skeletons in the closet. I hang them out on the line in the front yard." And nobody had bothered to notice them.

One explanation for the avoidance of Jarmin could have to do with his personality. He is certainly cooperative and agreeable enough when a reporter approaches him. But he has the shifty eyes and deep-seated wariness of a man with a past. Much as you would like to like him, you feel he is not anybody you could ever trust. You have a distinct feeling that this man could and would hurt you if he took a notion.

Jarmin was born October 21, 1949, in Eureka, California. His parents came west from Kansas, where they were married in 1939. They moved from Eureka to Whittier and then settled in Desert Hot Springs, a suburb of Palm Springs.

His mother was a devout Baptist, his father "was a very good person, a very moral person, but not deeply religious." When Gary was seven, he and his two older sisters were all baptized one night at the Baptist church. "It was just sort of let's-get-the-whole-gang-baptized kind of thing."

His father bought a set of those "great books of the world or great books of all time. I loved to read and one day I started reading Charles Darwin. Voltaire. You name it. These so-called enlightened thinkers, they all had a humanist approach, not a spiritual approach. I began to have a lot of doubts. About the Creation theory versus evolution. At the same time I was having this internal conflict. I became more interested in girls and going out and less interested in Boy Scouts."

Two important events changed his life at age fifteen. "My father died and I got a set of drums. I no longer had a father figure to keep me in line. At the same time, I got a band going. Ironically, one of the names we had was The Monks. It was a typical rock band with drums, three guitars, and a singer. We did Beatles, Kinks. Our repertory got pretty good. The band played for money on just a couple of occasions. Some guy in Palm Springs, very wealthy, his father had a party for him and we played. High school dances. But ninety percent of the time, we just played for the enjoyment of it.

"I got into drugs about this time, too. Bands and drugs go together like honey and bees. Marijuana, pills, LSD—never the hard stuff, smack. I ran away from home a few times. The archtypical screw-up."

The first time he was arrested and put on probation was for stealing a T-shirt in a drugstore. As he told me that story, and what follows, his tone was not that of a man confessing his crimes, but of one whose transgressions were so trivial the police shouldn't have bothered him.

Once, Jarmin and his buddies decided they were going to spend their days surfing in Hawaii; how to get there didn't seem so difficult as they planned it. So they caught a Greyhound bus to Los Angeles and spent the night on the San Pedro docks, where they asked about hopping a freighter to the islands. "We just got laughed out of the place by the old salts on the dock. We ended up working at a car wash." At night they slept in one of those bell-shaped collection bins for Goodwill Industries. There were three of them and they took turns sleeping in the middle, the only position where anyone could lie straight. The police nabbed them one night when they were slipping into their little home away from home. They were taken to the station and sent back to their parents.

Another time, Jarmin and a friend hitchhiked to the freeway, and just took the first ride that came along. The driver happened to be going to West Virginia, so that's where they went, too. They then traveled South, "two long-haired hippies from California" trying to get through Mississippi at the height of racial upheavals in the state. A band of white boys nearly did them in, but they convinced them they didn't even know about any demonstrations in Jackson that day.

Back in California, he said, "I wound up spending ten months in Twin Pines Ranch. Sounds like a place you'd want your kid to go for camp." In fact, it was a prison for young criminals.

"The dastardly deed I committed, the crime I committed against the people of the State of California, was stealing my sister's car. My sister was very angry that I took it. [And so she swore out a warrant for his arrest.] I was gone for five days, went up to Lake Havasu on Labor Day Weekend, 1966."

When he got back home, his sister delivered a five-minute tirade and then she was all right. However, he says now, the police would not drop the charges, and he was tried and convicted of grand larceny.

"The bottom line was my probation officer hated my guts. I think he was convinced I was a drug dealer—which I was not. I was a user, but I wasn't selling. He tried to talk me into being an informer, a snitch. I refused. From then on, he had it in for me. Let's face it, taking my sister's car was a minor offense—but I had to go to court on grand larceny charges. Juvenile court is a strange business . . . kids in New York are killing old ladies and they walk right out. I got ten months."

He's glad he had the prison experience. "If for no other reason, it gave me the opportunity to discover things about other people and about myself." It was also a chance to read. The others called him Doc because most of them didn't—or couldn't—read. His sister sent him Viktor Frankl's *Man's Search for Meaning*. He was beginning to move from being a "confirmed atheist" to thinking that God might exist.

On June 28, 1967, he got out of prison. Two weeks later, he was back in jail. The police had caught him and two friends smoking marijuana in a park. "One in the group managed to escape with the stash, so all they caught us with was a few seeds. I spent that night in jail and that was the lowest point in my life. I knew I would have to go to the Youth Authority [instead of Twin Pines] and that was for your hardcore rapists and murderers. But I managed to beat the rap."

The police had relied on the testimony of three girls who had been smoking with the boys. "They were just afraid they were going to jail, so they signed all this testimony. While we were waiting for trial, we ran into these girls at a dance. We explained to them that the consequence would be very bad for me if they went ahead with it—and they did feel very bad being a fink. When the court day came the prosecutor expected them to sing and they didn't. They denied everything."

Not long after this, Jarmin went to visit a cousin who was a devoted follower of the charismatic Korean evangelist, Sun Myung Moon.

"While I was there, each day I became more and more interested in what they were doing, their conceptualization of God. I had always grown up with the belief that God was distant and apart from man. Whatever was good or bad was God's will. I came to the conclusion if God existed he must be a cruel God to allow what was going on. The greatest awareness I came to was that God is not responsible for evil. Man is responsible. God suffers and loves us and blah-blah-blah.

"What impressed me was the community itself: no smoking, no sex, no drinking." Like most teenagers of that time, he had sampled all of these abundantly, but now he felt good about giving them up, sacrificing his personal wants and needs for the good of a community, a family. "Having that experience contrasted with jail, which was also a communal environment, but where you had to fight to survive and where there was very little or no human affection shown."

Jarmin joined Moon's Unification Church in October 1967 and stayed with it for six and a half years. "There's nothing ritualistic about becoming a member. You hear the Divine Principle and merely fill out an application and that's it. Most people do not live in the center before they become a member: I moved in with my cousin and was living in this community while studying." Otherwise, he might never have joined, if he had gone through the regular routine, "just been dragged off the street and taken to a lecture."

Meanwhile, at Los Angeles City College, where Jarmin was a student, the Students for a Democratic Society had taken over the student government and used student funds to post bail for students arrested in demonstrations. Jarmin became the leader of the Student Alliance for Education, which engineered a recall election and threw out the leftist student administration. "I'd be up till three o'clock in the morning, printing and putting up literature. . . . Although we had a titular head of our group, I ended up doing all the work."

In the summer of 1970, Jarmin moved to Washington to become secretary general of Moon's Freedom Leadership Foundation, which publishes *Rising Tide*, an anti-Communist newspaper. "I had met Reverend Moon before that—he had come to the U.S. in 1969. Then I met him a second time in 1970. He's hard to describe. He's a very warm, friendly person. Very intense spiritually. A pretty dynamic speaker." Here Jarmin gestured sheepishly as he said, "It's all in Korean, of course. He does have a translator. I haven't seen him in eight years; I understand he now speaks English."

After some years as secretary general of the Moon group, Jarmin was not getting along with some of the other leaders. He was also in love with a woman in the church and they wanted to get married. "We knew we wouldn't have gotten permission—so we didn't even try. You can't go to Reverend Moon and say, 'I've found this girl I like a lot.' The only right you have in marriage is refusal. When they have a marriage ceremony it's a very special time, and unless they have that you can't get married. You have to be in the church for three years before you can even be considered to be matched or blessed. If we had waited, it would have been 1975."

On December 6, 1973, he and Susan Miller were married. For a long time, Jarmin had no place to go spiritually; sometimes he would wander back to the Unification Church to be with his old friends. The criticism of the Moonies is "grossly exaggerated," Jarmin feels. "I think the people in the Unification Church are very good, loving, devout. I don't think they are evil. I lived in that experience for six years and I was not brainwashed."

After four years, Jarmin and his wife were having problems and they separated for a while in 1977 and then permanently in December 1978. She and his daughter now live in an ashram in Portland, Oregon. He was married again on October 12, 1980, to Gina Mondres, his assistant at Christian Voice.

In March 1975, Jarmin went to work for the American Conservative Union, a senior group founded by Young Americans for Freedom, and stayed there as legislative director for four years. While there, he became friends with Colonel Doner (Colonel is his given name), who was a fund raiser and consultant for the ACU and also for a California-based group called Christian Cause. Doner, Richard Zone, and Robert Grant, two ministers and political activists in California, had started Christian Cause. In 1977, Doner and Grant had lunch with Jarmin in Washington and discussed setting up an active lobbying organization there. Christian Voice was set up in October 1978 as a charitable and educational (meaning lobbying) organization, which is tax-exempt. In January 1980, the same people set up a political action committee called Christian Voice Moral Government Fund, so that they could work directly in political campaigns.

Christian Voice's statement of purpose includes these words: "We believe that the unmistakable signs of moral decay are all around us: sexual promiscuity and perversion, pornography, legalized abortion, the disparaging of marriage, family, and the role of motherhood—all are rampant in our schools, our government, and even in many churches. . . . The Primary Objective of Christian Voice is to slice through this murky sea of non-values and clearly focus public attention on the basic moral implications of each issue along with its ultimate potential consequences."

Gary Jarmin says, "Christian Voice has been my salvation. It's the best thing that's ever happened to me. Through it I had a special purpose. Even in the first year I was representing them I was drinking heavily and doing other things that were hardly representative of the Christian viewpoint. All that is in the past. I can talk about it because I am very stable now. Ten years from now, who knows? Who can say?"

By his own timetable, Jarmin was still something other than a Christian at the time Christian Voice proudly proclaimed in a newsletter: "We are extremely fortunate to have the top Christian Conservative lobbyist in Washington, D.C. to head this office—Mr. Gary Jarmin. . . . We are very fortunate to have this unusually gifted man to serve us. Our new man in Washington, D.C., your Christian Voice spokesman, is praised . . . as being highly *effective*. And that's what we are going to be on your behalf—effective. Not just a lot of talk—but action."

The most despised—that is, effective—device used by Christian Voice is a rating system similar to that used by the labor unions for several decades and by the old Americans for Democratic Action and Americans for Constitutional Action. There is one important difference. Christian Voice doesn't rate a congressman as to whether he is conservative or liberal, it says only whether a vote is "Christian/Moral" or not. The clear message here is that a wrong vote is un-Christian and immoral.

How could a Christian group be so judgmental? I asked. "First of all," Jarmin replied, "you have to make a value judgment based on the Bible about the truths in there, what's right and wrong. In our society in the last few years, the humanist trend denies there are any absolutes, any good or evil. It's okay to be gay; if it feels good, do it. That's a hedonist mentality. There are absolutes and we have to make judgments about what is right or wrong. We don't call ourselves *the* Christian Voice, but we certainly believe ours is the correct one. The competing values right now are theistic and humanistic. You will have competition between them, but you cannot have peaceful coexistence because they are so totally opposite one another. This argument of pluralism is nonsense. You can have different political philosophies, but most in a society must agree with each other."

Number one on Christian Voice's report cards is support for Taiwan or "Free China." Jarmin can give you a moral or Christian explanation as to why the issue is there, but there is one practical reason: he is a paid lobbyist for the American Council for a Free Asia, making several trips back and forth to Korea and Taiwan each year and representing their governments' interests on Capitol Hill. "I'm listed as a consultant, so I can wear two hats. I can represent any group I want to."

In addition to the overall report card on Congress, Christian Voice provides individual ratings of particular congressmen who are targeted for defeat. In my talks with various political workers, they all mentioned that these leaflets—passed out mainly at churches—were the most effective weapons used against them. "How can you defend an 'immoral' vote?" one of them asked bitterly. Christian Voice also produces radio spots from a half-minute up to a full half-hour program; these are broadcast over the various religious networks.

The most sensational issue that Christian Voice has latched on to is that of homosexual rights. The group campaigned vigorously and expensively, although unsuccessfully, for the Briggs Initiative in California. The group also lobbied in support of Larry McDonald's resolution in the House that would specifically deny any special or separate consideration of homosexual rights in Congress. McDonald is on the boards of Christian Voice and the John Birch Society.

A Christian Cause poll against gay rights was written about in long articles in the *Los Angeles Times* and the *Washington Star* as if it were a legitimate, objective poll. Said the *Times* headline: "Poll Reveals Strong Bias Against Gays." The *Washington Star* said in a headline: "Conservative Christians Show Strong Anti-Gay Bias." The poll cost $40,000 just for postage and printing. A questionnaire was sent out to 2.75 million conservative Christians, including 250,000 Catholics. Of these, 1.6 million responded. The remarkable point, not appreciated by either newspaper's religious writer, was that anybody responded in favor of gay rights at all, considering the mailing list. But, while 91 percent said they were against homosexual teachers, only 42 percent objected to gay policemen and only 13 percent to gay firefighters. Also, 97 percent said they felt all sex laws should be reexamined and explained better to the public. As for X-rated movies, an astonishing 12 percent of these conservative Christians said there should be no laws restricting such films.

After the election of 1980, Christian Voice crowed in a newsletter: "We turned the evangelical vote for Reagan. . . . Final results among white evangelicals: 66 percent voted for Reagan. HOW DID WE DO

103

IT? . . . Perhaps our most exciting effort was the use of our hard-hitting 30-second TV spots that caused Jimmy Carter, Vice-President Mondale, Press Secretary Powell, and numerous other Carter aides to attack us by name. . . . What was our strategy? Very simply, to break Carter's hold on Southern evangelicals who vote for Carter from regional pride or Christian brotherhood, but who are very conservative on social and family issues. We concentrated these spots in crucial Southern states that were considered 'too close to call.' Our spots tied Jimmy Carter to the Gay Rights movement which he, his family and his aides had been courting for the last year, culminating in the Carter-approved Gay Rights plank in the Democratic platform. We are indebted to Mike Thompson of Long Advertising in Florida, the brilliant creator of these spots. Mike formerly handled all the media specials for the American Conservative Union and Anita Bryant."

These television spots were planned for use throughout the South and Midwest; in fact only a small number of stations would allow them to be aired. They were timed for the very last days of the campaign so that the issue would be raised but not resolved. One of the spots showed a parade in San Francisco of "militant homosexuals . . . flaunting their lifestyles." The voice-over continues with: "And now the march has reached Washington, and President Carter's platform carries his pledge to cater to homosexuals' demands. Carter advocates acceptance of homosexuality. Ronald Reagan stands for the traditional American family." "They elected a mayor in San Francisco; now they're trying to elect a President," says a sinister voice as the camera zooms in on the most bizarre-looking characters in the Halloween-like parade.

The second spot focused on an older woman who says, "As a Christian mother, I want my children to be able to pray in school. I don't want them being taught that abortion and homosexuality are perfectly all right. I was sorry to learn that President Carter disagrees with me on all these issues."

To me, these Christian Voice spots were among the sleaziest tricks pulled in recent American campaign history. If they were anything, they were not moral or religious. Their method was distortion and exaggeration and there was no reason why they should have been mentioned in news reports on the campaign.

I asked Jarmin how he could participate in something like that when he knew full well that a number of his new-right colleagues were homosexual. What about the homosexuals he worked with? His boss at the American Conservative Union had been Bob Bauman, the Maryland congressman involved in a world of homosexual hustlers that the FBI finally unveiled because he was so vulnerable to blackmail.

"I didn't know him personally that well. I admired him very much; I thought he was a tremendous legislator, a master of parliamentary rules. No one was more shocked than I was when his problem of homosexuality came out. In our opinion, if he was sincere when he repented, then he deserves our sympathy and our support." He had, however, nothing but disdain for another conservative Republican congressman, Jon Hinson, who resigned his seat after being arrested during a homosexual encounter in a men's room of a House Office Building.

"Bob Bauman had been involved [in conservative politics] for many years before he came to Congress; he was well known among Conservatives. Jon Hinson was a freshman congressman who hardly knew anybody. The way a guy votes does not necessarily reflect on his moral character." This last statement is something the readers of Jarmin's report cards might keep in mind.

The day the anti-homosexual television spots were to be released in selected campaign areas, Gary Jarmin called a press conference and presided proudly at a preview showing of the spots. The reporters watched and then took their press kits and left. Few of them mentioned Christian Voice in their stories, fewer still mentioned Gary Jarmin. All of them mentioned Jimmy Carter's spluttering attempts to defend himself in the face of such "vicious" attacks on the eve of the election.

But the power brokers on Capitol Hill knew Gary Jarmin's name and knew he was involved in delivering this killer blow. As the votes began to come in on the various "Christian/Moral" issues in Congress, it was obvious that a majority of the legislators were not about to cross such a man. Something else was just as obvious in a key vote in the House of Representatives that would have removed all criminal sanctions against sexual acts between consenting adults in private in the District of Columbia. One hundred and nineteen representatives refused to be bullied in a massive telephone, mail, and publicity campaign staged by Christian Voice and Moral Majority. These people took the risk, stood up, and were counted: their names are on the record to be used and abused as the new right sees fit. Every new-right group I mention in this book has published this long "hit list" of names as a first step toward defeating these people in the 1982 elections. Gary Jarmin and others of the new right may find that the electorate responds more favorably to a legislator's strength and courage than it does to some pressure group's narrow view of what is right and wrong.

7

GAULEITER JEW

That a person is Jewish is not unusual or important enough to mention in most areas of American life today. However, it is a fact one is always told about Howard Phillips, head of Conservative Caucus. It is a self-contradictory assertion; the need to mention it belies the ecumenicism it is meant to express.

In the company he keeps, Howard Phillips is often the only Jew on the speakers' platform, and more often than not the only Jew in a whole auditorium. Any suggestion that there is anti-Semitism in the new right is invariably met with the statement, "Howard Phillips is a Jew." However, anti-Semitism is very much present among the forces of the new right, even if it rarely surfaces except in the slips of the tongue of the less sophisticated preachers. The most notable example came not from a preacher and it was hardly a slip, since it was included in a carefully prepared press release from John G. Schmitz, a California state senator running for the U.S. Senate seat being vacated by S. I. Hayakawa. Schmitz, a prominent member of the John Birch Society, was the presidential candidate in 1972 of the American Independent Party, to which some of the leaders—such as Richard A. Viguerie—and many of the followers of the new right once belonged. Schmitz's statement resulted from a hearing over an anti-abortion bill that he had written. He said the committee hearings, held in four California cities, were attended by "imported lesbians, anti-male and pro-abortion queer groups in San Francisco and other centers of decadence." He said the front rows at the hearings were filled "with a sea of hard, Jewish, and (arguably) female faces." As a result of this statement, the leadership of the California legislature promptly took the extraordinary action of taking away Schmitz's chairmanship of one committee and vice-chairmanship of another.

Schmitz's statement offers specific documentation that such virulent hatred of one group can easily be extended to another—and another. Thus it is understandable that while Howard Phillips's religious background is not a difference he tries to hide, neither is it one he chooses to emphasize. One is led to the inescapable conclusion that along with his hatred of homosexuals and his denigration of women, he also shares this other hatred of Jews, his own kind, himself. Phillips was the only new-right leader I interviewed who was evasive and reluctant to talk about his childhood. He had his stock political answers and he didn't seem to notice or care that they were not answers to my questions.

When I asked Phillips about his religious upbringing, he told me about his years under Richard Nixon; when I asked if he had gone to Hebrew school at a synagogue, he said, "I can't emphasize enough my experience at the Office of Economic Opportunity." I had to ask what his birth date was three times in order to elicit the fact that it was February 3, 1941.

He was born in Boston, the son of Fred and Gertrude Phillips. His father was in the insurance business, his mother a housewife. "Religion was part of my life. I'm Jewish. My grandparents emigrated to this country in the early part of this century. I was brought up with a religious education.

"But here again, probably the most compelling religious experience I had was my service in the government back in the early 1970s." How was that religious? "Basically, I had to decide what was important in my life."

But what kind of religious instruction did he get as a child? "I attended religious instruction after public schools. But again . . ." What had he learned as a child at the synagogue? "Basically, I learned that our rights came from God. I went to Boston Latin School—you had to compete to get in—and I have always been fascinated by history." (He described Benjamin Franklin as a graduate of this same school, but in his *Autobiography*, Franklin says he went only a few months to what he describes as a Latin school in one place and a grammar school in another; otherwise, Franklin was self-taught.)

Just like all the others I interviewed, Phillips had to explain the three kinds of politics or governmental power. In his case, the three labels were liberal, libertarian, and conservative, the latter being the highest and best, with all power and authority coming from God. "That's why Jefferson argued for *in*alienable instead of *un*alienable rights," he said. I asked if he knew why Jefferson had used the word "Creator" and the words "Nature's God" instead of just "God." He said he did and left it at that. "There are lots of things I disagree with Jefferson on." Such as? "He had an excessive faith in the essential goodness of man. Liberals hold that the state is the final arbiter and there are no absolute standards. I was taught there is good and evil: homosexuality is wrong; abortion is wrong; strong families are important. The primary responsibility of man is to provide. The responsibility of the wife is to help the husband; her role is the transmission of values."

The Boston Latin School he attended was founded in 1635, he said. "Harvard was a year later. Even when I was there it was very competitive." One very strong influence on Phillips was a Latin teacher named William Roach, who later became a professor of philosophy at Boston University. "I learned more philosophy than Latin. He inculcated in every student a healthy skepticism. He had no scale in grading. Most of us were in the low sixties. If anybody made a seventy he was a scholar. He had tremendous moral insight. He instilled in us the belief that there was no substitute for high standards and hard work; a belief in competition; a belief that the world does not owe anybody a living. . . . He respected no man, none of the sacred cows. He attacked everything from school boards to welfare to promiscuity.

"My political views were conservative from the time I was in high school. I helped organize for Eisenhower. My parents are essentially nonpolitical. They voted for FDR, Truman, and Eisenhower."

At Harvard, Phillips was president of the student council in 1960–61, and that took him to the National Student Association Congress, which was then dominated by liberal activists. He was offended by the resolutions and statements that came out of this congress. In particular, he hated the resolution saying students constituted a "world class" that should join in the fight for human rights throughout the world. He felt it was a contradiction to be upset about violations of academic freedom and civil rights in this country while praising Fidel Castro's Cuba, where such violations were rampant.

There was one happy outcome of this congress for Phillips, however. He found himself paired with Carol Gene Dawson of Indianapolis, Indiana, who later that year would marry Robert E. Bauman, a future congressman from Maryland. Phillips and Dawson were a debate team in support of Richard Nixon's candidacy for President. She told him, "You'd be interested in going to this meeting in Sharon, Connecticut." This was the historic gathering of ninety-three college students, where the "Sharon Statement" was drafted.

Phillips says, "Actually, I was the one who proposed the name 'Young Americans for Freedom.' " He was on YAF's board of directors for the next year, then he left because of the "infighting and careerism among the leaders."

In addition to founding YAF, Phillips was chairman of a conservative student group, the Committee for a Responsible National Student Organization, set up to oppose the liberal National Student Association. He became increasingly involved in party politics—serving as state chairman of the Massachusetts College Republican Federation from 1961 to 1963, president of the Republican City Committee of Boston from 1964 to 1966, and then chairman of "Opportunities Unlimited," with the Republican National Committee, 1966–68.

Phillips's political career was tied to Richard Nixon from the very beginning. He believed that Nixon was the best hope for bringing America back to Eisenhower conservatism. "I identified with Nixon. He epitomized the American dream. He was able to succeed and conquer. He, more than any other politician, spoke to the causes I believed in." Phillips served as acting director of the President's Council on Youth Opportunity from 1969 to 1970. Then he was a Republican congressional nominee in Massachusetts's Sixth District. He took part in one more unsuccessful campaign, his last as a candidate, this one for the Democratic nomination for U.S. Senator. He explains the switch simply: "I wanted to show you didn't have to be a Republican to be conservative." One of his opponents in this race was Elaine Noble, an openly lesbian state senator. Perhaps because of her presence, Phillips invited Anita Bryant to stage a benefit concert in his behalf. When the date approached and most of the tickets had still not been sold, Phillips canceled the show and blamed it on the threat of violence from gays.

Phillips's most memorable assignment, and what he would most like to talk about, was being named in 1973 by Nixon to be acting director of the antipoverty agency set up as the hub of Lyndon Johnson's Great Society: the U.S. Office of Economic Opportunity (OEO). Phillips thought he had been put there to "dismantle" the operation. He made brash statements about what he was going to do, and began to cut programs left and further left. "You have no idea," he said to me with deep earnestness, "what it is to come to work and look in those offices and see Mao's picture or Che Guevara's on the wall."

During this time he was asked about all the young ex-members of YAF whom he had appointed. Phillips replied, "We're the Gauleiters," borrowing a word used for Hitler's political enforcers in the *gau*s or districts of Nazi Germany. His burning cause became the elimination of federal grants to such liberal organizations as the National Association of Social Workers, the American Friends (Quaker) Service Committee, the National Urban League. (All of those he named to me as examples were involved in the movement for black civil rights.) "To understand our viewpoint," he said, "consider if Jerry Falwell were getting such grants."

In the weeks that followed his appointment to OEO, Phillips faced wall after wall, disappointment after disappointment. He received no support in his ax wielding from the White House. He sent memo after memo to the President, but nobody bothered to acknowledge them. Right after he took the job, he discovered that a Chicano activist in Texas, "an avowed Marxist," was receiving "millions from the OEO." Phillips promptly stopped the grants. The man in Texas responded just as quickly with a call telling Phillips he couldn't do that to him. Nixon and his campaign staff had promised the man those grants in exchange for his support of Nixon's candidacy. "I discovered that Fred Malek and others had promised OEO money to minority groups all over the country. . . . I discovered that Richard Nixon didn't believe in a whole lot except exercising power. . . . The Great Society policies were actually expanded under Nixon."

The reason, Phillips believes, was that Nixon had such a fear of conflict that he would promise anything to keep people quiet. I asked Phillips if he hadn't had suspicions about Nixon's wrongdoing all along. He believed in him right to the last, he says, and turned against him "only when the evidence was overwhelming."

He tells a poignant story about trying to get through to Nixon.

Somehow he heard that Nixon's top aides would be going to a Boy Scouts of America reception; he got himself invited too, so that he could confront H. R. Haldeman and John Ehrlichman in person. He wanted to find out why nobody was answering his memos.

Egil Krogh was the only White House official who showed up. Phillips recalls that Krogh seemed amused and said, "Oh, you're the one who's been sending all those memos." He says Krogh explained that the staff didn't show them to the President because they didn't want to upset him. Phillips got Nixon's attention "only when we showed him they [the liberal groups] were using government funds to attack him personally."

The dichotomy Phillips couldn't stand was that Nixon was more or less conservative in his politics, but liberal in the policies he acted on. Phillips felt it should have been the reverse. In 1974, Phillips left the Nixon administration just before it sank. He and Richard Viguerie and others formed what they called CREEP II, the Conservatives for the Resignation of the President.

"I was wrong," Phillips says about Nixon. "The scales were over my eyes. I had blinded myself, I heard what I wanted to hear. I wanted to believe there was a way to turn the country around."

The preceding paragraphs reflect what Howard Phillips told me about his relationship with Richard Nixon and his tour of duty at the OEO. Another man who worked in the same office, Dan Bradley, who later was named head of the Legal Services Corporation, told me the facts were somewhat different.

In January 1973, when Nixon was assuming command of his second administration, one of his chief lieutenants, H. R. Haldeman, is supposed to have told Phillips that they were finally going to run things the way they wanted to: specifically, they were going to destroy the antipoverty agency set up by Lyndon Johnson's administration.

Bradley, who had started out as a young lawyer in the legal services division of the OEO in Washington, was by this time regional director of the same division in Atlanta. He was responsible for making policy decisions and actual grants for projects in the South. He remembers Howard Phillips's first contact with his holdover subordinates. It was titled, "Memo to the World" and it ordered all regional offices to cease and desist everything—all travel funds and all grant funds were frozen until Phillips himself released them.

Phillips installed himself in the director's office and ordered new steel bolt locks for his doors. One of his YAF buddies was installed as general counsel, another as head of legal services, still others quickly replaced old-line civil service professionals. Bradley describes it as a "malicious, methodical program of destruction . . . a reign of terror." One of the most successful programs in the South was the legal services operation in Jackson, Mississippi. Phillips took away its funds and presented them to a radical-right leader long identified with ultra-racist causes in Mississippi.

Meanwhile, several of the antipoverty agencies that were the objects of Phillips's destruction got together and hired a lawyer to represent their interests. They were joined in a suit against Phillips by four liberal senators who sat on the committee that should have been asked to approve Phillips's nomination as head of the OEO, according to the terms of the act setting up the agency. President Nixon had figured he could bypass the law by naming Phillips through an executive order not to be director, but to oversee the dismantling of the office.

A federal judge ruled that Phillips had been named illegally and, furthermore, his successor was ordered to review every decision he had made in that time—nearly all of them were rescinded. The successor, Alvin Jones Arnett, wanted Dan Bradley to move up as head of legal services, but Phillips and others managed to block that appointment through pressure from the conservative press. Arnett then named Bradley as his assistant—holding the same job, in other words, without the title. Under Jimmy Carter's administration, the Legal Services Corporation became a separate agency and Bradley was named to head it until April 1982, when right-wing pressure finally forced him out of office.

The truth is that Howard Phillips was acting director of OEO for only five months. Nixon did not oppose his dismantling of the various antipoverty agencies—that's why he named him to the position. Nixon just refused to support him when Phillips wanted to appeal the lower court ruling to the Supreme Court. That's when he couldn't get through to the President and that late date is when his anti-Nixonism actually began.

Phillips moved from the Nixon administration to CREEP II to The Conservative Caucus, which he founded in 1974. He has been its national director ever since; he also serves as an officer on all of the various committees, foundations, and subgroups formed as offshoots of the original group.

The Conservative Caucus claims 300,000 members, with organizations in every state. As such, it is the largest conservative organization in the country—but that, again, is a claim it must share with at least three other groups. It led the fight against the Panama Canal treaty and against SALT II and helped in the pioneer "targeting" that led to the defeat in 1978 of Thomas J. McIntyre (whose account of this is printed as an appendix to this book) in New Hampshire and Dick Clark in Iowa because they had supported these issues.

It was inevitable that such an operation would encounter the forces of the emerging religious right who were upset over many of the same issues. "At some point in my work with Conservative Caucus," says Phillips, "I ran into Ed McAteer. He started talking to me about various things. . . . He was with the Christian Freedom Foundation, which folded. I was impressed by several things he said. He said there was a tremendous untapped resource among fundamentalists, who were basically conservative. He began introducing me to various religious leaders. I spent a lot of time with him that year. Ed had been working on it for twenty years, the idea you can't separate morality from government.

"One day he said he'd found the key guy who could put it together. It was in January 1979. I went down to Lynchburg and suggested an organization to tie it all together. I suggested the name 'Moral Majority.' We put together another meeting and Weyrich went down. Since then, we've had good lines of communication. . . . We are involved in a continuing effort to get together people of diverse faiths. . . ."

Phillips has said of the religious right, "On the national level, they've got a community of television. As opposed to a place of education or work, the place of worship, you assume, there is a shared community of values."

I sat in Phillips's spacious office in a suburban Virginia shopping center, trying to comprehend the man's muddled sentences—and his equally inconsistent career in politics. Much of his life's story was told by the framed photographs and other memorabilia that virtually covered two walls. There were pictures of his wife and children, of his parents—beside whom he looms like the oversized cartoon duckling, Baby Huey, a foot taller and seemingly twice as broad as either of his parents. There are unsigned photographs of Richard Nixon and Spiro Agnew. There is a framed happy-thirty-ninth-birthday letter from Jesse Helms, on Senate stationery. There was also a letter of thanks

signed by the office staff of Richard Schweiker's unsuccessful senatorial campaign in 1968. That was another phase of Phillips's development that seems out of character—for Schweiker was regarded as a
liberal in those days. Phillips had served as Schweiker's campaign
manager.

It was difficult to take seriously Phillips's pronouncements on absolute right and wrong, good and evil, when his own thoughts and affili-
ations—from Republican to Democrat, from conservative to liberal
and back again in both cases—had changed so often in such a relatively short space of time.

There is no indication of such an equivocal past when Phillips
speaks for The Conservative Caucus. He told the 1979 YAF annual
convention: "Our country is going down the drain. . . . We may have a
majority, but we lack power. . . . What is power? It is the ability to tell
others what the issues are, what the issues mean, and who the good
guys and bad guys are. That is power." In a statement presented to the
White House Conference on Families, he sounded like an echo of Jerry Falwell: "According to the Bible, God has charged parents, not civil governments, with responsibility for the rearing of children. All
education is rooted in values. The question is, whose values shall prevail? Those of the parent, or those of the state? In a free society, the
family, rather than the state, ought to determine whether children
shall be subjected to pornography, amorally premised sex education,
atheistically based textbooks and curriculum, or proselytization for
doctrines of homosexuality, abortion, and extramarital sex."

An introductory note to the *Conservative Digest* interview with Phillips said, "Of all the New Right leaders, Phillips is clearly the best
stump politician. His powerful oratory seldom fails to excite
crowds. . . ." It is curious that the wording describes him as a stump
politician instead of a speaker, because a great speaker he is not. I sat
at the back of a Moral Majority seminar Phillips addressed and noted
that the crowd did not seem to be moved at all by his rambling
thoughts and conservative slogans, which they already knew.

The most salient point Phillips made in response to the controversial appointment of Sandra Day O'Connor to the Supreme Court was
that "we have to preserve the coalition that came together in the
1970s—pro-family, defense, free market." He explained that if people
were promised something and then didn't get what they wanted, they
would break away, embittered. "We have got to put up a fight or we

will lose our clout. The only battles we lose are the ones we fail to fight." He said 1980 was the first time Americans had been offered a conservative alternative since Goldwater:

—In 1968, "Fifty-seven percent of the people voted against the Great Society." (That was the combined vote for Wallace and Nixon.)

—In 1972, Nixon "had the good fortune to run against George McGovern so he didn't have to defend his record."

—"Then, in 1976, a fellow named Jimmy Carter came along. I remember in 1972, Mike Mansfield said, 'If we Democrats are ever going to break that Republican stronghold, we're going to have to find a 'Southerner.' . . . Jimmy Carter during the campaign said, 'Hey, fellows, look at me, I'm from the most conservative region in the country and I'm a deeply religious man.' Going against that was Jerry Ford's wife, who had become a symbol of liberalism through her statements on her daughter's sex life and on the ERA. Conservatives voted for Jimmy Carter and against Betty Ford."

Phillips said the basic principle of the new right is that "our rights came from God. They [liberals] think our rights come from the government. They think those eight men and now one woman [on the Supreme Court], whatever they say is right: forget the common law, what the Bible says."

Phillips concluded with a sequence of one-line slogans: "politics is religion"; "all law is morality"; "you cannot separate law and morality"; "the government is trying to impose its values on us"; "good and evil cannot live side by side"; "peaceful coexistence won't work for us." These read like emotional catchwords that should have been weighted with feeling and meaning, yet Phillips was tossing them off as if by rote. Does he mean it when he now speaks of moral absolutes? No more, I think, than he meant it when he campaigned for Richard Nixon as the great conservative hope—and for Schweiker, and for the Republicans and for the Democrats. . . .

At that Moral Majority seminar, Phillips also told about visiting a small, desolate church in Moscow where the attendant proudly explained that Communists also believe in the separation of church and state. When you visit the Soviet Union, said Phillips, "you see the logical conclusion of American liberalism." He did not tell his audience what the logical conclusion of American conservatism might be.

8

EDDIE McATEER'S
SWIMMING AX

The *Conservative Digest* cover story on Edward E. McAteer described him as "the music man of the religious right. When he talks, people listen."

McAteer was, in fact, a salesman and his rapid patter does bear some resemblance to that of the lovable huckster, Professor Harold Hill, in *The Music Man*. In one of his Religious Roundtable brochures, he writes in breathless (if awkward) phrases: "Righteousness exalteth a nation. But sin is a reproach to any people. . . . Twenty-one million Americans smoke marijuana. . . . Over nine million alcoholics in the U.S. . . . There is currently proposed legislation that prohibits employment discrimination on the basis of sexual orientation (i.e., male or female homosexuals, bisexuals, or heterosexuals). . . . The U.S. will soon be the porno capital of the world—780 X-rated theaters. . . . The fact is that we can no longer survive as a free nation if we follow the same course we now are pursuing with breakneck speed. Something must be done."

But if Eddie McAteer can draw a crowd, they're either not buying his message or not paying enough for it. He and Ed Rowe run the Religious Roundtable out of a tiny office that could fit into one corner of the spacious quarters of the National Conservative Political Action Committee down the hall. When I stopped in, McAteer held out his latest brochure with some embarrassment. There hadn't been enough money to do it right, and the design had to be changed so that it wouldn't cost so much.

But if he lacks the financial empire of his new-right colleagues, McAteer makes up for it in the value of his connections. He was, by all accounts, the original link between the preachers and the politicians that formed what is now known as the religious right or, more specifically, Moral Majority, Inc.

Somewhat portly in shape, his graying hair slicked back from the last few wisps on top, his apple cheeks so red they look rouged, McAteer is the only new-right leader a casting director might say looked the part. In fact, he looks so much like the late character actor, Ed Begley, I had to remind myself that I was involved in a conversation and not watching a stage performance.

McAteer was born on July 29, 1926, in Memphis, Tennessee. His father was a Roman Catholic, but he had already deserted the family by the time McAteer was five, the year his mother died. "I'm about as much an orphan as you can find who wasn't raised in an orphanage. I was raised by several relatives and I lived with a friend. I was converted to Christ in a Methodist church at fourteen. The little Bible learning I got was under a pentecostal preacher in Wichita, Kansas."

How would he describe his born-again experience? "I told a fellow I went to law school with after my conversion experience. I said, 'Bill, people tell me that's a figment of the imagination. But I couldn't explain the spiritual experience any more than you can tell me why a black cow eats green grass and gives white milk.' "

He speaks of it as a conversion, but he admits he wasn't much of a sinner before that. "I never did get into any notorious things," such as drinking and gambling. After high school, he went into the U.S. Navy Air Corps and was on the U.S.S. *St. Lo* when it was hit by a Japanese kamikaze plane and sunk in the Leyte Gulf in the Philippines.

Later, when he was a college student, McAteer represented the mid-South in the Golden Gloves national boxing championship in Chicago. In 1948, he took a job as salesman for Colgate-Palmolive Company and remained with it until 1976, when he resigned to devote his full time to politics. "For twenty-eight years, I marketed the world's finest toothpaste—cleans your breath while it cleans your teeth." He speaks of the enemy toothpastes as he would a current political opponent: "Crest—crust; Gleem—glum." He helped to test-market two of the company's most successful products, Ultra-Brite toothpaste and Palmolive Rapid Shave.

The Lord had a plan for him, this Eddie McAteer firmly believes. His marketing of soap and toothpaste coincided with another career in religion, and both of them would lead to the successful position he is in now. Starting out as a deacon in the Meadow Heights Baptist Church in Collinsville, Illinois, in 1954, he also taught a Bible class and was Baptist Training Union director of youth programs as well. After the family moved back to Memphis, he was first chairman of deacons and chairman of evangelism at Bellevue Baptist Church.

As a layman, he claims to have preached the Baptist version of Christianity in India, Kenya, Australia, Finland, Denmark, Ireland, England, France, Italy, Hong Kong, Spain, and Japan. One high point in his religious globe-trotting was being arrested and jailed in 1957 in the town of Zaragoza in Colombia, for passing out Wycliffe Bible Associates' translation of the Gospel of Luke. He also preached among "the tribal people of Mexico." According to the *Southern Baptist Advocate*, McAteer "holds the distinction of being the only Christian ever to present the Gospel of Jesus Christ in a series of meetings in a public building in Islamabad, Pakistan, whose population is 98 percent Muslim."

His involvement in politics coincided with the civil rights movement in the South, although he is careful—as Southern whites were at the time—to avoid the code words that would brand him a racist. He told *Conservative Digest*: ". . . in the early seventies the busing legislation went through. I knew that was not only—well, it wasn't even practical—it wasn't good. [The legislation, of course, was the 1964 Civil Rights Act; the busing was ordered as a result of the widespread refusal of whites to abide by the Supreme Court's 1954 ruling that segregated schools were unconstitutional.] Economically it was a disaster, and talking with people I could see that the various races, regardless of who they were, did not like that. So it was an accumulation of these things. It was the accumulation of things that began to concern a lot of people in the sixties and seventies."

In 1976, McAteer's twin careers of religion and selling found a home at the Christian Freedom Foundation, which had been founded in 1950 through a $50,000 grant from J. Howard Pew. The Pew Freedom Trust, endowed by Sun Oil Company money, contributed

$300,000 to the foundation in 1974, and Richard DeVos, a co-founder of Amway, gave $25,000 that same year.

Through the foundation, McAteer started seminars to get evangelical leaders involved in politics. The first of these was held at the Crystal City Marriott Hotel just across the Potomac from Washington. There were twenty-five fundamentalist leaders at the meeting, among them Jerry Falwell of Thomas Road Baptist Church in Lynchburg, Virginia. Falwell was known among the religious for his "Old-Time Gospel Hour" on radio and television. But he had just begun to be noticed in the newspapers. He flew in to help Anita Bryant with her crusade in Miami, and was merely one in a long list of speakers mentioned in the news accounts the next day. More important, Falwell had "taken on" Jimmy Carter because of the *Playboy* interview in which Carter confessed that he had lusted in his heart a few times. That made news. Every story that quoted Carter also quoted Jerry Falwell. The media were noticing him finally, and so was Eddie McAteer.

McAteer knew the preachers and he knew the politicians. "I started doing some marrying." Howard Phillips was so impressed by McAteer's work, says McAteer, that he offered him his own job at The Conservative Caucus. McAteer said no, he didn't want to be executive director (with Phillips moving over as director of The Conservative Caucus Foundation); he wanted to be a field director under Phillips. He took the job and that naturally led to talk about involving evangelical leaders in the work of The Conservative Caucus.

"I had talked with Jerry about the need of speaking out on the issues and what I saw in him as a real key leader. I said, 'I've got a guy I want you to meet.' " He said something similar to Phillips about Falwell. Waking up to a snowstorm one morning in January when he was supposed to meet McAteer at Falwell's in Lynchburg, Phillips asked his field director, "Do you really think it's necessary that I come down there?" "I said, 'Yes.' "

McAteer flew from Memphis to Roanoke, rented a car, and drove on to Lynchburg; Phillips drove down from Washington. "I told Howard to have his gun loaded; he'd get one hour, so get right to the point." As they talked with Falwell about his possibilities as a new kind of religious political spokesman, the Lynchburg preacher's interest grew and grew. They began their meeting over lunch around noontime; they didn't leave until 9:00 P.M.

One project they discussed was converting Falwell's newspaper into a national publication, with the possibility of a circulation of five million. They set up another meeting to talk about the newspaper. And that was when Paul Weyrich of the Committee for the Survival of a Free Congress came along. Scott Stanley, editor of the John Birch Society's *Review of the News,* also came to inspect the Lynchburg facilities and give his opinion about such a newspaper.

It was at this meeting that the magic phrase "moral majority" was first spoken. Avoiding sides on this point of history, McAteer says it may have been Weyrich who first mentioned the words to Falwell, "but Phillips had written on it before." Whoever said it and when, "that was when Jerry's ears really perked up."

A national newspaper of the religious right did not emerge, however. Falwell's fund raiser, Jerry Hunsinger, was insistent that it would involve more money than they could raise. "Then I had a buddy of mine shoot us out of the saddle," says McAteer. This was Art De-Moss, founder of National Liberty Insurance Company in Valley Forge, Pennsylvania. McAteer had served on the board of DeMoss's Freedom Foundation. DeMoss said a newspaper was "too parsimony [*sic*] a thing" to get involved with.

At the next meeting, the lawyers for Jerry Falwell and Allen Dikes, representing The Conservative Caucus, drew up the charter for Moral Majority, Inc. "At that time, Jerry asked me to come with him and set up Moral Majority. I told him I would, but then I made my decision to start my own organization."

Religious Roundtable was formally organized in September 1979, but McAteer continued to work at The Conservative Caucus until the end of the year. Originally, The Roundtable (as it is now called) was to involve regional meetings of evangelical and political leaders, workshops and seminars teaching the religious about politics. There were fourteen of them in 1980, including the one in Dallas whose speakers included Presidential candidate Ronald Reagan. Considering his Baptist origins, McAteer was remarkably conservative in his numbers. He said only forty thousand people had attended those meetings, not a very impressive count in a field where others speak of millions. But McAteer aims to catch up fast. He wants to organize Roundtable chapters in every state, one hundred chapters in 1981, three hundred in 1982.

With Moral Majority and Christian Voice already in the business, was there really a need for another religious-right group? Well, Mc-Ateer thought of it the same way he had about a new soap or tooth-paste. You ask yourself: (1.) Is there a need, a market? (2.) Is there a point of difference that would sell your product? As with Ultra-Brite and Rapid Shave, he answered yes to both questions. "What is the greatest need in America? One word: leadership—in the home, churches, government."

"Is there not a cause?" is the biblical slogan The Roundtable marches under. That comes from 1 Samuel 17:29, when little David comes down from the mountain and his big brother Eliab says: "Why camest thou down hither? and with whom hast thou left those few sheep in the wilderness? I know thy pride, and the naughtiness of thine heart; for thou art come down that thou mightest see the battle."

And David said, "What have I now done? Is there not a cause?" According to the Living Bible, David's words could also be translated: "What have I done now? I was only asking a question."

Two other biblical quotations inscribed in oversized bronze plaques also adorn the Roundtable's office walls. One of them is, "The Sun Stood Still," which, of course, refers to the time Joshua needed for it to stay daylight "until the people had avenged themselves upon their enemies." But the second one stopped me. It read, "The Iron Did Swim." I found that in 2 Kings 6:6. The sons of the prophets tell Elisha "the place where we dwell with thee is too strait for us." So Elisha says they can go unto Jordan and build another place. Using a bor-rowed ax, one of them starts to work, only to have it break off and disappear in the water. That's when the man of God comes and throws a stick in the water where the ax fell in, "and the iron did swim."

These are not just parables to Eddie McAteer; he believes in an Old Testament God of absolutes, a God seeking vengeance on a whole country full of sin. One wishes that McAteer, like the original music man, were selling a product that is more fun—or humane—and less potentially harmful than the radical changes he has in mind.

122

9

IGNATIUS WEYRICH'S
FAITHFUL SON

Of all the new-right masterminds, Paul Weyrich is surely the best liked. One network political analyst—who strongly disagrees with much of what Weyrich says—speaks of him as a friend, and they often have lunch together when he's in Washington. A reporter for a gay newspaper told me that Weyrich was always accessible and treated him with more courtesy and respect than the liberals did.

I also liked Weyrich more than I did the others I met in connection with this book. He seemed secure in his beliefs and betrayed none of the condescension that characterizes so many of his colleagues. Others call his Committee for the Survival of a Free Congress the "flagship" of the new right. Weyrich is more than willing to accept that honor because he feels he earned it after waging "the longest political crusade in American history."

If Weyrich is secure, it is surely because the beliefs about life, religion, and politics he espouses now are the very same ones he inherited intact from his father. Ignatius Weyrich came from southern Germany to this country in 1923, at the age of twenty. He was Roman Catholic, and so was Virginia Wickstrom by the time they were married in 1939. She was fifteen years younger than he, the daughter of Protestants from Norway. Her father had worked in the shipyards in Oslo before emigrating to Racine, Wisconsin. That is where Paul Weyrich was born on October 7, 1942, the only child in a desperately poor but intensely proud household. He remembers one winter when he and his mother knelt on the threadbare carpet in the living room and prayed because there was no money and they were running out of coal.

How much he earned was something his father would never have mentioned, but Weyrich's mother once spoke of it as sixty cents an hour. The elder Weyrich worked for fifty years shoveling coal at a Catholic hospital. Other kids' fathers talked about sports and hobbies; Weyrich's dad had no time for such foolishness. Although he had dropped out of school in the eighth grade, Ignatius Weyrich read whenever he had free time and he was avidly interested in politics, starting out at a campaigner for his fellow Catholic, Al Smith, and going on to the first campaign of Franklin Roosevelt, with whom he soon became disillusioned.

Also unlike other fathers, Ignatius Weyrich didn't say one thing and do another. He lived his religion and his politics and there was no separating his personal sense of right and wrong, good and evil, moral and immoral from either one. He was bitterly opposed to unions, partly because a mandatory forty-hour week would have kept him from working the extra hours (at the same hourly wage, of course) that bought the precious few luxuries the family had. Whenever there were strikes, Weyrich would calculate the cost in lost wages, and he always figured that the workers lost more than they gained by staying out of work.

The Weyrichs borrowed no money, and they bought nothing on time. Their furniture and carpets were worn, but they were theirs and nobody could take them away. Their house was small, but it, too, was paid for. During the Depression, Weyrich had to sell for four hundred dollars a 1928 Nash he had bought for one thousand dollars. Then the family had no car until 1957. After carefully shopping around for months, Weyrich purchased a four-door Chevrolet for $2,464 cash. In order to save that amount, Weyrich had gone to his eight-hour job at the hospital and worked all night. When he got off that job, he went to mass and then took two buses out to the suburbs, where he worked another four hours in a foundry. It took two years for him to save enough for the car.

There was no place for debate or questioning in the Weyrich home. Their rigid Roman Catholic faith did not allow for doubts of any kind. When young Paul went to visit his Protestant grandmother, he noticed that the Methodist youth magazine had been left out for him, and Billy Graham kept appearing on television. But his faith—then and now—remained as strong as his father's. Recently, Weyrich joined the Eastern or Byzantine Rite of the Roman Catholic church, not because he had changed but because he felt the regular Roman Catholic church had grown too liberal.

Part of the Weyrich faith was that the Republican Party offered the best answer to America's problems. By the time he was five years old, Weyrich could name the members of Harry Truman's cabinet, although as the enemy; when he was seven, he was taught his father's view that the Taft-Hartley Act encouraged corruption in unions.

At Holy Trinity grade school, Paul Weyrich knew no others who claimed to be Republicans; at St. Catherine's High School, he may have been one of fifteen Republicans—out of three hundred students. What struck Weyrich at a very early age was that his Catholic relatives were just as conservative as his Protestant kin who were voting Republican. This was dramatically impressed on him in 1960 when his family gave him a trip to visit relatives in Philadelphia and New York. At seventeen, he was already a board member of the Wisconsin Young Republicans. For the trip East, he brought along a transistor radio to keep up with the campaign between Republican Richard Nixon and Catholic Democrat John Kennedy. His Catholic relatives in Philadelphia were dumbfounded that he and his father were opposed to Kennedy, and they called in all the neighbors to hear the reasons why. It was, says Weyrich now, "providential for me." It was his first chance to explain what he hasn't stopped explaining since: people should forget about ethnic, regional, and party traditions and vote for the philosophy that suits their consciences. Conservatives at heart were helping to elect liberals just because they happened to be Democrats or Catholics or Southerners or Protestants.

From this humble beginning, Weyrich traces the now-successful alliance between urban Catholics and rural Protestants, and the marriage of the two to the Republican Party. It was a long time coming. When he had asked his relatives why they voted Democratic, they said the Democrats took care of them; he was the first Republican they had ever seen. At the Young Republicans, he was the only board member who wasn't a young executive. "Nobody would listen," when he talked about getting away from the limousine/country club set and getting down to the level of working people who were true conservatives. In terms of "absolute values," Weyrich always felt that conservative Protestants, Catholics, Orthodox Jews, and Mormons had the same beliefs.

There was no branch of Young Americans for Freedom in either his college or hometown. The only place he could read about that new group was in the *National Review* at the public library. He continued to work in the regular Republican Party during two years of college, after which he dropped out and got a full-time job as a radio station manager. "I thought, well, I'll drop out for a year or so and meantime I never got back to school, which I sort of regret." In 1963, he married Joyce Smigun, whose father was a Russian emigrant and whose mother was the daughter of an Italian emigrant. "Between the two of us, we have all of our country's known enemies." They have two daughters and three sons.

After working with WLIP and WAXO in Kenosha, Wisconsin, Weyrich became a reporter for the *Milwaukee Sentinel*. As such, he debated as a conservative on WISN, the CBS television affiliate in Milwaukee, during the 1964 elections. The turning point in his career from journalism to politics came after he had taken a job with radio station KQXI in Colorado. As news director, he did a series of half-hour programs on the 1966 election. One of those who listened and liked what he heard was a successful conservative candidate for Congress, Gordon Allott. Allott hired Weyrich as his press aide, a job that took him to Capitol Hill, where he has remained ever since.

The most important connection Weyrich made in Colorado, however, was not a politician but a brewer named Joseph Coors, successor to his brother William as president of the Adolph Coors Brewing Company in Golden, Colorado. Although Coors Beer is sold only in fourteen Western states, it ranks fifth in sales for the whole country. It also has a cultlike following that has included Presidents Eisenhower and Ford, who stocked it aboard Air Force One, and actor Paul Newman, who used to insist that Coors Beer always be available on the sets where he was working.

When Weyrich first met him, Joseph Coors was, according to Weyrich, "politically naïve." There was no question about his ultra-conservative bent. He was already an active supporter of the John Birch Society. But there were better and more effective ways to spend his money, and Paul Weyrich was there to show them to him. After six years with Allott and a brief part-time stint with Carl Curtis, Republican senator from Nevada, Weyrich set up the Heritage Foundation with Joseph Coors's money. This was a research and educational foundation, prohibited by law from engaging in political campaigns. It was designed as a conservative answer to the liberal Brookings Institution. Many of the Reagan administration's decisions and policies are based directly on position papers and reports from the Heritage Foundation, located in the Joseph and Holly Coors Building, a few blocks northwest of the Capitol.

Weyrich was more and more anxious to get into the thick of the campaign fighting, and in 1977 he persuaded Coors to back another venture of his, the Committee for the Survival of a Free Congress, a political action committee that finds and instructs potential candidates and then does everything it can to get them elected.

"After a year I left Heritage precisely because it was prohibited from doing political things by its tax-exempt status. . . . In 1974, I went to Carl Curtis and Jesse Helms, both senators from the distant far right, and got them interested in backing something like CSFC. Joe Coors, who had helped with Heritage, didn't think it was the best idea in the world." The implication is that Coors backed it all the same and has not been unhappy with its success, since he continues to back the group.

With $5,000, Weyrich launched his first direct-mail campaign. In two years, CSFC had raised more than $2.3 million.

Meanwhile, the mix of beer money and politics proved to be an unhealthy one for the company. By 1981, sales were down by 15 percent in California, where 45 percent of Coors beer was sold. Paul Newman switched to Budweiser and so did a majority of those drinking at San Francisco's gay bars.

The decline in sales came about because of a boycott of Coors called by what *Newsweek* described as "a formidable, if somewhat incongruous alliance of activists that includes women's groups, Chicanos, homosexuals, and civil libertarians." The Coors brewery had been a union shop for forty-two years, but what caused the union's last and fatal strike in 1977 was not low wages but management's low regard for civil rights. Job applicants at Coors were asked in a lie-detector test: What are your sex preferences? How often do you change your underwear? Have you ever done anything with your wife that could be considered immoral? Are you a homosexual? Are you a Communist?

David Sickler, a union officer and Coors employee before the strike, said, "When you get through being grilled on that lie detector, you feel dirty." The first boycott against Coors was started in 1967 by a Mexican-American veterans' group. Sickler has said, "At that time, I was aware of only one black and approximately five Mexican-Americans within the brewery." No women were employed in the production side of the company until 1971, and no separate rest room facilities were provided for them until 1973.

Although Coors succeeded in breaking the strike and driving the union out, a symbolic protest continues among union officers and former Coors employees. The most effective protest they were able to make came through an alliance with gay rights groups in San Francisco, where one hundred bar owners agreed to stop buying and selling Coors Beer. This was a reaction to Coors's support of groups that had supported Anita Bryant's anti-homosexual crusade in Miami. In May 1981, the union Solidarity and a group called Gay-Lesbian Liberation in San Francisco threatened to picket a Coors Day benefit by a local television show, and the event was canceled.

All of this was hitting Joseph Coors where he hurts. He did some reading up on homosexuals, or so he wrote in a letter to the *San Francisco Chronicle* columnist, Herb Caen. Caen couldn't believe the letter was genuine, so he called Coors's office to confirm it. Yes, indeed, Coors had come around. He said none of it was true about homosexuals; they couldn't help being the way they were. The company also initiated a massive publicity campaign to announce that the strike was over, the lie-detector test had been changed, Joseph Coors had never supported Anita Bryant. The strike was finished, but so was the union; the lie-detector test had been reworded but it was still there; if Coors had not contributed directly to Anita Bryant, the groups he funded had done so and also had come up with some anti-homosexual proposals of their own. Such gaps as these had to be filled in between the lines of full-page ads that Coors took out in ten newspapers in and around San Francisco, including *The Advocate*, a national gay newspaper whose publisher, David Goodstein, had never supported the boycott and who urged non-union gays to go back to drinking Coors.

Meanwhile, Coors's man in Washington apparently hadn't gotten the word or, more likely, did not consider himself so closely identified with the brewer that he couldn't say what he really felt. In a March 1980 interview with *Christian Life* magazine, Paul Weyrich said: "Now, we're talking about homosexuality we're talking of course about one of the gravest sins condemned in the Scriptures, a sin which is described and condemned more explicitly than most others. So we are not talking about someone's creed, someone's race, someone's private beliefs. We're talking about the question of morality, which, of course, affects society as a whole. To elevate that sin to the level of a civil right and thereby legitimatize this kind of lifestyle, I think sets a dangerous precedent."

In another interview he said, "Homosexuals are not just people who have a particular viewpoint different than yours or mine. They are people who seek to induce others to follow their lifestyle. Perhaps because they don't have children and don't propagate their race, therefore they proselytize," he said, borrowing a thought and similar words from Anita Bryant.

In his talk with me, Weyrich had mentioned homosexuality only in the most discreet and polite way. Reading over these harsh phrases, I realized he was not just the simple congenial fellow who had been so nice to me. Later I would be shown videotapes made of Weyrich during his training sessions. In these, the genial guy becomes cold, severe, as he delivers such cynical pronouncements as these:

—"We are talking about Christianizing America. We are talking about simply spreading the Gospel in a political context. We are in this for the long haul. If we really want to turn around America, then we're going to have to turn around the legislature. And the only way that we can do that is for people to be informed and, frankly, outraged at what is going on in the nation's capital. Therefore, you have to be able to put things in, if you will, simplistic, polemical terms. Ultimately, everything can be reduced to right and wrong. Everything."

—"Many of our Christians have what I call the 'goo-goo' syndrome. Good Government. They want everybody to vote. I don't want everybody to vote. Elections are not won by a majority of people, they never have been from the beginning of our country, and they are not now. As a matter of fact, our leverage in the elections, quite candidly, goes up as the voting populace goes down."

Weyrich has never been one of those who felt the social issues should be pushed aside while Congress considers matters affecting the economy and defense. He doesn't speak of a "pure conservatism" in relation to individual privacy, if that privacy happens to include homosexuality, abortion, or equal rights for women. His associate at

CSFC, Connie Marshner, was an author of the Family Protection Act, an omnibus bill that would provide for mandatory prayers in schools, prohibit busing, allow parental review of textbooks, and bar homosexuals or anyone advocating a homosexual lifestyle from teaching in public schools.

Like Weyrich, Marshner is a Roman Catholic. At the University of South Carolina she became friends with a group of fundamentalist Protestants. "They were the only people who politically were sympathetic with my views at the time. In addition they had a dynamic, fervent faith, which I shared. I used to go to prayer meetings with them. Instead of becoming a fundamentalist, they encouraged me to reexamine my own Catholicism and to become more appreciative of it and to discover a greater fullness of my own personal faith." She had planned to teach, but she took a job with YAF's *New Guard* magazine in Washington. After a few weeks at *New Guard*, she moved over to the Heritage Foundation, after which she followed Paul Weyrich to CSFC. Marshner edits the group's monthly *Family Protection Report* and is head of the Library Court Group, an umbrella association of religious and political leaders that meets regularly in Washington to swap ideas, grants, and research.

In addition to the subgroup that Marshner heads, Weyrich also has the Kingston Group, founded in 1979 as a weekly forum for conservative congressional aides and political activists, and the Stanton Group, which meets every two weeks to talk about national defense. All of these activities are carried out from two elegantly restored townhouses in a stockadelike arrangement in what is still a poor black neighborhood beside the railroad tracks behind Washington's Union Station. Twenty-foot-high chain-link fences, topped by barbed wire, protect the parking lot and offices of CSFC in a closed-off cul-de-sac.

Throughout his rise to power in the new right, Weyrich has carried with him that original cause of forging a Republican Party with a truly grass-roots conservative membership. "I was a great admirer of many of the Southern conservatives in Congress," he said. He would ask them why they were Democrats, and they would talk about the Civil War. "Okay, that was a hundred years ago."

"Orthodox Jews had always been part of my idea of a coalition. In the early 1960s, I met with leaders of orthodox Jews and found that we were in agreement on a number of issues. And then we had a wonderful meeting with them in New York [in early 1981]."

The path away from the limousine Republicans and down to the ordinary Catholics and fundamentalist Protestants became more clearly defined after Weyrich became friends with Ed McAteer of The Conservative Caucus. "He was a Southerner who had come to the same conclusions I had. In his travels around the country he had found that Mormons, Baptists, Lutherans all agree on the same set of issues. We began to talk about it in 1977. It was his dream to have that coalition. It was like meeting a long-lost brother.

"Then, in 1979, he took me down to Lynchburg to meet Jerry Falwell. Howard Phillips was with us. I said, 'Out there is a moral majority waiting to be tapped,' and he (Falwell) said, 'What!' He said, 'That's a great phrase.' And that was the beginning. Right after that, Moral Majority was announced."

10

HOMOSEXUALS AND ANTI-HOMOSEXUALS

With the arrest of the John Birch Society's most prominent spokesman of the late 1950s and early 1960s, former U.S. Army General Edwin Walker, in a homosexual encounter in a Dallas park, and of Richard Nixon's unsuccessful appointee to the Supreme Court, G. Harrold Carswell, in a similar situation in a men's room in Florida, it should be obvious that liberals hold no franchise on homosexuality. There is an interesting and important difference, however, in the kind of person who moves in a society that does not condemn homosexual feelings and another kind who is clearly defined by himself and his society as a deviant, but who places himself among the most rigid defenders of that same society—among those he should naturally regard as enemies.

Lucian Truscott IV examines such a character in *Dress Gray*, his novel about a homosexual cadet who is murdered at West Point. The deviant was the perfect cadet; the Spartan life of "don't's" suited him much better than it did those whose lives weren't so sharply defined. In telling him so specifically what he could not do, the society was also telling him what he could get away with. At the time, there were dozens of restrictions at the all-male academy against showing affection or having sex with a woman, but there were no such rules about doing the same things with other men. Roommates were "wives."

I am told by several friends who worked and went to parties with them that many of the key people sent in by Ronald Reagan to plan his inauguration and the transition from the Carter administration were secretly but actively homosexual. During the Christmas–New Year's holiday season just prior to the inauguration, they held several private parties. One that was described to me took place in the Foggy Bottom townhouse of a man who has been one of Reagan's closest advisers from the beginning of his political career. Although he is married and has children, he lives in Washington with a male lover. The guests at his party and the others I heard about were all white, all male, and—except for a few young Democrats looking for work—all Republicans. Two handsome young California lovers arrived at the Foggy Bottom party driving matching sports cars and wearing identical shoes, slacks, shirts, ties, and V-necked sweaters.

The kind of stories that were told at these parties were the kind that little boys tell about getting away with breaking the rules. The thrill was that they were passing for straight. One man—known as "Reagan's Capote"—came up with a flamboyant idea of having the military units in the inaugural parade march with American flags instead of rifles. The Pentagon was dumbfounded. "Why," some military spokesman was quoted as saying, "we'd just as soon march down the street with our pants unzipped." But, the gay revelers whooped, didn't the Pentagon understand that this was exactly what Reagan's friend would love to see?

All of these people are part of an underground society of very wealthy and powerful homosexuals, some of whom were at the heart of the earlier anti-Communist and anti-homosexual crusades of Joseph McCarthy, and all of whom are active in the new-right groups. Their true sexual identities keep them from any kind of public roles, but this vulnerability has also put them in touch with some of the country's biggest sources of money, however corrupt. Like the women, Jews, or blacks who succeeded in spite of societal attitudes about their kind, these men have a stake in preserving their own oppression. They don't see it as oppression at all. They see it as privilege conferred on them because they are special; if other homosexuals suffer from oppression, then they deserve it because they are so weak or just not clever enough.

It is the best of both worlds that these men enjoy. They are lawyers, real-estate men, construction contractors who—in terms of financial success—are at the very top of their professions. They have everything that money can buy, including a gay lifestyle in the midst of a disapproving (in earlier times, at least) world.

In Washington, a group of such men meets on a regular basis and stages lavish parties fairly often. They actually make up names for their little club, "the RPQs—rich and powerful queens" or "the Thirteen Richest Fairies." The lover of one of them was handed two hundred dollars and told to prepare a party for the new Republican arrivals in town around the time of the inauguration. He laughed contemptuously at such pocket change, carried the money down to a male go-go place on Ninth Street, and gave it to one of the young dancers to come do a strip-tease for the Republicans. The liquor and food for the party cost several times that amount, and everybody got a laugh out of the lover's introduction of the dancer: "This is just to show you that two hundred dollars can still buy something worthwhile." The young man began to bump and grind and remove his clothes on top of the dining room table. One of the distinguished guests promptly turned away from the dancer and faced a wall until he had finished. Why do you think he did that? I asked a friend who was there. "Oh, it wasn't the impropriety of it, I can assure you. I know him. He just felt that anything erotic should be kept in the dark."

A cheaper customer—at fifty dollars a turn—of the young dancers on Ninth Street for many years was a young congressman named Robert E. Bauman. Born April 4, 1937, in the rural town of Easton (population 8,500) on the Eastern Shore of Maryland, Bauman had spent half his life on Capitol Hill. He started out as a page, worked as a congressional aide, and then was elected in a special election on August 21, 1973, to succeed a congressman who died in midterm. A Roman Catholic, Bauman was a member of SS. Peter and Paul Church in Easton. In 1960, he married Carol Gene Dawson and they subsequently had four children.

Bauman was no mere conservative Republican, he was a militant fighter against any and all things liberal. He and his wife were both among the ninety-three founders of Young Americans for Freedom, and he served for a time as national chairman of that group. He was co-founder and national chairman of the American Conservative Union. As the energetic and aggressive head of these groups in the 1960s and 1970s, Bauman was one of a very small number of activists who decided on the issues and tactics and laid the groundwork for the new-right victories at the polls in 1980. The religious right, said a victim of one of their campaigns, "just took the same issues laid down by the ACU and baptized them and called them 'moral.' "

A short, scrappy fellow, Bauman saw himself as the feisty "watchdog" of the U.S. House of Representatives. Like Jesse Helms in the Senate, his tactics often served to embarrass his colleagues and slow down the legislative process, but they also served his purpose by constantly putting liberals on the spot with controversial issues through published roll-call votes. For no other reason than to get liberals to commit themselves in public, he would raise these issues, which would normally have been calmly worked out through compromises. He was so despised that once, when he stayed home because of the snow, his colleagues mustered up a quorum and forced through as many votes as they could. The conservative Americans for Constitutional Action gave him a perfect 100-percent score for his voting record, and so did the oil lobby. The National Council of Senior Citizens rated him zero.

In an exclusive interview with John Rees in the John Birch Society's *Review of the News*, Bauman was described as the "bulldog of the House." He said, "Anytime the House is in session, America is in danger." Liberal Republicans, he added, were nothing more than "Democrats in drag."

But in the 1980 elections, the year of the conservative and of Republican victories nationwide, Robert E. Bauman himself went down to defeat against an inexperienced young Democrat. The reasons why go back to the bars on Ninth Street where the male hustlers hang out in Washington.

The Maryland congressman was charged with soliciting sex from a teenage boy, after an extensive FBI investigation showed that Bauman was a prime target for blackmail. Although Bauman later denied it, the FBI report noted several instances where he had already paid blackmail. The mother of one of his sex partners had also asked Bauman to have another of her sons discharged from the navy after the boy got in trouble for going AWOL. At the same time, proceedings were begun in Baltimore against a twenty-six-year old man who had worked as a street hustler in Washington since he was thirteen, the year he claimed he first met Bauman. They met at a sleazy bar in Washington, but the two were born just seventeen miles apart on the Eastern Shore of Maryland. This man had tried to extort two thousand dollars from Bauman by threatening to tell his family about his extramarital affairs. He was apprehended when an FBI agent posed as an aide to Bauman to hear his offer.

The newspaper accounts all mentioned Bauman's anti-homosexual votes in the House. He was a co-sponsor of a bill that would amend the 1964 Civil Rights Act to allow employers to discriminate against homosexuals without federal interference; it would also have prevented federal interference in discrimination suits where homosexuals were involved. In July 1980 Bauman voted for an amendment that prevented the Legal Services Corporation from representing homosexuals; he had voted for the same measure in 1977, when it was defeated. Bauman was also among the original signers of the Family Protection Act, which contained a number of anti-homosexual provisions.

Bauman responded to the solicitation charge with an extraordinary statement that said, in effect, he must have been drunk and didn't know what he was doing. "In recent years, I have had an increasingly serious personal problem with the consumption of alcohol. Last winter my drinking problem reached what I now realize to be the stage of acute alcoholism, although I did not know it at the time. . . . I have confessed my sins, as my religion requires, and I am in the state of grace and will remain so with the help of God." The eleven-paragraph statement carried only this reference to the charge: "The charge involved is solicitation." He did not mention homosexuality.

Meanwhile, Bauman's longtime friend and physician, Albert Dawkins, back home in Easton, told *The Washington Post*: "I would not consider Bob an alcoholic. I define an alcoholic this way: when the use of alcohol interferes with the person's productive life or his health, his ability to function. There is no evidence I know of in the lifetime I've known Bob Bauman that alcohol interferes with his productivity, his ability to function."

Although his conservative friends urged him to resign, Bauman refused and continued to run for reelection. He did finally resign as chairman of the ACU—at the urging of William F. Buckley, Jr., among others. But he remained on the ACU's national board of directors. Paul Weyrich of the Committee for the Survival of a Free Congress said, "It's not that I don't forgive him. It's that he has brought dishonor to the movement in which he has been involved." Weyrich said Bauman had done "considerable damage to the movement" and "can no longer be a credible spokesman for causes." Bauman, of course, had served that movement longer and in a far more important position than had Weyrich.

After a few weeks of silence, Bauman called a press conference to announce that he'd been cured. "I do not consider myself to be a homosexual," he said in answer to a reporter's question. "I will not discuss the clinical details," he snapped in answer to another question. "I don't owe it to anyone but my God, and I have confessed to him and am going forward. I have changed. I am not going back to this grave problem in my life. I have not had a drink since May 1." Bauman refused to understand that nobody really cared about his drinking, or—more to the point—he was frustrated that the reporters wouldn't follow along when he tried to shift their attention from his homosexuality to his drinking. Most of us who live in Washington were still telling jokes about a similar attempt by the congressmen involved in Abscam who, one by one, claimed they had a problem with alcohol and that must have been what made them take money from FBI men posing as Arabs.

At least one of Bauman's supporters didn't care what he did, as long as he voted right. This was Joseph Kesner, who had sponsored a bull roast for Bauman's reelection campaign. He said, "If he was working with children where he was forming little minds, I might take a different view. But Bob Bauman, whether he's a homosexual or whether he's got four legs, expresses my views in Washington." Kesner's words, in my opinion, suggest that the attitudes in the hinterlands about homosexuals are not nearly so rigid and inflexible as many of the new-right leaders seem to think.

The solicitation charge against Bauman was eventually dropped after he agreed to go through a six-month rehabilitation program. Although he was defeated in his bid for reelection, Bauman's conservative pals apparently accepted him as cured. He was hired by Trent Lott of Mississippi, the House minority whip, at one thousand dollars a week to instruct the freshmen Republicans on House procedures—using a manual Bauman had written on the subject.

Such a personal crisis played out in public brings out the best and worst in small-town Washington. I mean, we all laughed at Bauman. The curious thing is that at the same time, another conservative Republican congressman found himself in a similar predicament over his homosexuality—and we did not laugh at him. This was Jon Hinson of

Mississippi, a member of the national advisory board of The Conservative Caucus, who, it turned out, had been one of the survivors of a fire at a gay movie theater in Washington in 1978 in which five men were killed. Hinson's involvement became public when he filed a deposition in support of the families suing the owners of the theater. It was a noble gesture that took real courage, I thought, and I wrote to Hinson and his wife and told them so.

Back home in Mississippi, there were dark rumblings that this would be the end of Hinson's political career. But one of his supporters, W. D. (Billy) Mounger, an independent oil man, said: "You'd think a man who had acknowledged frequenting a homosexual theater would have been run out of Mississippi. But some folks would rather have a queer conservative than a macho liberal, and they may be right." Hinson was reelected, but during his next term he was arrested during a homosexual encounter in a public men's room in a House office building, after which he resigned. It was then revealed that he had previously been arrested on similar charges in a park in Arlington and at a bookstore in Alexandria.

A Democrat who went to the same Baptist church Hinson attended had also noted the difference in the way people responded to his troubles and to Bauman's. He told me: "Hinson was a man with real problems and he hadn't been up there demagoguing it on the subject; and he didn't lay it all to alcohol once he got caught, either."

Meanwhile, the Bauman jokes continue: he's head of the "oral majority"; he was born on the Eastern Shore but reared in Washington; give him back his seat, boys.

There was one line in a *Washington Post* story that must have reflected a general attitude at the time. An Easton neighbor of Bauman's said: "It kind of makes you wonder: Who else?"

Who else? I know of at least ten other prominent leaders of the Republican right who have either had sex with friends of mine or gone to gay parties with them. According to people I trust, there are at least twenty members of Congress right now who are homosexual; not all of them are conservative Republicans, but most of them are. This is not to suggest in any way that a man who is over thirty and unmarried these days is automatically assumed to be homosexual. In fact, most of the homosexuals I've mentioned are married. But that is an attitude that did exist in Washington in the 1950s, when more than ten thousand government employees were fired because they were believed to be homosexual.

The late H. L. Hunt—one of the great-uncles of the new right—spelled this out in his plan for the reconstruction of the Republican Party through a "Public Service Education Institute" for candidates in the early 1960s. He said, "Prospects are needed, age twenty to sixty years. If a man is more than twenty-six years of age, he should be married and preferably the father of one to four children. . . ." Hunt could use that as a measure, since he had fathered children by each of three wives. While still married to the mother of his "first family," as Hunt's biographer, L. J. Davis, calls it, Hunt married another woman in Florida and had children by her. He later fathered children by a third woman, whom he married after his first wife's death.

In her book about Washington, Rita Jenrette speaks of two senators from the same state who are "big in the Moral Majority" and make a point of being seen with the town's best-looking women, but are known to be homosexual. Paula Parkinson, the blonde lobbyist who created a scandal by talking about going to a house party with six conservative Republican members of Congress, was amazed that one of them wanted her to keep quiet because she felt the affair might help counter rumors that he is homosexual.

During the peak years of the new right, one of the most widely discussed secret homosexuals in Washington was Terry Dolan, head of the National Conservative Political Action Committee. Long before Dolan's homosexuality became a news story in mid-1982, I had known several people who had been to gay parties with him; I knew one man who had had sex with him; a young congressional aide whom I knew (conservative, Republican, homosexual) was one of his close friends.

Every gay activist in Washington and New York, every political reporter in the capital, knew about what Dolan himself apparently thought nobody knew. I can't imagine anyone living the way he felt he had to live for so long, but I still regarded it as his choice. Even as I headed into his office one afternoon in the summer of 1981, I was not sure I would actually confront him with the fact that I knew he was homosexual.

All I could think about was the American Nazi Party spokesman who had killed himself immediately after a *New York Times* reporter told him the paper was going to print the fact that he was a Jew. I did not know—until Terry Dolan himself told me that day—that he was close enough to Jerry Falwell and James Robison to be included in this book about the religious right. Robison has suggested that "like cancer," homosexuals must be removed from our society; Falwell is more careful with his language, but his message is just as clear.

Dolan is a member of the advisory committee of the National Defeat Legal Services Committee. While this group was set up to seek the destruction of the entire program of Legal Services, one of its specific complaints was that the group aids homosexuals and homosexual groups. Also, NCPAC's National Conservative Foundation has challenged the FCC license of the Pacifica radio station in Washington, and among the complaints listed is that the station broadcasts programs by and for homosexuals. In a fund-raising letter for NCPAC in 1981, signed by Dan Crane, congressman from Illinois, are these words: "Our nation's moral fiber is weakened by the growing homosexual movement, the fanatical ERA (Equal Rights Amendment) pushers (many of whom publicly brag they are lesbians). . . ."

At the January 1981 convention of religious broadcasters in Washington, Terry Dolan had been one of the featured speakers. He said, "I would make the point over and over that your movement is separate, that your motivations are vastly different than mine and [those of] the people I represent." But he went on to say: "Now that does not mean we are not allies. We certainly are. I can think of virtually nothing that I do not endorse on the agenda of the Christian right. My guess is that there is very little if anything that the people on the Christian right don't endorse concerning what we stand for." Of course, homosexuality is at the top of every list of things the Christian right has declared war against, and the congressmen whom Dolan's NCPAC has helped to elect vote right down the line in favor of every anti-homosexual proposal that comes up.

Dolan is a hyperactive, boyish-looking man with a trim body, neat dark mustache, and short haircut. Some would describe his as the stereotypical look in gay bars now. His dark eyes look right through you—and then wander here, there, and everywhere as he adjusts first one leg and then another up under him in the big swivel chair behind his desk. His is the office of one who lives to work. There are no pictures or mementoes of family, no memorabilia of friends; there is no evidence whatsoever of any interest in art, literature, or music. There is one plaque on the wall, making Dolan an honorary citizen of Texas, signed by the Republican governor. There are two eight-by-ten photographs in plain certificate frames, one showing Dolan with David Stockman, the other showing him with Philip Crane, the erstwhile presidential candidate and new-right congressman from Illinois.

He welcomed me with a firm handshake, as if he meant it. He said he didn't think of himself as part of the religious right, but he would be glad to answer any questions I had.

John Terry Dolan was born on December 20, 1950, in Norwalk, Connecticut. His father was then a manager for Sears, and now works as a fund raiser for a Catholic hospital. His parents were Democrats, but conservatives. His mother, Peg, converted in late 1981 in order to head up the "Republicans to Replace [Lowell] Weicker" in the 1982 Senate race in Connecticut. Dolan's brother, Anthony, is chief speech writer for the President; his sister, Maiselle, is also on the White House staff.

"I was raised a Catholic; spent all except two years in prep school in Catholic schools." He graduated from Georgetown University in 1972, and in 1979 completed work on a law degree through night courses there. "I was not a particularly strong Catholic in college. If there is such a thing, I'm a born-again Catholic. I believe in most of the basic tenets of fundamentalism . . . a more profound belief in faith than most Catholics are taught—less concern about extra-biblical things than Catholics have."

Dolan dates his conservative activism from 1974 "when I saw what Richard Nixon was doing to the country—all in the name of conservatism. I thought he was the most liberal president we've ever had, in terms of federal involvement in people's lives. The bureaucracy increased in droves . . . when he came in we had 40 percent going for defense; it was down to 26 percent when he went out. The loss of Vietnam. The recognition of China."

This was what Dolan told me about Richard Nixon. He admitted to another interviewer that his first political campaign had been when he was nine, in 1960; the candidate was Nixon.

If he felt so strongly about winning the war in Vietnam, why had Dolan avoided military service? "I was in college during the draft and then afterwards in the lottery my name was nowhere near the top." Did it occur to him to drop out of school and join up—as thousands had in earlier wars? "No, well, it occurred to me, but now I'm glad I didn't. I was supportive of the war, but not of not to win. . . ."

The year when he became disillusioned with Richard Nixon's conservatism, 1974, was also the year Dolan says he got interested in the Bible. He was working in the unsuccessful Senate campaign in Alaska for a member of the John Birch Society's national council. Many of his co-workers were born-again Christians; one woman in particular helped spark a new interest in religion and reading the Bible.

In 1964, when he was thirteen, Dolan had worked in Barry Goldwater's campaign for President. "That's when I became familiar with a man named Ronald Reagan—his 'rendezvous with destiny' speech for Goldwater. . . . I still have a record of that and I still listen to it. In 1968, I went down to the Miami convention as a volunteer for Reagan, and I supported him in 1976 and 1980." He was a member of Teenage Republicans and YAF in high school, YAF and College Republicans, and then the Young Republicans Club. In 1975, he set up the National Conservative Political Action Committee with Charles Black and Roger J. Stone. Black had worked on Jesse Helms's staff in the Senate; Stone had been identified during the Senate Watergate hearings as a political spy for Richard Nixon during the 1972 campaign. In 1977, Stone went to work for Arthur J. Finklestein Associates, the polling company used by the new-right affiliates of The Viguerie Company.

Dolan's NCPAC is not only the richest of the political action committees; it is also the meanest by all accounts, including Dolan's own. He has bragged that he could get away with any kind of distortion and this would never reflect on the particular candidate he was supporting. In his book, Viguerie praises Dolan as a pioneer in the "independent expenditure campaign." In cruder language, Dolan figured out a way to get around the limits on individual contributions to campaigns. One provision of the 1974 campaign reforms allows for a group operating independently of the candidate to spend any amount of money it wants to. In other words, a Joseph Coors, for example, is forbidden by law to contribute more than one thousand dollars to the campaign of Ronald Reagan. However, Joseph Coors can give any amount he wants to a PAC set up independently to support the same candidate. As Viguerie puts it in his book: "A PAC called Conservatives for Reagan could legally spend five million dollars or whatever it could raise to help elect Ronald Reagan President as long as none of the PAC's leadership was in contact in any way with Reagan or his staff."

Such maneuvers by NCPAC were challenged in the courts, but the

Supreme Court voted four to four—with Sandra Day O'Connor abstaining for unexplained reasons—and that left standing the lower court ruling in favor of NCPAC. There is no way a reasonable person could possibly believe that amounts of money in the millions could be spent in behalf of a candidate and he and his staff wouldn't be involved in the process. The presence of Terry Dolan's brother and sister on the White House staff is solid evidence that he is much closer to Ronald Reagan and his top advisers than is ever publicly acknowledged.

Dolan himself confirmed my suspicion of his closeness to Reagan in a later interview with Larry Bush, a press officer and speech writer in the Agriculture Department during the Nixon administration who is now Washington editor for two gay newspapers, *The Advocate* and *New York Native*. Dolan explained to Bush that NCPAC was started in 1975 and "we were putzing along for almost a year and not doing badly. We were making state legislative contributions and a couple of federal races. And then when Reagan lost the Republican nomination, he took an interest in NCPAC and signed fund-raising letters that raised us, I would guess, eight hundred thousand or a million dollars in a period of about three months."

"So," Bush started to ask, "you really have a debt, as it were—"

Dolan interrupted: "Oh, no question about it. Well, not only a debt, but a long-standing relationship. I was for Ronald Reagan in 'sixty-eight when I was seventeen years old and 'seventy-six and in 'eighty. Charlie Black became the chairman of NCPAC, then went to work for Reagan. Roger Stone was the treasurer of NCPAC [and he] also went to work for Reagan—this is 'seventy-six. And then both of them worked in 'eighty again, so it was a very close relationship."

In another case challenging Dolan's "independent" expenditures, George McGovern's 1980 senatorial campaign proved beyond any doubt in my mind—after reading specific allegations and documents at the Federal Elections Commission offices—that Dolan and his staff had participated in selecting the candidate who would oppose McGovern, and then personally participated in various stages of that campaign. The FEC ruled straight down the party lines of its members; it was another tie vote, meaning there was no ruling for Dolan, but none against him, either.

Another bald attempt at getting around the law was made by Dolan in a reverse bribe offer to a congressman from North Carolina, a Democrat named Steve Neal. In a messenger-delivered letter on

NCPAC stationery, Dolan had tried to persuade Neal to vote in favor of Reagan's tax-cut package:

If you will make a public statement in support of the President's tax-cut package and state that you intend to vote for it, we will withdraw all radio and newspaper ads planned in your district. In addition, we will be glad to run radio and newspaper ads applauding you for your vote to lower taxes. Of course, your constituents will be greatly upset if you say you support President Reagan's tax cut and subsequently vote against it.

Sincerely,
John T. (Terry) Dolan
National Chairman

Neal was outraged by Dolan's bullying and fired off a letter of protest to William French Smith, the Attorney General and Reagan's longtime personal friend and political ally. Smith passed it to a subordinate who informed the congressman that no investigation would ensue because no money had been exchanged and so no actual bribe had taken place. But Neal fired back yet another protest letter to the Attorney General, saying that if he had accepted Dolan's terms *he* would have been guilty of taking a bribe while Dolan, meanwhile, was not even investigated because he offered one. The Democrat's protests fell on deaf Republican ears, and his letters were politely but firmly answered in the negative; there would be no investigation of Terry Dolan or of NCPAC by this administration. It is absurd to assume that Dolan tried to change that congressman's vote without first informing someone in the White House (his brother, if no one else) about what he was up to. It is hard to believe that his actions have been upheld by Republicans on the Federal Elections Commission and on the Supreme Court as anything but a matter of political expediency.

That afternoon in his office in Arlington, Dolan and I seemed to be talking comfortably, so I started asking Dolan more specific questions about his connections with the religious groups in the new right and the issues for which they were crusading. How did he feel about the Family Protection Act? He stammered and flip-flopped in his response, and said the bill wasn't all bad: "All in all, it's pretty good legislation." But he said he was against "any section that is using federal power to enforce social or moral standards." But, I asked, hadn't he supported those who had written this and other moral and social legislation? "I support everything the Christian right is doing that will permit a man or woman personal salvation, that will get the government out of their personal lives. . . . From my conversations with Jerry Falwell and James Robison, they feel the same way. I have asked them, and their biggest desire is to be left alone."

Hearing that, I knew the confrontation would have to take place. There was no way that Dolan could not have known about Falwell's and Robison's tirades against homosexuals. I asked if he hadn't seen all the stuff they were sending out, especially Falwell's "declaration of war" against homosexuality. He looked away and didn't answer.

I asked him how well he knew these men. He said he talked with Falwell "several times a week—and we make all our polls and research available to them." He implied that he was even closer to Robison.

Perhaps he sensed what this line of questioning was leading to, for he seemed to be telling me what I might agree with. He said it was "very wrong to have the federal government interfering in the area of morality . . . but to a degree we do have the government involved in morality and we always will . . . I mean, murder's a moral issue. Traditionally, in America, it has been defined as locally as possible. My objection to liberals is not that they have bad social policies, which they do, but that they are using the strongest and most dangerous power on the face of the earth to enforce them."

Had he actually said the federal government was needed only to defend us and deliver the mail? "That was an exaggeration to make a point; yes, I said that."

Abortion is the one exception to everything he had said about government interference in moral and social issues. "I think that Roe versus Wade was one of the most unconstitutional decisions since the Dred Scott decision. I happen to believe that abortion is killing."

What about homosexuality? "I happen to believe that's a local issue. I don't care what they do in San Francisco; I don't care to live there." What about homosexuality as a political issue? "I'm against gay rights. As I understand it, they are demanding quotas and special treatment." He said individuals had always been allowed to discriminate in America, and the government should make no laws saying they had to rent or sell to anybody they didn't want to. However, he said he didn't think the government should discriminate against homosexuals or anybody else. "Except in security risks. If they determine a homosexual is a risk, then—but somebody who is a bigamist would be as well. . . ."

This kind of double-talk was beginning to rattle me. I had arrived in his office fully in sympathy with Dolan's predicament. I was nervous, sweating, in my discomfort over what to say and how to say it. But the more equivocal he got about "those people," the more angry I got about his duplicity. And, as if he were reading my mind, he—a master at holding an interviewer's attention, if nothing else—unbent his leg, put his feet on the floor, reached in his desk drawer, pulled out a Bible, and proceeded to read to me. "If you want to read Romans, you'll see there's no hierarchy of sinners." He then read out a list that included fornication, murder, deceit, disobedience, adultery, envy. Dolan said, "I know I've done at least four of them. Why should homosexuality be any higher sin than adultery?"

After reading the list, which I had heard quoted many times before in other interviews, Dolan continued to read a concluding paragraph with which I was not familiar: "Do you, my friend, pass judgment on others? You have no excuse at all, whoever you are. For when you judge others, but do the same things that they do, you condemn yourself."

I was struck by this turn of phrase and delighted that Dolan seemed to be leveling with me. If he wasn't saying it was all right to be homosexual, what was he saying? So the moment arrived and the question came out quite calmly: "Several of my friends have been to gay parties with you, and they wonder how you can reconcile your own homosexuality with your lifestyle among these groups you're aligned with?"

But I had misjudged his mood. Maybe he had been saying it was okay for others to be gay, but once I associated his name with that word, he became uncharacteristically flustered. His words came out in scattershot, disconnected thoughts and half-sentences.

"In the last two years I've been accused of all kinds of things. . . . A man came in here and said I was a crook . . . he claimed he had evidence I'd taken bribes. . . . In the last two years I've been accused of being a womanizer. . . . One of the stories had . . . [a Republican congressman] was supposed to have been involved with another man and a woman. . . ."

"Wait a minute," I said, stopping him. "You mean [the congress-man] was supposed to have had an affair with you?" "Yes," Dolan said, "that's what they said."

After all this meandering, Dolan's mind apparently returned to my original question about the gay parties. He wanted to know who the people were who had been to these parties, and where the parties had been. I mentioned the party in Foggy Bottom with the Reagan adviser, and another one on Capitol Hill, where Dolan had made a spectacle of himself by hovering over the host's lover, the best-looking young man at the party. (One of the other guests explained to me that this was not only unseemly, it was also unsportsmanlike.) Dolan said he had never been to the house in Foggy Bottom, although he knew the man; he said I had the wrong first name for the man who was his host on Cap-itol Hill.

Every other sentence, it seemed, Dolan was with me; then, in the next one, he was against me. The clear impression he gave on the one hand was that it was all right to be gay, with the implication that he was; then he would counter that with an explanation that contradicted the previous impression. My restraint finally broke: "Listen, are you homosexual or not?" "No, I'm not," he said, "but I don't see that that's a question."

I stood up, we shook hands, and I assumed the interview was over. We had been dancing around in circles until I felt I was never going to get any answers to my questions. But as Dolan moved around from his desk, he kept talking face on to me, eyeball to eyeball, in a way that carried me along with him through the narrow doorway, and on out the door of his outer office, into the hallway to the elevators. He asked, "You got the names of those people who said that about me?" I told him they were friends; if I hadn't known who they were and trust-ed them, I would never have repeated what they said to me. I looked up, then, to see that Dolan was leading us right into the men's room. He was still talking and leading me on, but that is where I stopped. I will never know what he might have said to me in the privacy of that rest room; at that point I didn't want to know, I just wanted to get somewhere and down a few drinks and try to forget about a man like Terry Dolan. I felt such shame for him. I knew he was lying, and I knew he knew I knew. How long could such a charade go on? That afternoon, I worried that the confrontation might have caused him to do himself in in that men's room and never go back to his double life.

It also crossed my mind that he might send somebody out to take care of me. But no, I thought, he is not a man to face up to anything. Like Bauman, he had obviously not thought about what he would do if his homosexuality was disclosed, because he has lived in two worlds as separate as darkness and light—and when he was in one, the other didn't exist.

In March 1982 there was a bizarre sequel to my confrontation with Dolan involving him and Larry Bush, who had sought an interview with Dolan about homosexuality for several months. Bush, who told me about attending gay parties with Dolan, and who also made available his extensive files for my use in this book, finally had a date and time for his interview, arranged through a young press aide to Dolan. However, the day before this interview, he received a curt telephone message from Dolan's secretary saying the interview had been canceled. That morning, he later learned, the young aide had been fired on the spot by an infuriated Dolan who said the interview was "unauthorized."

Bush, however, persisted and within a matter of days, Dolan agreed to a preliminary "off the record" discussion after Bush explained that every other new-right leader—including Jerry Falwell and Gary Jarmin—had been interviewed by him for gay publications. When Bush showed up at Dolan's office, Dolan summoned two male assistants to sit in as "witnesses." Dolan finally agreed to an actual interview to take place the following week. At that time, Bush was introduced to an older man whom Dolan described as "the office enforcer." The man said nothing during the hour-long interview which was taped by both Bush and Dolan.

Dolan obviously was better prepared for questions about homosexuality than he had been with me. He said that "sexual preference is irrelevant to political philosophy." He said, "The rhetoric that some of my friends in the right have used on gay activism has been excessive." When Bush asked him about the Dan Crane letter quoted earlier in this chapter, Dolan issued an apology: "I truly regret that we ever put something into print that would ever question the morality, the patriotism of any other person." Although he spoke in complete sentences and paragraphs, Dolan's interview with Bush contained the same kind of confused double-talk that he had given me. On the one hand, he said, "if there isn't a law there ought to be a law" to protect gays from discrimination by the government. Then, he said, he was against all laws except those for national defense. He said the 1964 Civil Rights Act was "irrelevant," and the Voting Rights Act was "absolutely silly." There were also the following words which I leave to the reader to interpret. I have transcribed them directly from Bush's tape of the interview.

Dolan asked: "You ever been to a Republican meeting?" Bush said: "Yes." Dolan said: "Ugliest women in America. No, no, that's not true, the second ugliest women in America." Bush asked: "The first being?" Dolan: "Democratic conventions. I don't think that anybody who has really—my guess is like most political organizations they tend to attract—to be charitable—an *interesting* group of people. I don't know why that is—but in the nature of politics in America, but they are not what I would call normal people." Bush asked: "People in politics?" Dolan answered: "Yeah . . ." Both then stopped in a long pause over what the answer had to do with the question.

The clear message in the interview, however, was that Terry Dolan was breaking with his colleagues on the new right by coming out for gay rights—and that is how the story was reported in *The Washington Post* and the *San Francisco Chronicle* after those papers were given advance copies of Bush's interview from the gay *Advocate*. The *Chronicle* headlined its story: " 'New Right' Leader Supports Gay Rights."

However, in an extraordinary letter answering a flood of inquiries from the right about his comments, Dolan swore, "I do not, nor have I ever endorsed gay rights. . . . I have also discussed this matter with Jerry Falwell and other leaders of the Christian right. While we may and do disagree on a few issues, we all support the same conservative goals." He tried to twist the blame onto *The Washington Post* for trying to "split apart" the new right. He tried to blame the interviewer for misrepresenting him and the aide for granting an "unauthorized" interview. And then he did one more curious thing: he granted another interview to Bush on the subject of homosexuality, this time for an article in *The Village Voice* of April 20, 1982. This article, without answering the question, was all about whether Terry Dolan is or is not gay. The main source was, incredibly, Terry Dolan himself. "I got a call from a reporter who said the fact that you gave an interview with *The Advocate* leads one to believe you are gay. I have gotten other calls from people who ask: Are you? I enjoyed them very much because they were ashamed to ask and they should have been. I have had calls from other friends who said other reporters were doing the same thing. I am used to life in the big city and I emphasize this with all reporters: It's irrelevant; it's not true; and aren't they ashamed of asking."

Dolan couldn't understand that it wasn't his homosexuality but his hypocrisy and duplicity that brought him all this unsolicited attention. A high point in his ludicrous attempt to shift the blame came after he had referred to the way the press covers up liberals' "adulterous affairs." He said, "Adulterers always protect adulterers. Liberals always protect liberals." Bush asked, "And do gays always protect gays?" Dolan sighed: "*You*'ll have to answer that question."

But after reading all of this, there were no more questions in the mind of any reporter I talked with about Terry Dolan's homosexuality. The only questions were in his own mind, the only problems with the subject were his.

I met a young man from Dolan's dark side of life. Unlike Dolan himself, Richard Anderson did not live two lives; he was not ashamed of being homosexual or of having had sex with Terry Dolan; he wished they had become friends.

Their eyes locked as if on a reflection in a mirror. They looked enough alike to be brothers. Both wore the regulation plaid shirt and jeans of the Levi's-and-leather set. Both wore their dark hair in short military cut; their mustaches were neatly trimmed, and so was Richard's beard.

The two were instantly attracted to each other; perhaps the need for a brother/lover was more strongly felt because it was the holiday season, December 22, 1980, the Monday before Christmas. Richard Anderson had seen Terry Dolan on television several times; he despised his politics, but he liked his looks. Who did he think he was, challenging the man who had just been elected Vice-President? Dolan had threatened: "George Bush better mind his p's and q's, or he'll find himself out of a job."

However, Anderson did not recognize the face he saw at the entrance to the back bar at the Eagle that night. (On reflection, it seemed more rounded in person than it had on television.) The Eagle is Washington's oldest and most popular leather bar. I know executives in New York who think it's the best gay bar in the country, and they often come down on weekends just to hang out there. The crowd is a nice mix of people in costumes of plastic leather and a larger, less flamboyant group who come there seeking "real men," or at least men who aren't fluttering with affected gestures and language.

Richard had just gotten a job as an information specialist with a government agency, and he was sporting a new leather jacket and vest that night. He doesn't remember the exact time he got to the bar—it wasn't happy hour, but it wasn't the desperation hour toward closing, either.

He's not the sort who can stand back in such a scene; he has to keep moving. So he passed by Terry Dolan several times, always saluting him with a smile. After Dolan returned the attention, he walked over and started talking. They introduced themselves, first names only. Richard mentioned his new job; Terry said he was a lawyer for a lobbying group.

By then, they both knew what they wanted. When it turned out they also both lived in Arlington, the only questions were whose place to go to and how to get there. Richard and his roommate never kept their place in any condition to receive guests, so he eagerly agreed when Terry suggested they go to the apartment he had just moved into.

The two cars traveled south down Seventh Street and over the Fourteenth Street Bridge, and then on I-395 to the Ridge Road exit. Terry led the way into a parking lot beside the high-rise building, 511 South Four Mile Run Drive. They rode the elevator up to the twelfth floor and opened the door into apartment 1209, two barren rooms and a kitchen with none of the extra attention to details that makes a place look lived in.

There was a small kitchen on the left, and it, too, seemed bare except for a note pad on a countertop. The living room was straight ahead, with windows overlooking the railroad tracks along U.S. 1 in south Alexandria. The two wasted no time in there, but went straight to the bedroom and quickly undressed.

Afterwards, they went into the kitchen for some supermarket chocolate-chip cookies and milk. That was when Richard saw the note pad with *National Conservative Political Action Committee* at the top, with the nearby Wilson Boulevard address. Still, he did not connect this Terry with that Terry.

Anderson said, "I hope that's not the lobby you work for?" Terry said, "As a matter of fact, it is." Richard then made a mock protest about NCPAC's Terry Dolan: "That cute little asshole, who does he think he is, telling George Bush he better mind his p's and q's?" Terry said in serious defense, "*He* never said that." He went on to say that Dolan had been misquoted. This led to a political discussion, the kind Richard normally avoids. He just isn't a very politically oriented person, and he never has the facts and figures at hand to defend what he feels on an emotional level.

But he was curious about Terry as a person. How could he live such a double life—being gay and being associated with the Moral Majority people all the time? Terry explained that he had no direct connection with "those people"; they just happened to share some of the same goals. He said he was a "pure conservative" who believed strictly in government non-intervention. Homosexuality, said Terry, was something the government should not be involved with; there should be no laws one way or another. He did say that it would be disastrous for him if some of the people he dealt with were to find out about his homosexuality. He said he didn't go around telling everyone about his sex life, because he didn't want them to know, and that was the way he wanted to keep it. He maintained a low profile in the gay community, he said, and almost never went to gay bars or parties. At the office, he said, he just didn't discuss his social life. His gay friends were asked not to call him at work. As he was writing out his telephone number and address on a slip of paper that Anderson still keeps, Dolan asked him please not to give it to anybody else. He said he got so many death threats, he had had to change his number.

The two then went back to bed. Richard had been as impressed by Dolan's mind as he was by his body. As they talked, he leaned up on one elbow and lightly caressed him, kissing him every now and then. Terry said he had to fly down to Florida for the holidays the next morning; Richard said he'd be staying with his family in Washington.

By the way, Richard finally thought to ask, what was Terry's last name? "Dolan," said Terry. Suddenly a buzzer went off in Richard's head, and he felt like a fool. He lay back and slapped his forehead. "Oh, shit," he said. How had he not guessed before? "Don't worry," consoled Dolan, "at least you said I was a cute asshole."

It is a lovely story, I think, and nothing whatever to be ashamed of.

PART THREE

11

THE LAWS OF GOD AND THE JUDGE IN WAUWATOSA

The legitimate powers of government extend to such acts only as are injurious to others. But it does me no injury for my neighbor to say there are twenty gods, or no God. It neither picks my pocket nor breaks my leg.

—Thomas Jefferson in *Notes on Virginia.*

SCOREBOARD:

Number of times Holy Bible mentions U.S. Constitution   0
Number of times U.S. Constitution mentions God   0

The way some religious absolutists talk about the laws of God, you'd think it was the U.S. Constitution instead of the Ten Commandments that Moses brought back from the mountaintop.

"The foundation for our government, our laws, our statutes, our civilization, the structures of our homes, our states, and our churches have come from the Word of God," says Jerry Falwell in *Listen, America!*

A young man and woman in Wauwatosa, Wisconsin, were convicted of fornication recently by a judge who explained: "I guess we really go back to some of the most fundamental law of all, the law of Moses." Charles Couey, pastor of South Bay Baptist Church in Homestead, told the Miami-Dade Council: "May I remind you our laws today in America were based on one law—the Word of God."

A few of the religious spokesmen have had the grace to concede that there might be a difference between the laws of God and those of man. Although he never stopped to explain what he meant by the phrase, Jimmy Carter was constantly referring to the laws of God, and so was his wife. He told *Christianity Today* and *Playboy* magazine: "If there's a conflict between God's law and civil law, we should honor God's law but we should be willing to accept civil punishment." Speaking for his resolution supporting Anita Bryant's crusade, Tom Collier told the Arkansas House of Representatives, "When God's law and the country's laws conflict, God's law should be supreme."

When I pointed out to a number of the "Washington for Jesus" marchers that God is nowhere present in the U.S. Constitution, they wouldn't believe me, but they responded to a man or woman: "If He's not, then it's time we put Him there."

Bobbie James, wife of the governor of Alabama, wrote that she had decided that nobody in her state would be allowed to participate in the White House Conference on Families because she felt it did not "establish traditional Judeo-Christian values concerning the family, the foundation of our nation under God."

It's difficult to understand precisely what these people mean by God's law, especially after asking them to explain. Are they speaking only of the Ten Commandments? Or do they include all of the lists of do's and don't's in the Bible as the sum of God's law?

In the books of David, Samuel, and Deuteronomy it is written that a man may have more than one wife: Solomon had seven hundred wives and another three hundred concubines; God himself had children by two whores, according to the story in Ezekiel 23. In Exodus, Deuteronomy, and Leviticus, one reads that a father is within his rights to sell his children into slavery in order to get out of debt. While there are several mentions of wedding feasts in the Bible, nowhere is a religious marriage ceremony set forth; it was a business contract between the father and bridegroom, a simple exchange of property.

In Leviticus, we also read that it is as much an abomination for a man to lie with a man or a woman with a woman as it is for a woman to cut the hair on her head and a man to cut the hairs on his face.

But the most relevant question in all this talk of the laws of God and man is almost never mentioned. Miami–Dade County Commissioner Ruth Shack kept trying to explain to Anita Bryant and her followers that she was not elected as a theologian; it didn't matter in her role as a commissioner what the Bible said about anything. It is an argument the fundamentalists are utterly incapable of hearing or understanding because in the Old Testament world they would like to establish, all the laws come directly from God.

Most reporters covering the various groups have been just as blind to this larger question as have the extremists they are trying to describe. Only in one obscure letter to the *Wall Street Journal* did I find the layers of emotional arguments stripped away to reveal the point of it all: "The real question is whether it is the law's function to enforce the Bible. Clearly it is not."

Who can say what kind of government we would have in this country—or even in the modern state of Israel—if we had relied totally on the "repulsive and anti-social" laws (as Thomas Jefferson called them) of those primitive desert tribes. History does offer at least one pure example of an attempt to reinstate the "Kingdom of Zion" in sixteenth-century Munster. An excessive reading of Revelations (the Apocalypse), said one historian, led John Bochold to style himself John of Leyden and King of the New Zion. A rigid interpretation of the scripture led him and his followers to abolish all laws of property and marriage, causing all manner of excesses, fanaticism, lust, and cruelty. Following God's command, John brought one of his wives into a public square and cut off her head. In 1535, this Kingdom of God was destroyed by several Protestant princes uniting with the Catholic bishop.

In America, we have the example of the theocratic government of early Massachusetts, whose most memorable act took place in 1692, when nineteen good and decent men and women were hanged because three or four hysterical young girls said that God had pointed them out as witches.

We owe no small debt to the Greeks and Romans for our ideas of a republic and a democracy, but Thomas Jefferson found that there was a more immediate source for our tradition of justice. As designed by Jefferson, the Great Seal of the United States of America would have included the figures of the two brother chieftains who led the Saxon tribes into what is now England. It would have carried this legend: "Hengist and Horsa, the Saxon chiefs, from whom we claim the honor of being descended, and whose political principles and form of government we have assumed."

There was a reason why Jefferson wrote of our "Creator" instead of "God," and why he spoke of "life, liberty, and the pursuit of happiness," instead of property. Inspired by Locke and other European humanists, Jefferson believed not in any God-given rights, but in the natural rights of man. He was fascinated by the way the illiterate and un-Christian tribes had governed themselves in this country, and he also spent a great deal of time studying the ancient tribes who were our ancestors in Great Britain and Europe.

In his biography of Jefferson, Phillips Russell observes: "In reading English law, Jefferson was amazed to learn that the Bible was part of the law of the realm. In the words of Sir Matthew Hale, 'Christianity is parcel of the laws of England,' and this dictum had been used by Lord Mansfield in his decisions. 'The essential principles of revealed religion,' Mansfield once ruled, 'are part of the common law,' and Blackstone in his commentaries had rubricated this precept. In this field, precedent had been piled upon precedent, so that it occurred to no one at that day, to question the saying. But Jefferson questioned it; moreover, he tracked it to its cradle."

Jefferson proved that parts of the Bible had been inserted into the common law as a "pious fraud." The old monks charged with copying King Alfred's Saxon laws had simply inserted five books—20 through 24—from Exodus into the laws. The legal historians who said that the common law derived from the "Holy Scriptures" had misunderstood the words *ancien scripture*, said Jefferson. He said this was another example of "the alliance between Church and State in England" which "has ever made their judges accomplices in the frauds of the clergy."

Jefferson asked: "Has not every restitution of the ancient Saxon laws had happy effects? Is it not better now that we return at once into that happy system of our ancestors, the wisest and most perfect ever yet devised by the wit of man, as it stood before the eighth century?"

I know from asking them that the religious absolutists would answer no to Jefferson's questions. They are content with knowing only what they want to know, seeing what they want to see. And they will never acknowledge that their very freedom to exist in this country comes not from Moses or Jesus, but from our pagan ancestors' natural belief in being fair and just.

One can only speculate about who and how many wise men and women would be denied a voice in the Christian republic the absolutists would like to create. But we can look backward and see that some of the brightest and best of our founding fathers would have been silenced if such a rigid definition of a Christian nation had prevailed at that time.

Jerry Falwell quotes Benjamin Franklin as saying, "God surely was no idle spectator when this great nation was born in his name and with his grace." But he does not seem to know about these words of Franklin's: "As to Jesus of Nazareth ... I think the system of Morals and his Religion, as he left them to us, the best the World ever saw or is likely to see; but I apprehend it has received various corrupting Changes, and I have, with most of the present Dissenters in England, some doubts as to his divinity. . . ."

Falwell refers to Thomas Paine's statement that "What we obtain too cheaply, we esteem too lightly; it is dearness only that gives everything its value. Heaven knows how to put a price upon its goods, and it would be strange indeed if so celestial an article as freedom should not be highly rated." But this same Paine, whom George Washington credited more than any other man with the success of the Revolutionary War, also wrote: "I do not believe in the creed professed by the Jewish Church, by the Roman Church, by the Greek Church, by the Turkish Church, by the Protestant Church, nor by any church that I know of. My own mind is my own church.

"All national institutions of churches, whether Jewish, Christian, or Turkish, appear to me no other than human inventions, set up to terrify and enslave mankind, and monopolize power and profit. . . .

"It is impossible to calculate the moral mischief, if I may so express it, that mental lying has produced in society. When a man has so far corrupted and prostituted the chastity of his mind as to subscribe his professional belief to things he does not believe, he has prepared himself for the commission of every other crime.

"He takes up the trade of a priest for the sake of gain, and in order to qualify himself for that trade he begins with a perjury. Can we conceive any thing more destructive to morality than this?"

Falwell also quotes Thomas Jefferson as saying, "Man is not made for the State, but the State for man." But he is apparently unaware of Jefferson's feelings about the divinity of Jesus:

"I consider the doctrines of Jesus as delivered by himself to contain the outline of the sublimest morality that has ever been taught; but I hold in the most profound detestation and execration the corruptions of it which have been invested by priestcraft and established by king-craft, constituting a conspiracy of church and state against the civil and religious liberties of mankind," wrote Jefferson in one letter. In another, he said that "The day will come when the mystical generation of Jesus, by the Supreme Being as his Father, in the womb of a virgin, will be classed with the fable of the generation of Minerva in the brain of Jupiter. But we may hope that the dawn of reason and freedom of thought in these United States will do away all this artificial scaffolding, and restore to us the primitive and genuine doctrines of this most venerated Reformer of human errors."

Preachers, said Jefferson, "dread the advance of science as witches do the approach of day-light and scowl on the fatal harbinger announcing the subversion of the duperies on which they live."

12

MORAL SEASONS COME AND GO

Harry Truman's advice to those who wanted to understand the present was to read about the past. Nothing had prepared him better for the presidency, he said, than his reading of history.

"Almost all current events in the affairs of governments and nations have their parallels and precedents in the past," he wrote in his *Memoirs*. "History taught me the periodic waves of hysteria which started with the witch craze during colonial days, produced the abominable Alien and Sedition Acts of the 1790s, flourished again in the Know-Nothing movement, the anti-Masonic hysteria, anti-Catholicism, the Ku Klux Klan, the Red scare of 1919. When the cycle repeated itself during my administration in the form of anti-communist hysteria and indiscriminate branding of innocent persons as subversives, I could deal with the situation calmly because I knew something about the background. . . ."

Truman may have dealt calmly with the witch hunts he faced, but he was not able to curtail or stop them. A knowledge of the past does not necessarily save us from repeating it. That we faced up to and endured an ugly situation before does not guarantee that we can do it again.

What is most comforting in any review of preachers and politics in America is the number of times in history that preachers have been put in their place, when responsible leaders have put a stop to the recurrent movement to convert our democratic republic into a Christian dictatorship.

Like bank robber Willie Sutton, the preachers have always known where the money was, and from the first settlements they have by and large aligned themselves with the wealthy and powerful. Thomas Jefferson thought his Act for Establishing Religious Freedom in Virginia was a greater accomplishment than being President. But it took ten years before the opposition of the wealthy clergymen could be overcome and the act could become law.

"The clergy, as a class, have always been ready to come in for a share in the advantages of the privileged classes, and in return for the ease and convenience accorded to them by these classes, to spread their broad mantle over them," wrote a Massachusetts congressman in 1834.

There is nothing new about the coalition of the interests of the wealthy few with the religion of the poorer majority. Alexander Hamilton was the first to put forth the idea of a Christian Constitutional Society as a means of strengthening the Federalists against the anticlerical Jeffersonian Republicans. In *The Age of Jackson* Arthur M. Schlesinger, Jr., says, "Though Hamilton's particular scheme never came to anything, the alliance he had in mind was rapidly consummated. Religion, in exchange for protection against Jeffersonian anticlericalism, would hedge the aristocracy of wealth with divinity. To the clergy were assigned the essential functions of reconciling the lower classes to inequality and binding them to absolute obedience to the laws. 'Christian morality and piety, in connexion with the intelligence of the common people,' declared Calvin Colton, Episcopalian preacher, later Whig pamphleteer, great friend and biographer of Henry Clay, 'are the last hope of the American Republic, and the only adequate means of bridling and holding in salutary check that rampant freedom, which is so characteristic of the American people.' "

That God meant for some to be rich and most to be poor was a sentiment preached throughout the states, then and now. A minister friend of Daniel Webster's named Hubbard Winslow said, "That there should be an inequality in the condition of men, as there is in all the other works of providence, is clearly a wise and benevolent ordinance of heaven ... it was the levelling disposition that cast down the shining angels from their starry heights." A New York preacher of the same time denounced "the pompous doctrine that 'all men are born both free and equal.' The axiom of equal rights is infidel, not Christian, and strikes at all that is beautiful in civil, or sacred in divine, institutions."

As now, the critics of religious politics were branded as immoralists, enemies of God threatening the very security of the nation with their blasphemy. Lyman Beecher, a popular Presbyterian preacher, wrote in his *Spirit of the Pilgrims*, "Whoever contended with his Maker and prospered? Does He not hold at His disposal all the sources of national prosperity, and all the engines of national chastisement?"

In 1815, Beecher proposed that the government hire a religious instructor for every one thousand citizens in the country. That brought this response from the former President, Thomas Jefferson, in a letter to H. G. Spafford dated January 10, 1816: "You judge truly that I am not afraid of priests. They have tried upon me all their various batteries of whining, hypocritical canting, lying & slandering, without being able to give me one moment of pain. I have contemplated their order from the Magi of the East to the Saints of the West and I found no difference of character, but of more or less caution, in proportion to their information or ignorance of those on whom their interested duperies were to be played off."

One of the most colorful opponents of the political evangelists of the early 1800s was Anne Royall, now chiefly remembered for catching the President, John Quincy Adams, at his early-morning swim in the Potomac and sitting on his clothes until he had answered her questions. She attacked the young women of Washington who went to prayer meetings just because there were boys there. "It is painful to see handsome young females who might grace a levee, caterwauling about with a parcel of ignorant young fellows (for their singing is more like cats' mewing than anything else) every evening. Here they sit, flirting their fans and suffocating with heat for hours while some cunning Missionary tells them a long story about the Lord's doings. They have the Lord's doings in the Bible better told than any Missionary tells it. Why do they not, if religiously inclined, stay at home in their father's house and read the Lord's doings? But there are no young men there. Now if these young ladies were really Christians, instead of dressing and flirting about at night with young fellows they would hunt up the destitute and afflicted and relieve their sufferings."

Royall cut through the highfalutin prose of the distinguished gentlemen of theology and the government with a clear voice of reason and fairness. She was what seemed a contradiction at the time, both pro-Mason and pro-Catholic. Actually she was anti-intolerance, no matter who the despised happened to be.

"A Catholic foreigner discovered America, Catholic foreigners first settled [it]," she wrote in the face of a periodic nativist rising. "When the colonies were about to be enslaved, foreigners rescued it. . . . At present, we verily believe, that the liberty of this country is in more danger from this native combination than from foreigners."

The idea of a Christian party for a Christian government was clearly defined on July 4, 1827, in a sermon at Philadelphia by Ezra Stiles Ely, titled "The Duty of Christian Freemen to Elect Christian Rulers."

"I propose, fellow-citizens," said Ely, "a new sort of union, or, if you please, a Christian party in politics." Of course, Ely saw only "five classes of true Christians." These were Presbyterians, Baptists, Methodists, Congregationalists, and Protestant Episcopalians. He said Christians should pledge to vote for no candidate who "is not professedly friendly to Christianity, and a believer in divine revelation." A Christian political force, he said, would force the politicians to appear to be religious even if they weren't. "It is a matter of thankfulness if they are constrained to *seem* such persons," he said. "We are a Christian nation: we have a right to demand that all our rulers in their conduct shall conform to Christian morality."

The response to Ely's proposal was immediate and loud. The crusading libertarian, Frances (Fanny) Wright gave a sarcastic description of the kind of capital this Christian nation might have in an article in the newspaper *The Free Enquirer*: "Washington carried by a storm; a Baptist senate; a Methodist House of Representatives; an Episcopalian cabinet; and a Presbyterian President! And to perfect the odor of sanctity of this New Jerusalem upon earth, you must imagine a Supreme Court, compounded of Bishops, Presbyters, Elders, Deacons, and high-seat Fathers of double-refined orthodoxy, propounding the soundest theology of all the sound churches, and trying every case, domestic and foreign, national, international, and individual, by the church catechism, the thirty-nine articles, the Westminster confession of faith, the apostle's creed, and the revelations of the apocalypse!"

William Moore, a Universalist leader of Nantucket, asked of Ely's plan: "What would liberty be, or the right of suffrage, but a name to such as belonged not to the union, if five of the most popular religious sects in this country should unite, and succeed in getting the reins of government into their own hands?"

One of the most widely quoted responses to Ely came from another Universalist named Zelotes Fuller in Philadelphia in a speech titled "The Liberty Tree," for George Washington's birthday in 1830. "Never, I beseech you, encourage a certain 'Christian party in politics,' which under moral and religious pretenses, is officiously and continually interfering with the religious opinions of others, and endeavoring to effect by law and other means, equally exceptionable, a systematic course of measures, evidently calculated, to lead to a union of church and state. If a union of church and state should be effected, which may God avert, then will the doctrines of the prevailing sect, become the creed of the country, to be enforced by fines, imprisonment, and doubtless death! Then will superstition and bigotry frown into silence everything which bears the appearance of liberality; the hand of genius will be palsied, and a check to all further improvements in our country will be the inevitable consequence."

In the year following Ely's appeal, a national organization called the General Union for Promoting the Observance of the Christian Sabbath was founded specifically to stop the transportation of mail on Sundays. This group's petitions came to a committee in Congress headed by Richard Mentor Johnson of Kentucky, a gregarious, burly character remembered for having killed an Indian chief thought to be Tecumseh at the Battle of the Thames in Ontario, Canada, October 5, 1813, and also for living openly with a Negro mistress and attempting to bring their children "into society." He was later the seventh Vice-President, under Van Buren, but was so out of favor by the next campaign that his party nominated no Vice-President rather than endorse him.

Johnson rejected the Christian petitions with a statement that was reprinted and embroidered in wall decorations as another Declaration of Independence. He said, "It is not the legitimate province of the Legislature to determine what religion is true, or what false. . . . Our government is a civil, and not a religious institution."

It was in Andrew Jackson's campaigns for the presidency that the Whig religious coalition emerged in full force. Jackson was a regular churchgoer, although he never joined the church until he was near death because he didn't want anybody to think he was doing it for political effect. The contemporary historian, George Bancroft, wrote of the campaign against the Jackson Democrats: "The community was made to believe that there was danger the Bible be taken out of their hands . . . Democracy was said to be a branch of atheism . . . a perfect fever was got up."

One of Jackson's most active opponents was Theodore Frelinghuysen, who was a U.S. senator from 1829 to 1835, the Whig candidate for Vice-President with Clay in 1844, the chancellor of the University of New York until 1850, and then president of Rutgers College until his death. Frelinghuysen himself represented a classic union of big business and religious activism. He supported the U.S. Bank of Nicholas Biddle and volunteered to serve as lawyer against journeymen shoemakers in Newark if they went on strike. He was also a prominent member of the American Bible Society, the American Tract Society, the American Sunday School Union, and the American Temperance Union. A history of "political irreligion" in America, published in 1838, was attributed to him. Citing the refusal of Jefferson and Jackson to declare national fast days, he asked: "Is liberty of conscience to be confounded with the license that acts against conscience? Are Christian institutions to be administered by un-Christian agents? Without religion, law ceases to be law, for it has no bond and cannot hold society together."

In the *American Whig Review*, Taylor Lewis, a professor, stated the party's purpose: "Religion—revealed religion, Christianity—should regulate legislation."

In spite of all the sermons against him, Jackson won and soon found himself embroiled in a tawdry scandal stirred up by none other than the preacher from Philadelphia, Ezra Stiles Ely, who, oddly enough, had previously supported him. Ely wrote Jackson that he happened to know that his Secretary of War, John Henry Eaton, was married to a woman—a witty beauty named Peggy O'Neal—who had a past. She had been married to a navy man named Timberlake who later committed suicide. Too long after he once left port, said Ely, Timberlake's wife found herself pregnant and was delivered of a miscarriage in 1821 by a certain Washington physician.

This scandal of major proportions never seemed to have anything to do with whether the Secretary of War's duties were in the least affected by his wife's background. All that mattered was Peggy Eaton's virtue. All that really mattered was Jackson's loyalty to his old Tennessee buddy, Eaton. "Eaton is the last man on earth I ought or would abandon," he said. "I would sooner abandon life."

It turned out that everything Ely said was secondhand gossip. He heard it from Jackson's Washington minister, a Presbyterian named John N. Campbell, who confessed to the President that he was the source of the rumors and that he had been told them by a physician who had since died. Jackson promptly contradicted the story and "read his pastor an explosive lecture on Christian charity." Jackson then moved to clear Peggy Eaton's name by calling in all of the cabinet, except for Eaton himself, to hear the stories of Ely and Campbell—in fact, to hear them denounced. Ely said he knew nothing bad about Eaton himself. "Nor Mrs. Eaton either," said the President. Ely said, "On that point, I would rather not give an opinion." Said Jackson: "She is chaste as a virgin!"

Jackson thereafter refused to attend Campbell's church. Campbell was invited to dinner by a member of the cabinet; Jackson suspended cabinet meetings. "The strain of this lashing defiance was great," recalled Jackson's secretary, Jack Donelson. "The old veteran's hair turned from gray to white." After all the fuss, Eaton still had to resign, although Jackson named him governor of Florida and then ambassador to Spain.

Another President from Tennessee, James K. Polk, wrote that none of his visitors in the White House had disgusted him as much as one Presbyterian minister, whom he told at the time that "Thank God, under our constitution there was no connection between Church and State, and that in my action as President of the U.S. I recognized no distinction of creeds in my appointments to office." Later, Polk wrote, "I have a great veneration and regard for Religion & sincere piety, but a hypocrite or a bigoted fanatic without reason I cannot bear."

The most successful of the nativist groups was the Native American or American Party that grew out of the Supreme Order of the Star Spangled Banner, founded in 1852, and the American Republican and the Order of United Americans, both founded in 1845. "No one can deny that ignorant foreign suffrage had grown to be an evil of immense proportions," wrote one contemporary observer. The nativists would have denied the vote to all Catholics and all others who were not born in this country. The party made two indelible marks on our culture. One was the nickname "Know-Nothings," by which its members were known, not for their ignorance or lack of class, but because

167

they answered all queries about their secret doings by saying, "I know nothing."

The other mark is a real one about a fourth of the way up the Washington Monument. You'd think George Washington had never been anything but a monument, from all the simplistic rhetoric you have to wade through to get to the truth of him. But the actual monument—first authorized, without appropriation, by the congress of 1783—was not completed until 1885, eighty-six years after Washington died, in 1799.

Nearly every Congress argued about a monument to Washington, but they kept not putting any money where their resolutions were. Finally a private citizens' group started the obelisk that is now a part of the landscape. It took this group sixteen years to find a site and acquire the money to start. The monument rose to 160 feet when work had to stop because money had run out. What had been done was accomplished largely through contributions such as the blocks of marble from Americans in China, from the Mormon territory of Deseret, and a piece of the Temple of Concord in Rome, from Pope Pius IX. The Know-Nothings were outraged by the papist gift and demanded that it be removed. When their protests were ignored by the monument society, masked party members broke into its offices, seized the records, and then took possession of the monument itself. Tradition has it that a piece of the Temple of Concord lies somewhere at the bottom of the Potomac. Congress, meanwhile, withdrew its offer of a $200,000 appropriation and the nub stood there for forty years—a backdrop to the Washington Monument Slaughterhouse Company during the Civil War—until Congress finally authorized the Corps of Engineers to complete the work. The line where the work stopped is clearly visible on the monument now—a prominent reminder of what effect intolerance can have, but also that it can be overcome.

The Know-Nothings may be remembered as a joke, but they were a serious threat in their time. In 1855, the governors and a majority of the legislatures of Massachusetts, New Hampshire, Connecticut, New York, Rhode Island, California, and Kentucky were Know-Nothings. The party inspired bloody riots in several cities, but by 1856, it was falling apart over the slavery question. Its national candidates—former President Millard Fillmore and Andrew Jackson's wife's nephew, A. J. Donelson—carried only one state, the original Catholic refuge, Maryland.

The Roman Catholics were conspicuous and convenient scapegoats of the several nativist movements in the 1800s. They worshiped in an alien language; they bowed down to idols of gold and silver; their priests and nuns took the seemingly unnatural vows of chastity, poverty, and obedience; they were subservient not just to God but also to an earthly prince in Rome. According to the Catholic historian John Gilmary Shea, there were only 24,500 Catholics in the United States at the time of the first census in 1790. Of these, 15,800 lived in Maryland, 7,000 in Pennsylvania, 200 in Virginia, and 1,500 in New York. Several states barred Catholics from holding public office up to the time of the Civil War.

The story of Roman Catholics—who are now the largest single denomination in America—is a classic case of the oppressed becoming the oppressor, of the downtrodden losing their feeling for others once they make it to the top. In 1843, the Catholic bishop of Philadelphia asked the school board to let the Catholic children use the Douay translation of the Bible in their daily readings instead of the King James version, which carried the original preface describing the Pope as "that man of sin." Catholic churches were attacked thoughout the city as a result, and two were destroyed by fire in the suburbs. A convent was also burned, and many inhabitants of the Irish quarter were shot as they fled houses that had been set on fire. The bishop temporarily closed all the churches.

In 1854, a Jesuit priest urged the parents of Catholic children in Ellsworth, Maine, to defy a town order on reading the King James Bible in the public schools. The school committee met and voted to tar and feather the priest if he showed his face in town again. He did, and they carried out their threat.

In 1859, eleven-year-old Tom Wall was beaten on the hands for thirty minutes, until he finally agreed to read the King James version of the Ten Commandments at school, which his parish priest had ordered him not to do.

In 1870, in Cincinnati, the school board solved such sectarian squabbles over whether to read the Protestant or Catholic translations in schools by forbidding Bible reading altogether. The ruling was upheld by the state supreme court. Rutherford B. Hayes wrote in his diary that the judge involved in this case, Alfonso Taft, would have gotten the Republican nomination—instead of Hayes himself—if that ruling hadn't tainted him as soft on Catholicism. The Ohio opinion is a model of clear reasoning and fine language: "Legal Christianity is a solecism, a contradiction of terms. When Christianity asks the aid of government beyond mere impartial protection, it denies itself. Its laws are divine, and not human. Its essential interests lie beyond the reach and range of human governments. United with government, religion never rises above the merest superstition; united with religion, government never rises above the merest despotism; and all history shows us that the more widely and completely they are separated, the better it is for both."

A hundred years later, we find the Catholic cardinal in New York, Francis Spellman, speaking of the separation of church and state as "an outworn shibboleth." On the day following the U.S. Supreme Court decision against Bible reading in the public schools, June 17, 1963, three of the five Roman Catholic cardinals in the United States spoke out. Spellman said, "No one who believes in God, and I say believes in God, can approve such a decision." J. Francis McIntyre of Los Angeles said the ruling "can only mean that our American heritage of philosophy, of religion, and of freedom, are being abandoned in imitation of Soviet philosophy, of Soviet materialism, and of Soviet-regimented liberty." Richard Cushing of Boston called the decision "a great outrage."

Many Americans in the nineteenth century—as do many of us today—felt that the Roman Catholic, or any, religious hierarchy was by definition antagonistic to our faith in free will and the individual's right to privacy. In *Cornerstones of Religious Freedom in America*—the revised edition, published in 1964—Joseph L. Blau summarized this tradition of anti-clericalism: " . . . while religious organization is a good and a necessary thing if each individual is to have free choice, any organization, religious or not, must be watched; any organization contains the threat of becoming in its expansion, a self-perpetuating, oligarchic danger to free individuals. Churches are especially likely to develop into a menace because of the necessarily oligarchic character of their ministry. Any ministry contains the germs of a priesthood, and must be prevented from developing into a priestly class. In a word, the middle-of-the-road American attitude was pro-religious, but anti-clerical and anti-ecclesiastical."

The most tragic involvement of preachers in politics took place in the decades surrounding our Civil War. Fifteen years before the state governments vowed they could not live together, most of the major

Protestant denominations—Baptist, Methodist, Presbyterian, and Lutheran—split apart in bitter public disputes. The Methodists got back together in 1939; the other three are still divided 115 years after the war ended. The Southern Baptists owe their cohesive organization to this split: otherwise, they would have carried on the Anabaptist tradition of strict local autonomy, with no kind of church hierarchy at all.

As in the civil rights movement of the 1960s, a few ministers in the North spoke out and were leaders in the movement to abolish slavery; the vast majority of them remained quiet or spoke out for tolerance of slave owners.

In the South, ministers cited the Bible in their holy crusade in defense of slavery: the blacks were cursed by a different color and ordained by God to be servants forever. The Southern Presbyterian Church resolved in 1864 that "we hesitate not to affirm that it is the peculiar mission of the Southern church to conserve the institution of slavery, and to make it a blessing both to master and slave." In the same church's pastoral letter of 1865, after slavery was officially abolished, this attitude was solemnly reaffirmed. "One of the most pernicious heresies of modern times," it said, was the notion of the "inherent sinfulness" of the relationship of master and slaves.

One Baptist editor in Illinois said of the Southern newspapers exchanged for copies of his paper (a common means of sharing the news then), "We have been accustomed to observe, for years past, the most violent and radical pro-slavery men in that quarter were ministers."

Henry Clay wrote in 1852, the year of his death: "I tell you, this sundering of the religious ties which have bound people together I consider the greatest source of danger to our country." In his book, *The Story of Religion in America*, William Warren Sweet wrote: "There are good arguments to support the claim that the split in the churches was not only the first break between the sections, but the chief cause of the final break."

"We are charged with having brought about the present contest," wrote a Northern Methodist, Granville Moody. "I believe it is true that we did bring it about, and I glory in it, for it is a wreath of glory around our brow."

The modern historian, James W. Silver, concludes his book, *Confederate Morale and Church Propaganda*, by saying: "The church in the South constituted the major resource of the Confederacy in the building and maintenance of civilian morale. As no other group, Southern clergymen were responsible for a state of mind which made secession possible, and as no other group they sustained the people in their long, costly and futile War for Southern Independence."

As a professor at the University of Mississippi, Silver was to be a front-line witness and chronicler of some of our more recent civil-war battles in the 1960s, when there was violent resistance to the integration of the university and of the public schools and public facilities in the rest of the state. In his award-winning account of that time, *Mississippi: The Closed Society* (1966), Silver cited numerous examples that showed how the churches and religious leaders joined—either by their silence or in fact—the hateful forces of the (white) Citizens' Councils who, again, considered themselves Christian soldiers. The Mississippi Baptist Convention defeated resolutions that would have urged everyone to pray "that we may live consistent with Christian citizenship." The churches, of course, were among the last institutions to be integrated in the South.

Methodists in Jackson led the court battle to keep the churches segregated. Said the president of their ministers' and laymen's association, "Either John Wesley's principles will triumph or the radicals will take over and our church will disintegrate." At least sixty-eight seminary-trained Methodist ministers were forced to leave the state because of their tolerant views on integration. One of the twenty-eight young Methodist ministers who signed a "Born of Conviction" statement favoring a reasonable attitude on racial matters said, "A Citizens' Council member strode into my office, newspaper in hand, and said, 'You've messed yourself up good, boy!' " Another said, "In Mississippi, a Christian minister is free only as long as he is willing to run and bay with the pack."

An Episcopal minister who also felt he had to leave the state wrote to Silver: "The great disappointment was that persons of prominence who would give you to understand they never paid dues to the Citizens' Council gave all the support the CC could hope for by their silence."

One of the most eloquent comments about Mississippi in those days came from a cousin of the racist governor, Ross Barnett. A Southern Baptist missionary, she wrote from Nigeria to the *Baptist Record* back home: "You send us out here to preach that Christ died for all men. Then you make a travesty of our message by refusing to associate with some of them because of the color of their skin. You are supposed to be holding the lifelines for us, and you are twisting them into a noose of racism to strangle our message. Communists do not need to work against the preaching of the Gospel here; you are doing it quite adequately."

During the Civil War, the discussion of God's role grew all the more exaggerated and absurd as the bloody conflict went on and on. A minister named Byron Sunderland said to Abraham Lincoln: "We are full of faith and prayer that you will make [a] clean sweep for the Right."

Lincoln replied: "Doctor, it's very hard sometimes to know what is right! You pray often and honestly, but so do those across the lines. They pray and all their preachers pray honestly. You and I don't think them justified in praying for their objects, but they pray earnestly, no doubt! If you and I had our own way, Doctor, we will settle this war without bloodshed, but Providence permits blood to be shed. It's hard to tell what Providence wants of us. Sometimes, we ourselves, are more humane than the Divine mercy seems to us to be."

In his second inaugural address, Lincoln said of the opposing armies: "Both read the same Bible and pray to the same God, and each invokes His aid against the other." The tragic final comment on Lincoln's quandary over a God who would let men kill in his name is found in one of the last notations in the diary of his own killer, John Wilkes Booth: "I can never repent it, though we hated to kill. Our country owed all her troubles to him, and God simply made me the instrument of his punishment."

After the war, clergymen again took the lead in sustaining the bitter feelings that had caused the war in the first place. Sydney E. Ahlstrom says in his *A Religious History of the American People*: "Southern Baptists, Methodists, Presbyterians, and Lutherans . . . with one voice proclaimed their loyalty to the Lost Cause, accepted or arranged for the transfer or separated status of Negro 'members,' and in some cases even won accessions among whites in the loyal border states where slavery had once existed."

Except for its very first meetings, when it was supposed to have been a joke of an old boys' good-time club like Mark Twain's E. Clampus Vitus, the Ku Klux Klan has largely been led by uneducated fundamentalists, many of them Southern Baptist ministers. At a Klan rally I covered in 1964 for the *Chapel Hill Weekly*, five of the six speakers were Baptist preachers.

A mimeographed creed of the Klan read, in part: "We the Klan believe in God and the tenets of the Christian religion, and that a Godless nation cannot long prosper. We, the Klan, will never allow our blood bought liberties to be crucified on a Roman cross; nor will we yield to the integration of white and Negro races in schools or anywhere else. We will follow the teaching of the Bible and not the unwise and one-sided ruling of the U.S. Supreme Court which is not in keeping with the Constitution of the United States of America."

One of the preachers speaking to this rally was Roy Woodle, a Baptist radio evangelist from Lexington, North Carolina. "I go to as good a Baptist church as there is in town. If I knew there's a better one, I'd go to it. . . . Do you think your children got enough wisdom you can send 'em down in Niggertown and they won't be pulled into sin too? Mine don't. They passed a law now saying the Jews are not responsible for crucifying Christ and the stupid, ignernt American people is stupid enough to believe it. Doctor Martin Luther King professes to be a preacher. I've saw him on television. Bless God, the Pope in Rome's done put his hand of approval on him. Why can't he go to Africa where people's eatin' people?

"Jesus wasn't a Jew because he was God-inspired. 'My beloved is white,' the Bible says. Then some ignernt preacher get up and say he's a colored man. . . . I know people says the Klu Klucks is a mean outfit. But I've met some of the nicest people in it, finer people than some in my church, better'n them Pharisee hypocrites in church."

On February 3, 1863, the leaders of eleven Christian denominations met at Xenia, Ohio, because they felt it was God's judgment that the Union cause had not been won by then. The absence of God in the Constitution and the lack of orthodox Christian belief by the first six Presidents, they felt, was being paid for on the battlefield. The Xenia conference led to the organization of the National Reform Association.

In 1867, the NRA began publishing the *Christian Statesman* and launched a campaign to amend the preamble to the Constitution with these words: "We, the people of the United States, acknowledging Almighty God as the source of all authority and power in civil government, the Lord Jesus Christ as the Ruler among the nations, and His will, revealed in the Holy Scriptures, as of supreme authority, in order to constitute a Christian government, form a more perfect union, establish justice. . . ."

(A hundred years later, John B. Anderson, U.S. Representative and a trustee of the First Evangelical Free Church in Rockford, Illinois, proposed the same thing, but with different words: "This nation devoutly recognizes the authority and law of Jesus Christ, Saviour and Ruler of nations, through whom are bestowed the blessings of Almighty God." Anderson was then a member of the advisory board of Young Americans for Freedom and a favorite of the Americans for Constitutional Action and the Liberty Lobby. He was born again as a liberal in the 1980 presidential election.)

The National Reform Association didn't have a President encouraging it, but it did have an even more prestigious membership than Moral Majority does today. A justice of the Supreme Court, William Strong, was one of its presidents, and its vice-presidents included four former state governors; among educators supporting the association were the president of Amherst College and the commissioner of public schools in Rhode Island.

In the Congress, Charles Sumner of Massachusetts led the opposition to the Christian amendment proposed by the NRA. In one dramatic gesture, he presented the senate a petition 953 feet long, bearing 35,000 signatures of people opposed to rewriting the preamble to the Constitution. The *Daily Globe* in Boston wrote of the "absurdity of the proposed constitutional plan of salvation" and said "the most truly religious men in the country are opposed to the amendment."

This piece of religious legislation was shunted aside and forgotten as other issues took its place.

Just as anti-Catholicism united the Christian activists in the earlier part of the nineteenth century, Prohibition was their burning cause in the latter part. Again, their main bastion of strength lay in New England. Starting with Maine in 1846, all of the New England states had banned alcoholic beverages by the time of the Civil War. Oddly, states in the Southern "Bible belt"—as it would become known in this century—were among the last to vote for local Prohibition before the national law was enacted. (Maybe they were just slow—the same states were among the last to vote "wet" after national Prohibition was repealed.)

It was the Women's Christian Temperance Union, founded in 1874, that popularized and Christianized the Prohibition movement. A coalition of various local women's groups, the WCTU's national organization was able to get regular columns featured in eight thousand newspapers, and its aggressive president, Frances Willard, spoke in every state and territory and in every city with a population of ten thousand or more.

Willard wrote: "The women who went forth by an impulse, sudden, irresistible, divine, to pray in the saloons, became convinced, as weeks and months passed by, that theirs was to be no easily won victory. The enemy was rich beyond their power to comprehend. He had upon his side the majesty of law, the trickery of politics, and the leagued strength of that almost invincible pair—appetite and avarice." It was, however, the more political Anti-Saloon League that carried the cause to victory, largely because its leaders didn't care what a politician did in private, so long as he voted dry. Will Rogers summed it up: "Americans will vote dry so long as they can stagger to the polls."

The temperance movement also made women aware of how powerless they were without the vote. Women's suffrage thus became another of their issues. A number of other progressive measures were backed by them, including the income tax and direct election of senators, both of which became law in 1913. Alcoholic beverages were banned in the United States in 1920, the same year women were first allowed to vote.

Although Prohibition was made part of the Constitution under a Democratic President, Woodrow Wilson vetoed the enforcing Volstead Act; and it was the next Democrat, Franklin Roosevelt, who oversaw Prohibition's repeal. The preachers, meanwhile, lined up with the Republicans, and that's where they have remained. A Methodist bishop in Virginia, Charles Cannon, was the "Dry Messiah," as his biographer calls him, in the Prohibition movement, but he was also one of those who led the "solid South" out of the Democratic fold when the party nominated a Roman Catholic for president in 1928. According to surveys at the time, more than 85 percent of Protestant clergymen voted against Franklin Roosevelt in his four presidential campaigns.

In *Cornerstones of Religious Freedom*, Joseph L. Blau calls it "the masking of political and economic activity behind a false front of religion": "For example, in 1947, six hundred and thirty-seven Protestant clergymen signed a statement issued by the American Council of

Christian Churches, asserting that the closed shop violated the basic teachings of the Bible as well as freedom of conscience."

The most inflammatory political preacher of the 1930s was a Canadian-born Roman Catholic priest named Charles Edward Coughlin, who had a radio program broadcast out of Detroit. Coughlin was eventually silenced by his bishop for his anti-Semitism, but he made a career out of attacking every phase of Roosevelt's New Deal. He organized the National Union for Social Justice and mounted a campaign against Roosevelt in 1936. Coughlin had bragged about the ten million votes the party would get; it got 891,858.

In his *Secret Diary*, published in 1953, Roosevelt's confidant, Harold L. Ickes, tells of an attempt to blackmail the President by Coughlin. "As I recall it, the demand was that the President put on pressure to get the Frazier-Lemke bill through, failing which Father Coughlin would attack the President." Coughlin's representatives were told "that this savored very strongly of blackmail" and the President would not even be told about it.

Thereupon, the priest-politician attacked. Ickes wrote: "From what the President quoted to me, Father Coughlin must have made a very violent attack. It sounded outrageous to me—arrogant and blustering and altogether presuming. In the Monday morning papers Congressman O'Connor invited Coughlin to come to Washington and give him the pleasure of kicking him all the way from the Capitol to the White House. He said that he was a disgrace to the Catholic Church, of which Congressman O'Connor is a member."

Another minister involved in the anti–New Deal, anti-Semitic campaigns of the 1930s was Frank Buchman, a Lutheran pastor and a lecturer in personal evangelism at Hartford Seminary. Buchman founded Moral Re-Armament after getting a call from God to convert the world. Like the Moral Majority of our time, the MRA lived comfortably. The field workers and recruiters—who were still active in the 1960s, when I was in college—always had introductions into the best of homes, where they were provided with the best of accommodations, all free of charge, of course. At a certain point, the host and his or her friends would be asked for contributions. "Good food and good Christianity go together," said Buchman of this method. In the 1920s, Moral Re-Armament had gained supporters throughout the United States and in many foreign countries. Queen Marie of Romania was among its followers.

Buchman became more and more friendly toward fascism as he became more and more anti-Communist. Although he lived until 1961, he never lived down the sentiments expressed in a 1936 interview: "I thank heaven for a man like Adolf Hitler, who built a front line of defense against the Antichrist of communism. Think what it would mean to the world if Hitler surrendered to the control of God. Or Mussolini. Or any dictator. Through such a man, God could control a nation overnight and solve every last bewildering problem." Without the references to Hitler, of course, evangelist James Robison of the current right has expressed precisely the same sentiments.

Most of the political preachers in our time have been more diplomatic than Coughlin and Buchman. They know how far they can go, which code words to avoid to keep from being labeled a racist or a bigot. Billy Graham, some of the time, has contended that he has no politics but God's. God seems always to lead him among conservative Republicans, where the money—if not always the political power—is.

Graham tried to be friends with Harry Truman. But Truman told Merle Miller years afterward that the big-time evangelist was no friend of his. "He's one of those counterfeits. . . . All he wants to do is get his name in the newspapers." Actually, Graham wanted to get his picture in the papers, too, and that's how he came to be declared persona non grata in the Truman White House.

In his biography of Graham, Marshall Frady describes the evangelist's moment of truth with Truman. Graham and two of his aides, Cliff Barrows and Jerry Beavan, showed up at the White House in white suits, white buckskins, and flower-print ties. Truman welcomed them into the Oval Office, saying he was a Baptist himself. "Well, I immediately began trying to preach to him," said Graham. Truman said he lived by the Sermon on the Mount and the Golden Rule. Then, Graham quoted Truman as saying, "If it just weren't for these goddamn newspapers after me every day, and that columnist Drew Pearson, the sorry SOB. . . ." Graham then asked if it would be all right if he said a few words of prayer. He put his arm around Truman and stood praying "that God would bless him and his administration and that God would give him wisdom in dealing with all the difficulties in the country and the world." Barrows was punctuating the prayer with "Amen," and "Tell it," and "Yes, Lord."

When they got outside, reporters and photographers were waiting with questions. Graham was more than obliging. He and his two aides knelt down and "recreated" the praying scene on the White House lawn for the photographers. The pictures in the newspapers the next day infuriated Truman, and his staff was told that Graham was never to be invited into the White House as long as he was living there.

From then on, Graham was almost as much a figure of Republican politics as the elephant. He was especially close to Dwight D. Eisenhower and Richard Nixon, and frequently found ways to mention them on his radio and television broadcasts during their campaigns.

During the Nixon administration, a Baptist minister told Marshall Frady: "What we have right now is the most powerful man religiously in this nation, Billy Graham, giving the government and its policies and the power community in this country his conspicuous blessing—not just in his preachments, but through all his friendships, all those pleasant little prayer breakfasts, but more than anything else, all his silences in the face of the most arrant outrages by that government. He has especially become a spiritual sanction to this particular administration. What we've got is almost a Graham-Nixon axis. I don't mean to sound intemperate. But the truth is, Jesus went to the cross because he alienated the powers of his day. Not for nothing do the scriptures say, 'Beware when all men speak well of you.' What I want to know is, how can a man spend thirty years preaching the Gospel, and with maybe only two or three exceptions, not have one mayor, one governor, one banker, one chairman of the board, one president of a chamber of commerce, one Defense Department official, one political party chairman—*not one!*—speak a single ill word against him. You ask me if there's anything finally tragic about Graham in all this? Lord knows, it's tragic."

Graham is now trying to present himself as the elder statesman of the religious right, the voice of reason in a milieu of malcontent fanatics. He said in an interview published in the February 1, 1981, *Parade* magazine that it would be "unfortunate if people got the impression all evangelists belong to that group [the Moral Majority]. The majority do not. I don't wish to be identified with them.

"I'm for morality. But morality goes beyond sex to human freedom and social justice. We as clergy know so very little to speak out with such authority on the Panama Canal or superiority of armaments. Evangelists can't be closely identified with any particular party or person. We have to stand in the middle in order to preach to all people, right and left. . . . "

In spite of Graham's denials about politics, his sermons for three decades more often than not concerned the news of the day. He had opinions on Douglas MacArthur's removal, and about the Korean War, and later about the war in Vietnam, and he didn't hesitate to express them. What people outside the South may not have realized was that his comments about preachers in politics were directed at Martin Luther King, Jr. and a very small number of ministers who were active in the civil rights movement.

When Graham's dear friend Richard Nixon was finally forced to resign from the presidency in disgrace, the evangelist could only comment about how shocked he was that such a nice man could use such dirty words as those revealed in the White House tapes, as if that were Nixon's only crime.

Although in somewhat duplicitous fashion, Graham himself had said it best: "I have really stayed out of politics purposely. It's pretty hard to do, since so many of my friends are in politics. . . . You must remember that the worst part of history was in the Dark Ages, when the church ran everything. Too many ministers think they're social engineers."

Graham may not have heeded his own sound advice, but there is some comfort in our history, which shows that we can and will heal ourselves when this current mood of divisiveness is over. For every bigot we've produced, there's been another voice that spoke out for reason and human decency.

The Salem witch trials of 1692 offer an example. While nineteen good men and women were hanged, several times that number were in jail waiting to be hanged when the people came to their senses and put a stop to the hysterical proceedings. And all of this happened through no outside influence; the people simply saw that what they were doing was wrong. Within twenty years, the religious hierarchy had rescinded the excommunication of those hanged as witches, and the legislature had paid remuneration to their survivors.

In a book entitled *The Devil in Massachusetts*, published at the height of the investigations of alleged Communist infiltration of Hollywood, Marian L. Starkey, a descendant of a Mayflower passenger, concluded her history of the witch trials on a note of hope. "Moral seasons come and go. Late in the nineteenth century, when it was much the fashion to memorialize the witchcraft delusion, honest men discussed it with wondering pity as something wholly gone from the world and no longer quite comprehensible. But such condescension is not for the twentieth century. . . .

"One would like to believe that leaders of the modern world can in the end deal with delusion as sanely and courageously as the men of old Massachusetts dealt with theirs. . . . What one feels now for deluded Salem Village is less pity than admiration and hope—admiration for men whose sanity in the end proved stronger than madness, hope that 'enlightment' too is a phenomenon that may recur."

13

WE HEATHENS WERE
ALSO PRESENT

The following are just a few of the "facts" from history that Jerry Falwell mentions in his book, *Listen, America!*

"Let us never forget that as our Constitution declares, we are endowed by our Creator with certain inalienable rights" (page 20). (Nowhere in the Constitution will you find the word "Creator" or the words "inalienable rights." The Declaration of Independence contains these words: " . . . that they are endowed by their Creator with certain unalienable rights. . . .")

"America must not forget her motto, one that was founded and established in the early days of her history" (page 29). (Congress did not designate "In God We Trust" as our national motto until 1956. The phrase was first used on coins in 1864, but it was not used consistently until 1955, when Congress ordered its use on all coins and paper money.)

"In 1607 Puritans established the first settlement in this country at Jamestown" (page 30). (If the Puritans had ever landed at Jamestown or later Virginia they would have been arrested—as many of the Quakers and Falwell's own Baptists were, right up to the time of the Revolution.)

If Jerry Falwell mistakenly believes that the Puritans landed at Jamestown, he is surely not alone. That Sunday-school picture of the pilgrims getting off the boats all dressed up for Thanksgiving is such a neat and tidy image, we seem to have adopted it as a metaphor for the settling of the whole country rather than of one tiny region of the North by a very unusual group of immigrants.

Not only do Falwell and his brother evangelists confuse the settlement of New England with that of the rest of America, they are also confused about the history of New England itself. As Oregon's senator Mark Hatfield, said to me, "You know, if these people would only read their own history . . . "

Falwell and the others have swallowed whole the myth that the Puritans came here to "escape religious persecution." In fact, as Gore Vidal has written so bluntly, the Puritans left Europe "not because they were persecuted for their religious beliefs but because they were forbidden to persecute others for their beliefs."

To these non-conformists and dissenters from the Church of England, religious toleration was about as foreign an idea as it was to the Roman Catholic church at the time. Transplanting their religion to the open space of America only made their beliefs more rigid and intolerant than they ever could have been in Europe. The Puritans strictly enforced what they considered God's law, and allowed no dissension from their dissent. The Baptists were among the first to be persecuted, causing Roger Williams and others to flee into the wilderness that became Rhode Island.

Williams wrote in *The Bloudy Tenent of Persecution* in 1644 "that the blood of so many hundred thousand souls of Protestants and Papists, spilt in the wars of present and former ages, for their respective consciences, is not required nor accepted by Jesus Christ, the Prince of Peace . . . the doctrine of persecution for cause of conscience is proved guilty of all the blood of the souls crying for vengeance under the altar. . . . It is the will and command of God, that (since the coming of his Son the Lord Jesus) a permission of the most Paganish, Jewish, Turkish, or Antichristian conscience and worships, be granted to all men in all Nations and Countries: and they are only to be fought against with that Sword which is only (in Soul matters) able to conquer, to wit, the Sword of God's Spirit, the Word of God."

William Penn said it more succinctly in 1670: "Were some Christian as they boast themselves to be, it would save us all the labor we bestow in rendering Persecution so unchristian as it most truly is."

The Quakers in Massachusetts were more persistent than the Baptists, and suffered with their lives because of it. One Mary Clark refused to give up her faith or be quiet about it; she was sentenced to twenty stripes of a three-corded whip "laid on with fury" and twelve weeks in prison. When King Charles II read that four Quakers had been hanged for their faith in New England, he ordered that from then on, any Quakers arrested should be sent back to England for trial. When England's own Act of Toleration became law, the King chided the New Englanders for ignoring it and for sustaining that from which they had supposedly fled.

In *Listen, America!*, Falwell speaks fondly, if ignorantly, of this early American theocracy and with disdain for the modern democracy to which he and his followers owe their right to exist. He says, "Our Founding Fathers would not accept the tyranny of a democracy because they recognized that the only sovereign over men and nations was Almighty God."

From the records, it is apparent that this God of our fathers moved in some very mysterious ways. In his diary of the *Mayflower* voyage, William Bradford tells of a "very profane young man, one of the seamen, of a lusty, able body, which made him the more haughty; he would always be condemning the poor people in their sickness and cursing them daily with grievous execrations . . . but it pleased God before they came half seas over to smite this young man with a grievous disease, of which he died in a desperate manner. . . ."

Likewise, it was "divine confirmation of the community's sentence" on Anne Hutchinson when she was butchered by the Indians after being expelled by the religious government of Massachusetts. And when the Indian tribes were rendered defenseless by disease, this too was an act of God. What it signified when one of the pilgrims died on the Mayflower or when half their number died that first winter, Bradford fails to explain.

But the history of New England is not the history of America. John Wesley and his brother, Charles, found out in blunt and brutal fashion that the New England brand of piety and intolerance was not so easily transplanted to other parts of America. While it may be true that many or even most of the early settlers of America were religious, they were never all religious and that was never the only reason for their coming here.

Writing in 1765, John Adams said: "Under the execrable race of the Stuarts the struggle between the people and the confederacy of temporal and spiritual tyranny became formidable, violent, and bloody. It was this great struggle that peopled America. It was not religion alone, as is commonly supposed; but it was a love of universal liberty, and a hatred, a dread, a horror, of the internal confederacy that projected, conducted, and accomplished the settlement of America."

In fact, the first settlers were sent by investment companies, part and parcel of business deals. Eugenia Walker Howard explains this nicely in the June 1968 *National Genealogical Society Quarterly*: "Fortunately, the settlement of this country, no matter which colony is considered, was thoroughly documented. The kings and queens who invested fortunes in this venture, as well as the private entrepreneurs, such as the trustees of Georgia, were not fools nor were they empty-headed visionaries. They were in this colonial business for coolly calculated profit and increased trade which might be gained on the side."

When the bawdy King Charles II decided to grant all of what is now the Carolinas—clear to the Pacific Ocean—to eight of his drinking buddies, he knew their interests were purely mercenary. But, as "lords proprietor," they came to him as humble Christian missionaries. "Here," laughed the king as he tossed a pet spaniel to one of them, "make this your archbishop." His sarcasm is spelled out in the language of the charter itself: the petitioners, "excited with a laudable and pious zeal for the propagation of the gospel, have begged a certain country in the parts of America not yet cultivated and planted, and only inhabited by some barbarous people who have no knowledge of God."

At Jamestown, the leaders of that ill-fated settlement may have been strict adherents to the Church of England, but the ordinary settlers were something else again. Since there were no women among them for twelve years, they could hardly be cited for fostering Jerry Falwell's ideas of the perfect family. And if there was a God, they must have concluded, he didn't like them very much. In one dreadful "time of starvation," only sixty of five hundred people at Jamestown survived.

In his widely praised *Jamestown, 1544–1699*, Carl Bridenbaugh says: "Whatever the rulers at Jamestown may have thought, the temporary and unstable populace of this waterfront settlement, having few compelling religious convictions, tended to frustrate all piety and missionary endeavor."

The first settlers of the backcountry on the Eastern seaboard were the Scotch-Irish, my own people, who have (I learned from a speech by Edward Kennedy) produced seventeen of the country's Presidents. Sydney E. Ahlstrom writes with disdain for the typical historian's view of these people: "The Scotch-Irishman was, as historians keep saying, 'the typical frontiersman,' bold, courageous, lawless, individualistic, resentful of constituted authority, a hard drinker, a hater of Indians, and an inveterate 'squatter' on land he had not bought. Historians also speak of his 'rigid Calvinism' as if he were invariably a psalm-singing covenanter; but such was not the case. He had been twice uprooted. Both the migration to Ulster and that to America were made by people who were more restless than pious. And to America, at least, he brought with him little of his religious tradition and very few ministers."

After the Indians had defeated the naïve and pompous General Braddock and his men in 1755, Benjamin Franklin was put in charge of the militia assigned to build a series of forts in western Pennsylvania. One day the minister serving as chaplain came to him and complained that none of the men were showing up for the worship services. Franklin offered a solution. He put the preacher in charge of doling out the men's ration of rum each day—and he got his congregation.

While the absolutists seem to think that our national motto reflects the religious nature of the country's founders, the story of its origin is quite the opposite. It was the absence of God in the Constitution and the influence of deism on the first six Presidents that caused a preacher named M. R. Watkinson of Ridleyville, Pennsylvania, to write to the Secretary of the Treasury on the subject on November 13, 1861. "From my heart I have felt our national shame in disowning God as not the least of our present national disasters," said Watkinson in a letter to Salmon P. Chase. It would surely help to turn the Union Army away from defeat toward victory if there was "recognition of the Almighty God in some form on our coins." The first "In God We Trust" coins were minted in 1864.

For all their latter-day importance, our national emblems developed quite casually, almost haphazardly. Nobody knows for sure who designed the flag or what it means, although it bears suspicious resemblance to the Washington coat of arms. The Pledge of Allegiance to the flag was not written until 1892, when it was published in *Youth's Companion* magazine. It wasn't officially sanctioned by Congress until

December 22, 1941. The words "under God" were not inserted in the pledge until June 14, 1954.

One reason our national anthem wasn't adopted for 127 years after it was written had to do with the pious opposition of certain temperance leaders. Francis Scott Key set his words to the melody of a then-popular drinking song, "Anacreon in Heaven," written in 1770 by John S. Smith. Anacreon was a Greek poet who celebrated the joys of wine and beauty and was memorialized by a statue on the Acropolis showing him in a state of drunken hilarity. The ridiculous range of the melody of "The Star-Spangled Banner" is explained by its origins at a club of roisterous fellows in London, who would lift their mugs on the high notes.

In that long litany of evidence for a union of church and state, the religious politicians always mention the national holiday of Thanksgiving and the presence of chaplains in Congress. It is true that both of them are now part of our government, but it should also be remembered that both of these were considered unconstitutional by none other than the two men who wrote the two great documents that created and sustain the country itself.

Thanksgiving goes back to the first harvest of the pilgrims at Plymouth in the fall of 1621, and the day—not always of feasting, but often of fasting—was regularly celebrated in religious New England. However, once the government of the United States was organized, the enlightened Southern leaders considered such a day "a relic of Puritanic bigotry." George Washington declared national days of thanksgiving only twice in his eight years as President. President Madison called for such a day of reflection following the War of 1812, in 1815. Otherwise, it was not observed until October 3, 1863, when Abraham Lincoln felt that such an observance might help the war effort.

When the Danbury Baptist Association of Connecticut petitioned President Jefferson to declare an annual Thanksgiving day to commemorate the Revolutionary War, he responded with a declaration that he clearly meant to be government policy, since he had his Attorney General examine it before it was made public. Jefferson wrote:

> Believing with you that religion is a matter which lies solely between man and his God, that he owes account to none other for his faith or his worship, that the legislative powers of gov-

187

ernment reach actions only, and not opinions, I contemplate with sovereign reverence that act of the whole American people which declared that their legislature should "make no law respecting an establishment of religion, or prohibiting the free exercise thereof," thus building a wall of separation between Church and State. Adhering to this expression of the supreme will of the nation in behalf of the rights of conscience, I shall see with sincere satisfaction the progress of those sentiments which tend to restore to man all his natural rights, convinced he has no natural right in opposition to his social duties.

I reciprocate your kind prayers for the protection and blessing of the common Father and Creator of man, and tender you for yourselves and your religious association, assurances of my high respect and esteem.

Andrew Jackson, in rejecting petitions for a national day of prayer and fasting to avert a cholera epidemic in 1832, said he would do nothing to "disturb the security which religion now enjoys in this country, in its complete separation from the political concerns of the General Government."

To his dying day, James Madison considered the presence of chaplains on the national payroll a violation of the Constitution he had written. Said Madison at the time the position was first proposed: "Is the appointment of Chaplains to the two Houses of Congress consistent with the Constitution, and with the pure principle of religious freedom? In strictness the answer on both points must be in the negative. The Constitution of the United States forbids everything like an establishment of a national religion. The law appointing Chaplains establishes a religious worship for the national representatives, to be performed by ministers of religion, elected by a majority of them; and these are to be paid out of national taxes. . . . The establishment of the Chaplainship to Congress is a palpable violation of equal rights as well as of Constitutional principles. . . . If Religion consists in voluntary acts of individuals, singly or voluntarily associated, and if it be proper that public functionaries, as well as their own constituents, should discharge their religious duties, let them, like their constituents, do so at their own expense."

Years later, Madison wrote on the "immunity of Religion from civil jurisdiction," and said: " . . . this has always been a favorite principle with me; and it was not with my approbation that the deviation from it took place in Congress, when they appointed Chaplains, to be paid from the National Treasury. It would have been a much better proof to their constituents of their pious feeling if the members had contributed for the purpose a pittance from their own pockets."

My favorite story of excessive piety confronting common sense in America occurred between the first settlers of Georgia and the founders of Methodism, the brothers John and Charles Wesley. In his book, Jerry Falwell refers to John Wesley as one who "came to America preaching the Gospel of Jesus Christ and spreading revival throughout the land."

The truth is somewhat more complicated. The spartan General James Oglethorpe had brought Charles Wesley along as his private secretary, and John Wesley as the resident minister of the Church of England. In their own diaries, the two are depicted as moaners and malcontents, and Oglethorpe seems to have despised them from the start.

Charles Wesley was gossiping with two women at Frederica, on St. Simon's Island, south of Savannah, one day when they told him they both had had sexual relations with the general. The women promptly told the general that Charles had called him an adulterer. This was only one of the many squabbles that plagued his brief stay in Georgia, for after six months he was happy to be shed of the place. Waiting for the boat at Charleston, he was delighted to find that one of his Georgia friends would be a fellow passenger. "His ingenuous, open temper, and disengagement from the world, made me promise myself a very improving and agreeable voyage," he noted in his diary.

But after a month at sea, the friend "laid aside his mask" and told Wesley what he really thought of him: "He began by telling me all Mr. Oglethorpe had ever said to him, particularly his inmost thoughts of my brother and me; that he ridiculed our pretended fasting in the ship; that he took all my abstemiousness for mere hypocrisy, and put on for fear of my brother, for he saw how very uneasy I was under the restraint; that he much blamed my carelessness, my closeness, my frightening the people, and stirring them up to mutiny &c. &c.; that he found I apprehended being turned out of my office, and therefore pretended to be weary of it; that to save my reputation he had found me an errand to England. . . ." In a few words, the friend said, Oglethorpe believed himself "to have a little sincerity, but more vanity," but Wesley "to have much vanity and no sincerity at all."

Wesley asked his friend if he agreed with Oglethorpe's assessment. "He answered, 'Yes.' "

John Wesley's troubles were even more serious than his brother's; in fact, he came within hours of ending his stay in America in jail. He had become smitten with a young woman named Sophie Hopkey and they would take long walks together and meet for prayers and Bible readings that went on for hours. Then she married another young fellow. The Anglican priest retaliated by refusing her communion the next Sunday. Her family brought charges of defamation, but Wesley said it was a church matter and he would not answer the constable's questions. A grand jury was then convened, and it indicted Wesley on ten counts. He announced that he was ready to go back to England, after all, and this was met by orders for his immediate arrest. He was able to escape that night across the river, where he promptly got lost in the woods and swamps on the way to Charleston.

The people's attitude about Wesley is preserved in his diary. He asks a certain "M——" why he is being so cold, and the man responds: "I like nothing you do. All your sermons are satires upon particular persons, therefore I will never hear you more; and all the people are of my mind; for we won't hear ourselves abused. . . . And then your private behavior: all the quarrels that have been here since you came, have been 'long of you. Indeed there is neither man nor woman in the town who minds a word you say. And so you may preach long enough; but nobody will come to hear you."

Wesley's private reason for coming to Georgia was to be a missionary among the Indians. Here was a whole continent of lost souls, a body-count higher than the combined converts of all the saints and martyrs in the Bible. But by the time the English settlers arrived, the coastal Indians had endured a hundred years of persecution in the name of the white man's God, through the Spanish.

The Indians of the Southern barrier islands were both bisexual and polygamous and often ruled by women chieftains when the Spanish priests arrived in the sixteenth century to impose their unnatural rules of behavior. When they found a Frenchman living among the Indians on Guale (now called St. Catherine's Island), the priests lured him away with the promise of gifts on another island and then secretly had him garroted. According to a memorial written in 1566, the man was a

"Lutheran and noted sodomite," but he was also much beloved by the Indians, especially the chief's son, who lived with him. The chief's son cried as his friend was led away, "because he loved this man very much."

John Gilmary Shea's *History of the Catholic Church in the United States* records the Indians' revenge. "In September, 1597, the son of the cacique [chief] of the Island of Guale, wearying of the restraints on his passions required by the Christian law, fell into great excesses, and at last went off to a pagan band." This band killed every missionary north of St. Augustine. The Spaniards decimated the Indian tribes in retaliation. And later, when the priests heard of widespread starvation among the Indians because of a drought, they thanked God for His retribution.

One of those who managed to endure the judgments of both God and Spaniards was an old chief named Chicali, to whom young John Wesley explained his dream of converting the Indians to Jesus. Chicali replied: "He that is above knows what He made us for. We know nothing. We are in the dark. But white men know much. And yet white men build great houses, as if they were to live forever. But white men cannot live forever. In a little time, white men will be dust as well as I."

We heathens were also present among the first settlers and the founding fathers. As Will Rogers (a descendant of the Cherokee) said, many thousands of us were already here to greet the boats of those European Christians.

PART FOUR

14

WHY JERRY FALWELL

Months after the picture appeared in *Life* magazine, Jerry Falwell was still upset. Piloting a car from his walled-in hilltop estate through the surrounding cramped development of lesser houses with tiny yards down to his church and school buildings along Thomas Road, Falwell told *Newsweek*'s Wally McNamee that it just wasn't fair. The other photographer had spent hours, taken hundreds of shots from every possible angle, and then chosen the one that showed Falwell in the worst light.

Alone among the thousands of pictures published of him in the last few years, the one in *Life* had really made Jerry Falwell mad. It shows him driving an expensive tractor mower on the lawn of his executive mansion; it also shows a frightened security guard whom Falwell is mockingly trying to run down with the big machine.

As Falwell was telling McNamee about the *Life* photographer, he eased the car onto the wide parking lot beside his church. At that moment, a security guard was walking across the space between them and the church. McNamee watched in disbelief—and frustration that he couldn't capture it on film—as Falwell gunned the engine, aimed the car at the hapless guard, and grinned happily as the man stumbled out of the way.

McNamee may have missed another shot illustrating the ruthless small-town bully playing games with his power and weaker people's lives, but he managed to get a picture that—to outsiders, at least—was far more damaging to Falwell's sacred image. Seeing the swimming pool behind Falwell's house, McNamee had asked if he could take a picture of Falwell in swimming trunks beside the pool. Falwell first resisted, but then—anything to please the press—agreed to go through with the pose on condition that he be shown reading the Holy Bible. Falwell then obligingly stuffed his pink, porcine figure into a clashing outfit of red shorts and a maroon and white T-shirt, and reclined on a chaise longue—the Bible perched just under his belly.

Not only were Falwell and his public-relations staff unashamed of this picture, they ordered a seemingly endless supply of that issue of *Newsweek*, September 15, 1980, which also featured Falwell's picture on the cover for a "Born-Again Politics" report. A year and a half later, a copy of the magazine was still included in Falwell's elaborate press packet, a far more expensive production than anything the Kennedys ever put together for their campaigns.

This dichotomy—how Jerry Falwell and his people see him, contrasted with the view from outside—is at the heart of any explanation of his success. To me, the man appears totally lacking in any redeeming qualities whatsoever. His opportunism shows through every one of his various causes. The facts of his life don't add up to a dedicated man of God, but to an entrepreneur using the only avenues available to him to pursue a multimillion-dollar empire and an international jet-set lifestyle. Time and again, I hear other writers and reporters using the ultimate rationalization in explaining Jerry Falwell: at least he is sincere. To which I say: nonsense. To borrow H. L. Mencken's words about William Jennings Bryan: "This talk of sincerity, I confess, fatigues me. If the fellow was sincere, then so was P. T. Barnum. The word is disgraced and degraded by such uses. He was, in fact, a charlatan, a mountebank, a zany without sense or dignity."

Obviously, many people would disagree with this admittedly harsh view of Jerry Falwell. The more I learned about how he got so much money and political power, the more I wondered why. What was it about him that made the political professionals in Washington choose him to head this new "moral majority"? What is it about him that causes so many of the faithful to dole out their hard-earned cash so that he can live in luxurious comfort they can only dream about? There are dozens of other electronic evangelists who are better showmen—Jim Bakker can command real tears at a second's notice on his "PTL Club," and he's a master at spending time in elegant Hawaiian quarters in tax-exempt service to the Lord. James Robison is a far better exhorter than Falwell, and he's also a handsomer man, with real charisma. Pat Robertson of the "700 Club" and the Christian Broadcasting Network is more articulate and better educated—he holds a law degree from Yale, having turned to the ministry after he failed to pass the bar in New York State. Carl McIntyre of New Jersey had a far stronger claim to the role of political preacher dating back to his highly publicized pep rallies in support of Richard Nixon's war policies.

I think the political pros wanted Jerry Falwell precisely because he had none of these qualities. He had no publicly identifiable politics, so they could mold him as they saw fit; he could head up their new coalition of single issues because he hadn't spoken out on any of them (except homosexuality) before. They didn't want a James Robison, who just might become too popular; they didn't want a Pat Robertson, who might be too smart. Falwell would continue to need them as much as they needed him; it was a marriage of convenience that would last because of mutual need.

Why Falwell continues to hold the audience he does—even when the facts show it's only a tiny fraction of what he claims it is—is the enduring mystery of the man and his success. How is it possible that his followers don't see in the man what is so obvious to those of us outside the fold?

Baldly stated, the man is a hypocrite. While claiming to be some sort of authority on American history, he constantly exhibits a profound ignorance of the subject—not just of the fine points or little facts anybody might slip up on now and then, but of what history means. His ignorance of the past is matched and surpassed by his approach to the present. His misstatements of fact regarding the here and now are not mere slips of the tongue, they're revelations of character flaws. Whereas Anita Bryant's distortions of certain "facts" in her anti-homosexual crusade might be attributed to her zeal or even to her accepting misinformation that was being fed to her, Jerry Falwell can claim no such excuse. Time and again, he has been caught in exaggerations and outright lies that could not be explained as anything but a calculated attempt to bolster his public image.

Falwell might see such distortions as innocent "fudging," but a clear pattern of deliberate deception emerges from these incidents. In one, Falwell announced to his radio, television, and live audiences that

"Thank God, Senator Byrd and Senator Warner from Virginia have said, 'We will not ratify'" the Strategic Arms Limitation Treaty (SALT II) then being debated in the Senate. Neither senator had made up his mind about his vote at that time, and neither had talked with Jerry Falwell on the subject. Warner demanded and got a public apology from Falwell.

Falwell's first successful effort to rise from the obscurity of Lynchburg and electronic evangelism to mainline political media attention was during the 1976 campaign of fellow fundamentalist Jimmy Carter. Carter had told *Playboy* magazine: "I've committed adultery in my heart many times—something that God recognizes I will do, and God forgives me for it." Falwell staged interviews with *The Washington Post* and the *Los Angeles Times*, and then went on to devote two full broadcast sermons attacking Carter for saying what he did and for allowing an interview of himself with *Playboy*. But Falwell had enjoyed his brief moment in the limelight and wasn't about to let the matter drop. In a story headlined, "Falwell Attracts Ford Campaign," the *Lynchburg Advance* reported: "Following release of Carter's remarks to *Playboy*, Falwell said, Ford called him. 'The President called simply to assure me that he disagreed totally with the language and philosophy of Mr. Carter to these moral issues,' Falwell said."

That the Thomas Road Baptist Church pastor was getting calls from the President was certainly a newsworthy story. It just didn't happen to be true. The same newspaper reported on October 1, 1976: "Falwell said earlier reports that Ford had called him last week to talk about the Carter interview were in error. Falwell added that he took full responsibility for the error. He and White House Assistant Press Secretary Bill Roberts said today a call was made Thursday from a White House aide to Falwell. The aide expressed no opinion on the Carter interview for himself or Ford, Roberts said."

The most widely quoted incident in which Falwell rearranged the truth to suit his needs involved a simple exchange between himself and Jimmy Carter at a White House prayer breakfast on January 22, 1980. According to a transcript of a tape recording of the meeting later released by Carter's staff, Falwell had asked: "Does your concept of the family include homosexual marriage?" The President had answered, "No."

Seven months later, however, Falwell told a group in Anchorage,

Alaska, that he and Carter "were discussing national events, all these issues, and I asked the president, 'Sir, why do you have known practicing homosexuals on your staff in the White House?" He said the President responded, "Well, I'm President of all the American people; I believe I should represent everyone." Falwell then quoted himself as saying, "Why don't you have some murderers and bank robbers and so forth to represent ..." His sentence was interrupted by cheering and applause, otherwise the Falwell exaggeration might have gone on and on. Later, he would try to explain this away as a "parable" or an "anecdote." On "Meet the Press" that week Falwell insisted he had not lied, and when asked if he had apologized to the President, he said, "I'm doing it right now," and said no more on the subject.

A more subtle brand of deception masks Falwell's racist background and his anti-Semitism, both of which he now denies with vehemence. Although the grade school housed in buildings behind his church now admits some blacks, that was not its policy in the beginning. There can be no doubt that—like hundreds of other such schools set up throughout the South and elsewhere in the country—Falwell's Lynchburg Christian School was set up to avoid integration.

Falwell told Robert Scheer of the *Los Angeles Times* that his father was a segregationist and so was he, "even in the early years of my ministry. It wasn't until I spiritually developed and matured, as I see it, that I came to realize it was an unscriptural position." He said it was "probably 1963–64 that I totally repudiated segregation. It was a carryover from my heritage. I would say that 99 percent of all Southerners, maybe Northerners too, but certainly Southerners—I can speak to that—were segregationists, and once we became Christians, many of us were still in that cultural society—an all-white church and pastors who preached it as the Gospel. I don't think they were guilty of racism. They just believed it was a scriptural position and sometimes misapplied scripture to support it. It was only as I became a real student of scripture that I saw it's not in the Bible. As a matter of fact, the opposite is there. And when I began to repudiate segregation, it cost me."

Like Jimmy Carter, Falwell would now like to rewrite his biography on the subject of racial prejudice. Although he sets the date in the early 1960s when he had a change of heart on segregation, Scheer pointed out to him that he was denouncing civil rights leaders as late as 1965. And as late as 1967, the other ministers in his hometown were denouncing his own actions in setting up a "Christian" school whose sole purpose was to ensure that white children would not have to attend integrated public schools.

To those who have any doubts about the purpose of Falwell's Christian School, I refer to an article in the April 13, 1967, *Daily Advance* in Lynchburg: "The Lynchburg Ministerial Association in a prepared statement concerning its April 5 meeting attacked the use of the word 'Christian' in connection with the private schools which exclude Negroes and other non-whites. The allusion apparently was in reference to the newly formed corporation, the Lynchburg Christian Schools, which plans to build a private school exclusively for white students. . . ." The list of guest speakers on Falwell's "Old-Time Gospel Hour" reads like a *Who's Who* of Southern segregationists, including Lester Maddox of Georgia and George Wallace of Alabama. Falwell returned the visits, addressing both houses of the Alabama legislature and visiting with Wallace in the governor's office.

In November 1979, Falwell made a trip abroad to what might seem an unlikely trio of countries: Rhodesia, South Africa, and Israel. The two white regimes in Africa, of course, suited Falwell's own attitudes about the roles of blacks and whites, but Israel? The Jewish state has been a quiet but consistent and loyal supporter of the white South African government, but why it should become a supporter of Jerry Falwell makes no sense at all, unless it is for similar purely practical reasons. That an opportunistic evangelist would court public figures when and where he can says nothing new about such a man; that Israel would encourage and support Jerry Falwell speaks volumes about how far its leaders are willing to go in securing and holding friends of power and influence, no matter what their philosophy or politics. There is a "Falwell Forest" in Israel, named and endowed by the man himself. When Falwell is in that country, he is received as if he were an ambassador or chief of state by the prime minister, Menachem Begin; and when Begin has been in this country, he has always included a visit with Falwell on his schedule.

In early 1980, the Jewish National Fund honored Falwell for his support of Israel; later that year, Begin himself presented Falwell with the Jabotinsky Medal at a banquet in New York, where Frank Church was also scheduled to be honored. Church, one of the six liberal senators "targeted" and defeated in a massive new-right crusade in the

1980 elections, refused to attend or to accept an award that was also going to Falwell.

In one of the most telling—and hilarious—episodes involving Falwell's involvement with the Jews and Israel, he managed to come down on all sides of the debate over whether God hears the prayers of Jews and, if so, whether he bothers to answer them. The fuss began at that historic gathering of religious politicians in Dallas during the 1980 campaign, when Bailey Smith, pastor of the First Southern Baptist Church in Del City, Oklahoma, and president of the Southern Baptist Convention, proclaimed: "With all due respect to those dear people . . . God Almighty does not hear the prayer of a Jew. For how in the world can God hear the prayer of a man who says that Jesus Christ is not the true Messiah?"

Falwell's involvement in this controversy is carefully documented in the book, *Jerry Falwell, an Unauthorized Biography*, by Bill Goodman and Jim Price, two ordained ministers with earned doctorates of divinity who teach at Lynchburg College. When first asked if he endorsed Bailey Smith's view, Falwell responded: "I believe that God answers the prayer of any redeemed Jew [meaning one who believes in Jesus] or Gentile and I do not believe that God answers the prayer of any unredeemed Gentile or Jew." In a subsequent broadcast of NBC's "Meet the Press," Marvin Kalb asked Falwell: "I want to quote you on something that's been in the press. 'I believe God does not hear the prayers of unredeemed Gentiles or Jews.' Did you say that?"

"All right. Yes, I've made that statement. I believe . . ." Here Falwell was interrupted by Kalb, but later he continued: "I think it very unfortunate that the press today, and present company excepted, is making a point of putting a wedge between some very healthy relationships in the past twenty years that have developed, for example, between evangelical and fundamentalist Christianity and the Jews. I told several rabbis this week in New York, and they agreed, that the best friends the Jewish [*sic*—Falwell also consistently says 'anti-Semitics' when he means anti-Semites] in America, Israel, around the world have are among the Bible-believing Christians in America. . . ."

Not since medieval philosophers argued solemnly over how many angels could dance on the head of a pin have so many words been wasted on so little. To one removed from either side of the controversy, its most hilarious aspect was the seriousness with which it was taken. But Jewish leaders correctly perceived that despite Falwell's and, later, Bailey Smith's disclaimers, there was a clear undercurrent of anti-Semitism in everything they were saying. After a meeting with Marc Tannenbaum, a rabbi who is director of interreligious affairs for the American Jewish Committee, Falwell released a statement saying, "God hears the cry of any sincere person who calls on him."

Meanwhile, Jimmy Carter's campaign staff ran a commercial on 251 radio stations for four days, saying, in part, " 'God doesn't hear the prayers of Jews.' That's what Jerry Falwell, the leader of Moral Majority, backing Ronald Reagan, said recently in a rare moment of candor. . . ." This commercial was withdrawn after Moral Majority filed a ten-million-dollar defamation suit against the Carter campaign. Ron Godwin of Moral Majority said, "That commercial totally misrepresents us. We're tired of being misquoted and maligned." As Price and Goodman point out in their book, Godwin was technically correct: Falwell had been misquoted. He had said that God *hears* the cries of all people; but the real test is whether he *answers* them. No, Falwell had said, God does not answer the prayers of unredeemed Jews or Gentiles.

Falwell was thus able to duck out of the whole thing, but the underlying meaning was still there, and it didn't take him long to let that meaning slip out once again. At an "I Love America" rally in Richmond, he said: "I know a few of you here today don't like Jews. And I know why. He [a Jew] can make more money accidentally than you can on purpose." In the uproar that followed this remark, Falwell could not see anything wrong in a "humorous" remark perpetuating the Shylock stereotype.

This controversy did serve to point out what many of us from that culture knew all along—the fundamentalists are much too independent as individuals to be lumped together under any one banner, including "moral majority." Southern Baptists in Virginia and the District of Columbia denounced those who were stirring up religious bigotry over God's selectivity of which prayers to hear and answer and over anyone's attempt to speak for them. The 104th annual session of the District of Columbia Baptist Convention unanimously passed a resolution affirming that "God is sovereign, and that he hears and answers prayers from whomever he wills," and urging Baptists to "build relationships with our Jewish friends." The group went further by "rejecting as arrogant and inaccurate the claims of such groups and individuals to speak exclusively for God, the Christian church, or Baptists at large."

The whole controversy involved anti-Semitism from the start, and the president of the Union of American Hebrew Congregations said that in no uncertain terms. Rabbi Alexander Schindler, head of the group representing 750 reform congregations with 1.25 million members, said it is "no coincidence that the rise of right-wing Christian fundamentalism has been accompanied by the most serious outbreak of anti-Semitism in America since the end of World War II.

"When the head of the Moral Majority demands a 'Christian Bill of Rights,' when the president of the Southern Baptist Convention tells the Religious Roundtable that 'God Almighty does not hear the prayer of a Jew,' there should be no surprise at reports of synagogues destroyed by arson and Jewish families terrorized in their homes. I do not accuse Jerry Falwell and Bailey Smith of deliberately inciting anti-Semitism. But I do say that their preachments have an inevitable effect."

On reflection, it seems obvious that Smith and Falwell did their flip-flops and turnarounds concerning the ears of God only because they were worried about their public relations. Their colleague James Robison, however, was not so careful. Writing in the magazine *Life's Answer*, for January 1981, Robison defended Smith's words as based on "scriptures that clearly identify Christ as the one mediator between God and man, and man's only avenue of access to God. . . . Every born-again Christian should know that God hears only the prayers of those who seek Him and His salvation and those who have accepted Jesus Christ as the Messiah and, through Him, have been cleansed of their sin and received into the family of God. . . . I am certain the world and liberal religious spokesmen would cry out that it's unkind, unfair, unloving, not even scriptural to say that those who reject Christ will spend eternity in Hell. As hard as it may be to accept such an idea, it's still God's truth."

To Robison and Falwell and their kind of absolutists, other religions and other sects of Christianity are not just different ways of worshiping the same God, they are wrong, doomed, evil—the enemies of God. Jerry Falwell is only more diplomatic in his pronouncements; in the article I quoted from above, James Robison assumed the position of speaking for all of his brother evangelists. And he does.

Falwell's constant talk about his support of the Jews and Israel is nothing more than an attempt to widen his constituency, or at least to give greater coverage to his own narrow beliefs. There is no other explanation for it because his own published words contradict his seeming ecumenicism (a word he never refers to except as yet another curse of the liberals). In the 1965 sermon reprinted as an appendix to this book, he questioned the "sincerity and non-violent intentions" of black leaders such as James Farmer and Martin Luther King, Jr., because of their "left-wing associations." He also said that the blacks were being led by the Jews and that if the Jews didn't watch out, they were going to end up lost and wandering in the desert again for such actions.

In Falwell's most recent book, *Listen, America!*, his anti-Semitism is again stated in the concluding paragraph of a chapter ostensibly written in praise of the Jews and the state of Israel. "The Jews are returning to their land of unbelief. They are spiritually blind and desperately in need of their Messiah and Savior." The message contained in the key words of those sentences is the message of Revelations—the Apocalypse—that it is necessary for "unbelieving" (in Jesus) Jews to return to Zion or Israel before the Christ returns to earth. At that time, the true believers—that is, Christians—will rise in a body to heaven and the "unbelievers" will be slaughtered in God's own final holocaust. It is an attitude Jews have faced many times in history— that they must be destroyed in order to be saved. With friends like Jerry Falwell offering support based on such reasoning, the Jews won't need any enemies.

Who is this man who is able to indulge in such blatant, open duplicity and get away with it? His most devout followers think of him as a great man of vision who can do or say no wrong—to the point, I contend, where he can do and say anything he wants.

Falwell's ancestry of greatness is charted in an amazing little pamphlet prepared by Tobyann Davis and Ruth Tomczak for the Founder's Day service at Thomas Road Baptist Church on April 22, 1977. This booklet, titled "Jerry Falwell, a Man in the People Business," begins with Adam, who was created because "a man was needed to propagate and subdue" the world.

Then Moses was called forth to carry down the Ten Commandments from God. John the Baptist is the next great man on the list, and then the story jumps ahead a couple of thousand years to George

Washington and Abraham Lincoln. "Through the years as our nation turned from the 'Faith of our Fathers,' God sent faithful men to bring her to her knees in repentance—Jonathan Edwards, Dwight L. Moody, Billy Sunday and other great men of God.

"Today, when our nation, America, has reached the height of modern civilization and yet the depth of depravity, dangerously balancing on the brink of moral and spiritual destruction, God has again provided a man to meet the need and challenge of the hour. That man is Jerry Falwell. To God be the glory for sending him to us."

Falwell's comments about his family are as inconsistent as everything else he talks about. He has said in various interviews that his grandfather, Charles Falwell, was a bootlegger and an atheist. His father, Carey Falwell, was also described as a moonshiner by Falwell in one interview and as an alcoholic in nearly every description. Falwell seems to have come up with a "miraculous transformation" in his father that supposedly took place three weeks before his death, when Jerry was fifteen. The Sunday I went to his church, Falwell just started talking about his parents, although the stories had no connection to anything said before or after. "No preacher would go near him," he said of his dying father. But a layman was able to talk with him and convert him to Christ just in time. I have read no less than twenty-five descriptions of this scene attributed to Falwell—and something about the way he tells it (he always says he didn't know about it for many years afterwards) just doesn't ring true.

Robert Scheer of the *Los Angeles Times* (who also did the *Playboy* interview of Jimmy Carter that figured in Falwell's career) was able to get the most explicit information I could find from Falwell about his parents. "My father, as far as I know, never attended a church in his life. He loved his children, his family, he provided for us well, he loved us. Three weeks before his death, a layman visited him—I was fifteen years old at the time. That layman opened the scriptures and explained the plan of salvation to him. My father accepted Christ. I was not a Christian then, myself. I believe my father did become a Christian just before he died."

His father died of cirrhosis of the liver, Falwell told Scheer. "I think, frankly, that my father—I doubt if my father drank, I don't think he drank at all, until he and his younger brother had a shootout and his brother was killed. He had a very wild brother and very unmanageable. They never got along, and two years before I was born, 1931, in

205

one of the businesses that my father owned [a restaurant and tourist court across from the Merry Garden dance hall, which Carey Falwell also owned] his brother actually challenged him with a gun, and in an act of self-defense, he was forced to kill his own brother. There was no court hearing, there were no charges. But he never got over that. That was the beginning, my mother said, of his frustration, his drinking, and at times, after he was drinking, if he got despondent, his conversation would always center around that event."

One son, Lewis, had already been born to Carey and Helen Falwell, and the unplanned arrival of twins—Jerry first and Gene second—on August 11, 1933, could not have come at a worse time. Like many others in America in those days, Carey Falwell was broke; through a number of small ventures he was able to keep the family together and to die in relative comfort in 1948. The official Falwell biographies speak of Jerry's brothers as "aggressive, successful businessmen" who have added to "the family's extensive commercial interests." This is more Baptist fudging. When you arrive in Lynchburg, you are confronted with the name at every turn—Falwell Air Service, Falwell Airport, and a Falwell is the owner of the local baseball team, a farm club for the New York Mets. But these are properties of Jerry's first cousin, Calvin, not his brothers. His brother, Gene, who died in 1981, followed their father's and grandfather's example. Gene's wife, JoAnn, rode off to the Thomas Road Baptist Church on Sundays, but he stayed home and puttered about the trailer court he ran on the old home place, or went fishing. Gene must have been the genial opposite of Jerry. Cousin Calvin Falwell described him to Frances FitzGerald in an article in *The New Yorker*, "Aggressive? He's the most easygoing kind of guy you'd ever want to meet. Never gets mad. Has all the time in the world for you. I suppose he hasn't worn a tie since his mother's funeral. In fact, I'm sure he hasn't. Like someone once said to me, 'I guess Jerry got the other half.' " From his words, it sounds as though cousin Calvin admired the qualities of Gene's half.

Fairview Heights, where Jerry Falwell lived until he went off to Baptist Bible College, and where Gene Falwell lived until he died, is a working-class community far enough out from Lynchburg proper to think of itself almost as another town. It reminded me in every way of Woodfin, the community where I was reared a few miles outside Asheville, North Carolina. The little four-room frame houses had become just as drab and dreary. But I had a feeling that this place had been like the one I had known immediately after World War II. Then, there had been flowers in the front yard and everybody had a vegetable garden in back. The people had been proud of their little houses, and they did all of their own repairs and upkeep.

At the Mountain View Elementary School, the twin brothers were soon separated. Jerry was a better student and skipped a grade. Gene dropped out and joined the navy in the eleventh grade; Jerry—with a 98.6 average—would have been class valedictorian if the honor hadn't been denied him because he got involved in a prank that involved stealing lunch tickets and giving them to the school ballplayers.

Although Falwell now hints at the wild times he had as a young man, I think from all the evidence that he is like others who convert from their sinful ways—which, in fact, weren't all that sinful. He wasn't a drinker, for a start, and in that social setting, the only ones who had the really wild times—good and bad—were the drinkers. His boyhood pal, Jim Moon (now an assistant minister at Thomas Road), has said that Jerry was one of the rare ones' in their community who even entertained ambitious thoughts. You grew up, got a job, got married, and that was it. The options for careers weren't numerous enough to worry about: "You could go to work at the hosiery mill, the foundry, or the shoe factory. There wasn't much else. . . . But Jerry, he always wanted to be an engineer, and he was willing to do whatever was necessary to be the best."

The decision that led Falwell away from engineering into the ministry is one that is nowhere explained in any of the articles or books by or about him, or in any of the many recent interviews he's given. He was midway through his second year at Lynchburg College with—as his press biographies always note—the highest math average in the school, for which he was awarded a prize by the B. F. Goodrich Company. After finishing the two-year Lynchburg College course, Falwell planned to study engineering at VPI, Virginia Polytechnic Institute.

But that ambition was put aside for another when, as his Founder's Day biography explains, "a miracle took place." In more mundane language, Jerry Falwell and his friend, Jim Moon, decided they'd stop by a prayer meeting at the Park Avenue Baptist Church and see if they couldn't pick up a couple of dates for the evening. Jerry laid claim to the dark-haired organist, and Moon said the pianist was his. Eventually the two ended up marrying the opposite ones to those they'd picked up that night. Falwell married Macel Pate on April 12, 1958, and they now have two sons and a daughter.

How they managed to find the dates who would become their wives and get saved in the process is a combination of events that might confound one born outside a culture where the church is just about the only meeting place or social center that exists.

But on that first night, by Falwell's own accounts, he gave his life to the service of Jesus Christ. An official version says: "As the Reverend Paul Donnelson preached the reality of a hot burning hell, conviction gripped Jerry's heart. . . . An elderly white-haired gentleman put his hand on Jerry's shoulder and said, 'I'll go with you.' Garland Carey knelt with him at the altar, and there Jerry Falwell met Jesus Christ."

In 1952, when this took place, I was not yet eleven years old. But one of my brothers was the same age as Jerry Falwell. Career options—he chose the navy—were very much on his mind at the time because the draft board was aggressively pursuing all young men who were of age and in good health. Becoming a minister was one certain way of having your name removed from the draft rolls. I have no information at all that this was why Jerry Falwell chose the ministry, but he wouldn't have been the first or the last to do so.

Considering the many other embellishments Falwell has indulged in, it is curious that the story of his conversion does not have more to it than the simple fact of his walking down to the front and dedicating his life to God. But by the time Falwell wrote about it, such melodramatic accounts were somewhat out of fashion. Oral Roberts was struck down by the hand of God and lay on the floor in stunned paralysis for a while when he got the call—but that experience became tamer and tamer over the years until his latest biography records the event in the calm and decorous manner of Jimmy Carter and Jerry Falwell.

One bit of prophecy Falwell always adds to the story of his conversion has to do with the influence of the early radio evangelist, Charles E. Fuller. Every Sunday, Falwell's mother would get dressed up and go off to church by herself. But before she left the house, she would turn up the volume on the radio and set it to receive Fuller's "The Old Fashioned Revival Hour." The old man and the three boys were force-fed their Sunday sermons, as Falwell tells it, because they were too lazy to get up and turn off the radio.

Dropping out of Lynchburg College before finishing the full two-year course, Falwell next enrolled at Baptist Bible College in Springfield, Missouri, where he graduated. As a student, he assisted the pastor of a nearby church. He was put in charge of a "class" that consisted of one study book, one eleven-year-old boy, and a curtained-off space the size of a closet. It was his first numerical triumph. Praying to God two hours every afternoon for help, he toured the playgrounds and recruited his boys' class that numbered fifty-six by the time he graduated.

As a senior, Falwell preached at the Kansas City Baptist Temple. After his sermon, nineteen people came forward during the invitational. One woman said, "This morning I realized for the first time that I wasn't saved." These two stories about numbers and about Jerry Falwell's special calling are a key to understanding his success in the years ahead.

As for the numbers, this is a peculiarly Baptist obsession. It was another Baptist minister who told me the story about the final nuclear holocaust taking everybody off the face of the earth except for three men who find each other and discover that they are Southern Baptists: they agree to have six in Sunday school the next Sunday. It is comparable to the obsession American officials developed over the body-counts during the Vietnam war. The explanation would seem to be that such numbers don't merely validate our presence or our cause; they also reaffirm that we're winning and that we're right. In the following pages, I will be quoting a number of body-counts offered as evidence by Jerry Falwell in his rise to fame, fortune, and power. I have proved beyond doubt that enough of them are wildly exaggerated that I do not believe that any of the figures released by Falwell and his staff are to be considered reliable.

Returning to Lynchburg in 1955, at the age of twenty-two, Falwell became associated with a group of thirty-five people who wanted to break off from the church where he had been saved. There are various rumors in Lynchburg about what really caused the split, but you will not hear the story in any believable detail from Falwell or any of his lieutenants. In fact, none of his releases ever mentions that the group came from the same church where he met his wife. Some people told me the split arose because of a disagreement over church property; others said that there were personality problems involving the minister, who did subsequently leave town.

The splinter group asked Falwell to be their minister, and on June 19, 1956, Thomas Road Baptist Church was founded. Its origins were as humble as Falwell's own—both of which are constantly cited as evidence that only a miracle of God could have caused such success. The congregation's original meeting place was a small factory that had last been used for bottling soft drinks that carried the trademark of Donald Duck. There was so much syrup left around, they said you would stick to the floor if you stood in one place too long. The neighborhood kids called it "the Donald Duck church."

The original members went to work scouring the soda-pop syrup off the church building's walls and floors and combing the surrounding communities for new members. Out of such decidedly unpromising beginnings, a true empire has developed. The church itself—now in its third and grandest edifice, seating 3,600—claims 17,000 members. An early-morning radio show Falwell started soon after founding the church is now carried on 373 television stations that broadcast the Sunday worship services, and 300 radio stations that broadcast a half-hour daily version of "The Old-Time Gospel Hour." The Lynchburg Christian Academy—kindergarten through twelfth grade—was founded in 1967, and in the 1980–81 school year had 1,200 students enrolled. Liberty Baptist College was founded in 1971, and in the 1980–81 school year had 2,900 students. Liberty Baptist Seminary, founded in 1973, had an enrollment of 170 during the 1980–81 school year. Jerry Falwell has published three books: *Church Aflame*, *Capturing a Town for Christ*, and *Listen, America!*, the last one from Doubleday.

Jerry Falwell is, indeed, a man in "the people business." He would find nothing contradictory in comparing the role and methods of a religious administrator to those of a similar manager in the secular world of commerce. In *Church Aflame*, his 1971 book written with Elmer Towns, Falwell said: "Business is usually on the cutting edge of innovation and change because of its quest for finances. . . . Therefore the church would be wise to look at business for a prediction of future innovation."

This early creed of Falwell's is cited by a sociologist named Betty Gail Flint as a partial explanation not only of Falwell's success, but also of the larger popularity of fundamentalist religion in recent years. In a thesis for which she was awarded a Master of Arts from the College of William and Mary, Flint observes that fundamentalism "has received new packaging making it palatable to twentieth-century tastes. The fundamentalist religion, which many thought had disappeared into the hills and rural areas of the South, has re-emerged in many sectors of American life with new vitality, different techniques, and a wider appeal, making it a religion for *now*; the old-time religion with a facelift.

"In the South especially, which has long been a stronghold for this brand of religion, many groups espousing the 'fundamentals' of the Bible have amassed congregations numbering in the thousands, and have mobilized those outside their immediate location through televised ministries. This religion has been expertly adapted to the age of mass communication and has borrowed many of its techniques from the secular sphere."

During an eight-month period from October 1977 through May 1978, Betty Flint attended thirty-six different worship services on Sundays and Wednesday evenings at the Thomas Road Baptist Church. She worked as a volunteer in the mailroom for a time, sat in on missionary training sessions, and also conducted detailed interviews with church officials, ordinary members, and members of the community who are not members of the church. This was before the advent of Moral Majority and Jerry Falwell's active participation in the 1980 campaign, but Flint accurately predicted such a major role from her observations of Falwell.

Falwell, in *Church Aflame*, compared his success with that of a large shopping center as against just one big store: "The Thomas Road Baptist Church believes that the combined ministries of several agencies in one church can not only attract the masses to the gospel, but can better minister to each individual who comes. . . ." Flint said, "It is, it seems, a case of the supermarket replacing the old country store."

In Lynchburg, Flint found that people often referred to Falwell's ministries as one of the area's "largest businesses." In just over two decades, this one man had singlehandedly brought that business from nowhere to the top. The idea of charisma is important in understanding how Falwell did it, Flint says, "if one is mindful of the original limitations placed upon the term by Max Weber.

"According to Weber's original concept of the charismatic leader, the perception of the exceptional or superhuman qualities of the leader is a function of the interaction between the leader and his followers. To those outside the group, the exceptional personality may appear quite ordinary and the response will be neutral or antipathetic. This is

211

certainly true in the case of Jerry Falwell. To much of the Lynchburg community outside the church, Falwell's lack of distinctiveness and the banality of practically everything he utters is their strongest impression. As one interviewee put it, 'Whatever you make of him, he's still a hick. By God, he even looks like a hick.' "

This was one of the main points that had troubled me about Falwell. In his oratory, there was nothing whatever to excite or inspire the audience; there seemed to be no spark at all between him and his followers. And yet they were there. Such devotion to the leader, Flint says, citing Weber again, is actually devotion to "a common cause, to a rationally intended success." She explains: "The leader's extraordinariness obtains only inasmuch as he is seen as the vehicle and promise of a greater social or cosmological goal. . . . At Thomas Road this nexus is quite explicit. Falwell is the focus and director of the church's growth and activity, which in turn are seen as a 'spark' which will ignite a revolutionary transformation of the nation and the world.

"This absorption of the lives of individuals into a broader goal, vitally linked to the personality of the leader, is most likely to occur among classes of individuals who experience a certain alienation [from] and frustration with the *status quo*. Among groups content with their roles in the prevailing society, the vision of the utopia existing as a polar opposite to the present will lack clarity and importance. The concept of a religious sect, when reduced to its essentials, depicts the alienation of sect members from the dominant society. . . .

"The sectarian nature of their organization is proudly accepted by Thomas Road Baptist Church. Elmer Towns, editor-in-chief of all the church publications, who is very familiar with the sociological concept of sect, proudly proclaims that the church is definitely a sect and states that they intend to maintain this sectarian orientation." Thomas Road is not affiliated with the Southern Baptist Convention. And, unlike Billy Graham who would save people and then send them back to their own churches, Falwell is setting up what amounts to his own denomination in which he hopes to have five thousand "independent" churches by the year 2000. He refers to the older denominations as "religious morgues." Although Falwell speaks of his followers as "converts," Flint found that every person she interviewed in the church had been reared in a home where his absolutist moral code was practiced and believed.

Falwell's church met some definitions of a sect, but differed strikingly in others, according to Flint. She says it does not necessarily fit the kind of sect which Richard Niebuhr said was "by its very nature ... valid only for one generation." In addition to the stress on the born-again experience and the elite status of the saved—which fit the accepted definition of a sect—she found that Falwell had stressed "the need to train the young in the fundamentals of the faith, has a large and highly specialized pastorate, and displays a large and efficient organization" more comparable to an established denomination than to a sect.

"However, the main differentiation between the denomination and the sect remains that the former is accommodated to the dominant society while the most important element of the sect ... is that it is a movement of religious protest. . . . This religious protest is apparent at TRBC. In the estimation of the members, America is a 'sin-sick society' which is experiencing great difficulties and a loss of prestige as a result of its 'rebellion against God.' Present economic and spiritual problems represent 'God's judgment' on the country which fails to recognize His authority. . . ."

From the first, Falwell let his people know they were going to be part of something big. The membership rolls kept growing, and so did the construction of buildings to accommodate them. The first sanctuary building was completed less than two years after the group bought the Donald Duck building. Construction of an even larger auditorium, seating eight hundred, was completed in the spring of 1964; the 3,600-seat auditorium was finished in the spring of 1970. Meanwhile, three classroom buildings had been erected and the old bottling plant and the two previous sanctuaries were remodeled for classrooms. In the fall of 1967, the Lynchburg Christian Academy opened, using these same classrooms. That was also the year that Falwell's "Old-Time Gospel Hour" became a regularly televised weekly program, although there had been special telecasts staged by him since 1957.

All those numbers attracted even more numbers, and by the church's fourteenth anniversary the religious magazine *Christian Life* presented it a plaque for having "the fastest-growing Sunday school in America." In addition to numerous special events at the church itself, an annual Homecoming Service is staged at the town stadium. This service is described by church officials as "the largest Sunday school since Pentecost. . . ."

The members of Thomas Road are made constantly aware that they are part of not only one of the biggest, but one of the most important church congregations, as a steady stream of celebrities moves through on guest appearances. These have ranged from Anita Bryant to Elizabeth Taylor and John Warner, during his campaign for senator from Virginia. Name-dropping is a constant device Falwell uses to involve his ordinary followers in the important role he claims to play in Washington and Tel Aviv. By association, the church members participate in everything he does, and get to know every important figure he meets.

In 1971, Falwell established Lynchburg Baptist College, changing the name later to Liberty Baptist College. I describe the physical setting of that school in a later chapter. But it seems a sad irony that a school named "Liberty" operates as a kind of prison, under an extraordinary set of restrictions beginning with this one: "The college may alter, amend, or abolish its rules or regulations at any time."

Male students are required to wear ties on the campus until 4:30 P.M. every day. They are not allowed to have beards, mustaches, or sideburns, and their hair must be cut short behind the ears. Women are forbidden to wear "anything tight, scant, backless, and low in the neckline." This includes dresses or skirts with slits "shorter than two inches from the back of the knee. . . ." Women may not wear "hip huggers" and "will refrain from wearing men's cords or men's jeans or shorts." Shorts for men "are never acceptable."

Students are also "to refrain from listening to rock, disco, country and western, Christian rock, or any other music that is associated closely with these types." Any student leaving town for the weekend must get written permission from the dean of students; students wishing to get married must have written permission from both parents and "are not permitted to marry on weekends or holidays other than Christmas and summer vacation." Furthermore, the students can be punished and expelled for using profanity, dancing, smoking, drinking alcoholic beverages, or attending a movie theater.

Rounding out Jerry Falwell's religious shopping center are a small seminary at the college and the Thomas Road Bible Institute, which requires no previous education and involves instruction in the Bible either in classrooms or through cassette recordings.

The only serious threat to Falwell's empire came in 1973 when the Securities and Exchange Commission charged the church with "fraud and deceit" in the issuance of $6.5 million in unsecured church bonds. I found only one obscure interview in which Falwell admitted that the SEC was "technically right." One of his staff-written biographies actually says he and the church won this suit and were cleared of the charges. Such was not the case. The SEC agreed to remove the words "fraud and deceit" from the charges and the property was not placed in actual receivership until the bonds were paid off, but the church finances were put in the hands of a group of five local businessmen selected by the court to settle the mess. Falwell cut back on his free spending long enough to raise that money in the required time, and then he was talking of his grandiose schemes again: he would have fifty thousand students at Liberty College by the year 2000; he would build a huge church and gymnasium on the college campus seating twelve thousand. The latter, as he told Betty Flint when she was visiting his church, would be finished in 1978. The facility was not only not finished by 1982, it hadn't even been started.

According to Falwell, he is taking in well over one million dollars a week now—although his executives told Betty Flint in 1977 that by 1981 they would be bringing in more than one hundred million dollars a year. The bizarre machinations of Falwell's financial dealings have been the subject of continuing articles in *Penthouse* magazine. When the first one came out, Cal Thomas of Moral Majority dismissed the information as old news warmed over—implying, of course, that the information was true. Since then, the Falwell forces, who once were ready to march in the streets against *Penthouse*, have been strangely quiet. In the carefully researched pieces published so far, it is obvious that Falwell has involved himself and his people's money in every sort of shady and questionable practice known to the sleaziest of financial operators. That's not just my opinion, but also that of a former associate of his, a man as religious as Falwell. Arthur Weidel, a born-again Christian banker, with author L. J. Davis, wrote in the December 1981 *Penthouse* about an amazingly complex deal between a small Baptist church in New Jersey and Jerry Falwell's organization. "Before I was done," said Weidel, "I found myself involved with a confidence artist who doubled as a member of Falwell's board of directors, a missing million dollars, church bondholders literally scammed out of their money, dubious loans, and a very large question in my mind about whether some of the men of God I've encountered in all this have much to do with God at all."

Weidel said he was "especially disturbed because I am a born-again Christian. It is a conviction I take seriously, which is why I was all the more disturbed by my experiences with supposedly God-fearing men who use the name of God to exploit those around them. I have come to learn the wisdom of the Bible's teaching, especially those passages where Christ warns again and again about those who would use his name to cause division and gain worldly possessions."

Seven years after he first got involved in the bizarre world of Jerry Falwell's financial empire, Weidel says that now that he is out of it, "My faith remains strong. . . . Christ clearly foresaw what would happen when men begin to take advantage of His name—men whose gods, Saint Paul says, are their bellies. I began with little experience of men whose appetites for money had little to do with the piety they professed, but I have learned a great deal.

"And one of the things I have learned is this: there is no greater hypocrite than a man who will shamelessly use the name of God to gull the innocent, and there is no scam more effective."

But did this devastating moral indictment get through to Jerry Falwell? I have an idea he didn't even read it; he could always dismiss it as another page in a dirty magazine. Also, I don't think that Jerry Falwell could repent and disengage himself from the financial juggernaut he's set in motion, even if he wanted to. More than one person familiar with his operations has explained that it's a perpetual-motion machine he's got going: if something happened to halt his incessant fund raising, the machine would stop. If Falwell were taken ill for a time or died, his operations would also sicken or die. Betty Gail Flint's carefully posited findings about Falwell agree with those of nearly every knowledgeable observer I talked with about Falwell. Although he has more than forty assistant ministers helping him, and hundreds of employees in several locations, his is almost exclusively a one-man show. As his own fund-raising consultant said in a training session I attended in Springfield, Virginia, "People give to people." People don't give to Thomas Road Baptist Church or to Moral Majority; they give to Jerry Falwell.

In order to keep hitting their "hot button" and getting the cash he needs to survive, Falwell has got to keep coming up with crises that people respond to. One of his most effective devices has been to announce—about once a year, at least—that if he doesn't raise so many millions immediately, his shows will be taken off the air, or his students won't have dormitories, or some missionary effort (always involving children) will have to be canceled.

Here are a few such appeals addressed to me in the past year:

April 30, 1981

Dear Mr. Young:

It now appears that, after 25 years of broadcasting and televising the Gospel, the Old-Time Gospel Hour may go off the air. . . . Mr. Young, it breaks my heart to tell you this. But, it is the truth. The Old-Time Gospel Hour simply cannot continue with a 60 to 90 day deficit—especially when that deficit is increasing. . . . If we are unable to pay off this deficit in the next few days, we simply must cancel our programs. And, Mr. Young, this is why I am writing to you, asking you to prayerfully consider an emergency gift of $25 right now. I know $25 is more than you have ever given to the Old-Time Gospel Hour at one time, [for the record, I had never given him anything] but I must be absolutely honest with you; our situation is now at the crisis stage. . . .

July 9, 1981

Dear Mr. Young,

Because you have been a special friend to the Old-Time Gospel Hour—I want to share with you our current situation on Liberty Mountain. . . . Here is my problem, Mr. Young. In 30 days, thousands of students will be arriving here in Lynchburg to start classes on Liberty Mountain. But, Mr. Young, we're not ready! In fact, as you can see from the pictures I've enclosed for you today, we still have 3 dormitories on which construction is not complete. This means that many of our students may have no place to sleep on Liberty Mountain. . . .

Another urgent request carried with it a "telegram" received from the president of "Food for the Hungry International." You had to read it carefully to note that it had originated not in Southeast Asia, but in Scottsdale, Arizona. The dire warnings in Falwell's cover letter made it seem the message came directly from Southeast Asia. "As you see, the Mercy Ship is in serious trouble. . . . Because of this emergency and several other project needs, I'm asking you for a 'mercy gift' at this time." This, by the way, is a common device of Falwell's. Since all of his various agencies were combined into one kind of conglomerate after the 1973 SEC investigation, a contribution to one is technically a gift to all. The point where this borders on illegality, in my opinion, is that all of Falwell's appeals are pegged to one specific cause—but somewhere near the end of the long letters, there is always a vague explanation that the money may also be used for other projects.

In early 1980, Falwell launched the "Liberty Missionary Society" with an appeal for funds to help "thousands upon thousands of small children [who] are dying from starvation and malnutrition in refugee camps around the world. . . ." The first project of this society was to aid the Cambodian refugees in Thailand. As usual, Falwell covered himself by saying this was only "one of" the projects he needed money for. But when he published the projected two-million-dollar budget for these new "missions," $450,000 was earmarked for construction projects at Liberty College and another $450,000 was to go for training missionaries. Not one penny had been designated for food, although the appeal connected with this projected budget carried this message from Falwell: "In order to minister to starving people, we must first feed them. . . ."

The one issue Falwell keeps coming back to is his imagined threat of homosexuality: "Satan is waging a vicious war against our children today. He is destroying the lives of innocent little ones and their families. . . ." Most of those letters dealing with this subject come in "scare" packages with bold warnings in red on the outside of the envelope: "CAUTION: CONTENTS OF THIS MATERIAL MAY BE HARMFUL TO MINORS!" The "harmful" material is usually nothing more than the kind of pictures published in newspapers of Gay Pride marches in San Francisco and elsewhere—in fact, the Falwell "material" appears to be taken from newspaper picture files.

"With God as my witness," Falwell declares in one red-on-yellow urgent request for funds to fight the militant homosexuals, "I pledge that I will continue to expose the sin of homosexuality to the people of this nation. I believe that the massive homosexual revolution is always a symptom of a nation coming under the judgment of God. . . . Please remember, homosexuals do not reproduce! They recruit! And, many of them are out after my children and your children. . . . Your gift of $15, $25, even $100 will make a crucial difference at this time whether or not I can continue to cry out against the sins of our nation—including the sin of homosexuality. . . . Let me repeat, a massive homosexual revolution can bring the judgment of God upon this nation. Our children must not be recruited into a profane lifestyle. . . . Thank you for your help. Make your tax-deductible check payable to Old-Time Gospel Hour."

Jerry Falwell has fooled a lot of people for quite a long time. They believed him when he said there were children starving in Cambodian refugee camps, although they didn't read the details that explained that none of their contributions would ever reach those children. They believed him when he said that their contributions would help keep "The Old-Time Gospel Hour" on the air or Liberty College open to students—but they didn't stop to think that this cannot possibly be anything more than a temporary solution of such problems. If an organization must rely on such invented crises to stay alive, the question becomes not whether it can survive, but whether it should. Surely, more and more people are going to realize that the only crises their money helps to avert are those in the countinghouses of Jerry Falwell.

15

BASIC TRAINING FOR MORAL MAJORITY, INC.

Every time I had asked about attending a training session of one of the new-right groups, I was told that these were closed to the press. So, when I read in one of their newsletters that Moral Majority was staging a seminar on "Understanding Politics" at the Springfield (Virginia) Hilton just south of Washington, I enrolled as an interested citizen who "wants to listen and to learn."

No more than seventy-five people showed up for two days of meetings in a conference room set up for ten times that number with long, narrow laboratory tables and metal chairs. At least half of those attending were women who introduced themselves as "guests" of Phyllis Schlafly's Eagle Forum; eight others—the only blacks there—were "here with Reverend Sparrow," head of Moral Majority in the District of Columbia. Half of the others were officials of Moral Majority in Virginia, Maryland, North Carolina, and West Virginia. The president of the Maryland group was introduced as a "stable" leader, presumably to signal a shift from his predecessor, whose major crusade was a laughable failure to drive "pornographic" cookies out of an Annapolis bakery. The cookies—depicting gingerbread persons in naked detail—doubled in sales with the publicity.

The words *who, what, where, when, why* were written on a blackboard, and everyone in the audience was asked to stand up and answer the questions. Abortion was the burning cause of three-fourths of those who spoke, and all but one of these said he or she was Roman

Catholic. One of the four or five non-affiliated women came from Roanoke, Virginia, and said nervously: "I'm very new at this, and the reason I'm here is because the other side seems to know more than I do." Another woman from Maryland said, "I'm here so I can understand what my husband is saying when he talks politics."

The head of Moral Majority in Virginia said, "We are here to learn how to burn witches and everything else the press says we're about." I guess this sense of humor was what surprised me most at this meeting. It seemed to reflect a self-awareness that I had not detected elsewhere among the religious right. But I was to learn that even this, even the jokes and congeniality that had made my work so much more pleasant than I had expected, were all part of the good-salesmanship package.

The seminar was an example of the crossover among the different conservative groups. While it was listed as a Moral Majority presentation, it was, in fact, a cooperative effort that included the Eagle Forum, which provided the audience, and The Conservative Caucus and the Committee for the Survival of a Free Congress, which provided those speakers who weren't Moral Majority officials. The main handbook was Schlafly's "Citizen's Good Government Manual," which is complete with model personal thank-you notes from whoever the candidate is to whoever the campaign worker is.

If their timing was a bit off and their humor somewhat strained, the men from Moral Majority had their reasons this particular week of July 6, 1981. President Reagan had shocked them all by nominating to the Supreme Court a woman who had voted in favor of abortion while a member of the Arizona legislature. Howard Phillips would tell the seminar later that Reagan had "thrown down the gauntlet" and his staff had lied outright in a promise to Phillips that this woman would not be nominated. A coalition of conservative groups had called a press conference the day of the meeting I was attending, but they had been upstaged by the erstwhile godfather of conservatism, Barry Goldwater. When asked about Jerry Falwell's opposition to Sandra Day O'Connor's nomination, Goldwater spat out his response: "I think every good Christian ought to kick Jerry Falwell's ass."

Nobody seemed to notice the Christian right's reaction that such language was "beneath the dignity of a senator." Goldwater called yet another press conference the next day, not to deny the line about Falwell but to expound upon it. The Moral Majority officials were still monitoring the news as they went back and forth to the meetings in

221

the Springfield Hilton that day. Every speaker tried to respond to Goldwater's line somehow, but each of them stumbled and spluttered in embarrassed half-words and sentences. They couldn't even say "ass." The word became "derrière" or "rear" or "hind parts" or "blank" or "bleep."

Ron Godwin, vice-president and chief of operations for Moral Majority, was the first speaker, and he was introduced by Charles S. Judd, a financial consultant to the group. Judd said there was an ancient Greek who wanted to learn how to talk right, so he filled his mouth with rocks. As his speech improved, he would take out one of the rocks. Well, Godwin did the same thing, said Judd. Only he used marbles. "And when he had lost all his marbles, that's when he came to Moral Majority."

Godwin had a quick riposte all planned: "And one of the first acts thereafter was to hire Charlie Judd." But the microphone fouled up and he missed his timing and ended up muttering, "I really do think Charlie would make a great warm-up speaker for Tupperware parties." Nobody laughed at that, possibly because it was a Tupperware group he was addressing. There were no beautiful women, no handsome men. Some of the men sported early-1950s burr haircuts, and three wore white socks. Godwin said we would be hearing later from a speaker named Cal Thomas, and "I urge you not to wear white socks."

This was the first time Moral Majority had sponsored such a session; it was to be the prototype of training seminars throughout the country (although, six months later, only one other had been held). "Now, some of you may not agree on every issue," said Godwin. "I urge you to learn from one another. We need to be open-minded. We need to learn from other people." He also had some blunt words for those who were there to push their own causes. One woman had color pictures of dead fetuses, which she said worked "awfully good with groups"; another had big "Vote for Life" buttons for two dollars; another had pamphlets to give to women going into clinics to have abortions. Godwin said, "This is our show. You do your thing on your time and on your bucks, and you know what I mean."

The rumors of Moral Majority's demise "have been greatly exaggerated," said Godwin. "We are twice as big, twice as strong, twice as financially secure as we were on November 4 [1980]." There were, of course, no statistics to back this up and there would have been no means of verifying them, even if there had been. The organization was twenty-five months old at the time of this seminar. It had survived, Godwin said, because "we are not basically a political organization." To other audiences, Godwin and Falwell are forever saying they're not mixing religion and politics, because "Moral Majority is a political organization." Godwin explained the contradiction: "When a moral issue takes us into the political arena, we simply follow it there. I believe the pro-life issue was a moral issue hundreds and thousands of years before it became an American political issue."

Their newspaper, *Moral Majority Report*, he said, "goes to 840,000 homes a month. We hope to have over a million by the end of the year." He didn't explain that most of these homes either get it free at church or through one of the many contribution plans Falwell offers. The "Moral Majority Radio Report," he claimed, went to 333 stations at that time, and they hoped to have one thousand stations in 1982.

The group's immediate cause was the ultimately unsuccessful fight against the nomination of Sandra Day O'Connor to the Supreme Court. They would never say that President Reagan was wrong—he simply had been given the wrong information about this woman. "To ask these questions is not being a right-wing kook," said Godwin, "it's our constitutional right." Foreseeing a losing battle, he covered himself by saying, "We're not gonna throw the President out with the bath water simply because we disagree with him on this one issue."

The Coalition for Better Television was another project Moral Majority has supported. On February 2, 1981, 152 organizations formed the group to monitor television programs for three months with regard to sex, violence, and profanity. There was not one word on the news the night the coalition was announced at a Washington press conference, Godwin said. "I ask you, if 152 organizations came together to fight killing baby whales, would it have been ignored?" But when the three network presidents spoke out against the coalition, he said, suddenly there was coverage—and the number of supporting groups rose to 392.

He voiced a theme that I was to hear in every single speech and interview with a leader of the religious right. They complained bitterly about being ignored by the media—although they owed their strength if not their very existence to it—but once they had the spotlight, they behaved like petulant movie stars being pestered for their time. Donald Wildmon, the Tupelo, Mississippi, preacher who founded the television coalition, had been talking to himself for years, Godwin said. Then, suddenly, he had newsmen "following him literally twenty-four hours a day" and had to sneak out a back door if he wanted to go somewhere without being on camera. He publicly forbade pictures or interviews with any others in his family, although I find it hard to believe any reporter would have wanted to talk with them.

The Coalition for Better Television was so successful, Godwin said, "this fall you will be able to see a difference on television." The fall television season came and went and there was little or no noticeable change, but changes in the "coalition" itself seemed imminent. In a public-television documentary, Jerry Falwell said he couldn't see how a boycott of television sponsors would be necessary to impose the religious right's moral code; Donald Wildmon, on the same program, said it would be. Wildmon also seemed annoyed that Falwell was taking so much credit for the coalition's work. At the end of this documentary, Wildmon was asked if changing television was all he intended to do. Did God have other plans for him? Wildmon stared crazily into the camera, choked up, and muttered that he didn't really like to talk about that, but, yes, "God has bigger things in mind."

Another of Moral Majority's successful causes was the suit brought before the Supreme Court regarding the drafting of women for military combat service. Phyllis Schlafly, who holds a law degree although she is not a practicing attorney, was paid by Moral Majority to help prepare the case for presentation to the Supreme Court.

An ongoing cause of the group is pornography or, more specifically, the shutting down of pornographic bookstores. Godwin had particular praise for prosecutors in Cincinnati, Atlanta, and Jacksonville, and in Asheboro, North Carolina, who had managed to get court orders closing all of the pornographic shops in their cities and towns. At some time, Moral Majority hoped to get together prosecutors from fifty other towns and fly in the victorious prosecutors to tell them, in Godwin's words, "This is how you can do it. Now, sic 'em." This event took place in the Bahamas in late 1981.

Two other projects were just getting started. One was aimed at the "value alterators," public school teachers and literature that Moral Majority considers un-American or obscene. "Admitted, this is dangerous ground," said Godwin. But, he added, "We have not burned a single book or removed a book from a public library. We do say we have a right to say what our children are taught."

The final project had to do with "a group called the ACLU," the American Civil Liberties Union. "We've been losing to them for years—by default," he said. Moral Majority was setting up its own legal defense fund to fight whatever ACLU was for. "You know, we weren't paying too much attention to the ACLU until they started taking out full-page ads against us," he said. "Now they have our attention."

And so, Godwin concluded, "If you suffer from the blahs, join Moral Majority. We'll get you in more trouble before supper than you can say grace over."

If the humor represented here seems out of place, it seemed even more so at the time. None of it quite fit the occasion or the audience. The speakers all seemed to be straining hard to be upbeat and "with it." The result was an unfunny kind of cutting humor, of the type that was called "cruel" and "sick" in the 1950s.

Charles S. Judd, a short, jolly fellow, was the main speaker on raising money, compressing two days' lectures into two hours, he said. However, I think he would have rattled off his facts, figures, opinions, and jokes in machine-gun fashion even if he'd had more time. Like everything else the new right does, this too was calculated for effect. As a mumbler myself, I always notice the kinds of speaking techniques that hold an audience. Although Judd's words called for laughter several times, everybody was so intent on catching his next paragraph that they didn't dare interrupt with laughter. This technique also held everybody's attention to such an extent that when his text seemed to call for an audience response, it came without pause, as if the audience actually were reading the same script as the speaker. I had always wondered why carnival hucksters and auctioneers spoke so fast; hearing Judd and watching his audience, I understood that it was simply for this reason: if you were going to listen at all, you had to listen carefully.

Before everybody in the audience was seated, Judd had our attention as he moved among the first rows, using his rapid-fire technique from the beginning. "Quick, quick, I need a one, a five, a ten, who's got a twenty?"

"See how easy it is?" he said, pocketing the cash. "There, in twenty-five seconds, we raised thirty-six dollars."

As Judd opened his talk, he flashed a peculiar assortment of color slides onto a small screen behind him. The main feature of all of them was money. There was a shelf of quart jars of pickles and fruits, except for one jar full of ten- and twenty-dollar bills. There was another slide showing a formal table setting—fine linen, silver, crystal, china—with a salad bowl full of twenties and hundreds. The strangest slide of all came about halfway through the two-hour talk. "That slide doesn't mean anything," Judd explained, "I just like it." It showed a pile of pennies on top of an American flag.

From the beginning, Judd emphasized that he wasn't talking about what might be or could be or should be; he wasn't speaking about hopes and ideals, he was speaking from experience. "This is what works." Here, in his own words, are the highlights of Judd's advice on how to bring in the big bucks, regardless of your cause or candidate. I've also quoted the slides where necessary.

You start with people. There are givers and there are askers. We read about all this wealth. We're the wealthiest nation in the world and all that. There's all that money out there and we can't get any of it for our organization.

SLIDE
_____

$$\frac{42}{14} \qquad 28$$

We took a poll and asked people, "Were you ever asked to make a political contribution?" Fourteen percent said yes; 42 percent said they would have but they weren't asked. That 28-percent difference is what we're after. Those who if asked will give. The reason I got thirty-six dollars from you folks is I asked for it.

But you have to have a plan. I always quote Luke 14:28. [*He didn't, but it is: "For which of you, intending to build a tower sitteth not down first and counteth the cost, whether he have sufficient to finish it?"*] Plan your work and work your plan.

SLIDE
_____
START WITH A PLAN OR DON'T START.

Winning an election takes three things; it's like a three-legged milking stool. If you don't have three legs, you'll fall down.

One: You have to have a candidate or issues. We used to say you have to have a good candidate, but we've found out you can win anyhow.

Two: You need organization.

Three: What's the third thing you need?

AUDIENCE: **MONEY!**

Ah, music to my ears. Politics has become the largest spectator sport in America. You have 500,000 involved in the electoral process.

Raising money is like getting milk from a cow. Here's how. When you get ready to milk a cow, you don't take her up to the fence and show her a billboard and say, "Give," or plaster the pasture with posters. You don't write the cow a letter. You get personally involved.

SLIDE
---

1. Define Levels
2. Design Program
3. Project Income
4. Implement

You need to decide on the size of the contribution you're going after. Decide early whether you're going after twenty-five dollars or one thousand. You need to know about how much it's going to bring in. And you need to carry it out; it's one thing to talk about it, it's another thing to do it.

[*A slide showed a pyramid with "$1,000" at the top, with five levels down to "Under $100."*]

Are pyramids illegal in Virginia? In the old days before the election laws, you could turn that pyramid around. In jobs like mine you used to go into a phone booth and pick up a bag. The point is to have a program for people to give at one thousand, at one hundred, or under one hundred. Keep it simple. Five levels or four levels only. K-I-S-S: Keep It Simple, Stupid.

It's a basic rule as a fund raiser: Cardinal Rule Number One is, don't empathize with a contributor. Don't put yourself in their place so you make the decision whether they're going to give or not. The more you know about them, that's one thing; but don't empathize.

Cardinal Rule Number Two: Think big. Yeah, there are people who

227

can give ten thousand. If you don't have a way for people to give one thousand, you're losing big.

SLIDE _____

PROGRAMS

1. P____ to P____
2. Events
3. Direct Response

Person-to-person, peer-to-peer, people-to-people, one-to-one. That is the most personal and the cheapest and the most effective way to raise money.

For a fund-raising event, first rent a hall. Give 'em a three-dollar meal and charge 'em thirty-five. [*Our fee at the Springfield Hilton seminar.*]

Let me tell you about a very interesting dinner on the West Coast. It was a hundred fifty a plate, and you know what you got for a hundred and fifty dollars? The plate. No rubber chicken. And the best part was you didn't have to go to the dinner. The plate cost seven dollars and fifty cents.

The speaker does not sell tickets. I know all these people think if you can get Ronald Reagan or Jerry Falwell in here people will beat a path to the door. But these people aren't going to sell tickets.

Direct Response. What's that?

AUDIENCE: MAIL.

How many have gotten a fund-raising letter this week? [*The blacks were the only ones who did not raise their hands throughout this exchange.*] We call that junk mail. We don't want you to call it junk mail—you're empathizing with the contributor. You know why you get three or four of those letters a day? Because it works. It is the least costly and the most effective way to raise money.

Now, when you get ready to do that direct mail you get you somebody who can write that junk so it works.

Ten years ago, I heard about that hundred-dollar-a-plate, and I couldn't believe it; and then it was one thousand dollars a plate. *What did they eat?*

Do you know the difference in net and gross? Your net for each month should exceed what you're gonna need.

SLIDE

PEOPLE

People[1]
Give
To
People[2]

Remember this: People give to people. They don't give to letters, brochures, signs. You say, "Oh, people give to causes." Oh, no. They give to people.

Who are People Number One? Say it.

AUDIENCE: GIVERS.

Number two?

AUDIENCE: ASKERS.

[*A quick slide showed a wad of bills passing from one hand to another, and Judd said maybe it was two of the guys he used to work with.*]

SLIDE

WHY PEOPLE GIVE

1. Friendship
2. Habit
3. Reward
4. Access
5. Change Policy
6. Fear
7. Momentos [sic]

People give against, not for. And that's why you should start reading that mail you're getting. Somebody, the asker, hits their hot button. Everybody has a hot button. Who's the best person to hit a hot button, to get you stirred up? A friend.

Habit. Because it's that time again. And the United Way is the best

229

example. Boss comes around and say, "How do you like your job?" [*The audience groaned in recognition of the ploy.*] When there's a pattern established, you cash in on it.

Reward. Psychic satisfaction. Know what that means? A good feeling.

To establish access. I didn't say influence. We don't do that anymore, do we? I said access. What you appeal to here: that giver likes to think he's on a list that that candidate is going to read some day.

Change policy. The organization I used to be a part of raised $46 million because people give against, not for. We don't say we want you to give so we can provide good government, although that's what we believe in our hearts. I'm not here to try to tell you to be negative. I'm here to tell you what works.

Fear. In New Jersey they may be afraid of what happens to them if they don't give. [*Early in the session Judd had picked out four people from New Jersey as scapegoats for his banter, cashing in on yet another theme the new right uses in the hinterlands: New Jersey is New York and everybody hates New York.*]

Memento. Whether it's a lapel pin or a plaque to hang on the wall, in some fringe areas, these mean something.

But the most important one is the hot button. People give because somebody hit their hot button.

SLIDE

THE MORE YOU KNOW ABOUT YOUR CONTRIBUTOR
THE MORE SUCCESSFUL YOUR FUNDRAISING.

SLIDE

PEOPLE

w/ CLOUT
w/ Commitment
w/ Contribution
w/ No Fear
w/ P.M.A.

What kind of people make good askers? I've said that before, a lot of askers oughta be committed. The bottom line is you want to raise that money. You want them committed to your organization and no other.

Contribution. The askers have to make their own contribution first.

When you make a list of what you want them to do: Number one, make out your check; two, a list of contributors. The best asker is first a giver. If you get a lot of people on the list to sell tickets and they all buy tickets, you'll fill the hall.

How many people like to ask for money? [*Only one man raised his hand, saying, "I love it."*] I can identify with that. But I didn't used to. The best asker is not afraid to ask.

P.M.A. Positive Mental Attitude. Picture yourself being a success. If you're asked to raise five thousand dollars, then picture yourself coming back and saying to the board, "There it is." I can remember a little girl coming to the door and saying, "You don't wanta buy any candy for our band, do you?"

SLIDE
_____

1. Organize
   Plan for People

2. Deputize
   Involve People

3. Supervise
   Motivate People

[*The microphone went dead at this point.*] Okay, how far do I have to go back? What didn't you hear?

SLIDE
_____

MOTIVATION

1. Recognition
2. Communication
3. Special Treatment
4. Set Goals, Deadlines

Good askers ought to be treated like prima donnas. Some real ego food they have to have.

[*The last slide showed a little coin bank made of ten-dollar bills in the shape of a house.*] That's one of the things you can do with the money you raise. All right. Any questions?

QUESTION: What about the white socks? They told us you were going to say something about white socks.

231

No, that's the other guy, Cal Thomas. Big, tall, handsome guy. He's speaking to you tonight. He'll tell you about white socks. Any other dumb—uh, any other questions?

QUESTION: What about the group that raised $46 million? Who was that?

I was deputy finance director for the Republican Party until 1980, and before that I was working on the state level.

You had to examine the dates Charlie Judd had given for his career in order to understand that he was doing a bit of Baptist fudging again—like Jimmy Carter's claim of being a nuclear physicist and Jerry Falwell's of being an engineering student in college. Judd said he had been in the business of fund raising since 1975; then he said the organization he was with raised $46 million; then he explained that the name of that group was the Republican National Committee. But by the time he joined the committee, the election reform laws were in force and the hundred-thousand-dollar "bag drops" were a thing of the past. (After that, the same amounts would be funneled through political action committees.) Judd was thus not with the Republicans when they raised that monumental sum of cash in 1972 for Richard Nixon's reelection.

A similar bit of fudging was carried out by Cal Thomas, vice-president in charge of communications for Moral Majority. More and more, Thomas has taken the position of public spokesman for the group. When the president of Yale attacked the group, it was Thomas who said, "If I had done that kind of research for a class paper, I would have flunked the course." Again, when the first article in *Penthouse* magazine's investigation of Jerry Falwell's byzantine financial empire was published, Thomas dismissed it as poorly researched old news. (He and others in the organization became uncharacteristically silent, however, when the *Penthouse* articles continued to appear, with extensive details of Falwell's tawdry wheeling and dealing.)

Cal Thomas describes himself as a man with twenty-one years in broadcasting—seven and a half years of that with "NBC network news." To an outsider, that description might sound reasonable enough. But to one who knows the business, there is an important gap in the man's resumé. There is a distinct hierarchy among broadcast journalists; those on television make more money and have twice the prestige of those on radio. When I called the NBC bureau in Washington to find out about Thomas's days there, I was told, "He was here, but only on radio," a fact Thomas leaves it to you to find out.

Thomas did local television reporting in Houston and local radio work for NBC in Washington, where he would also do an occasional "feed" to NBC radio network news. That was his only "network" affiliation. If anyone wants to interpret his frequent references to "broadcasting" and "network news" as putting him in the company of John Chancellor, that's not Thomas's fault; he's not lying.

During the dinner preceding Thomas's speech about using the press, I was fortunate to be seated directly across from a genial white-haired gentleman named William Faulkner, Falwell's personal public-relations man. Yes, he had met the other Faulkner, "in airports; the similarity of the names and all." The other one was interested in family history and reckoned they must be related, since this one's people were from Alabama.

It was a chance for me to explain to Faulkner in front of others why I had refused to go through the kowtow of signing a decency pledge before interviewing Falwell. He cringed when I said there had been so many interviews already that I couldn't see that the man had anything new to say. Furthermore, I considered it a personal and professional affront. Falwell owed his very success to all those interviews he had given, and now he was trying to change the rules because two taped interviews of him appeared in an article alongside the naked ladies in *Penthouse.* I explained that writers—"even Faulkner"—often didn't participate in the sale of their articles to magazines and often didn't know or care where they would appear.

Seated between Faulkner and me was a Baptist preacher named John Bourne, from "wild, wonderful, almost heaven, West Virginia." Jerry Falwell normally didn't have that much time for him, according to the way he told this story, so Bourne had a friend tell Falwell that Bourne had just gotten the X rays back and it looked like "a terminal case." Falwell then said okay, he'd give him five minutes. Bourne produced an X ray that showed the ghostly outlines of his ribcage, with a Falwell "Jesus First" pin over his heart. "How'd you do that?" Falwell exclaimed. Bourne said he pinned it to his skivvy shirt. When a secretary from Moral Majority's Washington office mentioned that her husband was Polish, Bourne chimed in with another story, this one about the Pope's visit to America. They asked him what he liked most. The Polish Pope replied: "I like those M&Ms, but they sure are hard to peel."

As it came time for the speech, I could see several of the leaders of Moral Majority and other new-right groups huddled up front. Ron Godwin went back and forth to a television set in another room to report on the evening news. Howard Phillips and Paul Weyrich of The Conservative Caucus and the Committee for the Survival of a Free Congress were there to be introduced, although their speeches would come later, in another room. More than anybody else, these two men were responsible for putting together the coalition of religious and political groups that they felt had elected Ronald Reagan President. Now, it seemed to them, Reagan had betrayed the coalition. Adding insult to the President's injury was the remark by Barry Goldwater about Falwell. After a relatively brief moment of power and glory, Phillips and Weyrich had to feel somewhat like outsiders again—"right-wing kooks," as all John Birchers and their kind were in the 1960s. Standing there in their drab suits, white shirts, plain ties, and military haircuts, they looked for all the world like the pictures of the deadly intense labor organizers and Communists from the 1920s and 1930s.

Until he spoke, Cal Thomas displayed the classic good looks of an early Hollywood film idol—coal-black hair and piercing dark eyes, a neat mustache and a tall, lean body. But as he began to talk, the transformation was complete—Gary Cooper became Woody Woodpecker, or Don Adams as the smart-aleck secret agent on the old television series, "Get Smart." Thomas's rapid-fire delivery would have been comic if only he had allowed time for laughter. But we couldn't laugh at him and we couldn't laugh with him. His own humor was not merely condescending as was Godwin's and Judd's; he was downright vindictive. His was the voice of an embittered outsider, of one who had never made the team. In attacking the insiders with such feeling, he betrayed his own deepest yearning to be one of them. Although liberal New Journalists of the 1960s were his favorite targets, Thomas employed the very methods he deplored in attacking them. His sentences would run on to such length that they quite literally took his breath away.

Godwin came in from the evening news and gestured for attention. Thomas snapped: "Do you have a question, or do you have to go to the bathroom?" Godwin replied, "If I may interrupt your *half-witti-cisms . . .*" He reported that Goldwater had made the news again, and Moral Majority wasn't mentioned.

The problem with newsmen today, said Thomas, is "they all went to see *All the President's Men* and identified with Dustin Hoffman. . . . You see, in Washington they go to the same parties, live in the same world, and nobody can be invited into that world and if they get out-side that, they're lost. And, of course, if you don't dress in Brooks Brothers suits . . . and if you're religious, you qualify as a brain-trans-plant donor."

For too long, he said, conservatives and "pro-moral people" have been so busy attacking each other that they could never unite for the common cause. "Bees do not sting each other," he said with exagger-ated profundity. "If we're going to retake America, we have got to stop stinging each other. We have got to learn coalition from the liber-al Democrats. . . . They didn't care whether you crossed yourself or crossed the street. . . . And if we don't learn this lesson, we're gonna give it back to the people who've had it for the past forty years."

"How is it we've allowed others to say we're against everything?" asked Thomas. (Judd's words from the previous session came back to mind: "People give against, not for.") He lambasted George McGov-ern and all the others forming counter-groups to the new right. "That's giving liberals something to do while we're changing the coun-try. I wish George McGovern would get an honest job."

Much of what he said was predictable, but when he got into the spe-cifics of dealing with reporters and broadcasters, Thomas showed that he did, after all, have certain astute insights and perceptions about the people in the news business.

He advised his audience not to be afraid of the press. "Most of them are dumber than you are." He said they should try to meet those who are criticizing and attacking them, especially the local ministers. "If you can't convert them, you may be able to silence them." He had done this with "several of my friends in the Senate" by just arranging a meeting with Falwell, he said.

Take your local editor or station manager to lunch, he said, "or have him take you to lunch." The human contact alone would change things because "they think you're Attila the Hun. You show up and only have one head . . . they expect you to come dressed in a sheet, wearing a Nazi armband."

Thomas gave three specific examples showing where his own cooperation with reporters had paid off for his cause. He had recently been in New York and had taken a *Times* reporter out for lunch and a long talk. "That's one reporter who'll go back and know better when anybody says the Moral Majority is just a bunch of kooks."

Carl Stern of NBC television news had paid a visit to Moral Majority in Lynchburg during the time Falwell was trying to stop distribution of the issue of *Penthouse* containing the interview with him. "He came down and we had breakfast together and I had him interview Falwell. He went back and did a very fair, balanced piece." Thomas then read a letter he said had come from Stern about that visit: "Dear Cal: Many thanks for your help in the *Penthouse* matter. . . . The trip also made a convert out of me. Not to Jesus Christ, of course [here Thomas explained that Stern is Jewish], but to Jerry Falwell. I thought he was genuine and sincerely dedicated to serving his people. . . ."

And then there was "Frances FitzGerald—a very distinguished reporter, Pulitzer Prize–winning writer for *The New Yorker*, came down and did a very good piece."

The use of humor was another thing Thomas advised, although in his case it was obvious that he didn't understand the message conveyed by bitter sarcasm, as opposed to the congeniality that goes with real humor. "You can defeat them with a smile," he said, "particularly when they call you an Ayatollah or a Hitler."

This was his idea of a humorous response to such a situation: "Yes, you see, the cleaners didn't get back my sheet from the last Klan rally." One thing that angered him most about Falwell's image was the charge that he was trying to impose his ideas on other people. "People say, 'What do you do?' And I say, 'Oh, I'm in charge of forcing values down people's throats.' "

Thomas said that nearly every station or newspaper has "one responsible reporter with a religious background." He explained that they should never try to convert a particular reporter or complain to him about a particular story. If someone continues to be unfair, he said, then they should go to the editor or manager and say, "I'll talk with anybody but him."

Whenever a reporter was especially hostile about religion, Thomas said, it often had to do with a "latency" of bitter experience. He called it a "built-in religious bigotry. I want to put you down because I don't want to confront my own sinfulness." The best way to combat this, he said, was to "try to draw them out, try to confront them with their own religious background."

Finally, Thomas came to the issue of white socks, although someone in the audience brought it up. I realized then what the speakers had been working toward all day: by preparing the audience, they were humorously approaching a problem they considered very serious. By involving the audience in the joke, they were lessening the embarrassment of those who might be singled out for criticism. Thomas said in the 1960s he didn't see any liberal reporters going into William Sloan Coffin's kitchen and describing "his second braless wife" in stringy hair and flip-flop sandals. But "even Frankie FitzGerald" had felt obliged to "look for women with sprayed hair and men in polyester suits and white socks" when she wrote about conservatives.

"If you don't look the way they think you ought to look, then you're dumb. . . . I don't care how much you may love those polyester pantsuits, don't wear them. That's not an option. Don't do it. No white shoes and socks—especially in winter. No matter how much you like them. I'm serious. Take stock of your wardrobe. Some of you guys look like you got dressed in a closet with the lights off. . . . The way you look can speak volumes. . . . And go to a hairstylist—those of you who still have something to style. Sorry, fellas—no burrs and no flattops." (I counted three in the audience.)

Before staging a press conference, Thomas advised them, they should rehearse questions and answers as they would for any kind of stage show. That was what the coalition of conservative groups had done that morning when they met at the Capitol to announce their opposition to the nomination of Sandra Day O'Connor. "They got there an hour early and went through a rehearsal. Asking all the questions that might come up. The rehearsal was a disaster, but the performance was first-rate."

In the end, Thomas said, "you'll also benefit from the press's encounter with you." He said the press could be helpful to the cause, and it was important to know how other people see them. And then he quoted—complete with Scottish burr—from Robert Burns: ". . . to see ourselves as ithers see us. . . ." He didn't mention that the words referred to a louse.

16

VISITING THE FOLKS IN LYNCHBURG

. . . nothing would give me greater pleasure than to be useful to the town of Lynchburg, and to promote its prosperity. I consider it as the most interesting spot in the state. . . .

—Thomas Jefferson, October 7, 1817

Everything I had heard about Lynchburg was bad. Reporters who had been there told me it was an ugly spot with no decent places to stay or have lunch; and nobody would talk with you once you got there. In my mind, I pictured a hick town bullied by a tyrant preacher and his henchmen.

But I have rarely enjoyed proving myself wrong as much as I did on this trip. I had borrowed a fire-engine-red '68 convertible with a white top and interior, and it was springtime. From my childhood on the farm, I knew the flowers and trees along the way as intimately as I knew the two geraniums growing in the window of my city apartment. Even the car lots and trash dumps were embroidered with dogwood and redbud in the country towns I began to pass through south of the metropolis of Washington. I also began to see the faint outlines of the foothills of the Blue Ridge Mountains, my hills of home.

The Appalachians encompass the Blue Ridge to the east and the Alleghenies on the west, and end to the south of the more rugged Blacks and Smokies, where I was born. If fundamentalist America is said to have a "Bible belt" extending from North Carolina through Oklahoma, then the Appalachians could be described as the backbone of that region. In fact and fiction, out of those hills we hear of the uneducated preachers, the ignorant hillbillies. Like all stereotypes, these are based on truth, and I am painfully aware of these in particular. But I am also aware that the most extraordinary mind in American history came out of those people and that place. Thomas Jefferson was born somewhere in what is now an urban sprawl around Charlottesville, and he died in that magnificent temple to refinement and good taste on his "little mountain," from which he could survey his own idea of a university.

The road I was traveling, U.S. 29, followed roughly the same route my ancestors—out of Scotland, England, Wales, and Germany—had walked in the mid-1700s on their way south from the Quaker and Methodist meetings in Pennsylvania and Maryland, seeking cheap lands as long as they were available in the valleys, and then heading due west for greater elbow room across the mountains.

A young Quaker named John Lynch had started a ferry across a narrow point on the James River in 1757, when he was seventeen. He and his mother and his sister would remain pacifists and outspoken foes of slavery, but his brother, Charles, would become a wealthy slave owner in the next county and a military figure whose excesses gave the language the words "lynch" or "Lynch's law." Even though Lynchburg was named for the religious brother, the town is still very defensive about that term. On maps, tourist brochures, and place mats in restaurants, it is explained that the infamous lynching tree is located in another county, several miles south of Lynchburg. And furthermore, Colonel Charles Lynch didn't really hang anybody, he just ordered a bunch of Tories to be flogged thirty-nine times or until they cried "liberty forever." Whatever Lynch did under that old walnut tree, it was bad enough that the next state legislature felt it was necessary to exonerate him for it.

Although the Society of Friends itself did not endure the changing times in Lynchburg, the townspeople remain proud of their Quaker heritage. At the Quaker Memorial Presbyterian Church you will find the old graveyard preserved, and a reconstruction of the Quaker meeting house. More than one person pointed out to me that the resistance to integration in the 1960s was not nearly so violent in Lynchburg as it was everywhere else in Virginia and the South, because of this religious tradition.

The contradictions in the town's past are those you come to expect in Southern history. A public subscription bought the freedom of "Blind Billy" Armistead, a musician, and when he died he was buried in the city's white cemetery, with a tombstone showing a broken fife carved into its design. Meanwhile, in 1850, the Lynchburg Southern Rights Association was formed to prevent a slave rising, and a strict curfew was enforced at night against all blacks, free or slaves.

Roman Catholics and Jews were part of the town's population almost from the beginning. The first Catholic church was built in 1843—fifty years before the first Catholic church was erected in my hometown in North Carolina. The current state senator from Lynchburg is the Jewish owner of a furniture store whose wife has been honored for her work with B'nai B'rith. The assistant mayor of the town is black.

There has been a rare tolerance for other religions here, and also an unusually strong interest in education. According to tradition among Baptists, Thomas Jefferson became convinced that democracy could work by what he witnessed at a meeting of that denomination near Lynchburg. The town obviously took a special pride in its public schools; the high schools are set in grounds that look like college campuses. The local people had hoped that Jefferson would help to get the University of Virginia located in the town, but he favored the spot closer to Monticello, at Charlottesville, instead of near his "summer house" or "retreat" (if such a thing—from Monticello—can be imagined) near Lynchburg.

Other schools and colleges did emerge, however, and education surely employs more people in the town than any of the various industries—ranging from Fleet enemas to the color plates for *Penthouse* magazine to the factory that produced the faulty parts for the nuclear power plant at Three Mile Island, Pennsylvania. Just north of town is Sweet Briar College for women. On one of the beautifully landscaped hillsides in a nice old residential section is Randolph-Macon College, also for women. On yet another hilltop campus is Lynchburg College, a comparatively liberal school supported by the Church of Christ, or Christian Church. Out past the country club and the wealthier family estates is the Virginia Episcopal School, one of the state's best preparatory schools. Until very recent times, there was also a black Baptist seminary and college in Lynchburg, established in 1887.

As for the town itself, you behold the steep hills it's built on and wish that somehow the buildings could all be wiped off the striking geographical contours and redesigned with more respect for the remarkable beauty of the setting itself. It is not really a town, in terms of a planned community, but a whole sequence of settlements joined together at the courthouse and city hall. The central buildings are at the top of a high hill rising sharply from the river, five or six blocks, terraced in huge steps as high as some of the buildings themselves. It was all built helter-skelter—"just growed, like Topsy," as some townspeople explain. Others have an elaborate tale about the crooked roads being laid out by a drunken city council following a lost cow's trail one night. I was utterly charmed by the place and by the people I met there.

It was the week before Easter, and in a modern shopping center I found a mechanical bull being installed for the holiday weekend in a small-town version of Gilley's country-music disco in Texas. The young fellow setting up the controls for the weird-looking thrill machine sighed in mock disgust: "Friday, Saturday night, they'll all be in here—and, you know, crazy, you won't believe it, they *want* to get thrown." That night there were two broken fingers, one displaced shoulder, and two cracked ribs.

I began to ask around the bar about Jerry Falwell. Immediately, I heard what I would hear repeated throughout the town: they were sick of being described in the national media as a hick town that had never done anything but produce Jerry Falwell. "What the hell, he's a businessman," said one man. "He's given a lot of people jobs here," said another. "*I* don't have a big mansion with armed guards and a jet airplane." A young man in a business suit said he lived near Falwell's house, but he didn't go to the church or have anything to do with him. But, he said, "he's helped a lot of people. I mean, if somebody's down and out, depressed, and somebody comes along and makes 'em feel good, you can't say nothing bad about it. You can't put a price on peace of mind."

At another bar, I made friends with a tough woman bartender. You knew she'd seen some rough times, but she could still laugh about it. "I'll tell you why my kids go over there to his Sunday school," she said. " 'Cause they come after 'em in a bus and they give 'em candy." "Or hamburgers," added another customer. "Yeah, they take 'em to McDonald's. One time they even give away one of them little mopeds."

241

One of the regulars at this bar looked like an authentic cowboy, short hair, no mustache, big irregular teeth showing through an ever-present grin or smile. He wasn't grinning at anything in particular, he was amused at life itself. Oh, yes, he knew about Jerry Falwell, he'd been around him all his life. "My daddy got picked up for drunken driving and they put him in jail 'cause it was his third offense. And Momma went down there and got Jerry Falwell and he put in a call and the police let him go. I love my daddy and I don't wanta see him in jail, but you know that ain't right."

His body was lean and hard, as if the muscles had seen real work roping steers or riding the range; in fact, he had just taken care of himself. The women all gravitated to him, and he loved it. "Now you watch them two coming in there now." Two young college girls sat over near the windows, and sure enough, their eyes soon found the cowboy and he had them under his spell.

One of the women regulars stopped by to chat with my new buddy, and afterward he explained, "You know why I like that woman? Because she told me one time, 'God is what people invent to preserve their own sanity.' " I almost fell off the stool; that was not exactly what I had expected to hear in Lynchburg, much less in the part of town where Jerry Falwell had been born and reared.

My friend at the bar said, "It seems like ever' time I get involved with a woman, after about two months they all wanta drag me to church. And I tell 'em I don't want no part of any of that stuff; I just don't believe it. And you know, they just can't accept that. There was one woman, this last one I was living with, and she kept after me and kept after me until she got me to go over to Falwell's church, you know, Thomas Road. We went way down in that coliseum of a thing and we hadn't set there long until they come around taking up a collection. I put in a dollar. Well, they took that back and after a little bit they said, 'Now, we're gonna have a love offering.' So, I put in another dollar. Then they took that back and counted it and they said they didn't have enough money for that week's expenses so they were gonna pass it around again. [Other people confirmed that this frequently happens at Falwell's church.] This time I reached in and took out my two dollars, but my girlfriend said I couldn't do that and made me put it back in. Well, Falwell was saying nobody was gonna leave until they had however much money it was they needed. And I said there ain't nobody in this goddamn place strong enough to keep me from leaving. My girlfriend was a-saying, 'You can't do this, you can't do this, what'll people think, how'll I get home?' I said I didn't give a shit, she could take a taxi. And she did."

I was like Br'er Rabbit tossed back in the briar patch. These were the other voices out of my past, the real heroes, as far as I'm concerned, in that culture. They couldn't be bullied by Jerry Falwell or anybody else; theirs were the voices of common sense in the face of false piety, their humor and compassion confronting lives that were needlessly drab and stern.

At city hall, I did think I had met my first obstacle. I was curious about a tax case the city was pursuing against Falwell. There would have been no such case, I knew, if the town managers were genuinely cowed by the power of Falwell's empire. The first official I met rolled his eyes back, pulled me inside his office, and closed the door. "I wish I could tell you everything," he said, "but they've told me I can't talk about that case anymore."

Downstairs, in the city attorney's office, it was another story. William Clyde Erwin, the city attorney's bright young assistant in charge of the case, said he would tell me whatever I wanted to know. Falwell was just another citizen to them. He owned thirty-three pieces of property in the town that were not affiliated with his schools or his church, and they were either lying vacant or producing revenue, which in either case meant he should have been paying taxes on them. As Erwin explained it, a church could claim up to twenty acres as tax-exempt under Virginia laws, but anything over that was obviously not just for church use and could be taxed. Falwell had claimed that all of his property was either used for education or for religious purposes. Everybody in town knew that wasn't true.

In the clerk's office, a friendly woman helped me locate the Falwell files, 105 pages of deeds and other records. All of them involved complicated title changes whose only purpose seemed to be to enable the sellers or donors to avoid taxes somehow. The largest of these was a multimillion-dollar transaction involving a new shopping center, where the headquarters of Falwell's operations are located. As part of the purchase price, the owner deducted a huge amount to be marked off in $49,000-a-year gift installments—yearly contributions, in other words, to a tax-exempt charitable organization. This shopping center doesn't just provide office space for Moral Majority and "The Old-Time Gospel Hour"; it also includes an A&P supermarket, a huge singles bar, and other shops—all with nine-year leases with options to renew. It was clearly commercial property Falwell was trying to disguise as part of his religious operations.

This bar, by the way, had been described in a dozen different articles as if it were a redneck roadhouse. In fact, it's just like a typical big-city singles bar, only much larger. A part of every reporter's first visit to Lynchburg is a visit to this bar with Jim Price and Bill Goodman, two ordained ministers with earned doctorates of divinity who teach at Lynchburg College. With the tenacity of the young Hardy Boys, they have set up a local monitoring operation on everything that Jerry Falwell and his lieutenants do or say. A heavy percentage of everything that has been published in the outside media against Falwell has come from these two men and their archives, which are surely more complete than Falwell's own, since theirs also includes everything derogatory or damaging to him.

Goodman and Price have also published a paperback book entitled *Jerry Falwell, an Unauthorized Biography* that answers most of the questions about the man, especially the differences between what he says he is and who he really is. Is he anti-Semitic in spite of his pro-Israel pronouncements? Of course he is; they have tapes of everything he's said on the subject. Is he a racist? Of course he is; they know people who were at the organizational meeting for his first "Christian academy," which was set up specifically to avoid integration.

Either Goodman or Price tapes every Falwell broadcast and they collect everything printed or mailed out by him or Moral Majority or "The Old-Time Gospel Hour." And all of this is made available to visiting reporters and writers free of charge. They're having a good time while serving a cause of their own, as well. As Protestant Christian ministers and teachers themselves, they see what Falwell is doing as a perversion of the faith, turning trust into fear, love into hate.

A high point of any taping session is whenever Falwell speaks directly to them: "and I don't care if Mr. Goodwin or Goodman is taping this for his next book." This mispronunciation of another person's name was something I kept noticing in Falwell's sermons and speeches. The only explanation I can find for it is that it's his way of denigrating his local critics—Falwell is a household word; you, whatever your name is, are not. The implication also is that they're just too small and trifling to bother with. "But if we're really just gnats," said one of them, "why does he waste time talking about us?"

Another critic Falwell talks back to from the pulpit is a Lynchburg College instructor named Jere Real, a former writer with the *Richmond Times-Dispatch* and for columnist James J. Kilpatrick. Real, a conservative himself, has published numerous articles critical of Falwell in national magazines. He also follows up articles about Falwell in newspapers and magazines with letters of his own saying he's a conservative and he's bitterly opposed to what Falwell is doing. Real has, for example, had letters published that favor gay rights. In response to one of those, Falwell sniped at him on the air and then, his voice dripping with sarcasm, said, "That's spelled J-E-R-E."

A young woman reporter on the Lynchburg paper agreed to meet with me at a restaurant where liquor was served—ensuring that nobody from Falwell's church would see us. An intelligent and ambitious reporter, she had an eye on her career. In her hands was a daily story that was of national interest—the life of Jerry Falwell and the workings of his Moral Majority in an election year. With encouragement from her young editors, she had followed up every claim made by Falwell. He dramatically announced that all construction work was being suspended at his Liberty College until and unless enough people sent in enough money to start up again. This reporter did what any good reporter would have done. Suspecting it was just a ploy to raise more money, she visited the construction site with a photographer, and the story and pictures were published the next day, proving Falwell had lied.

One morning not long after this, she awoke to find that her garbage had been spread all over her front yard. There were anonymous phone calls to her home and office, carrying vague threats of what would happen if she didn't leave Jerry Falwell alone. She showed me just one of the letters she received. It was a death threat couched in the language of the Old Testament, but still a death threat in no uncertain terms. After some months of this, she came in to work one morning and her editor showed her a vicious six-page letter from a Falwell executive, attacking her personally and denouncing her abilities as a reporter. Nobody had ever said things like this to her. She broke down and cried. Her editor assured her he would not be pressured by Falwell's people; it would be her choice whether she stayed on that assignment or not. But she had just had enough of it and she asked for another beat.

I began to hear other stories about Falwell's bullying and about his hypocrisy. His students were forbidden to go places where alcoholic beverages were served or rock 'n' roll music was played, but he and his executives frequently dined in places where both were in evidence. When a young instructor in his college was considering a separation from his wife, he was ordered to stay married or be fired. Meanwhile, two of Falwell's top officials are divorced and have remarried. A man on his ministerial staff was arrested on sodomy charges in Lynchburg and in Knoxville, and Falwell not only disowned the man, but claimed that his salary had always come from a private foundation that Falwell had nothing to do with. One city official told me, "He tells all these kids to just come here to school and the Lord will provide. Well, the Lord provides by putting them on the federal dole. He's off making speeches against welfare, and I don't know how many of his students couldn't live without it." Falwell had a projected enrollment in the thousands at the college for 1982, but he has no medical facilities or a doctor on the staff; again, the students use public clinics—welfare, that is.

The geography of the land has provided natural enclaves for Lynchburg's clearly defined classes. The very rich live along the ridge road overlooking the river or the Blue Ridge; the middle classes live in smaller houses on lesser hillsides; the lower-income people live on the outskirts or in the cluttered valleys closer to town.

Falwell's childhood neighborhood is east of town, a working-class community of small four-room frame houses needing paint, with junked cars and useless rusted equipment in the yards. The church where he met his wife is a small tarpaper-covered building on a downtown street. His newer church is at the edge of an older downtown community with a new development of small tract houses on recently converted farmland on the other side. His house is a pretentious farmhouse on top of a hill smack in the middle of this new development. The Tara-like Greek revival portico in front and the bright blue swimming pool in back would be enough in themselves to set the house off from its neighbors, but there is also an enormous ugly dark gray concrete wall Falwell had built, completely enclosing his yard. The wall in some places has been built right up against the houses in the development. One of the neighbors told me that if you get close to the wall at night, sirens go off and spotlights come on.

In Frances FitzGerald's *New Yorker* article about Falwell, there was a puzzling mention of the architecture at the school. The author had heard that there was now a brick building there, erected since she had visited the site. What other kind of buildings could there be, I wondered, since the image that comes to mind of a college campus includes substantial buildings made either of brick or stone. Much of the fund-raising material Falwell sends out is geared toward making this school a kind of "fundamentalist Notre Dame." It was supposed to be located on "Liberty Mountain." I drove a few miles east of town to the narrow road down to the college. A young guard at the gate stopped me and put a big sign on my windshield reading "VISITOR." Presumably on instruction, this was the signal for students to salute me with "Good morning, sir," as I drove past. On the right, a short distance past the entrance, I saw a tiny white clapboard chapel, the only tasteful building on the site. It looked like what it should have been, a small country chapel. Elsewhere, there were eight or ten big metal prefabricated "Butler" buildings thrown up like the temporary base camps I had seen in Vietnam—in fact, the same structures were used in the war. They were set in the low slump between two hillocks. There was no mountain. There was no brick building. There had been no attempt to plant grass or to landscape the grounds around the buildings, which emphasized the impression of a temporary encampment.

I seemed to have arrived in Lynchburg at a turning point in the mood of the people there who don't care for what Jerry Falwell is doing. The educated people in town were fed up with the image Falwell had given them all, and they were ready to talk and agreed to my using their names. An Episcopal minister had attacked Falwell from the pulpit the previous Sunday. He had also procured one hundred "Immoral Majority" buttons from a friend of mine in Washington. Others had come up with "Jerry First" buttons to counteract Falwell's "Jesus First" pins.

I don't know whether the First Presbyterian Church deliberately sought an educated, articulate, liberal spokesman to counter Falwell's pronouncements from the other side of town, but that is exactly what they got when they hired John Killinger, an ordained Baptist minister, to be their new pastor—after he passed an examination and certification by a Presbyterian commission.

The author of twenty-five books, Killinger had been a professor of religion at Vanderbilt University for fifteen years before he accepted the call to this wealthy parish in Lynchburg. "The managers all live over here," he explained about the people who inhabit the castlelike estates surrounding the landscaped campus of his big new church building.

"I remember Falwell's coming to Nashville several years ago, giving pep talks on buses—using buses to get people to churches," he says. Falwell, of course, is opposed to "busing" when it means carrying students to integrated classes, but no child in public school in Lynchburg or Campbell County travels farther than the average student does to Falwell's own academy, where students are bused in from the surrounding counties.

Killinger said he didn't expect to have anything to do with Falwell or to say about him when he came to town. But after he got there, he felt compelled to speak out against him. He sensed, but didn't know for sure, that he was the first minister to do so. That Sunday morning, January 11, 1981, he could feel in the air that rare charge of electricity that comes when an audience is inspired by a preacher.

"Would Jesus Have Appeared on 'The Old-Time Gospel Hour'?" asked Killinger in his sermon. Regardless of what he might have thought of the show itself, he said, Jesus would have appeared on television with Jerry Falwell. After all, Jesus, "during his ministry in Galilee and Judea, appeared in some unlikely situations and interviews. He ate, for example, in the home of Simon the Pharisee, and entertained a member of the Sanhedrin, Nicodemus, at night. In an age when men were not seen speaking to women in public, even if the women were their wives, he visited the woman at the well. Another time, he scandalized everyone by going to eat in the house of Zacchaeus, a despised tax collector. . . .

"With a greater degree of probability, we can predict what Jesus' behavior would have been had he appeared on 'The Old-Time Gospel Hour.' He was an iconoclast. Always, without exception, when he was in the presence of so-called religious authorities, he flouted their traditions and expectations. 'You have heard it said,' he frequently responded to interviewers, 'but I say . . .' His thinking was original, pungent, incisive. He had a way of putting a spade under a question and turning it over, so that it smote the questioner. 'Who made me a judge over you?' he asked a man seeking his aid in a poorly distributed inheritance. 'You cleanse the outside of the cup,' he said to the Pharisees, 'until it sparkles; but inside you are filthy and diseased.' "

And then Killinger delivered the sermon he felt Jesus would have spoken to Jerry Falwell and his followers: "You appear to be very religious, before your television audience. But inside, you are rapacious, unconverted wolves, seeking a greater share of the evangelical TV market, without really caring for the sheep you devour.

"You take money from widows and children, promising the blessings of God; it is the blessings of God you take from them, only to build an empire.

"You have a college where you pretend to free young men and women from the bondage of ignorance. What you really do is indenture them to platitudes and prejudices darker than their ignorance ever was. You make them twice the sons and daughters of hell they were when they came to you.

"You speak glowingly of the great numbers of people in your Sunday school, your services, and your extended programs. It is better to be right with ten persons than it is to be wrong with tens of thousands.

"You talk of legislating morality as if the Father had given you the franchise on morality and you knew precisely what it is. You hypocrites! Have you not heard that it is immoral to decide for others what they shall read and not read?"

In three different broadcasts, Falwell claimed that people from Killinger's church had called him to apologize for this sermon. But nobody said a word to Killinger himself, except in congratulations and heartfelt thanks. There were hundreds of requests for printed copies of the sermon. I asked Killinger why he thought Falwell felt he had to answer everybody who criticized him. He said it had to be Falwell's insecurity coming to the surface. "He's pedaling awfully fast . . . he knows one of these days his empire is going to collapse and smother him."

On March 15, 1981, not long before I arrived in Lynchburg, Killinger had delivered another attack on Falwell, this one entitled "Could Jesus Belong to the Moral Majority?" In it he said, "The tragedy for the church, when it becomes identified with morality, is that then it unwittingly broadcasts the opposite of Jesus' message that God receives sinners. . . . At its center, most of Jesus' conflict with the Pharisees was over this very issue. They contended that God was the God of the righteous. And Jesus told all those parables whose single point was that God loves the unrighteous. . . .

"If Jesus were to show up at a Moral Majority rally—and who is to say he doesn't?—the persons he would really identify with would be the ones under attack, not the promoters of the rally. If you need a biblical paradigm for that, consider the story of the woman taken in adultery (John 8:1–11). Her proudly moralistic accusers thrust her into the presence of Jesus and announced that she had been caught in the very act of adultery. Did they think he would take their side? He didn't. With his rapier-sharp wit he drove off the priggish accusers, then tenderly forgave the woman's error and sent her away. . . . We are not called to be a society of gimlet-eyed critics, passing judgment on the morality or immorality of the world around us. We are called to be a community of love and forgiveness, where our meeting with the exalted Christ causes each one of us to fall down and cry, 'Lord, be merciful to me, a sinner.' It is from that vantage point and that vantage point only—on our face—that we begin to discover the inner nature of true morality."

That Easter dawn found me easing up to the little gathering in front of the Methodist Church in the heart of old Lynchburg.

I was moved by the scene itself. There were maybe as many as 250 people, black and white, old and young. According to a little mimeographed program, they came from Baptist, Methodist, Catholic, Unitarian, Episcopal, and Presbyterian congregations. A public meeting of blacks and whites, even for religious purposes, would have been illegal in this place, as it was in my hometown and throughout the South, just twenty years earlier.

The Salvation Army was represented by a band of two trombones, four French horns, and four cornets. Their renditions of the traditional Easter hymns were a bit ragged, but all the more effective because of that. "The Lord is risen," intoned one of the ministers. "The Lord is risen indeed," responded the crowd. I moved from behind a hedge and joined the worshipers in singing a lovely popular song by Cat Stevens, "Morning Has Broken." It seemed well suited to the occasion, and everybody knew the words. The story of the Resurrection was then read back and forth, minister and people, until the point where Jesus returns from the dead and tells the faithful, "Peace be with you."

A black minister named Phillip Terrell delivered the sermon "The Steadfast Majority." It was a sometimes incoherent jumble of sentences about sincerity and being good and being moral and what it all means in the end. He said something about "the macho aspect of Jesus," something else about how "Napoleon was sincere in his desire to unite Europe." He said Jesus could have had the most successful electronic evangelistic career he wanted, and the richest mail-order business too, if he had wanted that. But he didn't. Jesus had said, "I come not to save the righteous, but to save that which is lost."

Terrell's voice gradually rose, louder and stronger, as he reached his point and a dynamic proclamation: *"The world don't need no Moral Majority."* Few moments in my life have struck me as this one did. A spontaneous "Amen!" broke from the crowd in a shout. I turned to see if the white folks were joining in as another "Amen!" resounded. They were. I choked back the tears of appreciation for the people of my homeland who can endure such bitter contradictions—in Jerry Falwell's claims and in their faith—with dignity.

Terrell calmed his voice to a whisper as he concluded: "Remember before the church became a political institution? Before we started holding political rallies, we used to stand for Jesus. Can you remember that?

"I barely can. God bless you. Amen. Amen."

The band struck up one final rousing hymn, "Christ the Lord Is Risen Today . . . Alleluia." The members of the band struggled nobly with those *alleluias*, and so did we. I was as off-key and out-of-timing as a couple of the French horns (and I missed my tambourine), but it felt good singing out. For the moment, I was proud of being one of them—being myself, white, Southern, Christian.

I had just enough time for breakfast before the early service at Jerry Falwell's Thomas Road Baptist Church.

I opened the doors of the church and stood frozen in amazement at the noisy scene in front of me. This was not the simple foyer where one pauses before entering the quiet sanctuary of God. This was the busy, crowded lobby of a hotel during a political convention. To my right were head-high stacks of the latest issue of *Moral Majority Report*. Next to that were booths for various fund-raising drives. To my left was another booth, where Liberty College ties were being hawked for six dollars each.

Inside, the auditorium was color-coordinated shades of pale blue. It was spacious and cool, like a television studio—which, of course, it is. The cameras are concealed in an overhanging balcony, and one of them (I would see on a broadcast later) is equipped with a wide-angle lens to make the place seem even larger than it is. The setting was cold and sterile. The people crowding in came with little or no reverence, and quieted only when the service actually began.

At stage right were a grand piano and an electric piano; on the opposite side was a big, circuslike organ. No special decorations had been arranged for this holiest, most festive of Christian feast days. There were no Easter lilies, no live flowers at all. The only floral offering was a dried arrangement of brown and blue (matching the carpet) on a small cross in front of the central podium or pulpit.

On signal, the organist bounced in as if for a game show, took his seat, and started playing in one smooth motion. The choir marched in, also in quick-time, from both sides. They sang "He Lives," and at the first note of the second verse, Falwell himself emerged from a hidden doorway behind the choir and bounded down the steps to his throne at one side of the pulpit.

The choir and congregation then joined in singing another hymn, "Christ the Lord Is Risen Today . . . Alleluia." It was a smooth, professional performance. Unlike us amateurs, attempting the same hymn at the service downtown, they got all their *alleluias* just right. But Falwell turned to them and snapped out his first words of Easter morning: "By next Easter we'll know that one by heart, won't we, choir?" He sounded like a game-show host.

Another vocal selection was then called for by a bright-faced group of young people from the college, called the SMITE Singers. "Come on up here," said Falwell. "What is it? The Smite? Or Schmidt? Or is it Smut Singers?" ("SMITE" is an acronym for Falwell's "Student Missionary Intern Training for Evangelism.") What manner of man, I had to ask myself, would think such snide remarks were suitable for a holy service and addressed to young students at his college, who had doubtless worked long hours to prepare for the moment. I knew the answer, but I hadn't expected to have my opinion confirmed by the man himself so quickly. There were no instruments backing up this group from the college, but suddenly the whole place was filled with sound—big-band sounds getting louder and louder and more spirited. (Recordings of this kind of backup music are now being marketed in churches throughout the country.)

Falwell had a long list of announcements about the church's winning ball teams and track teams and about which television shows he'd been on and would be on next week. He said he'd be on the Easter broadcast of "Face the Nation." It was, he said, "a wonderful opportunity to talk about Easter, to spread the gospel." (I watched that broadcast and sure enough, Falwell was simply given a microphone to say whatever he wanted to say, with no interruptions about the truth of his statements or his validity as a spokesman.)

His sermon was a simpleminded, disconnected string of thoughts and quotations. "Christ died upon the cross for all your sins, although you weren't even born yet. I heard Oliver Green—an evangelist now in heaven for some time—say that the resurrection of Jesus Christ was the greatest bombshell ever to explode on an unbelieving world.

". . . Every so often, I hear anti-Semitics [sic] saying that the Jews were Christ-killers. That isn't true. You and I are Christ-killers. You helped nail God to the cross. We are all sinners deserving of hell."

He announced that he would be staging "I Love America" rallies the coming week in Wyoming and Colorado. "We fully expect to have to have security officers there to keep us alive. . . . The controversy is not between conservatives and liberals but between Christ and Satan. . . . If Jesus Christ is not risen from the dead, then forgiveness of sin is impossible. . . . If this is all there is, then we're in trouble. Thank God there's coming a day when it will all be good news."

The sermon was punctuated every now and then by a solemn "amen" from the audience—not that heartfelt, spontaneous "so be it" or "hosannah" or "hoorah" I had heard at the other service, but an uncommonly cold use of the word. It was as if the word had nothing to do with what had just been said or how the crowd felt; they seemed to be responding automatically, as if a television studio "applause" sign were cueing them.

The congregation here was also markedly different from the other. Although Falwell's assistant, Cal Thomas, has said that 17 percent of the church's membership is black, he must have drawn that figure from thin air. There was one young black man in the youth choir; there was one other black man in the audience.

Falwell said that morning, "The trumpet may sound before the church is out." In heaven, he said, "we'll all be thirty-three . . . perfect bodies; no more pain or suffering . . . no more dying, no more sickness. God himself will wipe away all our tears and there'll be no more lying."

This was a lead-in to the moment of confrontation, when everybody is asked a sequence of questions until finally all hands have been raised, either by the saved or the unsaved. With every head bowed, nobody looking, nobody leaving, the words, like a primitive intonation of doom, sounded from my past. "If you died right now," asked Falwell, "how many would not go to heaven?" A small number of hands went up. "God bless you," he congratulated them. "You may take your hands down now." The electric piano and the organ teamed up as background, with the choir singing softly as the members of the congregation were invited to come on down and rededicate their lives to Christ. The first "invitational" was "Have Thine Own Way Lord"; the second one was the more common hymn used at this time: "Just as I am without one plea . . . O Lamb of God, I come, ahhhhhh come."

It was an eerie spectacle that didn't remind me so much of anything in my own past. I couldn't help but think of those tapes of Jim Jones coldly exhorting his followers in Guyana. Falwell was the tough-talking sergeant, marshaling his recruits. "If you meant it," he charged, those who raised their hands should come on down. "If you need counseling, if you're headed for the divorce courts . . ." One young man was led down by his wife; others stood stiffly while "faith partners" came up and stood beside them.

"Counselors, go right to the prayer rooms, please. Keep on singing, please. [He said "please" as a command.] Just come and stand right here—someone will be with you in a minute. We need six or eight soul-miners downstairs. Right now.

"It's harvest time—oh, it is. For many of you it may be the last one. We don't want anybody to go to hell who came to church at Thomas Road at Easter."

As promptly as it had begun, the stage was cleared and the service was over. The odd thing was that I didn't feel outrage, frustration, or anger over this travesty of an Easter celebration; I didn't feel anything at all. The people around me didn't seem joyful or happy, as I remembered they had on Easter mornings when I was a child. I had the sudden realization that these people knew as well as I did that they had participated in an empty, hollow experience. And yet they did it. Why? To be friends with the bully? To be a part of the biggest, the best, the thing everybody's talking about, the only church in town on national television? Whatever the answers, I only knew I wanted to get out of that cold place. At the doors to the lobby, we were met by a surging crowd of people shoving to get the best seats for the next service. There was one frail old woman, frantically clawing the air as if she were in water, like some demented boxing fan ready to kill for a good seat at a championship bout. The carnival booths were in full swing now: ties for six dollars . . . read the *Moral Majority Report* . . . join the Women's Crusade for . . .

I repressed a messianic impulse to drive the money-changers from their stalls and to tell the people there was no God inside but Mammon. But I knew this was no temple of God. And I am no Preacher Sam.

Nobody I met in Lynchburg had ever been the few miles southwest of town to see Poplar Forest, the seat of a ten-thousand-acre estate that Thomas Jefferson owned through his wife's inheritance. Somebody mentioned the name of a contractor who was supposed to be restoring the house, but nobody seemed to know precisely where it was.

I found the state historical marker turned so that I had to park my car and get out to read it. "A mile and a half south is Poplar Forest, Thomas Jefferson's Bedford [County] Estate. He came here in June, 1781, after his term of governor expired, and while here was thrown from a horse and injured. During his recovery he wrote his 'Notes on Virginia.' " These "Notes," first published in French, in answer to a long list of questions about America, contain as clear and sensible a view of religion in America as has ever been written.*

But there was no sign of a road south from the marker. I took off west, crossing a precarious-looking little wooden bridge over some railroad tracks. I wound around back in the general direction that was more west than south, but there were no other roads to take. Finally, I spotted an old black woman putting down her grocery bags to open the picket-fence gate in front of a neat frame cottage that looked as though it had been right there since before the Civil War, if not the Revolution. "Excuse me," I said, reverting to an accent I lose in the city, "could you tell me where Thomas Jefferson's house is?" She threw back her head and laughed. "They law. You know, I lived around here sixty-five years and I'd never seen that. So I went over there the other day and tried to find it and you know something? I got lost."

In other words, you couldn't hardly get there from here, but you could see it if you were up in that big oak tree a ways. The reason you couldn't get there was the layout of another of those suburban devel-

*The essay is included as Appendix G of this book.

opments, this one with roads plotted in an obstacle course so nobody could go straight through. I spotted a young father walking his dog and little boy in front of one of the fresh new lawns and houses, and asked him. "Oh," he smiled, "you can't miss it. Go down there and turn at the recreation center." Actually, he said, it was straight through a clump of trees behind his house; he didn't know why the roads were laid out that way.

"Own a Part of History," proclaimed a huge billboard advertising lots in the development. There was a cheaply built recreation center, and spreading out from it was the golf course. Some of the houses were fairly well-built brick veneer, with two- and three-acre lawns, but as I got closer to the house Thomas Jefferson had built, I saw down at the edge of his old lawn two rows of cheap little brick tract houses that looked as fragile as cardboard.

There were no guards, no signs saying "Keep Out," and no fences. I parked my car and walked up the driveway. It was sacred ground to me.

There was no question that the ancient poplars in the back were from Jefferson's time. A recent windstorm had trimmed off the brittle dead branches, and a young black man was gathering them off the lawn. The boxwoods flanking the formal carriage entrance were thirty or forty feet high, meaning these slow-growing shrubs may well have been put there by Jefferson himself. And there was the house itself, as solid as a rock, its thick brick walls as sturdy as a fortress.

Jefferson had so despised everything English that he had turned against the plain but then-stylish "Georgian" architecture of colonial times and had introduced the classical style of Palladio to America. This house appeared to be an enlarged reproduction of the central portion of Monticello, the same octagonal shape, similar Greek Revival porticos in back and front. Inside, the plaster walls and flooring appeared to be in good shape, but there was no evidence anywhere that the place had been given the respect or reverence it deserved. The lawns were unkempt and overgrown, the shrubs and trees had been let go without trimming.

I walked past the remains of an herb garden beside the old kitchen buildings, and then down to an enclosure that must have outlined a formal garden at one time. Beyond it was a Hollywood-starlet, kidney-shaped swimming pool. Beyond that were the new houses.

Walking back up toward the big house, I wondered about two narrow little structures lined up with the house, about seventy-five yards out from either side. They looked like British sentry boxes, but that couldn't have been their real use. In many years of searching through old plantation houses and grounds, I'd never seen anything like them.

They were small replicas of the house itself; thick brick walls in octagon shape, both topped by domed copper roofs. I stepped up to the door of one of them, walked in, and collapsed in laughter. The heavy oak timbers were in good shape above, and so were those that formed the ledges with the holes in them on either side where four could be seated comfortably. Thomas Jefferson's crappers had endured. Like everything else he built, they simply had more substance than anything around them.

PART FIVE

17

TURNING POINTS

While there may be no sign of another Enlightenment of the kind that produced a Thomas Jefferson, there has been a growing chorus of important voices raised in opposition to the threats posed by the new right.

As early as March 1, 1978, Thomas J. McIntyre of New Hampshire told his Senate colleagues about "the desperate need for people of conscience and good will to stand up and face down the bully boys of the radical new right before the politics of intimidation does to America what it has tried to do to New Hampshire. . . . If you want to see the reputations of decent people sullied, stand aside and be silent. If you want to see people of dignity, integrity, and self-respect refuse to seek public office for fear of what might be conjured or dredged up to attack them or their families, stand aside and be silent. . . . If you want to see the fevered exploitation of a handful of highly emotional issues distract the nation from problems of great consequence, stand aside and be silent. . . . In the long run . . . I am confident that the forces of decency and civility will prevail over the politics of intimidation . . ."*

Eight months and six days after this speech, McIntyre, a native of New Hampshire seeking his fourth term in the Senate, fell victim to the forces he decried. A copilot for Allegheny Airlines named Gordon

---

*Further excerpts from this speech are reprinted in Appendix C.

Humphrey won the seat, although he had lived in New Hampshire only four years and his only political experience was serving as a field coordinator for The Conservative Caucus.

Nearly every major liberal candidate defeated by the new right in 1980 has since set up a national organization of some sort to fight them, but most seem too little too late, using the same tired techniques that led to defeat in the first place. The one new organization that has sparked real hope in liberal circles is television producer Norman Lear's People for the American Way. It is staffed by a talented group of young people as dedicated and energetic as any I saw on the right. In no time at all, Marcie Rickun has assembled a major collection of clippings, books, and original source material on the new right, which is used every day by writers, reporters, and broadcast people from throughout the world. With the avidity of a Civil War buff, she seizes on every new piece of evidence any visiting writer might have, and copies it for her own files. Frances Zwenig, meanwhile, fully matches any of her public relations counterparts in the right-wing groups, and surpasses them with a wit and humor that the right seems incapable of mustering.

The most effective tool Lear has, of course, is television itself. He assembled a sequence of public-service commercials using stars such as Muhammad Ali and Carol Burnett, who talk about being different and respecting those differences, which is the "American Way." The message is getting through, I know, because I hear the howls of reaction to everything Lear does in the new right's own broadcasts and their publications. None of the other new liberal groups is troublesome enough for them to respond to. Since the name sounds like something the right might have invented, the right avoids using it at all costs.

The most devastating weapon Lear's group possesses is used only for presentations to small liberal groups, although I would hope that they have some plan to show it to wider audiences. It is simply a sequence of actual film clips of right-wing training sessions, showing the same people I quote in this book, in action and using their most candid—and frightening—language.

But if all but one of the new liberal groups seem ineffective to me, I should add that some of the older groups have come back to life with strength and vigor I haven't seen in them since the most active days of the civil rights movement in the 1960s. B'nai B'rith's Anti-Defamation League and the American Civil Liberties Union are suddenly facing real enemies again. The number of anti-Semitic incidents doubled in the first year of the new right's rise to power, 1980–81. The Anti-Defamation League was there—as in the old days—with facts and figures and eloquent statments against such outrages.

The ACLU has been especially effective in its fund-raising drives and legal actions regarding anti-evolution suits and other causes being sponsored by Moral Majority. Borrowing tactics used by the right (which they borrowed from the old left), the ACLU has also been staging training seminars throughout the country so that liberal leaders can know their enemies and know what to do in the face of their actions.

There has been much talk about the "new liberal" in Washington after an *Esquire* article focused on a small number of young congressmen who are less concerned with traditional liberal issues and more concerned about issues that affect the economy and national defense. To borrow a phrase from the right's Robert Bauman, these people sound like Republicans in drag to me.

Edward Kennedy, meanwhile, has provided a consistent voice against the excesses of the new right. In particular, Kennedy has urged Democrats not to be defensive in the face of right-wing successes: "I am convinced that the answer to the problems of progressives is not for us to pretend that somehow we can join the other side . . . we cannot permit the gains of a generation to be set aside by the agents of special privilege. We must not permit our principles to be swept aside by the negativism of the new right—or by those who dare to call themselves the Moral Majority. As Democrats, we must be something more than just warmed-over Republicans. Let us resolve that we will not run from great political convictions for the convenience of the hour."

Leaders of the academic community have been understandably slow to raise their voices. The threat to freedom, I'm sure they feel, must be a real one before they have a legitimate cause to involve themselves in politics. From a more practical standpoint, their schools depend on the goodwill and generosity of many of the same men and organizations and corporations that created and sustain the new right.

The most eloquent statement against the new right came from the president of Yale University, alma mater of William F. Buckley, Jr.; new-right evangelist Pat Robertson; and Medford Evans, Sr., editor and author with the John Birch Society, for H. L. Hunt, and the Citizens' Councils of America.

On August 31, 1981, A. Bartlett Giamatti welcomed the freshman class to Yale with a forceful oration on what he sees as a very real threat to freedoms, academic and otherwise, in this country.*

> . . . A self-proclaimed "Moral Majority," and its satellite or client groups, cunning in the use of a native blend of old intimidation and new technology, threaten the values I have named. Angry at change, rigid in the application of chauvinistic slogans, absolutistic in morality, they threaten through political pressure or public denunciation whoever dares to disagree with their authoritarian positions. Using television, direct mail, and economic boycott, they would sweep before them anyone who holds a different opinion.
>
> From the maw of this "morality" come those who presume to know what justice for all is; come those who presume to know which books are fit to read, which television programs are fit to watch, which textbooks will serve for all the young; come spilling those who presume to know what God alone knows, which is when human life begins. From the maw of this "morality" rise the tax-exempt Savonarolas who believe they, and they alone, possess the truth. There is no debate, no discussion, no dissent. They know. There is only one set of overarching political and spiritual and social beliefs; whatever view does not conform to these views is by definition relativistic, negative, secular, immoral, against the family, anti–free enterprise, un-American. What nonsense. What dangerous, malicious nonsense. . . . I do not fear that these peddlers of coercion will eventually triumph. The American people are too decent, too generous, too practical about their principles to put up with the absolutism of these "majorities" for very long. . . . The "Moral Majority" is a cry of exhaustion, a longing for surcease from the strain of managing complexity.
>
> Those voices of coercion speak not for liberty but for license, the license to divide in the name of patriotism, the license to deny in the name of Christianity. And they have licensed a new meanness of spirit in our land, a resurgent big-

*The full text of this speech is reprinted in Appendix E.

otry that manifests itself in racist and discriminatory postures; in threats of political retaliation; in injunctions to censorship; in acts of violence. . . .

We must, therefore, civilly and clearly have the courage to reject bigotry and coercion in all forms and have the courage to embrace the intellectual and human diversity of our community and our country. We cannot as Americans succumb to the fatigue, the arrogance mixed with exhaustion, that claims an exclusive "morality" and that negates and denies. To do so would be to betray at the deepest levels what a free people have won, through struggle and pain, over three centuries.

A month after this speech at Yale, the president of Georgetown University, Timothy S. Healy, a member of the Roman Catholic Society of Jesus, raised his voice in a plea for reason and tolerance:

"America is in a rancorous mood these days, and our meanness tracks not escalating interest rates, but a sinking Dow Jones. In the United States such narrowing moods, such bouts of meanness have been recurrent. We deny our generosity, we constrict what used to be called in high rhetoric the 'bowels of compassion,' we pull away from the imperatives of our own history. These moods have found different names: 'Nativism,' 'Know-Nothingism,' 'America First,' 'the Ku Klux Klan,' 'McCarthyism.' Now we have the new righteousness and its prophet, 'the Moral Majority.'

"We are caught in a depression of the soul, a denial of our own powers, a betrayal of our historic instinct, a national change of mind and sagging of spirit far beyond the periphera of politics. No one administration, no one President, no one Congress can make us abandon cities, neglect the poor, the unemployed, and the aged, withdraw our support from children, students, and research at home, and lead us to bed down with tyrants and torturers abroad. It is we ourselves, most of us Americans, who go along, approve, and applaud this souring of self and society."

But, Healy warned: "The new righteousness runs counter to Western religion in three serious ways. First of all, unlike either Judaism or Christianity, it is anti-intellectual and simplistic. Chesterton makes Father Brown remark, 'To downgrade the human mind is bad theology.' Neither life nor faith yields to any quick and easy formula. The

Bible and the revelation of which it is a part, as well as the long history of synagogue and church have not ever pretended to solve all problems. ... If we stretch any revelation to cover items like treaties with Taiwan, and the Panama Canal, we make a mad world where the things of God and the things of man are confused. That will ultimately put the city of God and the city of man to a war in which both lose.

"More frightening than anti-intellectualism or oversimplification in the new righteousness is the moral pose of its political jeremiads. Its voice is the voice of hatred; its stand is against rather than for; it revels in a rhetoric of condemnation; its masterwork is political assassination. Ultimately, in this republic, these are the seeds of its death. The fairness of the American people will bring it down. Whether hatred comes wrapped in white sheets or the scriptures, it is still a denial of man and his works."

Perhaps, Healy was unaware of the prevalence of Roman Catholics in the new right or what he calls the "new righteousness." About midway through his speech, he stopped and said as an aside that the Moral Majority did not include him (as a Roman Catholic) when it referred to Christians.

Other Roman Catholics, however, are showing a growing concern over the number of their own faith involved in right-wing politics, and also with the direction the church's hierarchy in America seems to be taking on most of the major issues. Patrick J. Leahy, a Democratic senator from Vermont, wrote in an opinion-page article in *The Washington Post* of March 8, 1981:

During the past two years, the Catholic Church in the United States and extremely conservative Christian evangelical groups like the Moral Majority have formed a de facto political alliance. That alliance will ultimately benefit right-wing goals while diminishing many of the positive gains in justice, compassion, and human dignity made with the help of the Catholic Church during the past few decades. Many of the Catholic laity—myself included—are increasingly concerned that the church we love is being used in a dangerous way.

Throughout this century, the Catholic Church has been in the forefront of efforts to improve health care, strengthen civil rights laws, provide fair and decent housing, ensure safe working conditions and adequate wages, and guarantee religious tolerance.

The Catholic Church has also maintained steadfast opposition to abortion. Instructing its membership on the moral issues of abortion is the church's right and, many would say, its duty. The church, however, has done more than instruct. It has also sought legal strictures on abortions. In moving from the moral to the political arena, the church has allied itself with those who would turn aside nearly all that the Catholic leadership and laity have stood for in this century.

As a result of this alliance, the "pro-life" movement has become a stalking horse for the right. In a sincere belief in the respect for human life, many Catholics have been manipulated by far-right political action groups that run counter to the social teachings of the church. . . .

I'm sure all these speeches and statements have had an important cumulative effect, but they still reached only a small number of people, who happened to be sitting in an audience or to read them in the newspapers. Most of those who heard these criticisms already agreed with them.

But few Americans who watch television or read newspapers were unaware of the simple sentence that provided what I see as a crucial turning point against Moral Majority in particular and the new right in general. More important than the sentence itself was the fact that it was delivered by none other than Mr. Conservative himself, Barry M. Goldwater.

The senator from Arizona had proudly pushed for the nomination of Sandra Day O'Connor from his home state as the first woman Supreme Court justice. The President had announced this nomination on a Monday morning, and the new right immediately swung into action against it because of O'Connor's earlier support of legalized abortions while a member of the Arizona legislature.

Goldwater flew into Andrews Air Force base in Washington the next night, and there was a small group of reporters waiting to record his reaction to the nomination. He said how proud he was of O'Connor and how pleased he was that the President had nominated such a highly qualified person. The press conference had ended and all but one of the reporters had left when Allan Frank of the *Washington Star* approached Goldwater with one last question. What did the senator think about Jerry Falwell's statement that all good Christians should be against O'Connor's nomination?

"I think every good Christian ought to kick Jerry Falwell's ass," said the senator. Nobody before had voiced such blunt outrage in such earthy American idiom, and nobody could have said it with such effect as this man from within the right's own ranks. The Falwell forces were still reeling from the blow the next day when I joined them for a seminar in Springfield, Virginia. In many important ways, I don't think they will ever recover from it.

Throughout the days that followed that outburst, Goldwater was relatively quiet about O'Connor's enemies on the right. But the day after her nomination was confirmed, he entered an eloquent speech, "To Be a Conservative" into the record of the U.S. Senate.* It traced his own history from twenty years ago, when he was regarded as a reactionary, until now, when so many of his thoughts prevail that many people regard him as a visionary. In politics, as in life, he said, there can be no absolutes; every person and his or her opinions must at least be considered.

However, on religious issues there can be little or no compromise. There is no position on which people are so immovable as their religious beliefs. There is no more powerful ally one can claim in a debate than Jesus Christ, or God, or Allah, or whatever one calls his supreme being.

But, like any powerful weapon, the use of God's name on one's behalf should be used sparingly.

The religious factions that are growing throughout our land are not using their religious clout with wisdom. They are trying to force government leaders into following their positions 100 percent. If you disagree with these religious groups on any particular moral issue, they cajole, they complain, they threaten you with loss of money or votes or both. . . .

I'm frankly sick and tired of the political preachers across this country telling me as a citizen that if I want to be a moral

*The full text of this speech is reprinted in Appendix D.

person, I must believe in "A," "B," "C," and "D." Just who do they think they are? And from where do they presume to claim the right to dictate their moral beliefs to me? And I am even more angry as a legislator who must endure the threats of every religious group who thinks it has some God-granted right to control my vote on every roll call in the Senate. I am warning them today: I will fight them every step of the way if they try to dictate their moral convictions to all Americans in the name of "conservatism."

If the new right regards Goldwater as its father, as Richard A. Viguerie states in his book, *The New Right: We're Ready to Lead*, it is obvious that Goldwater himself does not recognize them as his legitimate offspring. His words also remind me that it was possibly unfair to lump together all conservatives with the radicals and extremists who came to the forefront during the 1980 campaign. However, the more reasonable conservatives themselves did nothing during that time to focus attention on divergent opinions in their ranks. They saw the chance for a real conservative victory for the first time, and they weren't saying no to anybody's vote.

In the aftermath, however, a number of voices were raised long before Goldwater's to indicate that there were important differences between the religious right and the overall conservative movement. My source for the statistics to prove this point about diversity among conservatives was a man named Robert Boege, 32, president of the National Conservative Foundation. Boege (pronounced "berga") was a college classmate and friend of NCPAC's Terry Dolan, who hired him in the summer of 1981 to head the foundation.

Dressed in conservative three-piece suits, Boege wears his dark auburn hair short on top, and a neatly trimmed mustache. He comes across as stiff and restrained in his fund-raising pitches and in his brief introduction of Dolan as the host of the group's weekly television talk show. But, in person, I found him to be unusually candid in his own opinions and genuinely concerned about what I and others might think of them. He said I should allow for other ways of solving the problems in society that I wanted solved by liberal means.

About a week after I interviewed Boege, he called me at home one night just to talk. He said he had found some opinion polls that he wanted to share with me. They proved his point about the diversity of conservatives.

An article in the February/March, 1981, issue of *Public Opinion* included these paragraphs:

> The General Social Surveys conducted by the National Opinion Research Center (NORC) show a slight increase since the mid-1970s in the number of self-described conservatives. Gallup, on the other hand, has found conservative ranks declining slightly over this period. While contrasting question wording accounts for some of these differences, the prime factor is the mushiness of the categories themselves. Most people just are not conservatives or liberals in any wide-ranging ideological sense. When the reality is soft, measures of it necessarily vary greatly.
>
> Within the general public, people who call themselves conservatives are consistently more likely to take conservative stands on various issues—but not that much more likely. Take the question of an amendment to the Constitution to permit prayers in the public schools as an example. In late March 1980, 87 percent of conservatives favored an amendment, but so did 77 percent of liberals. Affirmative action on behalf of jobs for blacks was endorsed by 76 percent of liberals in early 1980; it was also backed by a substantial majority, 61 percent, of conservatives. A Constitutional amendment banning abortion was *opposed* in August 1980 by 72 percent of self-labeled liberals—but it was opposed, too, by 57 percent of conservatives.

The next issue of *Public Opinion*, which Boege also sent me, contained an even more definitive poll by George Gallup, Jr., which further delineated the religious right from mainline conservatives. Gallup referred to polls he had done for *Christianity Today*, which showed that barely 20 percent of Americans could be described as born-again evangelical Christian; only 23 percent of all Americans considered themselves part of the "New Christian Right."

With specific reference to the Moral Majority, Gallup found that less than half of his national poll sample (40 percent) even knew about the group when the poll was taken in late November of 1980. Only 26 percent of those surveyed were familiar with the goals of Moral Majority; only 8 percent approved of these goals, and 13 percent disapproved.

When the numbers were all in, it was obvious that there was no "moral majority" in America in any sense of that phrase. And if there was a "religious right," it was hardly the cohesive block its leaders claimed it to be. The political preachers had boasted of a constituency of more than fifty million at the Republican National Convention in 1980. Jerry Falwell apparently told Richard Viguerie that his "Old-Time Gospel Hour" had fifteen million viewers, since Viguerie uses that figure in his book. The Nielsen and Arbitron ratings showed that his audience was never more than 1.5 million—and furthermore, that audience had dropped by 16 percent during the period of his greatest visibility and seeming power, the year between mid-1980 and mid-1981. Whatever their actual numbers, the "moral majority" hasn't been able to deliver. In the most important elections since the regular election of 1980, conservative Republicans have been beaten in almost every case. After Republican Marshall Coleman, with Jerry Falwell's last-minute blessing, lost the Virginia gubernatorial campaign, the word—according to *Newsweek*—came down from the President and other Republican and new-right leaders: Falwell and his kind were the kiss of death. The new-right operators can be faulted for many things, but they do know how to count.

One man who was never impressed by the religious right's boasts of untold numbers of supporters or fearful of their threats to would-be opponents was Senator Mark Hatfield of Oregon. I sought out Hatfield by reporter's instinct, knowing that his career bridged several gaps in the story. Mainly, I was puzzled by Hatfield's public defense of Jerry Falwell when everything I had ever heard about Hatfield indicated he was a liberal who should have loathed Falwell and everything he was trying to do.

Having never covered politics in Washington, I had no idea why Mark Hatfield's assistant was so petulant when I asked for an interview and expected to have it within a matter of days. "Listen," he said, "we didn't want this, we never expected it [he meant the Republican

271

majority in the Senate], and now we just don't have as much time for interviews."

Upon arriving at Hatfield's office in the Russell Building, I was quickly hustled down the elevator and into one of those rustic open-topped rail cars that scoot along underground from the office building to the Senate side of the Capitol. Up another elevator and down a long marble hallway, we opened the massive doors into the opulent office of the chairman of the Appropriations Committee. Although he had ran-kled his own party members more often than his opponents, Hatfield was nonetheless a Republican, and when the new majority took over in 1981, he was automatically elevated to the post of chairman of this powerful committee.

He is something of a paradox on Capitol Hill—a Republican, but also a liberal; a successful politician, but also a devout fundamentalist Christian.

Passing through outer offices that seemed to stretch farther than a city block in length, we came finally to another set of massive doors that opened into a long receiving room, where the senator sat alone in a fine wingback chair before a little log fire in a beautifully carved white marble fireplace. He looked like the institution he was: silver hair, impeccable dress and manners, so calm and wise. As he put down a newsletter on a table beside him, he said he just never had much time to read anymore. But there were no books in sight in the cavernous room, and no shelves or other places to put them if there had been. The museumlike space was more the size of a ballroom than of an office. An antique system of lights and buzzers in an old mantel clock interrupted the conversation every few minutes with loud signals from the Senate floor. "You get used to it," the senator said in apology.

No, said Hatfield, with calm, deliberate words, he is not afraid of any kind of right-wing takeover of the government. "This old ship of state is a lot more seaworthy than some people give it credit for." And another thing he believes: the Christian community is much more powerful than anything that can be done to it.

Mark Hatfield was born in Dallas, Oregon, on July 12, 1922, and reared in a conservative Baptist family. He graduated from Willamette University and then entered the navy as a lieutenant. Noting his religious background, the executive officer on his amphibious cargo ship said, "*You will* lead the services every Sunday." He continued to serve as a lay preacher at Stanford University, where he received an M.A. in 1948. He taught political science and was dean of students at Willamette.

The church of his childhood presented him a "legalistic" Christianity more concerned with superficial do's and don't's than with the more spiritual values of love and compassion. There was no smoking, no drinking, no messing around with women. "I did all of those and enjoyed them," said Hatfield. He believed in a "living Christ" and not in the historic Jesus argued over in endless and meaningless squabbles over the literal meaning of the Bible. He is a strong believer in the Christian community and practices that belief through a "covenant" of six couples who meet every week for prayers and Bible readings. Every Wednesday morning, he and a group of senators meet for a religious exchange over breakfast. This had started out with just Hatfield and Sam Nunn and Pete Domenici, but by the end of 1981 it had grown to the size of a regular church congregation.

Hatfield thinks of his religion as a separate and private matter from politics and the government. And that is how he believes it should be for everybody. If people start putting their religion into the government, he explains, then it won't be long before the government will be involving itself in religion. I told him I had heard that when the organizers of the 1980 "Washington for Jesus" rally marched into his office to tell him how he should vote, he sat them down and lectured them on the importance of the separation of church and state. Furthermore, I had heard, he warned them that he would personally take action to remove their tax-exempt status as a religious group if they didn't stop politicking. Hatfield said this group may have thought it was being so threatened, but he hadn't expressed himself nearly as bluntly as I had heard. However, a few years ago he became very concerned about a proposal that was the first step toward government auditing of church-related finances and the taxation of church investments. He called a meeting of the major evangelical leaders and put it to them directly: if they didn't start doing a better job of regulating their finances and making public their audits, the government was going to step in and do it for them. The Evangelical Council for Financial Accountability was a direct result of this meeting. One of those who protested the loudest against full disclosure of evangelists' financial dealings was George Wilson, Billy Graham's manager. Not long after that, the *Charlotte Observer* embarrassed the Graham operations by disclosing that the evangelist had a secret trust fund in Texas, worth more than $30 million, something never mentioned in the Graham crusades' appeals for money.

Hatfield and Graham have remained close friends over the years, and the question of full financial disclosure is just one of the issues Hatfield has seen him come around on. When he first met Graham, Hatfield says, the man was adamant about the arms race and would hear no talk about arms limitation. Now he supports it. That, explains Hatfield, is exactly why he has tried to keep a dialogue open with Jerry Falwell, whom he has defended publicly on several occasions. "You can't influence anybody you never see." He feels that Falwell is genuine in his stated religious belief, and he has particular praise for his recent hiring of a black minister as an adviser on social issues.

One reason Hatfield is so calm about the religious right is that he does not believe it has the force its leaders claim for it. Having been reared a Baptist, he knows the prevalence of a need for exaggeration among the believers, and takes it in stride. "Many of them claim credit for the election of the President and a majority in the Senate," he says. "I would challenge that. They may have played a part, but there were a lot of political contributing factors. To claim that massive credit is more self-serving than factual."

As for the issues, he says the religious political forces have presented a program replete with inconsistencies and contradictions. They talk about government interference and then invite more of it. They talk about the evils of abortion and the rights of the unborn, but, says Hatfield, "I hear too little about the post-natal child. . . . They talk about the need for prayers in the schools; but there is nothing to stop voluntary prayers right now. And if they get the right to mandatory prayers, whose prayers will they be? They talk about taking the life of an unborn fetus as if that's murder, and then go on to champion capital punishment and encourage killing on a global scale through the arms race."

An aide opened the door and stopped the interview by announcing that the foreign minister of Germany was waiting to see the senator. But I had just mentioned that I would be ending this book with a visit among some Anabaptist Brethren and Mennonites from Virginia and Pennsylvania. "Tell the foreign minister to wait," Hatfield said to the aide. And then he turned back to me, his face suddenly beaming with wistful admiration for the true Anabaptist believers. "Ah, those people," he said, "they practice—no, they *live* their religion." The old mantel clock blinked and buzzed a message from the U.S. Senate; the aide knocked again. A look of nostalgia came over the senator's face that told me of an inner part of the man that must often yearn to be out of the rat race and in a simpler time and place, better suited to his religious faith.

18

BACK TO BEGINNINGS

What I saw that hot, lazy afternoon at Rehoboth Beach, Delaware, was so incongruous to the setting that every detail has remained stuck in my memory like a photograph.

As I stepped over and around the loose groupings of greased and glistening bodies, I looked up toward the boardwalk and beheld two families of old order Brethren, Amish, or Mennonites, moving down the steps and through the bathers toward the water. Five hundred years out of time and place, they wore the heavy garb of medieval peasants. The only skin exposed was that of their hands and faces, and their faces were shaded by bonnets and wide-brimmed hats.

Later, I would learn that one of the bathers did make a snide remark to the group, but at the time it seemed that everybody on the beach was just as stunned as I was. Aside from the contrast in clothing, what made such a lasting impression on me was that these old believers clearly did not feel out of place. The men, women, and children moved with genuine self-confidence and grace, as if they were the only ones properly dressed. The youngest of them, a little girl with bright blue eyes and a fresh-scrubbed face, led the way. She scampered right up to the edge of the surf and reached down to catch a wave. She turned back to share the moment with her family, her face glowing with a look of pure joy.

These people have kept alive an important part of our Christian heritage. Their influence has always far exceeded their numbers in this country because they remind us of our culture's simple origins and of the inner strength and happiness that comes not from wealth and power, but from love and charity.

Why is it, asked Henry David Thoreau, "that the humble life of a Jewish peasant should have force to make a New York bishop so bigoted?" What is it that Jerry Falwell and others like him find in the life of Jesus that inspires them to take on the trappings of royalty and the lifestyle of movie stars and millionaires?

Actually, the old believers share a common ancestry with most of the others who today call themselves born-again or fundamentalist Christians. Both can be traced to the medieval Anabaptists who felt that Martin Luther hadn't gone far enough in his reformation, especially by holding on to the rite of infant baptism, which was neither sanctioned by scripture nor practiced by the primitive church. They also felt that since the scriptures mentioned no manmade hierarchy to stand between an individual and his god, there was no need for such an organization.

In an official Southern Baptist history, Frank S. Mead says, "The modern Baptist is the child of the sixteenth-century Anabaptist . . . the left wing of the Reformation; they were vagrant seeds in a vagrant wind, wild tares in the field of Rome, shooting up suddenly, unexpectedly, everywhere. . . . Advocating common property, pacifism, and the end of capital punishment, they rejected infant baptism as contrary to scripture and asserted the freedom of the soul and the conscience."

Without an organization remotely resembling that of a modern denomination, the Anabaptists managed to survive the radically shifting moods of tolerance and tyranny in the central European states. Like the American Indian tribes, they assumed the names that outsiders had first called them in derision. An "anabaptist" was one who felt he had to be "rebaptized" or "baptized again." To them, it was "to make a new beginning," a phrase adopted by Ronald Reagan apparently without any awareness or appreciation of its origins. To modern fundamentalists, the phrase that is used is "born again."

The various sects of Anabaptists were eventually known by the names of spiritual leaders. The Hutterites were followers of Jacob Hutter, who was burned at the stake in Innsbruck in 1536. They came to the United States in 1874, under the supposed assurance of President

Grant that they would be left alone in wartime in exchange for their agricultural expertise, which they would put to use on the Western plains. But, until the National Service Board for Religious Objectors was set up in 1940 as part of the World War II Selective Service Act, there was no official recognition of conscientious objectors in this country. Among the several hundred young men jailed for their pacifism in World War I were two young Hutterites who died from physical abuse, malnutrition, and pneumonia in North Dakota. When the wife of one of the men was finally allowed to see his body, she found it dressed in the uniform he died to keep from wearing. That was when many Hutterites quietly moved to Canada, where they still thrive, adhering to the faith their ancestors started 450 years ago.

The followers of Jacob Amen in Switzerland were called "Amish," and they still believe the excommunication of one partner dissolves the marriage. A rare case of such "shunning" occurred a few years ago in Pennsylvania, where a man was voted out of a meeting and subjected to strict silence from his wife and children. His wife was also forbidden to sleep with him. The man's attempt to bring legal action against the community was frustrated by their refusal to respond to his suit on the grounds that they are forbidden by scripture to swear any kind of oath.

To most of us, the continuing saga of this poor fellow was only an amusing story out of another century. But to other Anabaptist sects, it was thought to be embarrassing and unfair because it showed only the harsh side of one small sect's beliefs. The memory of that story was surely in my mind when I overheard two young men at a nearby table in a Washington restaurant during lunch one day in early 1981. One of them explained to a third person who joined them about the place where they lived: "It's a house for Amish, Mennonite, and Brethren exiles," he laughed. I asked if I might interview them for this book because it seemed yet another bitter story, not unlike my own break with the fundamentalist culture. They were willing and anxious to talk with me, curious to know about others, and for others to know about them.

I was in for a pleasant surprise. In most cases, they had not had to sever their ties with their families. "You see," a young gay Mennonite would explain to me later, "there was a great deal of love there. And we are still Christians." By such a happy coincidence, my search for answers in religious America had come to the hopeful conclusion I must have known I would find. At heart, I believe that most Christians are not like the Jerry Falwells and James Robisons and the Roman Catholic absolutists of the new right. Among the real majority, I insist, the simple spirit of love and peace propounded by Jesus still endures.

Among the Anabaptist sects, the followers of Menno Simons (1492–1559) have always been the least extreme. Although some of them had been involved in John of Leyden's Kingdom of Zion at Munster, they had repudiated his fanaticism. One historian observed: "They have never aimed at any social or political revolution, and they have been as remarkable for sobriety of conduct as the Munster sect was for its fanaticism."

Like the first Christians and Jesus himself, the Mennonites felt it was their duty to obey the laws of the land, not to live against society, but within and through it. They also took to heart the frequent criticism by Jesus of the noisy piety of the Pharisees, the Moral Majority of that day. They lived their religion and made converts by their example, not through bluff and bluster.

The Mennonites have been open to the world around them, unlike the Amish and Hutterites. These stricter sects could not have survived, however, without legal assistance from the freer Mennonites, who took their first political action in America in 1683 by joining in a protest against slavery.

They had remained apart from the Great Awakening of the 1700s—when Protestant evangelists inspired the masses in huge open-air meetings up and down the Eastern seaboard. And they had not been affected by the pre-millennial revivals of the evangelical missionaries among Baptists and Methodists who, in the early 1800s, said Jesus was coming back any day. But by 1900, the Mennonites were beginning to feel the weight of their own wealth, and along with it a greater responsibility to that vast majority who didn't believe as they did. One hundred years ago, there were no Mennonite colleges and no missionaries. Now there are six colleges and hundreds of missionaries. So successful were their missions to Africa in the 1950s and 1960s that there are now more members of the faith on that continent than there are in all of North America.

Among the Mennonite reformers of this century was a certain Amos Daniel (A. D.) Wenger, who was born into one of the old orders in a community in the Shenandoah Valley town of Harrisonburg, Virginia, in 1867. He was as devout as the others, but he also had an incurable yearning to see what lay beyond the confines of his own little community. Wenger went to New York, and on January 21, 1899, set sail on the liner *Servia* on a trip that took him first to the Holy Land and then on to China and around the world. His wanderlust satisfied, he moved to Millersville, Pennsylvania, and married Anna May Lehman, a descendant of an old Lancaster County Mennonite family. He then had to face the complex problems of earning a living and raising a family while holding onto the faith.

In Pennsylvania, there was only one cash crop that could provide such a living, and that was tobacco. But the Mennonites were opposed to smoking, and Wenger felt that if it was a sin to smoke the stuff, it was also a sin to grow it and sell it in the first place.

With the same kind of daring that had brought his people to America in the 1600s, Wenger organized a community and settled at the mouth of the Chesapeake Bay, southeast of Norfolk. There the Mennonites were able to support themselves quite comfortably on the health-giving fruit of their newly planted vineyards, peach and apple orchards, and farms.

Wenger's next venture was to join with other elders of the church in the founding of Eastern Mennonite College in the little town in western Virginia where he was born. From 1922 until he died in October 1935, Wenger served as president of the school, keeping it alive during the worst days of the Depression. His son, Chester, was among the graduates of that school and was among the first missionaries to Africa.

Chester Wenger, his wife, Sara Jane, and their eight children (four of whom were born in Africa), returned to the United States in 1966 after twenty-seven years in Ethiopia. Their return coincided with the social upheaval that had rocked the very foundations of this country. But, having faced communications problems in foreign countries, Chester Wenger had a practical approach to bridging the "generation gap" that everybody else in America was only talking about. He helped organize home missions in urban areas, specifically aimed at young Mennonites who had not only left farms and families but had also lost touch with their church. The Student and Young Adult Services of the church grew out of these missions.

If there were any controversies the Mennonites had missed through their ethnic isolation, these young people in the urban missions were soon bringing them all back home—if not in person, then through seminars and eventually their own publication. Their magazine, *Forum*, was called a "drifter" by its young editors because it had gone through three editors and changes of address in as many years. A confrontation arose about a year after Phil Wenger (A. D.'s grandson and Chester's son) and Marlise Horst took over as editors. Horst's parents had been born in Harrisonburg, but when she was twelve, her father, a historian, had been sent as a missionary to Amsterdam, where the family decided to settle permanently; for college, the daughter returned to her father's alma mater in Harrisonburg.

This was about the time I overheard Phil Wenger talking about exiles in Washington with his friend Philip Metzler, a classmate from college, who had written the controversial article. I found *Forum* a refreshing change from the strident and closed-minded publications of the religious right. In addition to its calm and intelligent discussion of all the major issues of the day, there was also a healthy sense of humor present that is nowhere to be found among other fundamentalist publications.

"How much of a pacifist were you?" asks a mock query in *Forum*, reprinted from its West Coast counterpart, *Shun*. The answers:

—I was such a pacifist that I thought the right to bare arms had to do with sleeveless shirts.
—I boycotted J.C. Penney's for selling tank tops.
—I never opened the window because I wanted to avoid the draft.
—I did not bat an eye.
—I refused to play the B-1 position in Bingo.
—The kids in my school are such pacifists that the school bully majored in peace studies.

The younger Mennonites are secure in their absolute pacifism because that is one part of their faith that has not changed in spite of all the outward changes in dress and the inner changes regarding sexuality and sex roles. A cartoon strip in *Forum* shows a nuclear power plant dome in one frame, and then the dome begins to crack like an egg. The "shell" finally falls off to expose the nuclear warhead underneath.

Although Chester Wenger had a letter in one issue advising the editors to avoid "scoff and scorn" in its pages, I found the magazine remarkably free of cynicism, a unique distinction among youthful publications in our time. I think possibly the church elders are too close to the situation, too involved in the fine points of doctrine to appreciate that their children are, in fact, carrying on the deeper spiritual values instilled in them.

One young writer routinely invoked the words of the founder, Menno Simons, in support of present-day pacifism. Another young Mennonite deplored the "practical" argument for supporting "the continued building of more and more weapons, which do not lead to a state of security. They just add to the paranoia that prompts building more and more nuclear weapons when we can already destroy ourselves several times over."

These young believers recall their martyrs to peace as other cultures celebrate the heroes of war. Along with this faith in man's goodness is a certain spirit of life that is worth recording: "Love!" exclaimed one *Forum* writer. "Ah, the joy of experiencing that universal power of love that transcends . . . borders, ethnic culture, numbers of personal visions. . . . How we need each other! Why? Because the earth is one global village. In today's world the old fences of lifestyle, geography, even theology, are surely crumbling under the realization that in this small world, when one hurts, all hurt."

One telling difference between the articles in *Forum* and those in *Moral Majority Report* was that the questions and opinions in *Forum* never presumed to represent what was *the* way or even what was a specific view of the Christian way. On the question of whether Mennonites should engage in elective politics, the answer was, ". . . only if this involves a clear call to prophetic witness and is not an opportunity for personal advancement or getting on a bandwagon, such as the 'Moral Majority'. . . . We are far too involved in our society professionally, economically, and emotionally to justify our political naïveté. We need to be as political as possible or be called irresponsible."

In response to the same question, Don Eberly, a conservative Republican who voted for Reagan and who works for a Pennsylvania congressman in Washington, said: "I grew up in a Mennonite family in a Mennonite area. A personal search which began in college led to a self-constructed standpoint concerning my beliefs. My standpoint is based on a total commitment to the historic truths of Christianity as communicated through the scriptures. So far my faith and my political involvement have not conflicted, due to my strong feelings about the separation of church and state. I am alarmed by the confusion of these two entities in the so-called new-right movement."

But politics and pacifism were easy external issues compared to the more personal questions involving societal changes in attitudes toward sex and sex roles. One writer for *Forum* said: "Mennonites are known for a wonderful stubbornness and singlemindedness of purpose, a refusal to budge on principle. On the positive side, our muleheadedness has kept us out of many bad but popular trends. On the negative side, it keeps us from grappling with awarenesses that challenge our perspective."

In the *Forum* article about psychiatric therapy, one man said: "The church is a very large part of me and can't accept me for who I am. There are two opposing forces in me. One is my sexuality, which I did not choose and can't deny. And the other is my Christian value system, which I did choose, but it rejects my sexuality. I'd like to get to the point where I can accept both, but I hardly see that happening.

"I don't want some therapist who is going to suggest kicking aside the value system. But I don't want one who will preach at me how Christ can heal—I'm not so sure he can yet. I have to come to know that on my own."

The church has withdrawn its support of the magazine and suspended publication three times. Each time, the point of controversy involved homosexuality. Each time, the elders revived the magazine with a pledge to "offer a few more answers and not so many questions," and each time, the younger generation insisted on raising the questions. The third time the magazine was closed down, it was because Phil Wenger had succeeded in getting his friend Phil Metzler's story published.

Like Wenger, Metzler had been born abroad, the son of a Mennonite missionary in Jamaica. The family came back to Pennsylvania in 1966, when Phil was ten years old. He was only twelve when his mother caught him masturbating and made him get down on his knees and pray for forgiveness. He can only remember tugging at her apron and begging her to please not tell his dad.

His father died when Metzler was twenty years old, and his chief regret about their relationship is that he wasn't able to tell his father he is homosexual. One summer after the father died, he made the first mention of it to his mother and two brothers. He said only that maybe he was "bisexual," and that was the end of it.

But when he had finished college and come back home to a good job at the water-treatment plant, Phil Metzler felt out of place. He couldn't go on living a lie. It was expected that he would follow his father into the ministry; it was also expected that he would marry and raise a family. In a very specific way, it was his religion that had inspired such honesty and integrity in him that he couldn't deceive people even if they were the ones with the misconceptions.

His mom was the first to be told. She heard him out and read the books and pamphlets on the subject that he brought home. Her only fear was that he might be hurt by what other people might think or say about him. Why did he have to tell everybody? It was none of their business.

At the Mennonite High School reunion, Phil wore a gay rights pink Lambda button just so people would ask. One friend wouldn't believe he wasn't joking. Another insisted that he be the one to tell her parents; they were too close and cared too much to hear such a thing about him through the gossip mill.

In this, the best of his encounters, Phil and his friend and her parents sat in their kitchen, capping strawberries for homemade ice cream. The parents were honest about their confusion over homosexuality. "Biblically, we just don't know, Phil." But there was no question about their concern for him and they were anxious to read any material he had on the subject. Two other couples he was even closer to were not so receptive. One of them was a strict fundamentalist husband and wife who saw everything in terms of the Bible. The other couple was the one Phil had assumed would be the most reasonable and the most supportive of him. They had been there after his father's death when he needed advice and counsel, especially in college, when he had questions about theology. The husband was a psychologist. Phil took them out to dinner and found they were not as sophisticated as he had assumed. "Are you sure?" the husband asked. "Just because you have certain fantasies," said the wife, "that doesn't mean you really know, does it?"

Later that summer, Phil's pastor said it was time they had a talk; it had been a long time since they had had breakfast together.

The pastor was obviously uncomfortable. After the usual morning pleasantries over eggs and coffee, he cleared his throat and brushed his hand over his mouth as if to muffle the words: "What about your, uh, homosexuality?" As Phil poured out his story, the minister responded with love and understanding. What shocked him most was Phil's announcement that he had quit his job and was going to live in Washington. The pastor didn't want Phil to go away angry with the church or with the people in it who loved him. In the age-old manner of their religion, he would call a meeting—not a council of bishops or any kind of formal inquest, but a meeting of friends.

Phil's chosen friends (the three couples) and his mom and the pastor gathered in the Metzlers' living room. The pastor explained why he had called the meeting, and then Phil explained himself: "I said I was no longer living like two different people. It was a positive, free thing I had done. I was sure that no matter who I was with from then on, I didn't have to worry."

All of them were worried about his leaving the community; they wanted him to stay so that they could help him to change. The men were not very judgmental, but two of his women friends were. The psychologist's wife said she couldn't accept what he was saying about homosexuality. "It is no clear-cut matter; there are people who have changed," she said. Because he had expected her to be the most supportive, her words hurt the most. The fundamentalist woman choked with emotion as she struggled to tell him, "You're going to hell unless you renounce your homosexuality."

His mother may have had difficulty dealing with his talk of homosexuality in private, but by the time of the meeting, she was ready to "come out" herself. She said, "I'm proud of Philip, I'm proud of his searching attitude. I love him very much for who and what he is. I have searched myself and I don't see where I have gone wrong." Her shedding of guilt was as important to him as his own actions in that regard.

In Washington, Metzler found an active chapter of the Brethren-Mennonites for Gay Concern and there were also the two houses of young Mennonites he had known in college. He hadn't really left the community, he had just moved from one part of it to another. And when he goes home now, he doesn't have to pretend to be anything or anybody but himself.

In his *Forum* article, Phil concluded: "With the acceptance of my gayness had come a feeling of wholeness that I had never before experienced. There was no longer the dichotomy of being outwardly one person and inwardly another. I was free to be myself—not just in 'safe' environments—but no matter where I was. I had come to see that what society or a local community desires is not always good—that norms and mores, like individual beliefs, can be based on irrational fears. One of the premises on which I base my life is that both 'differentness' and 'change' are good—that they are not to be feared. I also believe that it is only by observing one's reactions to various experiences that one truly learns about oneself, and that this self-knowledge is essential to growth."

Another who can go home again now with a clear conscience is Rebecca Dietz, a college classmate of the two Phils and a member of one of the "exile" households in Washington. Although her break with family and church did not involve sexuality, it did involve the traditional role of a young woman and was even more traumatic than Phil Metzler's break was. She, too, had been living a lie and the integrity of her upbringing only made it increasingly unbearable. Her conflict was across centuries instead of mere decades.

In introducing *Forum*'s special issue on women in 1980, an editorial read: "Many *Forum* readers like safe stories. They rejoice that *Forum* doesn't print confessions of premarital sex and they thank God it is not the godless paper they had imagined. But this magazine also attracts the anguished people whose suffering is real and unresolved. Their message is clear: The conspiracy of silence must end."

A young mother of two, who is also a university student, wrote in the same issue: "My great-grandmother who struggled to survive on the cold Manitoba prairie would have shaken her head in bewilderment at modern women's predicaments: a housewife's boredom, a working mother's guilt. How have we arrived at such an absurd situation, where 'work' and 'family' have come to represent two opposite extremes? Not just celebrities or world leaders, but ordinary citizens are forced to choose between them. . . . I envision a society in which work is not measured by promptness, perfect attendance, and profit, but by quality and usefulness to its members. A society where children and other dependents do not need to be sacrificed for the sake of efficiency and someone else's greed. A society in which love and achievement are not mutually exclusive but in fact harmonious despite the exhaustion, persecution, and guilt which must attend the working mother until it comes about. We will need a lot of help."

The simple facts concerning Mennonite women speak volumes about the radical changes that have taken place in the church in this century. There were no women pastors in the church until Annie Alle-bach of Schwenksville, Pennsylvania, was ordained in January 1911. Now, 18 of the 81 Mennonite pastors in Holland are women. And in America, 73 of the 211 students at Associated Mennonite Biblical Seminaries are women.

In many ways, Becky Dietz arrived as a student at Eastern Menno-nite College in 1978 not as herself but as everybody's great-grand-mother. She had a peculiar problem in this fierce time when women were fighting to be regarded as something more than sex objects. Becky's problem was that nobody saw her as a sexual being because she alone, among one thousand students, wore the ancient costume of their ancestors. Other students shied away from her as they would from a stern old ghost. Some reacted in amazement when she spoke up in class and voiced opinions as sharp and witty and modern as theirs. Her sparkling eyes and expressive mouth betrayed the feisty rebel un-der all those clothes, but nobody ever saw her without the full cover-ing, head to toe: heavy bonnet over a small lace cap, full-length cape behind and apron in front, over a heavy dress extending to the wrists and ankles. "My shoes were my one tie to modern life. I comforted myself in normal shoes."

The head covering was the specific symbol of women's subservience to men, as men are subservient to God. It is among the many stric-tures of the New Testament that come not from Jesus, but from the zealots who succeeded him as "Christians." The disciple in question was Saul of Tarsus, a rabbinical student of the great teacher Gamaliel. Saul was a rambling young rabbi who supported himself as a tentmak-er while preaching the Pharisees' doctrine that the laws of God were absolute. (Whereas Jesus himself said it was all right to break the Sab-bath sometimes and okay to sit among loose women and tight men at other times.)

Saul claimed he wasn't one of the superreligious Pharisees who shouted for Herod to get on with Jesus' crucifixion, but he did help in stoning Stephen to death. The rabbi Saul took the name of a Roman patrician, Paul, and, blinded by a vision of light one day on the road to Damascus, he also took Jesus as his savior. His new Christian dogma sounds suspiciously similar to the old Mosaic lists of right and wrong. In a letter to the Christians in Corinth, for example, he said if a wom-an prayed without her head covered, she might as well have her head shaved.

A good bit of modern Christianity would more accurately be called "Paulist" than Christian. Lawrence Durrell speaks to the two traditions in a character's tribute to D. H. Lawrence in the novel *Clea*: "How wonderful the death-struggle of Lawrence: to realize his sexual nature fully, to break free from the manacles of the Old Testament; flashing down through the firmament like a great white struggling man-fish, the last Christian martyr. His struggle is ours—to rescue Jesus from Moses. For a brief moment it looked possible, but St. Paul restored the balance and the iron handcuffs of the Judaic prison closed about the growing soul forever."

When Becky Dietz's grandparents—now in their eighties—were young, the three hundred members of the Old Order River Brethren were split into five different factions or groups over doctrinal disputes. Her mother was born into the Horse and Buggy Group, which had split off because its members felt the use of automobiles would lead to other changes that would disrupt the faith. (Among the Amish, there was a Black Bumper Group that agreed to use cars, but only after the shiny parts were painted black.) Becky's father was born into the Keller Group, which, like the Horst, Musser, and Stickler groups, was known by the name of its bishop. Some of the factional disputes had involved what powers these new bishops should have, because there was a firm tradition of the equality of men, and even this tendency toward a hierarchy was of very recent origin.

The Brethren were much closer to the stricter Amish than they were to many of the Mennonites in America, whose dress requirements—in the 1960s—were reduced to a small head covering for the women and a high-collared coat for the men on Sundays only. Many Mennonites had come to dress and worship a lot like Methodists and Baptists. They had ministers and bishops and missionaries, and they worshiped in regular church buildings, complete with musical instruments to accompany the modern hymns.

The Old Order River Brethren continue to worship in each others' houses or barns; they allow no musical instruments; the men and women sit apart from each other during services. Nobody is accepted into full membership as a brother or sister until he or she is old enough to make a personal decision about baptism. Women, of course, are expected to seek counsel from their husbands or fathers at home. Only

the men speak in the public services. It had been so for many years—
at least until young Becky Dietz came along.

While her grandparents and parents had lived within the church in
a time of factions and dispute, Becky grew up in a happier mood of
compromise and reconciliation. The strongest of the bishops quietly
agreed to relinquish certain powers and to abandon his edict forbidding new marriages (because he expected Christ's Second Coming any
day). Two mergers reduced the groups from five to three, and all of
the groups scheduled their love feasts at different times so that everybody could attend all three.

The love feasts in September, March, and June are a special time of
joy and sharing. All the members gather at a particular farmhouse just
at sundown on Friday. The women gather around a big table for the
first ceremony, kneading the unleavened dough that will be baked into
bread for communion. Lumps of dough are passed around so that each
woman has some to knead. As they do this, the women talk of being
better wives and mothers, of making their lives like this dough in the
hands of God.

All day Saturday is a time of examination. The brothers sit on one
side, the sisters on the other. Each person has to ask himself if he is
worthy of the Lord's supper. In the evening, two long tables are covered with white linen cloths and set in the center of the barn or basement.

Separated by sexes again, the communion starts with the washing of
feet, neighbor to neighbor, "beloved sister" to sister and "beloved
brother" to brother. Becky Dietz remembers playing about under the
table watching the women's bare feet, her Aunt Edith giving her a
conspiratorial wink of love and approval.

As the feet are washed and dried, a brother intones, "If I your Lord
and Master have washed your feet, so ought ye to wash one another's."

And the congregation sings: "There is a fountain filled with blood /
Drawn from Immanuel's veins / And sinners plunged beneath the
flood / Lose all their guilty stains."

Then the homemade wine and fresh-baked bread are passed around,
the body and blood of our Lord and Savior Jesus Christ. The brothers
and sisters softly weep as the image of Christ's suffering comes into
their minds at communion.

Although she had her doubts from the very beginning, Becky Dietz never thought about hers as an oppressive society. She doesn't recall anybody ever saying not to do something. There was no argument or discussion about smoking or drinking or premarital sex or going to the movies downtown. It simply wasn't done and nobody had to be told.

When she was in the second grade at the public school, she worried at first about her mother coming on visitors' day. But when the day arrived, nobody said anything about how her mother was dressed— they just responded to what a warm and loving person she was. It was the same with her father. Although he holds a master's degree in education, teaches at the Mennonite high school, and lectures often to church groups, he is known throughout York County as the good and gentle man with the egg and fresh vegetable route. "Myron Dietz's daughter?" people would exclaim when Becky identified herself. "He's such a wonderful man."

The doubts and confusion remained inside her head. But by the time she was fourteen, they were catching up with her. All of her girlfriends had seen the light, taken Jesus as their Savior, been baptized, and made a new beginning. In a society where real sin was not an option, Becky Dietz was plagued by her thoughts. Try as she might, she could not hear that still, small voice, she could not switch to the "low and narrow" path of God.

One old brother would often tell about his conversion. "I spent forty years outside the fold before I turned in. Afterwards I couldn't remember what the sermon was that day, but they told me old Henry Etter preached it on "What Lack I Yet?' I remember I sat up in the haymow and wept all day like a baby. 'What lack I yet?' the rich young ruler asked Jesus. He was a moral man.

"I was like that rich young ruler. I stayed at home and helped my daddy farm till he died. I lived a moral life. But it was not enough. I lived under such heavy condemnation. You young people who turn in early have it so good. You don't know what condemnation is."

Becky knew. She was the only one among her friends who still wore fancy (modern) clothes. In her group, the decision to "dress plain" was made at the same time one was born again or made a new beginning. In other groups, the children are dressed like their parents from the cradle onwards. The visible differences, then, made her feel like the only sinner in a roomful of saints. Her grandfather had seen angels dancing around his bed one night when he was ill; her father had a clear vision of God the night before he made his decision for Christ. Becky heard nothing and saw nothing. But whatever she was not experiencing was also keeping her awake at night.

One afternoon she was feeling miserable as she went about her housecleaning chores. Finally she got down on her knees beside her bed and told God she wanted to be a Christian. She pounded her fists into the mattress and said she hated herself for going ahead with what she knew to be an empty experience, but she cried, "I will try to change." She pinned her hair back and tried on one of her mother's head coverings. Yanking it off and throwing it at the mirror, she would have cursed her image, but she didn't know any dirty words.

She was properly baptized in the pond one Sunday, and then became a full-fledged sister of the Old Order River Brethren. But a part of her knew that she had lied in order to fit in. The pressures to conform were simply too strong in that small society. "When you join the church you're supposed to have this awareness. God is leading you. But I did it because my friends did it. I didn't have the religious experience others said they had."

In that life, a young woman had only a few choices for the future: she could get married or she could become an old-maid schoolteacher or a nurse. Becky Dietz knew she didn't want to be any of these. "There were problems and the answers were too simple. They set up these structures and a lot of people need them." But she didn't.

After a year in a local college, Becky wanted to go to school in England. Her family reacted as if she had proposed a visit to hell. They compromised by letting her attend Eastern Mennonite College.

When she was a child, nobody had ever left the church as far as she could remember. When she was a junior in college, three people left without explaining or saying goodbye. But Becky Dietz loved her family and, in deep and enduring ways, her religion too. She could never cut herself off completely from her family or her faith. She would face them and say what she had to say and then she would leave with a clear conscience—so that she could always return the same way.

On the morning chosen for her announcement, her family and friends were all gathered for the regular service in a pale blue basement, a big potbellied stove hissing warmth from a far corner. Only one of the brothers, who had a degree in psychology, looked at her eyes. Her father looked at the rug; her mother stared straight ahead.

She had never thought of the bishop as anybody but her friend's father. He was like the others, telling experiences and relating them to the Bible. One weekend, another brother in the group told about taking his family to see the ocean. He said when they walked through the crowds to get to the water, somebody had said, "Boy, those people must have a lot of problems." But, this brother had reasoned, "I think they're the ones with problems." (The more details Becky provided me about this story, the more I wondered if this might be the very same group I had seen on Rehoboth Beach.) And that was what Becky had always believed: It wasn't that others were so wrong, just that her people were more right. Now she had come home to say she no longer belonged.

The congregation finished singing an opening hymn and the bishop calmly announced: "And now a young sister has something she would like to say to us." It had been against church policy for several years for a woman to speak at meetings.

Becky closed her eyes and felt as if she were drowning in the Blood of the Lamb; she opened them and saw the blue walls closing in on her. She began haltingly by saying they had been right about what would happen when she went away to school. "I did change. You no longer know me and I don't know how to introduce myself." Each sentence was followed by a deathly silence; only the psychologist looked at her.

"I need to tell you I don't think I belong here anymore. I'm alien inside. This is not me and these are not my clothes. This is only a memory. You must accept it." Referring to some notes she had made, she spoke of the unnatural myths of the Bible that forced women into roles that did not fit. She spoke of the arts and of the need to be creative. All these things were in her notes, but they seemed ridiculously irrelevant when she said them aloud.

She struggled to hold back the tears until she had finished, but everybody else was crying. Becky had brought home the brutal truth of the illusory nature of their simple life in a complicated world five hundred years beyond them. If it could happen to Myron Dietz's Becky, it could happen to any of their sons and daughters—maybe even to one of them. She was not just a member of a club, offering her resignation. It was a kind of wake in which the deceased went on to a happier life.

None of the words seemed to speak for what was in her heart, and finally she came to the blunt point of her confession: "I'm telling you I'm leaving, withdrawing membership. It's a silly thing to say. What are boundaries? There are parts of me you can never throw out, parts that will never leave you.

"Please still love me."

She broke off then and collapsed in tears. The bishop quickly announced a hymn. Everybody was crying with her, but they tried to sing, grasping at the familiar words of the past to cover this awful confrontation with the present. Her grandfather grabbed her and wailed: "You'll go to hell, you'll go to hell if you take off your plain clothes." "Grandpa," she said, "you know that isn't true." And then a woman friend whispered, "I don't judge. I'm all mixed up too. And I love you."

Becky went back to her community of Mennonite-Brethren exiles in Washington, and that is where I met her and them. They seemed little different from me in the way they dressed; but unlike me, they were still Christians, in the very best sense of that word.

Three years after Becky left the church, I met her around lunchtime one day in Dupont Circle, near where I live in Washington. It was a crisp fall day in September 1981, and we sat on a wooden bench facing the sun. She was leaving Washington for a while, she said, going home again for a few months. Her grandparents were in their eighties and they needed her. The extra work was putting a strain on her parents. Going home now represented no kind of defeat for her, although at one time it would have. She was going back her own person in many ways, without the constraints that had weighed on her before. But in just as many ways, she was returning as the same loving daughter and sister she always had been and always would be.

AFTERWORD

It was important to me in the writing of this book to present the humane side of Christianity, in contrast to the narrow-minded and hateful bigots who have been hogging the spotlight for so long now in America. It is true that I knew my share of bigots in the past, but there was usually an equal measure of the simple love and compassion that Jesus talked about, if I would only look for it. There was my father's honesty and common sense in the face of unreasonable intolerance, for a start. There was my mother's refusal to measure anything human in simple terms of black and white; she knew that much of life comes naturally in shades of gray. This extended to the unique—even dangerous—view, in our community, that blacks had as much right to an education and to job opportunities as whites. In high school, I was encouraged in my involvement with an integrated group of students when the state law forbade racially mixed meetings in a public place. This was ten years before even token integration came to our schools. One of my brothers is a Christian preacher, the Methodist minister to Duke University. And he represents none of the things that Jerry Falwell and his kind do. As president of the student body at the University of North Carolina, he was an outspoken leader in the movement to allow black students at the school; when he graduated to the all-white divinity school at Duke, he carried the same cause with him. His associate ministers at the magnificent cathedrallike Duke Chapel always include women, and on certain occasions they have used the nonsexist version of the liturgy. In welcoming the freshman class, he is careful to explain that his counseling staff makes no judgments on anybody's life: whatever one's sex or sexual orientation, the counselors are there to help.

All of this developed out of our mother's lessons in tolerance. She had come to her reasonable attitudes by the most difficult path imaginable—by suffering through intolerance. She was a young woman of special intelligence and energy, a creative spirit crippled by the weight of dark forces nobody would explain but would still use to bully her. The man she thought was her father was a tyrannical Baptist evangelist, a fiercely repressed person whose inner confusion could only be calmed at times when he would chop wood for hours and hours on end. His rigid, unnatural view of the way life ought to be warps a scattered bunch of lives to this day; not one of his children ever took an interest in religion or church after they left home.

My mother made the connection between her secret anguish and mine immediately after I wrote to her that my first book, published in early 1975, would include the information that I was homosexual. Whatever the origins others wish to argue about, it was something I had always been, and it couldn't be changed without some radical change in who I was. It was also necessary for me as a writer to include this information for the reader in the books in which I myself was a character. I worried about what effect this revelation would have on my mother, but my being open and honest about who I was came as a direct result of the uncompromising integrity that she and my father had instilled in me.

Still, I felt an extraordinary weight lifted from me when my mother's letter of response arrived at the place where I was staying in New York. "Having loved you since before you were born, I cannot love you less knowing this," she wrote. "Come out of the shadows of guilt and live your life in the sunshine." I cried real tears of appreciation for this woman whose tolerance had somehow endured a life of real pain and suffering. "Everybody's a little strange except for me and thee," she used to laugh, "and thee's a little queer." "Little" did she know, I always add when telling that story.

But when she did know, she was loving and considerate about it. Mainly, she worried about my being lonely. She also worried about what people would do and say to me, and behind my back, over this very natural aspect of my being, which I had not chosen. She worried because she had been there herself. She could now tell her story to me. After instructing me to "burn this after you read it" (thus assuring its preservation), she proceeded to revise my family history in the best storyteller fashion. It was an excruciatingly painful confession for her, but she began it with a calm setting of the scene. "You know that farm Luther owns over toward Green Mountain. . . ."

Well, one time when Grandpa Fox had leased out the mining rights to some foreigners (meaning Virginians), a young college man came in as an engineer. The only name she ever heard for him was Beau, and he must have lived up to it. He was staying at the Fox house, and sometimes their oldest granddaughter would come over to help with the extra work for the boarders. This was Preacher Sam Tipton's girl, Lizzie, a willowy, dark-haired beauty of natural elegance and grace.

"The Tipton girls had been raised or were being raised very strict and since Lizzie was the oldest and prettiest at that time she said she was a pet of the aunts and Grandma Fox. The long and short of it was that she would slip over to help her Grandma. And fell in love. Evidently he loved her very much too. He gave her a beautiful ruby with diamonds. She let me wear it once and I never saw it after that. But her dad did so much 'forbidding' she wouldn't marry the guy and leave with him when the work was over, was scared to go to him, though he wrote and begged."

Beau was brought back for trial and convicted of fornication. "He was sentenced to five years *hard labor* and when they said that back then in the mountains they meant that. Course, it afforded the preacher victory over evil! and because they 'loved the daughter and sister' so much she became the outcast of the town. And I became not only their first grandchild but a bastard and the daughter of a convict!" Lizzie was then forced to marry the illegitimate offspring of a neighbor and his housekeeper. He died only recently, as illiterate and ignorant as he was born. The child, my mother, after being beaten by the new husband, was taken to live with her grandparents, who would die thinking she never knew who she really was.

Only after reading that letter could I understand the real meaning of an awful exchange between my mother and me the last time I had seen her. She is now in her seventies, too old for the kind of changes I've enjoyed, and every time I get near her, she throws out this web of memory like a fishnet, dragging me back into the "family" I ran away from. She recites the whereabouts and condition of every last brother, sister, nephew, niece, and cousin. (There are hundreds.) She recalls every little insult from her own hurt-filled life. But on this visit, she was situated in the best position she had ever known. She was running a restaurant attached to a beautiful old fishing lodge whose front lawn sloped down to the banks of the Withlacoochee River, near the Gulf Coast of Florida. She served fresh fish brought to the docks every day. She had a lively group of young people working for her, making her feel like a young girl herself. She and her new husband seemed as happy as newlywed teenagers. She had never known such happiness before.

Why did she have to dredge up all those family problems that seemed better off buried and forgotten? She started by telling me about going back up to the mountains in western North Carolina for Aunt Lizzie's funeral. I had dearly loved my old Aunt Lizzie. She was a gentle, dignified person who always seemed out of place in that grimy slum house she shared with Uncle John and a son who had been spooked by some World War II wound and who moped about with never a word for anybody.

Aunt Lizzie would sit and talk with me for hours about the old days in Yancey County. She carefully labeled a box of old pictures she gave me—except for one handsome young man beside her. (I fancy it's her Beau.) She would take me in and out of some nearby houses that had once been elegant mansions, and we would examine the woodwork and the paintings. She would tell me about a corpse she had just viewed at a funeral home after reading of some interesting death in the papers. (In many ways, the movie *Harold and Maude* recalled the happiest moments I had shared with Aunt Lizzie.) She encouraged my interest in history and writing, and she delighted in my small successes. But after I went away to college, I didn't go back to the mountains very much and I probably never wrote my Aunt Lizzie again. I had a brief moment of regret when Mother told me she had died; but I reasoned that she was old and the way she went was better than a long time of suffering.

Aunt Lizzie had specified in her will that my mother was to get five hundred dollars, a third of her life insurance money. Mother said Lizzie's daughter, Mary Lee, had gotten the whole thing and Mother was thinking of hiring a lawyer to get her share. At that point I lost control and started shouting at my mother over the absurdity of what she was saying. Poor old Aunt Lizzie had lived on welfare her whole life, died in a goddamn slum, and my mother was going to sue over a measly five hundred dollars. The lawyer would cost more than that. Hadn't she had enough of that with the litigation over my own father's will?

"Listen, Mother," I said, "all my life you've laid this family thing on me. I've been raised up with every hate you've ever known. But I got away from all that; I found that other people don't carry unresolved grudges through their lives. I don't have to live that way and I'm not going to live that way." She sat there with the hurt little girl's expression I had also lived with, but I walked out the door, and kept walking three miles to a grove of palmettos, where I sat alone, staring out at the Gulf just as I had taken refuge in a view of the mountains as a child.

My mother never mentioned this inheritance from "Aunt" Lizzie until the letter she sent me about her family and mine: "And that was why I wanted that five hundred dollars Lizzie left me. It was the only thing my mother ever gave me. . . ."

She understood what I had been through with my private guilt and shame over what people would think if they knew about my sexual orientation, because she herself had gone through the same experience. I can't change what she has already had to endure, but I can learn from that and go on to happier days for myself.

If I am outraged by the absolutist mentality of my supposed grandfather when I see it coming back with such force in the simpleminded slogans of the new right, I hope that my background explains why. Human behavior can never be so simply defined; and when somebody tries to impose unnatural limits and boundaries on other people's wants and needs, you end up with a solution far more destructive to the individual and to society than the so-called problems were to begin with. We have enough examples in our past, when love and compassion have overcome such movements as we are now facing, to be hopeful about overcoming the current one.

As the wise old survivor of the death camps said to a Miami reporter, "God is in your heart." As a Christian in Northern Ireland said to Robert Coles for an article in *The Atlantic*: "Hate feeds on hate, and someone has to break the circle, and Christ did that, and if we could only be Christians, we would, too."

APPENDIXES

The following appendixes are in three parts. In the first (Appendix A), I have included some samples of the direct mail being sent out by a few of the groups discussed in the text. In two cases, the original material was too faint to reproduce, so I have copied it in typescript, following the original text verbatim except where indicated. What appear to be handwritten notes and underlinings (in red on the original letters) are not my work, but were printed as part of the originals. They were obviously done to give the impression that this was a personal communication; they were also obviously mass-produced by computers and untouched by human hands. The second part (Appendixes B–E) consists of the texts of four speeches by Jerry Falwell, Thomas J. McIntyre, Barry M. Goldwater, and A. Bartlett Giamatti. The third part (Appendixes F–G) reproduces Thomas Jefferson's "An Act for Establishing Religious Freedom" in Virginia along with his answer to the query regarding religion in America in the book *Notes on Virginia*.

APPENDIX
A

JESSE HELMS
NORTH CAROLINA

United States Senate
WASHINGTON, D.C. 20510

Thursday

Dear Friend:

I have enclosed a 1976 Presidential Ballot for you.

Will you please fill it out and send it back to me today?

You just may save yourself hundreds of dollars in taxes in the coming years by sending me your Ballot today, and joining me in a new effort to halt the steady rise of taxes.

What I've done is help organize the National Conservative Political Action Committee (NCPAC).

And I want you to be a part of it.

Why? Because right now your tax dollars are being doled out to people who are perfectly able to work, but <u>refuse</u> to.

Because your tax dollars are being used to pay for grade school courses that teach our children that <u>cannabalism</u>, <u>wife</u> <u>swapping</u>, and the <u>murder</u> of infants and the elderly are acceptable behavior.

Because your tax dollars are paying for food stamps for teachers during their summer vacation . . . even if they <u>earn</u> <u>more</u> <u>than</u> <u>you</u> do.

Because your tax dollars are paying more than half of New York City's <u>massive</u> <u>welfare</u> costs, which amount to $314.81 a year per each of New York's 8 million residents.

I don't believe for a minute that you approve of any of this. And what's worse, it doesn't have to be this way.

Let's face it. You and I both know there is only one reason your taxes keep going up to pay for these radical programs. It's because of the kind of people who get elected to Congress and the state legislatures. People like George McGovern and Bella Abzug. People who vote for every give-away scheme <u>your</u> money can buy.

Now don't you think it's about time you and I got together and did something about all these dangerous abuses? I do.

In fact, as I've told you, I have agreed to help organize the National Conservative Political Action Committee to fight these

Not Prepared or Mailed at Government Expense

100 KEY LIBERALS ARE DEFEATABLE!

**That's why
I need
you on
my 1981
team...**

Dear friend,

We won't get a second chance. . .

The 1982 election can put an end to the "new deal" liberalism. . .or it can prove disastrous.

. . .and the election countdown is already well underway.

That's why I desperately need your help today.

Because 1981 is going to be the critical test year for you and me and all of us who have worked so hard, and so long, for a change. . .

In 1980, we won big. We made a lot of progress, but we have a lot of work ahead of us. . .

I would estimate that right now there are 36 reliable conservatives in the U.S. Senate. There are 39 committed liberals. And there are 25 moderate Democrats and Republicans.

Because the countdown has already started. . .and there's simply no time to lose.

I desperately need to hear from you by March 27th.

Sincerely,

Paul M. Weyrich

Paul M. Weyrich

P.S. Together we can defeat the "new deal" liberals once and for all. But the groundwork must be completed on schedule in 1981. Please make an especially generous 1981 contribution to CSFC today. I can't keep an effective effort going without your continued help. I really do need YOU on my 1981 team!

PLEASE READ THIS LETTER BEFORE OPENING THE SEALED ENVELOPE I'VE ENCLOSED.

August 13, 1981

Dear Friend,

I refuse to stop speaking out against the sin of homo-sexuality.

With God as my witness, I pledge that I will continue to expose the sin of homosexuality to the people of this nation. I believe that the massive homosexual revolution is always a symptom of a nation coming under the judgement of God.

Romans 1:24-28, Paul clearly condemns the sin of homo-sexuality. In verse 28, when a nation refuses to listen to God's standard of morality, the Bible declares, "God gave them over to a reprobate mind."

Recently, 250,000 homosexuals marched in the streets of San Francisco. Several weeks ago, 75,000 more were marching in the streets of Los Angeles. The homosexuals are on the march in this country.

Please remember, homosexuals do not reproduce! They re-cruit!

And, many of them are out after my children and your children.

This is one major reason why we must keep the Old-Time Gospel Hour alive! The Old-Time Gospel Hour is one of the few major ministries in America crying out against militant homo-sexuals.

So don't delay! Let me hear from you immediately! I will be anxiously awaiting your reply.

In Christ,

Jerry Falwell

Jerry Falwell

P.S. Let me repeat, a massive homosexual revolution can bring the judgement of God upon this nation. Our children must not be recruited into a profane life-style.

DECLARATION
OF
WAR

Be it known to all that The Old-Time Gospel Hour hereby declares war against the evils threatening America during the 1980's.

Furthermore, this shall be a Holy War, not a war with guns and bullets, but a war fought with the Bible, prayer and Christian involvement.

The Old-Time Gospel Hour hereby dedicates itself to spearhead the battle and lead an army of Christian soldiers into the war against evil.

In God's name we vow to fight against the following evils:

. . . legalized abortion — the murder of innocent babies

. . . pornography

. . . homosexuality

. . . socialism

. . . the deterioration of the home and family

With a firm mandate from God I fully commit The Old-Time Gospel Hour ministry in support of this Declaration of War.

signed

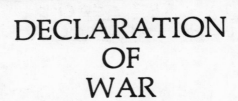

Jerry Falwell, President
Proverbs 14:34

THE OLD-TIME GOSPEL HOUR   LYNCHBURG VIRGINIA 24514

Urgent Communication

LATE BULLETIN

URGENT ** URGENT ** URGENT

FINANCIAL CRISIS AT CHRISTIAN VOICE MORAL GOVERNMENT FUND WORSE NOW THAN DON SILLS LETTER SAYS.

SO BAD I COULDN'T EVEN AFFORD TO MAIL THIS MESSAGE TO YOU SEPARATELY AND HAD TO INCLUDE IT WITH REV. DON'S LETTER.

SHORTAGE OF OPERATING FUNDS MAY FORCE US TO LITERALLY LOCK DOORS AND WALK AWAY FROM FIGHT IN 10 DAYS UNLESS FRIENDS COME TO RESCUE.

NEED GIFTS OF $15, $30, $60 OR $100 NOW TO PAY OVERDUE BILLS AND GO ON OFFENSIVE AGAIN. MUST ACT NOW TO DEFEAT HOMOSEXUAL RIGHTS LAWS, IMMORAL SEX EDUCATION, ABORTION. URGENT WE CONTINUE ALL—OUT EFFORTS TO BRING BACK SCHOOL PRAYER, HELP ENACT PRESIDENT'S GOOD STEWARDSHIP IN GOVERNMENT BUDGET.

CHRISTIAN VOICE MORAL GOVERNMENT FUND IS THE NATION'S MOST EFFECTIVE CHRISTIAN LOBBY AND POLITICAL ACTION COMMITTEE. CAN'T GIVE UP NOW. CAN'T LET MILITANT GAYS, ULTRA LIBERALS, ATHEISTS, PORNO PUSHERS, PRESSURE CONGRESS INTO PASSING SATAN'S AGENDA INSTEAD OF GOD'S.

URGE YOU, BESEECH YOU SEND MIRACLE WE NEED. PLEASE SEND SPECIAL OFFERING TO BRING OUR DRY BONES BACK TO LIFE AND INTO FIGHT AGAIN.

MAY GOD REWARD YOU A HUNDREDFOLD.

GARY JARMIN.

APPENDIX
B

Jerry Falwell, sermon delivered at Thomas Road Baptist Church on Sunday night, March 21, 1965, titled "Ministers and Marches." Quoted in full.

Under the Constitution of the United States, every American has the right to "peacefully" petition the government for a redress of grievances. This simply means that, in the present racial crises, all Americans, white, negro, or otherwise, have the legal right to "peacefully" demonstrate in order to obtain voting rights in Alabama—or elsewhere—if these rights are not allowed to the citizens. The purpose of this message is not to question such constitutional rights. Neither is it the intention of this message to discuss the subject of integration or segregation. It is my desire, in this sermon, to open the Bible and, from God's Word, answer the question—"Does the 'CHURCH' have any command from God to involve itself in marches, demonstrations, or any other actions, such as many ministers and church leaders are so doing today in the name of civil rights reforms?"

At the outset of this message, I do wish to speak frankly about one particular matter. There are, no doubt, many very sincere Christians who have felt a compulsion to join in civil rights efforts across the nation. At the same time, I must personally say that I do question the sincerity and non-violent intentions of some civil rights leaders such as Dr. Martin Luther King Jr., Mr. James Farmer, and others, who are known to have left-wing associations. It is very obvious that the Communists, as they do in all parts of the world, are taking advantage of a tense situation in our land, and are exploiting every in-

310

cident to bring about violence and bloodshed. But I must repeat that I do believe many sincere persons are participating. I must also say that I believe these demonstrations and marches have done more to damage race relations and to gender hate than to help!

Church Responsibility

Since all orthodox Christians accept the Bible to be the verbally inspired Word of God, let us look into this Bible and see what the commands to the church are. In the first book of the New Testament, Matthew 28:18–20, Jesus commissioned the church to: "Go ye therefore and teach all nations, baptizing them in the name of the Father and of the Son and of the Holy Ghost: teaching them to observe all things whatsoever I have commanded you." You will notice here three specific commands: (1) Make disciples, or as we sometimes say, win souls; (2) baptize these new converts in the name of the Trinity; (3) teach them the Christ-life. In Mark 16, you will find the same command in slightly different words. In Luke 24 and in John 20, the same commands are given. As we move to the Book of the Acts of the Apostles, we find in the 1st chapter and the 8th verse the very same command. As we search through the letters of Paul, and all the other New Testament letters, we see that the church is given no command other than this Great Commission to take the message of Christ to a dying world. As far as the relationship of the church to the world, it can be expressed as simply as the three words which Paul gave to Timothy—"preach the Word." We have a message of redeeming grace through a crucified and risen Lord. This message is designed to go right to the heart of man and there meet his deep spiritual need. Nowhere are we commissioned to reform the externals. We are not told to wage wars against bootleggers, liquor stores, gamblers, murderers, prostitutes, racketeers, prejudiced persons or institutions, or any other ex-prejudiced persons or institutions, or any other existing evil as such. Our ministry is not reformation but transformation. The gospel does not clean up the outside but rather regenerate the inside. I have had no greater joy as a minister of the gospel than to witness the marvelous changes wrought in the lives of many people to whom I have preached the gospel. Right here in the Thomas Road Baptist Church, I look into the faces of many people each Sunday who once were involved in the worst kinds of sin. Today they are God-fearing servants of Christ Jesus. What changed them? Did we go to Richmond and try to get laws passed which would send these persons to jail? No! In Christian love, we went to them prayerfully with the message of a crucified Christ. They received this Christ as their own personal Lord and Saviour. When Christ came in, sin went out. They no longer live their former lives. Not because we demanded they stop these things, but because now, they no longer want to do these things. As Paul says it in II Cor. 5:17: "Therefore if any man be in Christ, he is a new creature: old things are passed away; behold, all things are become new."

You may search the Bible and yet find no other command than the one mentioned above. Some, who are not acquainted with the Bible, will lift out such instances as Moses and his leading of the Jews out of Egyptian bondage, and thereby try to prove that Christians today are supposed to lead people out of bondage in situations where they are being discriminated against. Any Bible student would know first of all that the Jews spent 400 years in Egypt because of their own rebellion and because of a spiritual lesson which God was pointing out to all generations to come. Any Bible scholar would also know that the Jews were and are God's chosen people. His dealings with the Jews are very unique indeed. Likewise, the lessons of the Old Testament are related to the Law, while the New Testament lessons are all related to Grace. If we are going to lift out of the Old Testament things that are convenient for proving our contentions, we are also forced to accept other things. For instance, we would be forced to stone to death everybody who does any work on the Sabbath, or who commits adultery, or who fails to tithe. You can see how absurd such applications are under the Grace of God. The 400 years of Egyptian bondage is a type of the sinners experience before he is converted. We all live in bondage to sin until we know the truth of the new birth. When the Jews came out of Egypt, they immediately came into 40 years of wilderness wandering. This is a parallel to our infant and carnal Christian life as we struggle before learning the lessons of faith and rest in God. If church leaders are going to use Moses and the Jews in Egypt as a justification for what they are doing today with the negro in the South, they should also go on and tell the Jews that they are going to lead them into 40 years of wandering in which everyone of them except two will die. That is exactly what happened to all the Jews. Only Caleb and Joshua lived through that experience. Then, a new generation went into the Promised Land. The Promised Land is a parallel to the victorious Christian life on the earthly level, and our eventual Heaven on the eternal plane. To try to force any other meaning than this is simply making the Bible say what you want it to say. One atheist said that he could prove anything by the Bible. This is true, if you are not fair to the full and complete revelation.

The Christian's Citizenship

Philippians 3:20 is a key verse in getting to the heart of the matter. Paul said "For our citizenship is in Heaven." The King James version uses the word "conversation" in verse 20, but a study of the Greek reveals that the word should be "citizenship." The Christian has his citizenship in the Royal

Nation in Heaven. While we are told to "render unto Caesar, the things that are Caesar's," in the true interpretation, we have very few ties on this earth. We pay our taxes, cast our votes as a responsibility of citizenship, obey the laws of the land, and other things demanded of us by the society in which we live. But, at the same time, we are cognizant that our only purpose on this earth is to know Christ and to make Him known. Believing the Bible as I do, I would find it impossible to stop preaching the pure saving gospel of Jesus Christ, and begin doing anything else—including fighting communism, or participating in civil rights reforms. As a God-called preacher, I find that there is no time left after I give the proper time and attention to winning people to Christ. Preachers are not called to be politicians but to be soul winners. That is one reason why our church operates the Elim Home for Alcoholics. That is also the reason why we will be taking in 2,000 boys and girls without charge at Treasure Island this year. That is another reason why we support missionaries all over the world who are preaching the gospel of Christ. That is why we conduct daily radio and television programs. That is why we print tens of thousands of books and booklets with the Christian message in them. That is why we have established chapels and missions in needy areas in and around our city. When the 2,000 members of Thomas Road Baptist Church attend our services, they do not hear sermons on communism, civil rights, or any other subject except the gospel of Christ. If the many thousands of churches and pastors of America would suddenly begin preaching the old fashioned gospel of Jesus Christ and the power that is in His atoning blood, a revival would grip our land such as we have never known before. If as much effort could be put into winning people to Jesus Christ across the land as is being exerted in the present civil rights movement, America would be turned upside down for God. Hate and prejudice would certainly be in a great measure overcome. Churches would be filled with sincere souls seeking God. Good relations between the races would soon be evidenced. God is Love, and when He is put first in the individual life and in the church, God's people become messengers of love. May we pray toward this goal.

Jesus Christ and Politics

In Matthew 22:15–22, we have the story of the Pharisees coming to Jesus for the purpose of entangling Him in His words. They asked Him "Is it lawful to give tribute unto Caesar, or not?" There never was a more discriminatory and cruel government as that of the Roman Empire. Christians were slaughtered. Non-Romans were considered to be nothing. The tax system was most dishonest and unfair. The Pharisees assumed that Jesus would lash out at the Roman government. Surely He would take some political stand here. But He did not. He asked for a penny and, upon receiving the penny, asked whose image was on that penny. They answered by saying "Caesar's." He then said "Render therefore unto Caesar the things which are Caesar's: and unto God the things that are God's." In other words, he said: "Pay your taxes, forget politics, and serve Me with all your heart." He very tactfully sidestepped any involvement in a political argument. He was not here to reform the Roman Empire. In Luke 19:10, He said: "For the Son of man is come to seek and to save that which is lost."

On another occasion, John 4:6–13 gives the story of Jesus and His meeting with the immoral women at Jacob's well. Jesus was tired after his long journey into Samaria. A woman of Samaria came to draw water and Jesus asked her for a drink. She replied: "How is it that thou, being a Jew, askest drink of me, which am a woman of Samaria? for the Jews have no dealings with the Samaritans." This woman was saying to Jesus that the Jews were segregated from the Samaritans. They discriminated against the Samaritans. It was much like many of the situations existing today in America and in other countries between different nations and races. But as we read the rest of the account, we see that Jesus totally ignored her attempt to involve him in a discussion about segregation. He immediately began to tell her that her need was spiritual water. He told her all about her sinful life and her great need of salvation. She was converted and then, through her testimony, her home town turned to God. Jesus could have spent the rest of the day telling her how terrible it was for her to be a segregationist. He did not. He told her that her need was in the heart. She was a prejudiced person because she was a sinner in need of a Saviour. He did not work from the outside in, but rather from the inside out. When she became a Christian, she forgot all about any racial differences. She immediately became a soul winner herself. She even brought other Samaritans to this formerly despised Jew. What a wonderful lesson for Christians and churches to follow today.

Zacchaeus was a dishonest tax collector. When Jesus came to his town, he was very desirous to see Him. Being a very short man in stature, it was necessary for him to climb a tree in order to see over the heads of the throng who gathered around the Lord Jesus. If Jesus had been like some ministers and church leaders today, He would have led a demonstration against Zacchaeus and demanded that he give back all the money which he had wrongfully taken from the poor people. Instead, He looked up lovingly into the tree where Zacchaeus was. He asked Zacchaeus to come down, for He desired to go to his house and sup with him. This display of love won Zacchaeus to Christ. After his conversion, he offered to give back fourfold everything he had taken unfairly. This is another example of working from the inside out. Jesus was constantly found eating with publicans and sinners. The Pharisees, the church leaders of that day, criticized Him for such identification with sinners. He never attacked sinful people—but rather displayed love toward them. The only thing Jesus ever demonstrated against was the desecration of His Temple. When thieves, money changers, and ungodly people invaded the House of God, He quickly cleared them out with a barrel stave. I believe that if we spent enough effort trying to clean up our churches, rather than trying to clean up state and national governments, we would do well. Dances, parties, bingo games, many other forms of gambling, and other disgraceful things are going on right in the churches today. Worse than that, a liberal gospel has come in. The Bible is rejected as being the verbally inspired Word of God. Fundamental Christianity has been junked. And yet, there seems to be very little concern over this spiritual degradation inside our churches today. I'm afraid the church is casting stones while living in a glass house.

The Hypocrisy of the Social Gospel

One Bible teacher said that we should always require everything we say to travel first through three "gates of gold" before we allow these words to leave our lips. Those three "gates of gold" are: (1) Is it true?; (2) Is it loving?; (3) Is it needful? In relation then to this subject under discussion, I would ask a question: "Does this present civil rights program promote the Love of God?" The leaders are always crying out against prejudice and hate. They are always talking about love. Romans 12:9 says "Let love be without hypocrisy." I am fearful that all of the rioting and demonstrating has produced a great amount of hate as evidenced through the recent murders and other forms of violence. In Romans 13:13 we read: "Let us walk honestly, as in the day; not in rioting." In II Timothy 2:24, Paul says: "And the servant of the Lord must not strive; but be gentle to all men." The word "strive"could be translated in a modern form as "straining to have one's way." When we as Christians see an existing evil, it is our responsibility to pray. It is also our responsibility to preach the message of a living Christ to those who are in bondage to such sin. But it is never our duty as servants of God to exert physical force or effort which constitutes striving. In II Corinthians 10:3–5, we read: "For though we walk in the flesh, we do not war after the flesh: for the weapons of our warfare are not carnal, but mighty through God to the pulling down of strongholds; casting down imaginations and every high thing that exalteth itself against the knowledge of God, and bringing into captivity every thought to the obedience of Christ." The Bible teaching here is very clear and needs no explanation.

While the church leaders are so obsessed with the alleged discrimination against negroes in the South, very little is said about the same situation in the North. Likewise, very little is said about the very bad conditions under which American Indians live today. This leads one to believe that political expedience is somewhat involved in this so-called freedom movement. Could it possibly be that the American Indians do not present the potential of a strong voting block in the future. One cannot help but wonder. If church leaders feel that the church should take part in social reforms, then I am forced to ask why the church is not concerned about the alcoholism problem in America. There are almost as many alcoholics as there are negroes. Three times as much money is spent annually in America for liquor as for education. More money is spent annually for tobacco than for support of religious institutions. There seems to be a good bit of hypocrisy evident here. Why is the church not concerned about the liberal trend in our theological schools? Why is there not a like display of concern about the lowering of moral standards among young people today? Many other questions could be put forth. I believe that this suffices to illustrate the point.

The Church's Loss of Dignity

In I Corinthians 14:40 Paul said: "Let all things be done decently and in order." Also in I Thessalonians 5:22, he said: "Abstain from all appearance of evil." The Christian's testimony is the most precious thing he possesses as far as his relationship to others is concerned. If we are going to win people to Christ, they must see us living the same life seven days a week which we preach in the pulpit on Sunday. If the world does not respect us as children of God, then we have no hope of winning them to the Saviour. Many sinners have lost confidence in the church today because of its involvements in many questionable things.

I went to visit a man recently who is a very wicked person. When I began to tell him about the love of God and how that Christ could make him a new person, he quickly gave me a sharp word. He told me that he had been reading the newspapers and seen ministers and their involvements in the riots and mob actions in American streets. He said: "If this is Christianity, I'm glad I'm not a Christian." The world is losing respect for the church because it is lowering its standards. When any part of the church loses its testimony, the whole church suffers. All are judged by what some do. May God help us to run from all appearance of evil. Of course, we all recognize that there is a degree of discrimination in every place and in every land. As Christians, we detest discrimination. But we do need to see that we can never stop it through any other means than that weapon which was given the church 2,000 years ago—the preaching of the gospel of Christ.

Conclusion

Love cannot be legislated. Love is found in a Person—His Name is Jesus Christ. The church needs to become dedicated once again to the task of preaching Christ. Education, medicine, social reform, and all the other external ministries cannot meet the needs of the human soul and spirit. If money and education could raise the moral standards of a nation, America would be pure indeed. It cannot be done this way. When the light of the gospel shines into the sinner's heart, his entire life and attitudes are transformed.

I feel that we need to get off the streets and back into the pulpits and into the prayer rooms. I believe we need to take our Bible and go down into the highways and hedges and bring men to Christ. I believe we need to rededicate ourselves to the great task of turning this world back to God. The preaching of the gospel is the only means by which this can be done.

Prayer: O God, grant that this message shall be received in the same spirit in which it is given. May it please Thee to use the humble and simple truths embodied in this sermon to strengthen the hearts of many of Thy children. May Thy church be guided away from all secondary ministries, and into the true commissions of preaching the gospel of Christ to every creature. For we pray in Christ's name, Amen.

APPENDIX
C

Thomas J. McIntyre, Senator from New Hampshire, excerpts from a speech made on the floor of the U.S. Senate, March 1, 1978.

I want to express myself on the way the issue of the canal treaties has been politicized, and I will do so with no little anger and resentment. Perhaps what I am going to say is not precisely germane to the question before us, but I believe with all my heart that it must be said and said now. The campaign waged by certain opponents of ratification—in my state and across the nation—has impugned the loyalty and the motives of too many honorable Americans to be ignored or suffered in silence a minute longer.

Mr. President, I believe the techniques used to exploit the issue of the canal treaties are the most compelling evidencee to date that an ominous change is taking place in the very character and direction of American politics.

In his farewell broadcast several months ago, Eric Sevareid warned of the paradoxical rise of "dangerously passionate certainties" in a time of no easy answers.

One could speculate endlessly about the root cause of this development: A generation of disillusion and disenchantment with the lack of integrity and the misuse of power by leaders and institutions; the humbling experience in Vietnam; the unrelenting pressure of unfocused anxieties about national direction and purpose; and the all-too-human inclination to turn in frustration to the slogans and nostrums of a simpler time.

But whatever the cause, Mr. President, I see abundant evidence that these "dangerously passionate certainties" are being cynically fomented, manipulated, and targeted in ways that threaten amity, unity, and the purposeful course of government in order to advance a radical ideology that is alien to mainstream political thought.

Already we have seen the vigor of the two-party system sapped by this phenomenon. More and more Americans appear unwilling to abide by the essential ethic of the party system—that willingness to tolerate differing views within the party, and to accept the party platform, however unpalatable some of its provisions, in order to advance a general political philosophy.

As a result, the traditional role of the parties is slowly being usurped by a thousand and one passionately committed special interest, splinter faction, and single issue constituencies.

My colleagues know what I am talking about. They know, as I know, that on any given issue someone somewhere can depress a computer key and within hours or a few days at the most we are inundated by mimeographed postcards and custom-tailored letters and telegrams that vary scarcely a comma in the message they deliver.

Now let me make this clear, Mr. President. I believe in listening to my constituents. I do pay careful heed to all of their cards and letters. But I give special consideration to those that are obviously the individual product of the writer.

And let me say, too, that I believe in firm and outspoken commitment to principles and convictions. I would readily agree, as someone once said, that there are times when compromise offers little more than an "easy refuge for the irresolute spirit."

But I would make a distinction between commitment that is rooted in reality—commitment, for example, that recognizes the linkage between problems and the consequences of ignoring that linkage when applying solutions—and commitment that denies reality and is, in truth, but the blind and obsessive pursuit of illusion.

Extremists who deny reality in the pursuit of illusion deny something else, Mr. President, something of fundamental importance in our republic of free men and women. They deny the differences that distinguish one human being from another.

They deny the indisputable fact that each of us is the result of a unique combination of genes and chromosomes, of influences and impressions, of training and of faith, and of the milieu from which we sprang. In short, they deny everything that science and simple observation tell us about human nature and individual capacities and limitations.

By proceeding from the flawed premise that all of us are alike, it is easy for ideologues to conclude that we must see every issue as they see it—unless there is something sinister in our motivation.

And they proceed from that premise, Mr. President, with an arrogance born of the conviction that they and they alone have a corner on patriotism, morality, and God's own truths, that their values and standards and viewpoints are so unassailable they justify any means, however coarse and brutish, of imposing them on others.

Now I want to be fair about this, Mr. President. In the particular instance of the canal treaties, I am thinking about the kind of politics practiced by what has come to be known as the New Right. But I want to note that the record of extremists on the ideological left bears a remarkable, and regrettable, similarity. . . .

There have been times when some of us have felt the wrath of the purist left, Mr. President. And now—today—many of us are feeling the wrath of the New Right because we will not bow to their threats and vote against ratification of the canal treaties.

Indeed, Mr. President, one element of the New Right—the Conservative Caucus—did not wait for me to announce how I would vote on the treaties. They launched their attack months ago.

Last summer the national director of the Conservative Caucus, Howard Phillips, said conservatives should make "a political sitting duck" of Tom McIntyre over the canal treaties and that the Conservative Caucus could "make it a political impossibility for McIntyre to vote for that treaty."

On December 4, 1977, the Conservative Caucus of New Hampshire passed a resolution of censure and served it on me like a subpoena. I was "censured" for a speech I made last September, a speech in which I took neither side on the treaty issue but merely spelled out the pro and con arguments I would have to consider when I finally made my decision on how to vote. . . .

The resolution censured me for allegedly giving aid to a recognized dictator, one Omar Torrijos; for indicating I was willing to violate the Constitution and my oath of office by even considering a vote for treaty ratification; for failing to recognize through my speech and "personal ignorance" that the treaties would provide the Communist regimes with a legal beachhead from which they would eventually overpower all nations of Central and South America; for saying in the speech that however I voted I would vote in "good conscience"; for happening to be chairman of the Subcommittee on Financial Institutions when, the resolution said, "it is common knowledge that the financial institutions of the United States have more than a vested interest in the canal treaties. . . ."

Now I hope my colleagues are not surprised by the crude message and the abrasive, threatening tone of that resolution of censure. That is the lexicon of the New Right. And it makes a travesty of the movement's efforts to promote itself as respectable and responsible.

Hear, if you will, the revealing words of Howard Phillips on other occasions:

"We organize discontent. We must prove our ability to get revenge on people who go against us. . . . We'll be after them, if they vote the wrong way. We're not going to stop after the vote's past."

And hear the words of another spokesman for the New Right, Paul Weyrich, director of the Committee for the Survival of a Free Congress:

"We are different from previous generations of conservatives. We are no longer working to preserve the status quo. We are radicals, working to overturn the present power structure of this country."

Mr. President, these people are different from traditional conservatives. I know the traditional conservatives of my own state. I have competed with them in the political arena. I have worked with them in behalf of our state. They are people of honor, civility, and decency.

The New Right cannot comprehend how people of opposing viewpoints can find common ground and work together. For them, there is no common ground. And this, in my judgment, is the best indication of what they truly are—radicals whose aim is not to compete with honor and decency, not to compromise when necessary to advance the common good, but to annihilate those they see as enemies.

And if "conservative" in the title "Conservative Caucus" is an ironic misuse of the word, it is doubly ironic that destiny would link the national chairman of the Conservative Caucus—the governor of New Hampshire—with William Loeb, the publisher of New Hampshire's largest newspaper and the master practitioner of the politics of threat and vengeance.

Within the year, the governor, the head of the Conservative Caucus, made the following bizarre announcements:

He said the Carter administration was pursuing "a pro-Communist course." He said Martin Luther King "did great harm to the American way of life through his association with Communist-inspired organizations."

In South Africa a few weeks ago, he called our State Department "un-American" but called John Vorster "one of the great world statesmen of today." He said apartheid is a "local South African problem." As for detention without trial in South Africa, he said:

"You know, even Abraham Lincoln suspended habeas corpus during the Civil War."

Fourteen of New Hampshire's top religious leaders issued a joint statement, read from the pulpits of many churches, taking sharp issue with the governor's fawning appraisal of South Africa's leadership and policies. "Our Christian consciences," the clergy said, "will not allow (the governor's) statement to go unanswered."

So William Loeb immediately rushed to the governor's defense, declaring in a signed, front page editorial that the 14 clergymen "have been playing for suckers. . . . Their idealism and their innocence and almost complete ignorance about South Africa has been taken advantage of."

Mr. Loeb went on to give his own appraisal of John Vorster's South African regime. "The South Africans," Loeb said, "are doing the best they can to bring these blacks out of the jungle. . . ."

Mr. President, I cite the above public utterances by the national chairman of the Conservative Caucus and Mr. Loeb only to ask the obvious. If they hold such benighted opinions on those matters, how much credence can we give their views on the Panama Canal treaties?

But credibility may be too much to ask of men whose stock in trade is flag waving, sabre rattling and the politics of threat and vengeance.

In all of this nation, Mr. President, there may not be two more recklessly belligerent public figures than Meldrim Thomson and William Loeb. Though neither has ever worn the uniform of this country into battle, they are the first to demand the kind of precipitous action that could plunge young Americans back into combat.

Only a few weeks after the oil embargo of 1973 got under way, Mr. Loeb charged into this most sensitive situation with an editorial titled: "Let's Go After Our Oil." Calling the Arab leaders "heathen swine", he said that if they did not quickly yield to an embargo and blockade we could ask them:

"How would you like to have us bomb your holy cities of Mecca and Medina out of existence?"

And not many weeks ago, Governor Thomson went to Taiwan as the guest of that nation and promised that the day would come when the United States would support an invasion of mainland China.

Oddly enough, however, Chairman Thomson's high regard for military power and his willingness to use it is offset by his low esteem of the integrity of military leaders. Listen to his insulting appraisal of why the Joint Chiefs of Staff support the new canal treaties:

"Active commissioned officers," he contends, "will either say what the administration desires or remain silent."

Mr. President, what this notorious armchair warrior—and others like him—is telling us, in effect, is that a man like Admiral Holloway, a man who fought for his country at Saipan, the Southern Palau Islands, Tinian, Leyte, the Surigao Straits, Korea, and Vietnam, a man who has earned the Bronze Star, the Navy Commendation Medal, the Distinguished Flying Cross and three Air Medals, the U.S. Legion of Merit, and three Distinguished Service Medals, a man who rose to top command of our Navy by the age of 54, cannot be trusted when he tells us, as he did, that "the new treaties are in the best national security interest of the United States."

Mr. President, this is a prime example of what I meant when I said radical extremists believe that we would see every issue as they see it—if there was not something sinister in our motivation. In this instance, the national chairman of the Conservative Caucus—Governor Thomson of New Hampshire—would have us believe that military leaders like Admiral Holloway have compromised their integrity and the nation's security in order to ingratiate themselves with the administration. How insulting. How absurd. . . .

My political fate is not my concern here today. My concern is the desperate need for people of conscience and good will to stand up and face down the bully boys of the radical New Right before the politics of intimidation does to America what it has tried to do to New Hampshire. . . .

APPENDIX
D

Barry M. Goldwater, Senator from Arizona, speech entered in the record, September 16, 1981, U.S. Senate, "To Be a Conservative." Quoted in full.

It's a wonderful feeling to be a conservative these days. When I ran for president 17 years ago I was told I was behind the times. Now everybody tells me I was ahead of my time. All I can say is that time certainly is an elusive companion.

But those reactions illustrate how far the ideological pendulum has swung in recent years. The American people have expressed their desire for a new course in our public policy in this country—a conservative course.

President Reagan's triumphs at the polls and in Congress during the past year are, of course, great tributes to his skill as a politician. But they also resulted, I believe, from the long-developing shift of public opinion to traditional American values.

As far as I am concerned, that shift had to come. Government had been intruding more and more into every aspect of our lives. The people just wouldn't stand for it anymore.

I have seen it coming for a long time. Throughout my political career, since the day I took my seat in the United States Senate, I have preached one basic theme: the bigger government gets, the more it threatens our freedom.

Oh, I'm certain those who contributed to the growth of government had all the best intentions. As they started one federal program after another through the years, their motives always sounded good and the intent of the programs always seemed admirable.

Almost 150 years ago a young Frenchman came to this country and marveled at the success of the American experiment in democracy. Alexis de Tocqueville wrote after visiting this country that "the advantage of democracy does not consist . . . in favoring the prosperity of all, but simply in contributing to the well-being of the greatest number."

And the foundation of our form of government is not in the principle of prosperity for all but in *freedom* for all. That's what has attracted all those who have migrated to this country. That's what has made America the symbol of hope and prosperity for all the world. Freedom: that's what true conservatism is all about.

Being a conservative in America traditionally has meant that one holds a deep, abiding respect for the Constitution. We conservatives believe sincerely in the integrity of the Constitution. We treasure the freedom that document protects.

We believe, as the founding fathers did, that we "are endowed by our creator with certain unalienable rights; that among these are life, liberty, and the pursuit of happiness."

And for 205 years this nation, based on those principles, has endured. Through foreign wars and civil wars . . . through political scandals and economic disasters . . . through civil disorders and presidential assassinations, our flag has flown high. Through it all we've survived every possible attack on our freedom.

But where the guns of war and the breadlines of the depression failed, another force could succeed in dividing our country. The specter of single issue religious groups is growing over our land. In all honesty, I must admit that the birth of the so-called "New Right" is a direct reaction to years of increasing social activism by the liberal side of the religious house. Within that development lies a very serious threat to our liberty.

One of the great strengths of our political system always has been our tendency to keep religious issues in the background. By maintaining the separation of church and state, the United States has avoided the intolerance which has so divided the rest of the world with religious wars. Throughout our two hundred plus years, public policy debate has focused on political and economic issues, on which there can be compromise.

James Madison once wrote that "if men were angels, no government would be necessary."

Well, Madison certainly recognized that humans are not angels. He realized that they tend to group together in narrow interest groups, which he called factions. And he wrote extensively in the Federalist Papers about how the Constitution should protect us from the abuses of various factions.

Madison saw this as the great paradox of our system: How do you control the factions without violating the people's basic freedoms?

"In framing a government which is to be administered by men over men," Madison wrote, "the great difficulty lies in this: you must first enable the government to control the governed; and in the next place oblige it to control itself."

And in a well-constructed representative government like ours, Madison said, one of our greatest strengths is our ability to "break and control the violence of faction."

What he said is that the aim of the framers of the Constitution was to allow freedom of religion and freedom of speech for *everyone*, not just those who follow one religious faction.

"A zeal for different opinions concerning religion," Madison said, has occasionally "divided mankind . . . and rendered them much more disposed to vex and oppose each other than to cooperate for the common good."

Can any of us refute the wisdom of Madison and the other framers? Can anyone look at the carnage in Iran, the bloodshed in Northern Ireland, or the bombs bursting in Lebanon and yet question the dangers of injecting religious issues into the affairs of state?

Our political process involves a constant give and take, a continuous series of trade-offs. From this system of compromise, we get legislation that reflects input from many sectors of our society and addresses many needs and interests.

Obviously, not everyone can be pleased, but at least all sides are considered.

However, on religious issues there can be little or no compromise. There is no position on which people are so immovable as their religious beliefs. There is no more powerful ally one can claim in a debate than Jesus Christ, or God, or Allah, or whatever one calls his supreme being.

But, like any powerful weapon, the use of God's name on one's behalf should be used sparingly.

The religious factions that are growing throughout our land are not using their religious clout with wisdom. They are trying to force government leaders into following their positions 100 percent. If you disagree with these religious groups on any particular moral issue, they cajole, they complain, they threaten you with loss of money or votes or both.

In the past couple years, I have seen many news items that referred to the moral majority, pro-life and other religious groups as "the new right," and the "new conservatism." Well, I have spent quite a number of years carrying the flag of the "old conservatism." And I can say with conviction that the religious issues of these groups have little or nothing to do with conservative or liberal politics.

The uncompromising position of these groups is a divisive element that could tear apart the very spirit of our representative system, if they gain sufficient strength.

As it is, they are diverting us away from the vital issues that our government needs to address. We are facing serious economic and military dangers in this country today, and we need to make a concerted effort to correct our problems in these areas.

But far too much of the time of members of Congress and officials in the executive branch is used up dealing with special interest groups on issues like abortion, school busing, ERA, prayer in the schools and pornography. While these are important moral issues, they are secondary right now to our national security and economic survival.

I must make it clear that I don't condemn these groups for what they believe. I happen to share many of the values emphasized by these organizations.

I, too, believe that we Americans should return to our traditional values concerning morality, family closeness, self-reliance, and a day's work for a day's pay. These are the values our forebears clung to as they built this nation into the citadel of freedom it is today.

And I, too, have been pleased with the swing of the pendulum in recent years to the conservative, moral end of the spectrum.

But I object to certain groups jumping on that pendulum and then claiming that they caused it to swing in the first place.

And I'm frankly sick and tired of the political preachers across this country telling me as a citizen that if I want to be a moral person, I must believe in "A," "B," "C," and "D." Just who do they think they are? And from where do they presume to claim the right to dictate their moral beliefs to me?

And I am even more angry as a legislator who must endure the threats of every religious group who thinks it has some God-granted right to control my vote on every roll call in the Senate.

I am warning them today: I will fight them every step of the way if they try to dictate their moral convictions to all Americans in the name of "conservatism."

This unrelenting obsession with a particular goal destroys the perspective of many decent people with whom I think I agree on most issues. In the quest for moral righteousness they have become easy prey to manipulation and misjudgment.

A prime example was the recent nomination of Sandra O'Connor as a Supreme Court Justice and the ensuing uproar over her stand on abortion.

The abortion issue has nothing to do with being conservative or liberal. I happen to oppose abortion, but there are many fine conservatives who would go along with regulated abortions. In fact, my own wife believes that a woman should have the freedom of choice for herself whether she is capable of continuing the pregnancy and then raising the child.

I disagree with her on that. Yet I respect her right to disagree. Lord knows, if I expected her to agree with me on every issue we'd be in a lot of trouble.

And the same goes for prospective Supreme Court justices. *No* single issue ever should decide the fitness of a Supreme Court justice. To think otherwise is to go against the integrity of the Constitution.

There are many broad issues addressed each day by a jurist that are much more revealing of how that person might perform on the high court. A judge's attitude on private property rights, state sovereignty, statutory construction and treatment of criminals tells me more about whether a person is conservative than his or her stand on abortion.

Of course, the saddest part of the whole dispute was that Judge (Justice) O'Connor was attacked by these religious factions for a position she doesn't hold. She opposes abortion and says so. I firmly believe that she recognizes the authority of legislatures to regulate it.

She will make an excellent justice of the Supreme Court. She will make President Reagan proud that he chose her as the best of all candidates—men or women.

And the religious factions will go on imposing their will on others unless the decent people connected to them recognize that religion has no place in public policy.

They must learn to make their views known without trying to make their views the *only* alternatives.

The great decisions of government cannot be dictated by the concerns of religious factions. This was true in the days of Madison, and it is just as true today.

We have succeeded for 205 years in keeping the affairs of state separate from the uncompromising idealism of religious groups and we mustn't stop now.

To retreat from that separation would violate the principles of conservatism and the values upon which the framers built this democratic republic.

APPENDIX
E

A. Bartlett Giamatti, President of Yale University, Freshman
Address, August 31, 1981, "A Liberal Education and the
New Coercion." Quoted in full.

Ladies and Gentlemen of the Class of 1985:

You wondered all summer what these days and this place would be like. Would you be alone in your trepidation? Would everyone else be at ease and only you at loose ends? Would you *be* the loose end? If you were meant somehow to acquire a liberal education, would there be some way to recognize the creature ahead of time?

Here at Yale you will hear often about a liberal education. What is it? Is a liberal education a set of courses, fulfilling certain requirements, across a variety of disciplines? That is certainly a description of the mechanics of what might become a liberal education. Is it an education pursued, as Cardinal Newman believed, in a spirit that studies a subject simply for and in itself, without concern for the practical consequences of such study? That would be the description of the proper attitude to bring to your studies. There is, however, more to what I mean by a liberal education.

I believe a liberal education is an education in the root meaning of "liberal"—"liber"—"free"—the liberty of the mind free to explore itself, to draw itself out, to connect with other minds and spirits in the quest for truth. Its goal is to train the whole person to be at once intellectually discerning and humanly flexible, tough-minded and open-hearted; to be responsive to the new and responsible for values that make us civilized. It is to teach us to meet

329

what is new and different with reasoned judgment and humanity. A liberal education is an education for freedom, the freedom to assert the liberty of the mind to make itself new for the others it cherishes.

The order necessary to keep that freedom from collapsing into merely competitive appetites or colliding gusts of anarchy is, first, in this country, a respect for law and the processes of law. But it is also more than an order external; it is the internalized order that grows with self-government, self-civilizing. Order is the precondition of humane freedom, freedom the goal of responsible order. Your education here intends to do many things, but ultimately to bring you to comprehend the responsibilities and the pleasures of that essential, grand connection.

I speak to the nature of a liberal education, and of freedom and order, for three reasons. First, I believe it cannot be said often enough how precious and vital these ideas are to our daily lives. Second, I raise them because the practical application of these principles will be, I hope, the defining framework for your time at Yale and for your lives after Yale. And, third, I raise them because I think they must be asserted at this particular time in our country's history, in the teeth of a storm that blows across the landscape. I have said what I believe because there are now in America powerful voices which attack and will continue to attack these very ideas.

A self-proclaimed "Moral Majority," and its satellite or client groups, cunning in the use of a native blend of old intimidation and new technology, threaten the values I have named. Angry at change, rigid in the application of chauvinistic slogans, absolutistic in morality, they threaten through political pressure or public denunciation whoever dares to disagree with their authoritarian positions. Using television, direct mail, and economic boycott, they would sweep before them anyone who holds a different opinion.

From the maw of this "morality" come those who presume to know what justice for all is; come those who presume to know which books are fit to read, which television programs are fit to watch, which textbooks will serve for all the young; come spilling those who presume to know what God alone knows, which is when human life begins. From the maw of this "morality" rise the tax-exempt Savonarolas who believe they, and they alone, possess the truth. There is no debate, no discussion, no dissent. They know. There is only one set of overarching political and spiritual and social beliefs; whatever view does not conform to these views is by definition relativistic, negative, secular, immoral, against the family, anti–free enterprise, un-American. What nonsense.

What dangerous, malicious nonsense. What a shame more of our captains of commerce have not seized the opportunity to speak up *for* free enterprise. What a shame such denials of our country's deepest traditions of freedom of thought, speech, creed and choice are not faced candidly in open debate by our political and religious leaders. What a shame more of those from various parts of the society with the responsibility to lead have not made the point, clearly and unambiguously, that such beliefs have every right to be expressed but not to be imposed by intimidation.

I do not fear that these peddlers of coercion will eventually triumph. The American people are too decent, too generous, too practical about their principles to put up with the absolutism of these "majorities" for very long. Nor do I think that when these groups have finally gone back into their burrows of frustration and anger, to lie seething until the next time, that the value they now pervert will be done lasting harm. For what they claim they espouse— love of country, a regard for the sanctity of life and the importance of the family, a belief in high standards of personal conduct, a conviction that we derive our values from a transcendent being, a desire to assert that free enterprise is better than state ownership or state control—are not evil or pernicious beliefs. Quite the contrary. They are the kernels of beliefs held dear, in various ways, by me and millions of other Americans and you should not scorn these ideas simply because some extremists claim, whether sincerely or hypocritically, to have captured these beliefs for themselves. The point is, the rest of us hold to ideas of family, country, belief in God, *in different ways.* The right to differ, and to see things differently, is our concern.

What disgusts me so much about the "morality" seeping out of the ground around our feet is that it would deny the legitimacy of differentness. We should all be dismayed with the shredding of the spiritual fabric of our society, with the urging to selfishness and discrimination all around us. We should be concerned that so much of our political and religious leadership acts intimidated for the moment and will not say with clarity that this most recent denial of the legitimacy of differentness is a radical assault on the very pluralism—of peoples, political beliefs, values, forms of merit and systems of religion—our country was founded to welcome and foster.

Pluralism is not relativism. It does not mean the denial of absolutes or the absence of standards. Pluralism is not code for anything. It signals the recognition that people of different ethnic groups and races and adherents of various religious and political and personal beliefs have a right to coexist as equals under the law and have an obligation to forge the freedoms they enjoy into a coherent, civilized and vigilant whole. These different peoples have a responsibility, inherent in their freedom, to make a commonweal, that is, a public good whose abiding concern is the practical protection of the several individual freedoms that are ordered for the general welfare. If pluralism as a concept denies anything, it denies the hegemony of the homogenous, the rule by a single, overmastering sensibility which would exclude all those who are different from the general benefits of citizenship.

Pluralism is an inclusive, absorptive ideal; in practical terms, it encourages competition, compromise and consensus. It does not abide absolutism, decree and complete moral certitude. In political terms, a pluralistic democracy like ours is often messy; issues are not neat, edges are not clean, resolution is not swift in most cases because so many different interests must be attended to. One can, as I have, lament the special or single interest lobby; one can grow mightily impatient with a Congress, for instance, which always trades off and spreads the pain or the pork on a national basis. Nor is a pluralistic democracy any more immune to corruption than other aggregations of humankind. For the governors and the governed the consensual, complex, compromising mode of a democracy can be wearing and wearying. But how much better a system that does not assume one single voice shall forever have the last say; how much better a shifting, adaptive if imperfect public process, concerned finally to keep its questions open and essential freedoms strong, than one that would displace law with polyester mysticism and would presume to impose a final, complete, arbitrary contour on society and the behavior of individuals. The "Moral Majority" is a cry of exhaustion, a longing for surcease from the strain of managing complexity.

Those voices of coercion speak not for liberty but for license, the license to divide in the name of patriotism, the license to deny in the name of Christianity. And they have licensed a new meanness of spirit in our land, a resurgent bigotry that manifests itself in racist and discriminatory postures; in threats of political retaliation; in injunctions to censorship; in acts of violence.

In December of 1980, the Anti-Defamation League of B'nai B'rith stated that reported anti-Semitic episodes, including vandalism, arson and cemetery desecrations, increased by 192 percent in 1980—from 129 episodes in 1979 to 377 in 1980. The tip of the iceberg grew in a way that sickened all decent Americans. In the past few years, the Ku Klux Klan has increased its visibility again and claims to have founded or revived, in its name or in league with others, paramilitary camps and training activities in Alabama, California, Connecticut, Illinois, North Carolina and Texas.

Hating in public by the mad or the malevolent is only part of the story being told again. People who have no connection or sympathy with such forms of domestic terrorism nevertheless use the new atmosphere to apologize for other forms of terrorism; or they fall silent when it is imperative precisely to speak out; or they apologize for the excesses—the spiritual violence—of evangelical or political fringe groups. In the new atmosphere, it becomes possible to keep, as Jack Newfield among others has said, two sets of books on civil liberties, two sets of standards that can be applied as one's ideology demands, rather than the single standard set forth by the Bill of Rights, the "monism" of values, that a pluralistic society must maintain to be healthy, open and free. It is a new mood that can be quantified only up to a point, a mood that should not be dismissed as either inevitable—the consequence of a national "swing to the right"—or as historically predictable—the cyclic eruptions of Know-Nothingism or a recurrent "paranoid style" in American life. Neither of those "explanations" serves because each avoids the issue. The issue is that a reactionary mood, preying on the fears of those who feel dispossessed by change and bypassed by complexity, is growing and that there is a moral imperative, rooted in America's best traditions, to identify it and call for a cleansing of the air.

These efforts to deny others the freedom to be themselves wish for a closed society, a form of community similar to a vast, airless bunker. That is not the kind of community you have come to and that has been waiting to welcome you. Yale is a diverse, open place, receptive to people from throughout our society, and it must and will remain so. It is a University community given to the competition of ideas and of merit, devoted to excellence and dedicated to the belief that freedom of choice, speech, and creed is essential to the quest for truth that constitutes its mission. Those who wish such a place to teach only their version of the "right" values and "correct" views misunderstand completely the free market of ideas that is a great university; they misapprehend the extent to which the University serves the country best when it is a cauldron of competing ideas and not a neatly arranged platter of received opinions.

You will find, if Yale is at all successful, much that is different here. Revel in that diversity. Whether different idea or person, connect with it in order to understand it. Female and male, Christian and Jew, black, white, brown and yellow, you must find, as we all must, what binds us together, in common hope and need, not what divides us. You may or may not come all to love one another, but to be part of the best of this place you must have the moral courage to respect one another. This is not a community that will tolerate the sexism, the racism, the anti-Semitism, the bigotry about ethnic groups, the hysterical rejection of others, the closing off and closing in, that is now in the air. The spirit that sends hate mail, paints swastikas on walls, burns crosses, bans books—vandalizes minds—has no place here. We must, and we will, maintain at Yale a spirit that is tolerant, respectful and candid, for that spirit is the form of order essential to sustain the freedom of the mind inquiring.

Such a spirit in the service of the inquiring mind is the responsibility of everyone in this community—students, faculty, staff, alumni, all those affiliated with Yale in any way. We can all only fulfill our purposes in this institution of learning when we face that responsibility and what it means with zest and dignity. We must, therefore, civilly and clearly have the courage to reject bigotry and coercion in all forms and have the courage to embrace the intellectual and human diversity of our community and our country. We cannot as Americans succumb to the fatigue, the arrogance mixed with exhaustion, that claims an exclusive "morality" and that negates and denies. To do so would be to betray at the deepest levels what a free people have won, through struggle and pain, over three centuries.

I welcome you to Yale. We are proud to include you and we hope your pride in being here will lead you to include all the best of the traditions and aspirations of the place. You will find, if the past is any guide, that the burdens of that precious charge will begin to turn, before too long, into one of the many pleasures you will find here. It is all now yours.

APPENDIX
F

Thomas Jefferson, 1779, An Act for Establishing Religious Freedom. Quoted in Full.

Well aware that Almighty God hath created the mind free; that all attempts to influence it by temporal punishments or burdens, or by civil incapacitations, tend only to beget habits of hypocrisy and meanness, and are a departure from the plan of the Holy Author of our religion, who being Lord both of body and mind, yet chose not to propagate it by coercions on either, as was in his Almighty power to do; that the impious presumption of legislators and rulers, civil as well as ecclesiastical, who, being themselves but fallible and uninspired men have assumed dominion over the faith of others, setting up their own opinions and modes of thinking as the only true and infallible, and as such endeavoring to impose them on others, hath established and maintained false religions over the greatest part of the world, and through all time; that to compel a man to furnish contributions of money for the propagation of opinions which he disbelieves, is sinful and tyrannical; that even the forcing him to support this or that teacher of his own religious persuasion, is depriving him of the comfortable liberty of giving his contributions to the particular pastor whose morals he would make his pattern, and whose power he feels most persuasive to righteousness, and is withdrawing from the ministry those temporal rewards, which proceeding from an approbation of their personal conduct, are an additional incitement to earnest and unremitting labors for the instruction of mankind; that our civil rights have no dependence on our religious opinions, more than our opinions in physics or geometry; that, therefore, the proscribing any citizen as unworthy the public confidence by laying upon him an incapacity of being called to the offices of trust and emolument, unless he profess or renounce this or that religious opinion, is depriving him injuriously of those privileges and advantages to which in common with his fellow citizens he has a natural right; that it tends also to corrupt the principles of that very religion it is meant to encourage, by bribing, with a monopoly of worldly honors and emoluments, those who will externally profess and conform to it; that though indeed these are criminal who do not withstand such temptation, yet neither are those innocent who lay the bait in their way; that to suffer the civil magistrate to intrude his powers into the field of opinion and to restrain the profession or propagation of principles, on the supposition of their ill tendency, is a dangerous fallacy, which at once destroys all religious liberty, because he being of course judge of that tendency, will make his opinions the rule of judgment, and approve or condemn the sentiments of others only as they shall square with or differ from his own; that it is time enough for the rightful purposes of civil government, for its officers to interfere when principles break out into overt acts against peace and good order; and finally, that truth is great and will prevail if left to herself, that she is the proper and sufficient antagonist to error, and has nothing to fear from the conflict, unless by human interposition disarmed of her natural weapons, free argument and debate, errors ceasing to be dangerous when it is permitted freely to contradict them.

Be it therefore enacted by the General Assembly. That no man shall be compelled to frequent or support any religious worship, place or ministry whatsoever, nor shall be enforced, restrained, molested, or burthened in his body or goods, nor shall otherwise suffer on account of his religious opinions or belief; but that all men shall be free to profess, and by argument maintain, their opinions in matters of religion, and that the same shall in nowise diminish, enlarge, or affect their civil capacities.

And though we well know this Assembly, elected by the people for the ordinary purposes of legislation only, have no power to restrain the acts of succeeding assemblies, constituted with the powers equal to our own, and that therefore to declare this act irrevocable, would be of no effect in law, yet we are free to declare, and do declare, that the rights hereby asserted are of the natural rights of mankind, and that if any act shall be hereafter passed to repeal the present or to narrow its operation, such act will be an infringement of natural right.

APPENDIX
G

Thomas Jefferson, 1781–82, Notes on Virginia, *Query XVII, The Different Religions Received into That State. Quoted in full.*

The first settlers in this country were emigrants from England, of the English Church, just at a point of time when it was flushed with complete victory over the religious of all other persuasions. Possessed, as they became, of the powers of making, administering, and executing the laws, they showed equal tolerance in this country with their Presbyterian brethren, who had emigrated to the northern government. The poor Quakers were flying from persecution in England. They cast their eyes on these new countries as asylums of civil and religious freedom; but they found them free only for the reigning sect. Several acts of the Virginia assembly of 1659, 1662, and 1693, had made it penal in parents to refuse to have their children baptized; had prohibited the unlawful assembling of Quakers; had made it penal for any master of a vessel to bring a Quaker into the State; had ordered those already here, and such as should come thereafter, to be imprisoned till they should abjure the country; provided a milder punishment for their first and second return, but death for their third; had inhibited all persons from suffering their meetings in or near their houses, entertaining them individually, or disposing of books which supported their tenets. If no execution took place here, as did in New England, it was not owing to the moderation of the church, or spirit of the legislature, as may be inferred from the law itself; but to historical circumstances which have been handed down to us. The Anglicans retained full possession of the country about a century. Other opinions began to creep in, and the great care of the government to support their own church, having begotten an equal degree of indolence in its clergy, two-thirds of the people had become dissenters at the commencement of the present revolution. The laws, indeed, were still oppressive on them, but the spirit of the one party had subsided into moderation, and of the other had risen to a degree of determination which commanded respect.

The present state of our laws on the subject of religion is this. The convention of May, 1776, in their declaration of rights, declared it to be a truth, and a natural right, that the exercise of religion should be free; but when they proceeded to form on that declaration the ordinance of government instead of taking up every principle declared in the bill of rights, and guarding it by legislative sanction, they passed over that which asserted our religious rights, leaving them as they found them. The same convention, however, when they met as a member of the general assembly in October, 1776, repealed all acts of Parliament which had rendered criminal the maintaining any opinions in matters of religion, the forbearing to repair to church, and the exercising any mode of worship, and suspended the laws giving salaries to the clergy, which suspension was made perpetual in October, 1779. Statutory oppressions in religion being thus wiped away, we remain at present under those only imposed by the common law, or by our own acts of assembly. At the common law, heresy was a capital offence, punishable by burning. Its definition was left to the ecclesiastical judges, before whom the conviction was, till the statute of the I El. c. I circumscribed it, by declaring, that nothing should be deemed heresy, but what had been so determined by authority of the canonical scriptures, or by one of the four first general councils, or by other council, having for the grounds of their declaration the express and plain words of the scriptures. Heresy, thus circumscribed, being an offence against the common law, our act of assembly of October, 1777, c. 17, gives cognizance of it to the general court, by declaring that the jurisdiction of that court shall be general in all matters at the common law. The execution is by the writ De haeretico comburendo. By our own act of assembly of 1705, c. 30, if a person brought up in the Christian religion denies the being of a God, or the Trinity, or asserts there are more gods than one, or denies the Christian religion to be true, or the scriptures to be of divine authority, he is punishable on the first offence by incapacity to hold any office or employment ecclesiastical, civil, or military; on the second by disability to sue, to take any gift or legacy, to be guardian, executor, or administrator, and by three years' imprisonment without bail. A father's right to the custody of his own children being founded in law on his right of guardianship, this being taken away, they may of course be severed from him, and put by the authority of a court into more orthodox hands. This is a summary view of that religious slavery under which a people have been willing to remain, who have lavished their lives and fortunes for the establishment of their civil freedom. The error seems not sufficiently eradicated, that the operations of the mind, as well as the acts of the body, are subject to the coercion of the laws. But our rulers can have no authority over such natural rights, only as we have submitted to them. The rights of conscience we never submitted, we could not submit. We are answerable for them to our God. The legitimate powers of government extend to such acts only as are injurious to others. But it does me no injury for my neighbor to say there are twenty gods, or no God. It neither picks my pocket nor breaks my leg. If it be said, his testimony in a court of justice cannot be relied on, reject it then, and be the stigma on him. Constraint may make him worse by making him a hypocrite, but it will never make him a truer man. It may fix him obstinately in his errors, but will not cure them. Reason and free inquiry are the only effectual agents against error. Give a loose to them, they will support the true religion by bringing every false one to their tribunal, to the test of their investigation. They are the natural enemies of error, and of error only. Had not the Roman government permitted free inquiry, Christianity could never have been introduced. Had not free inquiry been indulged at the era of the Reformation, the corruptions of Christianity could not have been purged away. If it be restrained now, the present corruptions will be protected, and new ones encouraged. Was the government to prescribe to us our medicine and diet, our bodies would be in such keeping as our souls are now. Thus in France the emetic was once forbidden as a medicine, the potato as an article of food. Government is just as infallible, too, when it fixes systems in physics. Galileo was sent to the Inquisition for affirming that the earth was a sphere; the government had declared it to be as flat as a trencher, and Galileo was obliged to abjure his error. This error, however, at length prevailed, the earth became a globe, and Descartes declared it was whirled round its axis by a vortex. The government in which he lived was wise enough to see that this was no question of civil jurisdiction, or we should all have been involved by authority in vortices. In fact, the vortices have been exploded, and the Newtonian principle of gravitation is now more firmly established, on the basis of reason, than it would be were the government to step in, and to make it an article of necessary faith. Reason and experiment have been indulged, and error has fled before them. It is error alone which needs the support of government. Truth can stand by itself. Subject opinions to coercion: whom will you make your inquisitors? Fallible men; men governed by bad passions, by private as well as public reasons. And why subject it to coercion? To produce uniformity. But is uniformity of opinion desirable? No more than of face and stature. Introduce the bed of Procrustes then, as there is danger that the large men may beat the small, make us all of a size, by lopping the former and stretching the latter. Difference of opinion is advantageous in religion. The several sects perform the office of a censor morum over each other. Is uniformity attainable? Millions of innocent men, women, and children, since the introduction of Christianity, have been burnt, tortured, fined, imprisoned; yet we have not advanced one inch towards uniformity. What has been the effect of coercion? To make one half the world fools, and the other half hypocrites. To support roguery and error all over the earth. Let us reflect that it is inhabited by a thousand millions of people. That these profess probably a thousand different systems of religion. That ours is but one of that thousand. That if there be but one right, and ours that one, we should wish to see the nine hundred and ninety-nine wandering sects gathered into the fold of truth. But against such a majority we cannot effect this by force. Reason and persuasion are the only practicable instruments. To make way for these, free inquiry must be indulged; and how can we wish others to indulge it while we refuse it ourselves. But every State, says an inquisitor, has established some religion. No two, say I, have established the same. Is this a proof of the infallibility of establishments? Our sister States of Pennsylvania and New York, however, have long subsisted without any establishment at all. The experiment was new and doubtful when they made it. It has answered beyond conception. They flourish infinitely. Religion is well supported; of various kinds, indeed, but all good enough; all sufficient to preserve peace and order; or if a sect arises, whose tenets would subvert morals, good sense has fair play, and reasons and laughs it out of doors, without suffering the State to be troubled with it. They do not hang more malefactors than we do. They are not more disturbed with religious dissensions. On the contrary, their harmony is unparalleled, and can be ascribed to nothing but their unbounded tolerance, because there is no other circumstance in which they differ from every nation on earth. They have made the happy discovery, that the way to silence religious disputes, is to take no notice of them. Let us too give this experiment fair play, and get rid, while we may, of those tyrannical laws. It is true, we are as yet secured against them by the spirit of the times. I doubt whether the people of this country would suffer an execution for heresy, or a three years' imprisonment for not comprehending the mysteries of the Trinity. But is the spirit of the people an infallible, a permanent reliance? Is it government? Is this the kind of protection we receive in return for the rights we give up? Besides, the spirit of the times may alter, will alter. Our rulers will become corrupt, our people careless. A single zealot may commence persecutor, and better men be his victims. It can never be too often repeated, that the time for fixing every essential right on a legal basis is while our rulers are honest, and ourselves united. From the conclusion of this war we shall be going down hill. It will not then be necessary to resort every moment to the people for support. They will be forgotten, therefore, and their rights disregarded. They will forget themselves, but in the sole faculty of making money, and will never think of uniting to effect a due respect for their rights. The shackles, therefore, which shall not be knocked off at the conclusion of this war, will remain on us long, will be made heavier and heavier, till our rights shall revive or expire in a convulsion.

INDEX